OUT OF CHARACTER

OUT OF CHARACTER

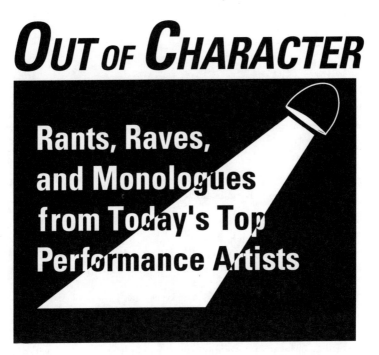

**Rants, Raves,
and Monologues
from Today's Top
Performance Artists**

EDITED BY

Mark Russell

BANTAM BOOKS
New York • Toronto • London • Sydney • Auckland

For Ethyl

OUT OF CHARACTER
A Bantam Book / January 1997

BOOK DESIGN BY JAMES SINCLAIR

Library of Congress Cataloging-in-Publication Data
Out of character: rants, raves, and monologues from today's
top performance artists/edited by Mark Russell.
p. cm.
ISBN 0-553-37485-0
1. American drama—20th century. 2. Monologues. 3. Monodramas.
4. Performance art. I. Russell, Mark, 1954– .
PS336.M65098 1997
812'.04508—dc20 96-18668

Published simultaneously in the United States and Canada

Bantam Books are published by Bantam Books, a division of
Bantam Doubleday Dell Publishing Group, Inc. Its trademark,
consisting of the words "Bantam Books" and the portrayal of a
rooster, is Registered in U.S. Patent and Trademark Office and in
other countries. Marca Registrada. Bantam Books, 1540
Broadway, New York, New York 10036.

PRINTED IN THE UNITED STATES OF AMERICA

FFG   10   9   8   7   6   5   4   3   2   1

Contents

Foreword

Over the past few years there has been considerable press attention given to Performance Art. It has been lauded, analyzed, pronounced dead, funded, defunded, hyped, and demonized.

This book is a collection of the work of some of the most influential and accomplished live performance creators that have come to national prominence in the last ten years. It is not meant to be a comprehensive study. It is a snapshot of some of the most adventurous voices in the field of what might be called Performance Art or solo theatre.

I don't like any of those titles. I just call it Performance.

In the eighties the solo show became the weapon of choice for many performing artists. It was a way of reflecting their lives and concerns in the most direct and low-cost way possible. As the information age grew more ambitious and attention spans and free time grew shorter, the solo show was the easiest and simplest way to tell one's story.

Our society is obsessed with fleeting fame, and personal stories are splattered everywhere, from the movies to the news to *Oprah*. Performance is a way to convey an even more intimate truth. Under the storm of electronic distractions, Performance touches the essentials of theatre; someone speaking, moving, and telling stories in front of a listening, watching live audience.

Performance surfed in on the wave of Punk Music in the late seventies. "Everybody can be a band" held for theatre and dance as well. Trash tradition—do what you know, what you feel, you don't have to be an expert to do it. The Judson school of dance makers experimented with pedestrian movements exploring the nature of dance. Actors and directors such as Spalding Gray and Elizabeth LeCompte were exploring the nature of a personal theatre. The action performances of visual artists on both coasts carried the flag of the European avant-garde from those nineteenth-century Russian cafés to the lofts of SoHo. Performance Art was here.

Performance fit with the politics of the time. "The personal is political," a statement developed from feminist thought, was gaining wider acceptance. The continuing liberation of women, blacks, Hispanics, gay men and women, and so many other marginalized cultures brought wider concerns to the national debate. What better way to reclaim your history than to speak it? What better way to celebrate your emergence into the national agenda than to sing out, in a rant, in a whisper, in a story, in a character? And what better way to get under the skin of one's enemy than to take on their voice?

Technology stepped in and added the Casio keyboard, the Walkman, the camcorder, the laptop computer, and loads of other consumer electronics to the mix. Fun tools that made it easier than ever to capture your world, to tell your story.

Many of the people pursuing performance hailed from a generation that was raised on TV and had no fear of changing channels at will. They could use whatever they felt they wanted to try. There were no rules. Filmmakers worked with live dance, dancers experimented with speaking onstage, theatre actors used their own life stories. Poets left the page behind. Performance took what it wanted from all fields including the time-based actions of Performance Art. Performance carried the torch of experimental theatre and dance all through the eighties. It was a form that wasn't a form, an ever-adaptable virus of theatre.

What mattered in performance was the honesty of the event, its originality and an element of surprise, its method of connecting to the truth and bringing that truth to the audience.

Performance shape-shifts along the blade of the cutting edge but it takes its greatest strength from the traditional. It constantly reinvents disciplines for its own time. It rediscovers rituals on the artist's own terms.

The great boom time of the 1980s that made the art world (for a brief moment) into Big Business also gentrified the industrial neighborhoods that had nurtured live artists such as Trisha Brown, Meredith Monk, Robert Wilson, the Wooster Group, Richard Foreman, and the many alternative spaces that supported their work.

The art world moved from SoHo to the East Village and eventually to Brooklyn in search of cheap shelter. Rehearsals for live events took place in storefronts or cramped apartments. The increased costs of staying alive in the eighties urban environment meant less free time and made it much more difficult to assemble groups for theatre adventures. At the same time, inspired by the success of Laurie Anderson, Eric Bogosian, and Spalding Gray, many theatre and dance artists started making their own solo work. A rash of small art spaces, clubs, and theatres came about to support this work. The off-off-Broadway theatre movement was supplanted by a ragtag spate of bar, living room, storefront, gas station, abandoned schoolroom makeshift cultural centers.

P.S. 122 was one of those cultural centers. I was lucky enough to become its grant writer, bookkeeper, programmer, and lone full-time employee in March of 1983.

Performance Space 122 was started by choreographer Charles Moulton and performance artists Charles Dennis, Peter Rose, and Tim Miller. Moulton was offered a chance to look at this big room in a newly colonized abandoned school building in the East Village by Sally Eckhoff, one of the painters who had taken a studio there. Moulton came to the room, which had been a classroom/assembly hall when Public School 122 was filled with grade-schoolers, and tore up a piece of the green linoleum. He found a beautiful tongue-and-groove white oak floor. Perfect for dance. Moulton started rehearsing in the space and invited Dennis, Miller, and Rose to help him share the rent.

In the summer of 1979 Alan Parker came to New York City to shoot the movie *Fame*. He was denied access to the original High School of the Performing Arts, and he needed a school building to shoot his film. P.S. 122 won the screen test. All of the tenants were moved out to other spaces around the city so that the *Fame* crew could have the run of the building. Moulton was offered a storefront loft on Warren Street. Moulton, Dennis, and Rose started holding performance parties in the storefront that attracted a host of young artists, such as Molissa Fenley, Eric Bogosian, and Karole Armitage. This burgeoning scene of dancers and theatre artists moved back to the school in the fall of 1979.

P.S. 122's first public performances were held that fall, one of the events being Avant-Garde-Arama, an irreverent multimedia minifestival organized by Charles Dennis and Jeffrey Isaacs. The space quickly became filled up with rentals for rehearsals and shows when the founding artists were not using it. Clip lights and a home stereo system were added.

The three artists along with Tim Miller (Peter Rose's boyfriend at the time) and a large core of supportive artists helped persuade the city to give the partnership of occupying organizations, the 122 Community Center, a long-term lease. Demonstrations in City Hall Park, the inclusion of a day-care center, backroom political deals, and long cold meetings in the old coal-heated building managed to do the trick.

Tim Miller designed the first P.S. 122 posters and calendars, a genius mix of New York tabloid in-your-face headlines and imagery photocopied from high school encyclopedias. These mailings and street posters had the naive and immediate quality of punk propaganda. Names large, bold, and italicized. The homemade urban-guerrilla nature of the space had found a visual face.

Miller also started taking Monday nights, his own rehearsal slot at the space, and turning them into weekly performances. These early performances were improvisational, filled with immediate autobiographical stories and dances, with props collected on the way to the theatre. Miller attracted critical attention and a cult following. Here was a gay man who had spent virtually no time in the closet, a new breed of free-loving, no-nonsense gay boyhood—the happy result of decades of struggle. He was proclaiming this fresh view of the world in an art form that was just as fresh. P.S. 122 was becoming the place to see the new generation.

In the early eighties P.S. 122 was in the middle of the East Village art scene, totally ignored in all the hype, literally left off the map of the crowded storefront gallery guides. The dancers and live artists just worked too hard and made too little money to get any attention in the fast and loose art scene. The art scene did, however, spend time in clubs and several popped up to give them a playground. The Pyramid Club, Club 57, 8 BC, Dorika, all featured performance and developed a generation of artists wild enough to deal with what was happening on the dance floor below them. Those artists moved on to the "art" spaces such as P.S. 122 where they could do longer runs without worrying about the 11 P.M. band moving in on them. John Kelly, John Jesurun, DanceNoise, the Alien Comic, and Ethyl Eichelberger, all created works for clubs which they then adapted to the slightly more formal stages at P.S. 122, Dance Theater Workshop, and La MaMa and other more established theatre organizations.

By 1983 the three founding artists' own careers were gaining momentum and they had less time for day-to-day management. Charlie Moulton's multiperson ball passing was being performed at Lincoln Center, Tim Miller was preparing to do a weekend as part of the Brooklyn Academy of Music's Next Wave Series, and Charles Dennis's *Safe at Home* performances were being seen all around the city. That is where I came in, having hung around the space since the beginning. I had been pursuing my own theatre projects as a young director while bouncing from survival job to survival job. The founding artists interviewed several candidates and selected me to help them manage this young and needy organization. I took on the basic maintenance of booking the space, getting its not-for-profit status sorted out, and trying to raise money.

P.S. 122 led a charmed life in the eighties. The city desperately needed and responded to the start-up of a new venue for theatre and dance. There was great curiosity about this thing called "Performance Art." The press, funders, and audiences found their way to our door. We added staff, we built a larger board of directors, we added performances and a downstairs theatre.

We didn't label any of our series "dance" or "theatre" or "Performance Art." We let the audience decide what they thought it should be. If they needed a label for what they saw, we just called it performance. The cheap rent of the space meant that almost anyone could afford to put on a show at P.S. 122. Our growing national profile meant we could exercise a certain quality control over what we put on. With funding, we started to offer artists fees and technical services and devote fewer and fewer weeks to straight rentals.

One of our most successful rentals was to Eric Bogosian in the summer of 1982. He developed what became his show *Fun House* in August 1982 before off-Broadway producers discovered him and took the show to the Actors' Playhouse. Eric continues to develop his solo shows at P.S. 122.

P.S. 122's flexible idea of what constituted an event allowed many things to happen: people built rope bridges in the space, cooked whole meals in the middle of performances, jumped from the roof of the building dressed as Maria von Trapp, and held twenty-four-hour marathon performances with bad jokes told on the hour.

The late eighties brought the rise of the Christian right and the scandal of the NEA Four, a national furor that erupted when NEA chairman John Frohnmayer, trying to placate right-wing criticism of the agency, rejected grants to Karen Finley, Holly Hughes, John Fleck, and Tim Miller, who had been recommended for funding in the solo theatre fellowship category. All four of these artists had performed within a two-month period at P.S. 122 in 1988 (the year before they were raked across the tabloid headlines). P.S. 122 was miraculously left alone in all of that turmoil while its fellow art presenters like the Kitchen and Franklin Furnace were stripped naked in the halls of Congress for daring to take NEA money for work they felt was of artistic merit. This was a cultural war and the arts community was ill prepared for the onslaught on their accepted values.

I think that P.S. 122 was overlooked because, well, we looked like a school. It messed up the sound bite. That season we did work that would have given Senator Jesse Helms hair, but it never came to his attention.

P.S. 122's story is just like thousands of other small art spaces and theatres' stories. A space holds forth a possibility and performers fill it: people come to watch, then more people come to watch. Critics come to see what is happening, the stage space is improved, the space becomes an institution, a pillar of the community. Generations of artists move through the building adding to its history. A dialogue between a community and its artists is shaped by a common place. There is probably a P.S. 122 in your community. There are more popping up each year.

Performance exists best in this environment. Intimate, specific, boundaries broken one evening can be replaced for the next. Different points of view rub against each other to create deeper meanings, wider resonances. The audience is there to participate, to be challenged.

I have spent many evenings watching the audiences watch the performances at P.S. 122. Waiting for the spark that will light both afire. It happens frequently enough for me to keep watching.

This book is structured very much like a season at P.S. 122. At P.S. 122 there are no themes, no series. The audience is left to its own devices to make connections between pieces and between artists. Each artist gets a time slot to bring forth their show, to add their voice to the ongoing dialogue. We think enough of our audience that they will do their own thinking.

The same holds true with this book. I could pull out trends and themes racing through all of these pieces but I think it is more interesting that readers discover them for themselves. Please understand that the artists and their works were not chosen at random, but each artist, once chosen, was given great freedom to choose their own selection, write their own introduction and their own biography questionnaire.

My own search through this project was an interest in what process each of these artists used to make their work, what made their work touch me, and how so many disparate individuals fit into this world of performance.

The artists included in this book probably don't want to belong to any club that would have them as a member. They all come from very different walks of life. They see their art as an act of cultural activism, a poetic vision, an expiation of demons, a rant of truth, a dance of the forgotten. They inhabit different selves, they take on different personalities, they exist in them completely, they comment on them as they perform them, they present them without comment.

Some work from the page, some improvise until they remember, some never know what they will say.

This is just a taste. To actually understand their work, closer study of each of them is required, starting with viewing them live. Not on video. Live.

Some of these folks are very difficult to see live. Ethyl Eichelberger is no longer with us. Many of the artists featured in this book get rare opportunities to perform outside a small circuit of arts spaces. The shrinking financial resources for these artists and the spaces that support them make their live appearances fleeting at best. Tours and long runs are rare. Critical attention and documentation for a field that isn't a field or an easily definable genre is also difficult to come by.

I've asked each of these artists to give the readers of this anthology an idea of how they go about making their work. It is a formidable task for anyone to put their work process down on paper. Some have written recipes, some have written rants, some have attempted to avoid the subject altogether.

I also asked them to fill out a very flippant biography questionnaire similar to the page facing the centerfold of a *Playboy* Bunny, a bachelor profile in a tabloid, or the back of a baseball card. A few were incensed and filled out their questionnaires under duress. Some enjoyed the fun, some took them seriously. I hope that these short profiles cut through the dry details endemic to any biography and give some sense of the unique history and energy of each of these amazing individuals.

Out of Character starts with Laurie Anderson and continues down the alphabet to David Rousseve. Laurie has wide fame as a multidisciplinary artist/rock performer and she is a seminal influence on many of these artists. She was one of the first to "make it" into the loved/hated heaven of pop culture. She was one of the first to be accepted under the rubric *Performance Artist*. Her wry observations on her life and the world around her set the downtown tone for the eighties: "Can you believe this nonsense?" It's also a very American voice. Optimistic, curious, cool, unflappable, Laurie can spin a fabulous dry yarn. She cuts through all of the state-of-the-art technology available to her and lands on our front porch, telling stories.

Most of the photographs in this book are by Dona Ann McAdams. Dona has been the house photographer at Performance Space 122 since its beginning. She has been a friend and champion of the artists as well, not to mention their best audience member. Dona is inevitably sitting in the first row with her Leicas quietly snapping away, capturing split-second moments of pure performance. Her trademark laugh supporting any good line, her attention palpable and supportive. For many years she was there live, every opening night. When P.S. 122 became more established, she had to move to dress rehearsal nights but still found time to shoot many events (if they were not too quiet) live. She can count on her hands the number of performances she has missed at the space, which is an achievement similar to baseball's Cal Ripkin's, considering the number of events we present each year at P.S. 122.

Since not all the artists in this book have performed at Performance Space 122, not all of them have been photographed by Dona Ann McAdams. We have included the work of other photographers where this is the case.

Again, not all of these artists have performed at P.S. 122—but a great number of them have. By dint of its activity Performance Space 122 was host to many of the New Yorkers creating work in the late eighties and early nineties. In other words, it was hard *not* to perform at P.S. 122. Still, many passed us by, and I've tried to include in this anthology the most influential of the legions that built their careers in other cities or through other spaces.

These artists come from many traditions and take on many different voices. They create characters that use their own given names, they inhabit complex individuals, they make plays of several characters played by one. What they do, many times, does not look like theatre as we expect it to be. It's different, it's basic, it asks for us to put away our artistic prejudices and let the artist take us somewhere else. It is many times a theatre of transformations, or dynamic transitions. It asks for participation in the illusion. The illusion that we are seeing Spalding Gray informally chatting about his life and that the chat is not as precisely put together as a fine watch. That Penny Arcade is the same Penny Arcade offstage. That Eric Bogosian is *not* that manipulative preacher, yet why does he do it so *well*?

This book is an anthology that is out of character with most anthologies, hence the bio questionnaires, the wide-ranging inclusion of artists, styles, and material. I consider it a collection of text and photo artifacts from a rich history of live performance. Do the texts work as great literature? No, they are meant to be *performed*. There are numerous elements of these live events that can only be hinted at on the page. Can or should they be performed by people other than the authors? That is a delicate question. What does it mean to play Spalding Gray playing Spalding Gray in a remembered life of Spalding Gray? Some of these monologues are more adaptable than others, but all of them would lose something once their original artist was not involved.

To hear the composer Philip Glass play Philip Glass solos, something I've been blessed with, is a rare experience. Though he is not a premier pianist, the direct connection between fingers, music, and heart brings something extra to the experience, untouchable by even the most gifted concert artist. The same is even more true of these performers and their work. In many cases this is their personal history they are evoking. The act of them revealing it before you is part and parcel of the event. As a gift, as a political statement, as a triumph over silence. The audiences' witnessing of the act implicates them in the action. It becomes more than just a theatre evening; we have a delicate truth to remember. We have been in a room with someone revealed.

Just telling secrets is not the point. It is how those secrets are told, with what artfulness the truth is given. Sometimes they are given with elaborate lies and grand theatrical artifice. Sometimes they are covered in someone else's voice and mannerisms. But eventually something is revealed, something is discovered. It comes out of the blue, out of character, but with the sting of truth.

Photo by Paula Court

LAURIE ANDERSON

Name: Laurie Anderson
Stage Name: same
Birthdate/Birthplace: June 5, 1947/Chicago
"Raised Up" Where: Next to a lake in Illinois; downtown Manhattan
Education: B.A., Barnard College in Art History 1969; M.F.A. in Sculpture from Columbia University, 1972
Honors/Grants: magna cum laude, Phi Beta Kappa 1969; NYSCA 1974, 1977; National Endowment for the Arts 1977, 1979; Honorary Doctorate from San Francisco Art Institute 1980; Villager Award 1981; Guggenheim Fellowship 1982; Honorary Doctorates: Philadelphia College of the Arts 1987; Art Institute of Chicago 1990; Distinguished Alumna Award, Columbia School of the Arts 1994
Influences/Mentors/Heroes: Ken Nordine, William Burroughs, Herman Melville, His Holiness the Dalai Lama
Places Performed: Just about everywhere except Russia
Pivotal Performance: The first time I performed in Europe was in 1965 when I was seventeen. There were fifty of us in the "Talented Teen U.S.A." troupe and we wore matching red blazers and did "up-with-America" type shows in town halls, fairs, and U.S. Army bases. I had never heard of "performance art." My act was a "Chalk Talk" and I talked about life in the United States (what Americans like to eat, wear, and drive; cowboys and Indians; high school, etc.) while I drew cartoons on a huge pad of newsprint. Since we did the shows in several different countries, the tour supervisors said, "Remember, you will be in foreign countries, so try to use a few 'foreign' words, you know, like *'Ich bin ein Berliner.'"* I'd had four years of Latin (which my teachers had always said would come in handy "someday") but when I tried it out, I found out what "dead language" really means.
Favorite Performance Experience: The first time I realized that I could work outside of the avant-garde circuit was 1978. I was scheduled to do a performance in a museum in Houston and since the museum itself wasn't really set up for this sort of thing, no stage, no chairs, no sound system, the performance was booked into a local country-and-western bar. The advertisements in the local papers made the performance seem like it might be some kind of country fiddling event, so a lot of the regulars came. They arrived early and sat along the bar, so when the art crowd showed up, dressed in black and fashionably late, there was nowhere to sit and they were forced to mingle. From my point of view, it was a pretty strange-looking crowd. About halfway through the concert, I realized that the regulars were really getting it. What I was doing, telling stories and playing the violin, didn't seem bizarre to them. The stories were a little weird, but then, so are Texan stories. I remember that I felt so relieved. I could talk to people who were outside the rarefied New York art world and they were getting it. It was a whole new world.
Most Terrifying Performance Experience: Kalamazoo, 1995: Performed in an old hemp house theater. We noticed during the load-in that the ropes looked a little bit, let's say, frayed, so Bill Berger, the stage manager, tried to simplify some of our fly cues. Unfortunately the fly guys missed their mark and one of our set pieces—a twelve-foot I-beam—came swinging in at a crazy angle. At the time I was facing the audience and I saw this look of horror on the faces of the first few rows of the audience. This is definitely not a good sign. Surprise, puzzlement, even boredom are expressions I can deal

with. But horror? I turned around (slowly) and watched this I-beam swaying around on its thin lines and just decided to keep playing the violin piece I was doing anyway, trying to imagine that this was a new and interesting part of the show. Even though I knew there wasn't really a danger this would come crashing down, there's always that nagging one in a million odd (can "odd" be in the singular? or is this one of the nouns that only comes in groups, like "scruples"?).

Favorite Prop or Costume: Digital audio gloves

Hobbies: Looking for a sheep ranch to settle down on

Reading List: Edmund Scientific Catalog, computer manuals

Favorite Music: Flamenco, Astor Piazzolla, Joey Baron

Favorite Quote: "Talking about music is like dancing about architecture." (Steve Martin)

Artist's Notes

—from an interview with Nicholas Zurbrugg, 1991

NZ: Can you remember your first performance as a storyteller?

LA: I can remember my first performance as a liar.

NZ: What was that? Was that as a child?

LA: Yeah. I'd just make things up for the other kids. And these sort of had to do with the Bible, but not too much. Based on the Bible, put it that way. I grew up in the Bible Belt and spent a lot of my childhood listening to these stories, at Bible school, Bible camp, Sunday school and so on. And these stories were completely amazing. Outrageous stories! About parting oceans and talking snakes. And people really seemed to believe these stories. And I'm talking about adults. Adults who mainly just did the most mundane things imaginable (mowing their lawns, throwing potluck parties). They all believed in these wild stories. And they would sit around and discuss them in the most matter-of-fact way.

NZ: So that was a kind of local surrealism.

LA: No, no, that was the local truth. Surrealism is an art term. We weren't artists.

NZ: How did you move from Bible Belt storytelling? When did you go through the art barrier, as it were?

LA: I haven't. I try to tell the truth as I see it. I'm just telling the same mixture of Midwestern Bible stories that I always have. They're a mixture of the most mundane things with a fabulous twist on them. It's only what I learned in Bible school. How Bible school related to public schools is what I'm interested in. Always have been.

My Voice

But the voice, my voice, what is it? It's a kind of mixture of my father's and my mother's voices. My father's voice, well, he learned English from Jimmy Cagney and Bob Hope and, way back, Abe Lincoln. He was getting a lot from the Lincoln style. (You know when that lawyer was teasing Abe about not having an office and schlepping everything around on his horse and Abe said, "My office? My office is in my hat.") And my mother's voice too, well, it's more of an academic voice, a Church of England voice. And I've mixed those up and found my own voice. Of course, that's not to say I've got only one. Everyone has at least twenty, bottom line, at least twenty. They have their hail-a-cab voice, they have their interview voice, and their most intimate voice talking to their dearest loved ones on the phone, to name just a few.

Voices on the Phone

People blame technology for a lot of things. They say, for example, that technology makes it harder to communicate, harder to have a real conversation. But I think it was probably hard to have a real conversation one hundred years ago, it was hard five hundred years ago, five thousand years ago. And by real conversation I mean improvising, really responding to what the other person just said, like jazz, not just repeating things that are already on your mind.

And anyway technology doesn't necessarily alienate people. Sometimes technology makes it possible to be intimate. For example, a lot of people have their first love affairs on the phone. You know, it's very sexy, you can whisper right into his ear and he doesn't have to see your face and if you say something stupid you can hang up right away.

New York Social Life
for Telephone and Tamboura

Well I was lying in bed
one morning, trying to think
of a good reason to get up,
and the phone rang and it
was Geri and she said:

>   Hey, hi! How are you?
>   What's going on?
>   How's your work?

Oh fine. You know, just
waking up but it's fine,
it's going Okay, how's yours?

Oh a lot of work, you know,
I mean, I'm trying to make
some money too. Listen,
I gotta get back to it, I just thought
I'd call to see how you are. . . .
And I said: Yeah, we should
really get together next week.
You know, have lunch,
and talk.

And she says: Yeah,
I'll be in touch. Okay?

Okay.

Uh, listen, take care.

Okay. Take it easy.

Bye-bye.

'Bye now. And I get up,
and the phone rings and it's
a man from Cleveland and
he says:

Hey, hi! How are you?
Listen, I'm doing a performance
series and I'd like you to do
something in it. You know,
you could make a little money.
I mean, I don't know how I feel
about your work, you know,
it's not really my style,
it's kind of trite
but listen, it's just my opinion,
don't take it personally.
So listen,
I'll be in town next week.
I gotta go now, but I'll give you a call,
and we'll have lunch, and we can
discuss a few things.

And I hang up and it rings
again and I don't answer it
and I go out for a walk and I
drop in at the gallery and they say:

Hey, hi. How are you?

Oh fine. You know.

How's your work going?

Okay. I mean . . .

> You know, it's not like it was
> in the sixties. I mean,
> those were the days
> there's just no money
> around now, you know.
> Survive! Produce! Stick it out!
> It's a jungle out there!
> Just gotta keep working.
> And the phone rings and she says:
> Oh excuse me, will you?
> Hey, hi! How are you? Uh-huh.
> How's your work? Good.
> Well, listen, stick it out,
> I mean, it's not the sixties,
> you know, listen, I gotta go now,
> but, uh, lunch would be great.
> Fine, next week?
> Yeah. Very busy now,
> but next week would be fine,
> Okay? Bye-bye.
> 'Bye now.

And I go over to Magoo's
for a bite, and I see Frank
and I go over to his table
and I say: Hey, Frank.

> Hi, how are you?

How's your work?
Yeah, mine's Okay too.
Listen, I'm broke you know,
but, uh, working. . . .
Listen, I gotta go now but
we should really get together,
you know.
Why don't you drop by sometime?

> Yeah, that would be great.

Okay.

> Take care.

Take it easy.

> I'll see you.

I'll call you.

> 'Bye now.

Bye-bye.
And I go to a party and
everyone's sitting around
wearing these party hats
and it's really awkward
and no one can think of
anything to say.
So we all move around fast
and it's:
Hi! How are you?

                      Where've you been?

Nice to see you.

                      Listen, I'm sorry
                      I missed your thing
                      last week, but we should really
                      get together, you know,
                      maybe next week.

I'll call you.

                      I'll see you.

Bye-bye.
And I go home and the
phone rings and it's
Alan and he says:

                      You know, I'm gonna have a show
                      on cable TV and it's gonna
                      be about loneliness, you know,
                      people in the city who for whatever
                      sociological, psychological,
                      philosophical reasons
                      just can't seem to communicate,
                      you know,
                      The Gap! The Gap!
                      It'll be a talk show
                      and people phone in
                      but we will say at the beginning
                      of each program: Listen,
                      don't call in with your
                      personal problems
                      because we don't want to hear them.

And I'm going to sleep
and it rings again and
it's Mary and she says:

Hey, Laurie, how are you?
Listen, I just called to say hi.
Yeah, well don't worry.
Listen, just keep working.
I gotta go now. I know it's late
but we should really get together
next week maybe and have lunch
and talk and . . . listen, Laurie,
if you want to talk before then,
I'll leave my answering machine on
and just give me a ring
anytime.

The Phantom Voice

In 1978, I spent time in California in the fall looking for a quiet place to live. I finally found what seemed to be the perfect apartment but the night after I moved in I heard a tremendous pounding sound. As it turned out, I had moved in right above a Hawaiian hollow-log drum school. Every other night, it was converted into a hula school with a live band of six Hawaiian guitars. I decided to soundproof my place but I didn't hang the door very well and all the sounds kept drifting in.

About this time, like a lot of New Yorkers who find themselves on the West Coast, I got interested in various aspects of California's version of the occult. We would sit around at night while the dust storms howled outside, and ask questions of the Ouija board. I found out a lot of information on my past 9,361 human lives on this planet. My first life was as a raccoon.

AND THEN YOU WERE A COW.
AND THEN YOU WERE A BIRD.
AND THEN YOU WERE A HAT

spelled the Ouija.

We said: A hat? We couldn't figure it out.

Finally we guessed that the feathers from the bird were made into a hat. Is this true?

YES, spelled the Ouija, HAT COUNTS AS HALF LIFE. And then? HUNDREDS AND HUNDREDS OF RABBIS.

This is apparently my first life as a woman, which should explain quite a few things. Eventually, the Ouija's written words seemed to take on a personality, a kind of voice. Finally, we began to ask the board if the Ouija would be willing to appear to us in some other form. FORGET IT FORGET IT FORGET IT FORGET IT.

The Ouija seemed like it was about to crash. "Please, please what can we do," we nagged, "so you will show yourself to us in some other manifestation?"

YOU SHOULD LURK.
YOU SHOULD L-U-R-K LURK.

I never really figured out how to lurk in my own place, even though it was only a rented place. But I did find myself looking over my shoulder a lot. Every sound that drifted in seemed to be a version of this phantom voice whispering in a code I could never crack.

My Voice as a Man

When I first began to perform in Germany, I noticed there was a lot of resentment on the part of the local crew. Gradually I realized that the all-male tech crew disliked the combination of women and electricity. Power was clearly a man's job. I discovered this when I didn't know how to make a connection and the Berlin crew proudly solved the problem. After that, they were nicer to me.

In performances, I loved to use the lowest setting on the Harmonizer, a digital processor that lowered my voice to sound like a man. This was especially effective in Germany. When I spoke as a woman, they listened indulgently; but when I spoke as a man, and especially a bossy man, they listened with interest and respect. And that was when I realized that I was in a country where people actually liked to be bossed. And since I like to boss, it was kind of perfect.

In 1980, I wrote a song for William Burroughs called "Language Is a Virus from Outer Space." This was a quote from one of Burroughs's books and it's a strange thing for a writer to say, that language is a disease communicable by mouth. It's also a very Buddhist thing to say. I mean, in Buddhist thought, there's the thing and there's the name for the thing and that's one thing too many. Because sometimes when you say a word, you think you actually understand it. In fact, all you're doing is saying it, you don't necessarily understand it at all. So language, well, it's a kind of trick.

I saw this guy on the train, and he seemed to have gotten
stuck in one of those abstract trances, and he was going
"Uuuuugh . . . ugh . . . uuuuuuuugh!!"
And Geraldine said: You know, I think he's in some kind of pain.
I think it's a pain cry. And I said:

If that's a pain cry, then language . . . is a virus . . .
LANGUAGE! IT'S A VIRUS!
LANGUAGE! IT'S A VIRUS!

I first met William S. Burroughs in 1978 at the Nova Convention, which was a three-day celebration of his work in New York City. During the day there were seminars about his work with Timothy Leary, Susan Sontag, and many other writers and intellectuals; at night there were concerts by musicians and poets who'd been influenced by his work. Frank Zappa read the talking asshole section from *Naked Lunch*, Patti Smith played the clarinet, Phil Glass played the piano. There were lots of other people too. It was a real scene.

Keith Richards was also supposed to appear, and even though the promoters of this event knew a week ahead of time that he wasn't going to show up, they didn't announce it. They just tacked up a note and posted it on the inside of the door to the theater.

"Keith Richards will not be appearing tonight"

it said in very light pencil. So a couple thousand kids poured through the door and a lot of them were looking for Keith. Phil would be playing a solo piano work and they'd be yelling

"KEITH! KEITH!!!!"

Nothing would shut them up and since I was one of the MCs, I'd have to keep going out to introduce someone else they didn't want to hear. "You know, just keep the ball rolling," the promoters kept saying.

Finally Burroughs shuffled out wearing a porkpie hat and carrying a briefcase and he sat down at a big wooden desk.

"Good evening."

Gravel crunching under a ten-ton truck. Plastic ripping in slow motion. That voice!

And he started talking about sex and drugs and alienation, things these kids thought they'd invented themselves and they couldn't

believe it.
"GRANDPA!"
But it was that voice that really got to people.
And you could never read his books again after that without hearing
that voice saying every word.

This Is the Language of the Future
for Harmonized Male Voice; the Nova Convention, New York, 1978

Last year, I was on a twin-engine plane coming from Milwaukee to New York City. Just over La Guardia, one of the engines conked out and we started to drop straight down, flipping over and over. Then the other engine died and we went completely out of control. New York City started getting taller and taller. A voice came over the intercom and said:

> Our pilot has informed us that we are about to attempt a crash landing.
> Please extinguish all cigarettes.
> Place your tray tables in their upright, locked position.
> Your captain says: Please do not panic.
> Your captain says: Place your head in your hands.
> Captain says: Place your head on your knees.
> Captain says: Put your hands on your head.
> Put your hands on your knees!
> (heh-heh)
> This is your captain.
> Have you lost your dog?
> We are going down. We are all going down together.

As it turned out, we were caught in a downdraft and rammed into a bank. It was, in short, a miracle. But afterwards I was terrified of getting onto planes. The moment I started walking down that aisle, my eyes would clamp shut and I would fall into a deep, impenetrable sleep.

> YOU DON'T WANT TO SEE THIS
> YOU DON'T WANT TO BE HERE
> HAVE YOU LOST YOUR DOG?

Finally, I was able to remain conscious, but I always had to go up to the forward cabin and ask the stewardesses if I could sit next to them: "Hi! Uh, mind if I join you?"

They were always rather irritated, "Oh, all right (what a baby)," and I watched their uniforms crack as we made nervous chitchat. Sometimes even this didn't work and I'd have to find one of the other passengers to talk to. You can spot these people immediately. There's one on every flight. Someone who's really on *your* wavelength.

I was on a flight from L.A. when I spotted one of them, sitting across the aisle. A girl, about fifteen. And she had this stuffed rabbit set up on her tray table and she kept arranging and rearranging the rabbit and kind of waving to it: "Hi!" "Hi there!" And I decided: This is the one I want to sit next to. So I sat down and we started to talk and suddenly I realized she was speaking an entirely different language. Computerese. A kind of high-tech lingo. Everything was circuitry, electronics, switching. If she didn't understand something, it just "didn't scan."

We talked mostly about her boyfriend. This guy was never in a bad mood. He was in a bad mode. Modey kind of guy. The romance was apparently kind of rocky and she kept saying:

"Man oh man you know like it's so digital!"
She just meant the relationship was on again, off again.
Always two things switching.
Current runs through bodies, and then it doesn't.
It was a language of sounds, of noise, of switching, of signals.
It was the language of the rabbit, the caribou, the penguin, the beaver. A language of the past.
Current runs through bodies and then it doesn't. On again. Off again.
Always two things switching. One thing instantly replaces another.
It was the language of the future.

PUT YOUR KNEES UP TO YOUR CHIN.
HAVE YOU LOST YOUR DOG?
PUT YOUR HANDS OVER YOUR EYES.

JUMP OUT OF THE PLANE.
THERE IS NO
PILOT.

YOU ARE NOT ALONE.

THIS IS THE LANGUAGE
OF THE ON-AGAIN
OFF-AGAIN
FUTURE.
AND
IT IS DIGITAL.

"Large Black Dick"
for Harmonized Male Voice

Let's talk about one of our hidden minorities: American men. White American men. I mean those get-out-of-town kind of guys, like Jesse Helms.

Washington, D.C.? It was a town that wasn't big enough for the senator and the artist Robert Mapplethorpe. Yeah, Jesse liked pictures of snowy landscapes, art that made you feel good. And Mapplethorpe?

He was after the big taboos, things like: What do sex and religion have in common?

So the senator looked at the artist's photographs and they were pictures of men with no clothes. And there were lots of chains and black leather and crosses. But the picture that bothered the senator the most was a very large black dick sticking out of a business suit. So he made a law that said:

WE'RE NOT GOING TO LOOK AT THIS
AND YOU'RE NOT GOING TO LOOK AT IT EITHER.

You know, I remember when I was a kid sitting in church and the preacher would point to pictures of Jesus Christ, who was wearing no clothes and bleeding profusely. And the preacher was saying:

LOVE THIS MAN!
LOVE HIS BODY!!
HE LOVES *YOU*!!!

And all the men and boys in church were squirming around, they couldn't look. They couldn't wait to get out of there.

And this of course was the reason for the invention of Sunday afternoon football.

It's been two years now since the Corcoran Gallery canceled Robert Mapplethorpe's show and Jesse Helms asked all the women and pages to leave the Senate so they wouldn't have to look at all the dirty pictures he was handing around. At the time, I thought this would blow over, that people would recognize Helms as just another hysterical crank desperate for a campaign theme. Instead he got reelected. And the issue of control, who controls what, has started to blend in with a whole new brand of puritanism.

But it's not hard to see that control is a major theme in America. Every episode of *Star Trek* is based on it. Losing control is the worst thing that could happen. The captain loses control of the ship for one reason or another and he starts yelling from the bridge,

"I'VE LOST CONTROL! I'VE LOST CONTROL OF THE SHIP!!"

And the plot of every show is how he manages to regain it. It's no coincidence that the whole drama is played out on the set of the control room. So who's really in control here? What's this morality play really about?

Since all this began, one of the things that happened is that everybody's gotten really preachy and puritanical, politicians, pop singers, cab drivers, artists. And it's actually really hard to avoid. I mean it's impossible to talk about puritanism without becoming one. I know this because my puritan ancestors came to this country from England for religious reasons. The King of England wouldn't let them punish people for playing games on Sunday. So they came to America to exercise this precious right to punish people who didn't agree with them. Welcome to America.

Listening to Women's Voices

Last spring I spent a week in a convent in the Midwest. I had been invited to do a series of seminars on language. They had gotten my name from a list in Washington, from a brochure that described my work as ". . . dealing with the spiritual issues of our time," undoubtedly a blurb I had written myself. Because of this and also because men were not allowed to enter the convent, they asked me to come out.

I stayed in a very spartan room. A wooden cross hung over the head of the single bed. It was quiet there at night but every morning at five A.M. precisely, there was a tiny tapping at the door. I'd jump out of bed and run to the door but I was never in time to see who was there. One of the sisters always left orange juice in a plastic cup, the kind they use for methadone, perfectly placed so that the door would just miss knocking it over when it opened.

The night I arrived they had a party for me in a nearby town in the downstairs lounge of the Crystal Lanes Bowling Alley. The alley was reserved for the nuns for their Tuesday night tournaments. It was a pizza party. The lounge was decorated to look like a cave. Every surface was covered with that spray-on rock that's usually used for soundproofing. In this case, it had the opposite effect. It amplified every sound. The tournament play-offs were going on and we could hear all the bowling balls rolling very slowly down the aisles, making the rock-glob stalactites tremble and resonate.

Finally the pizza arrived and the mother superior began to bless the food. This woman normally had a gruff low-pitched speaking voice but as soon as she began to pray, her voice rose, became pure, bell-like, like a child's. The prayer went on and on, increasing in volume every time a sister got a strike, rising in pitch. "Dear Father in Heaven."

The next day, I was scheduled to begin the seminar on language. I had been very struck by this prayer and I wanted to talk about how women's voices rise in pitch when they are asking for things, especially from men. But it was odd. Every time I set a time for the seminar, there was some reason to postpone it. The potatoes had to be dug out, or a busload of old people would appear out of nowhere and have to be shown around. So I never actually did the seminar.

I spent a lot of time there walking around the grounds and looking at all the crops, which were all labeled. There was also a very neatly laid out cemetery, hundreds of identical white crosses in rows. They were labeled: Maria, Teresa, Maria-Theresa, Theresa-Maria, Maria Teresa Maria.

The only sadder cemetery I saw was last summer in Switzerland. I was dragged there by a Herman Hesse fanatic, a very sincere Swede who had never recovered from reading *Siddhartha*. And one hot August morning, when the sky was white, we made a pilgrimage to the cemetery. We brought a lot of flowers and we finally found his grave. It was marked with a huge fir tree and a mammoth stone that said "Hesse" in huge Helvetica bold letters. It looked more like a marquee than a tombstone.

And around the corner was this tiny stone for his wife, Nina, and on it was one word, *"Auslander"* ("Foreigner"). This made me so sad and so mad that I was sorry I'd brought the flowers. Anyway, I decided to leave the flowers along with a mean note. It read:

> Even though you're not my favorite writer
> by a long shot!
> I leave these flowers
> on your resting spot.

Photo copyright © by Dona Ann McAdams

PENNY ARCADE

Name: Susana Ventura
Stage Name: Penny Arcade
Birthdate/Birthplace: New Britain, Connecticut
"Raised Up" Where: New Britain, Connecticut; Lower East Side, New York City;
Formentera, Spain; Canaan, Maine
Education: Reform school (eighth and ninth grades)
New Britain High School (dropped out of tenth grade)
Playhouse of the Ridiculous, New York (joined at age seventeen)
Influences/Mentors/Heroes: Jack Smith, John Vaccaro, John Giorno, Patti Smith, Van
Morrison, Dylan, Bina Sharif, Judith Malina, Anna Magnani, Ruth Malaczech
Places Performed: Poetry Project, St. Mark's; P.S. 122; La MaMa ETC; Theatre for the
New City; the Village Gate; the Ballroom; University of the Streets; Dixon Place;
Assembly Room, Edinburgh; ICA, London; Unity Theatre, Liverpool; Gallway Festival;
Olympia Theatre, Dublin; Everyman, Cork; Vienna Festival; Zurich Festival; Adelaide
Festival; Belvoir St. Theatre, Sydney; the Universe and Comedy Club, Melbourne
Pivotal Performance: Talking to the audience at the Loft Theatre, Tampa, Florida,
because I'd forgotten my *Between Characters* music
Favorite Performance Experience: When the audience spontaneously took over the
stage at the second performance of *Bitch! Dyke! Faghag! Whore!* at P.S. 122 in 1992 that
led to our dance break
Most Terrifying Performance Experiences: When Quentin Crisp answered five
questions in a row with "Mmm-hmmm" at the Vienna Festival.
Getting choked in the audience by a homophobic maniac I attacked at 8 B.C. in 1986.
Favorite Prop or Costume: Circle of psychedelic fish for Andrea Whips's *True Stories*.
Chiffon American flag from *Bitch! Dyke! Faghag! Whore!*
Hobbies: Reading, going out to see and hear bands, poets and photographers,
performers, painters and films, getting the best price on everything, finding unique people
Reading List: *Mists of Avalon, The Little Prince*
Favorite Music: Van Morrison, Shane McGowan, Nusrat Fateh Ali Khan, Jeff Buckley,
Loudon Wainwright III, Aretha, Solomon Burke, Dolly Parton, Mark Johnson, Al Green,
Marianne Faithfull, Patti Smith, Lonesome Val, The Roches
Favorite Quote: Hope is a killer.
　　　　　　Faith and love and action are everything.

Artist's Notes

I started out doing experimental improvisational rock and roll theater with
the Playhouse of the Ridiculous in New York City when I was seventeen
years old. This was in 1968. John Vaccaro, genius that he was, never gave
me a "role." I was always in the chorus, but always ended up with a "solo"
that I improvised. Years later, Vaccaro commented on how I was the only
one from the Playhouse creating my own work. "But, John," I replied, "you
gave everyone else real roles. I had to learn how to create theatre."

It has taken me years to accept my own way of working, to have it have validity in my own eyes because it wasn't and isn't the way anyone I know or who I've read about works. Usually I start out being obsessed with a person or an idea. In the early days of my work it was people. I would find myself telling that person's story to everyone I met all day long. Then I would end up alone at home, pacing the floor, smoking a lot of cigarettes, listening to the same song thirty times in a row—that evoked the essence of that character for me—and I would start to become that character. It was a feeling thing, not scriptural. Then I would go out to someplace and do the character improvisationally. I would almost always start out in the audience. I would build the text from what I remembered I'd said with what stuck with me. I never taped anything. That would make me very self-conscious, and I was trying to obliterate my "self" in those performances. I never wrote anything down for the first five years I was performing. I would say that one of my major skills is my memory. I called myself "an action performer," like Jackson Pollack, the action painter. I only develop work in front of a live audience, I don't sit at home and write.

I'm a talker and a "conceptualist," which is a fancy word for someone who lives in their imagination. When I started doing group pieces, I found that people weren't comfortable working this way. They wanted a script, so I started working with little dime-store notebooks. In them I would write down thoughts I had or visions. After a month or so, I would transcribe these thoughts and build on the original idea. Then I would cut up the pages and stack up the ideas that went together and then I would design the performance. Kinda like Brian Gysin's cutup idea that William Burroughs went on to develop and make famous. These days it's pretty much the same, but now I videotape all my performances because a lot of times I'm generating a lot of new material and my life is more complex than it used to be and I don't remember things in the way I used to because I'm performing for months at a time instead of once or twice a month. My process is obsessive talking, smoking cigarettes, standing around listening to loud music.

I'd have to say that I'm more inspired by visual art than by performance or theater—by paintings, photography, which is weird cuz I'm a text-based artist. I see a lot of theatre and performance because I love being an audience. I get a lot of ideas of my own while I'm sitting there, and I guess it's cuz I'm relaxed with no pressure to perform myself so I sit there and "dream" my work into being. This also happens to me when I'm walking around. All my work comes from my subconscious. I never work around a "theory." I've been in psychoanalysis for fourteen years, and I've used it mainly for my work. My life is still a mess but my work is very organized! New work seems always to be heralded by a lot of emotional pain—this indistinct feeling that there's something pressing that I can't quite think of. Sort of a pebble-in-the-shoe type thing. I also find that my last work has the seeds of my next work. Not surprising really but it always surprises me.

Aunt Lucy

I hope I die soon! The sooner the better! What I gotta do? Sit here an' look at these four walls? Wash an' wax the floor again? My floor's clean! I could drop dead now! I'm happy. My brother's a pig! I live with him fifteen years! He never lifts one finger. I told him, "You should burn in hell! An' when I go youse better do how I said or I'm gonna come back an' haunt youse! Heh, heh, heh."

This Cool Whip's good. It's better than ice cream! It's smooth going down, just like silk. Hey! Don't start with me. It's my only pleasure. That's twelve calories—the whole can! See? Protein—nothing. Carbohydrate—nothing. Sugar—nothing. It's all nothing. In the old days they had too much something. Now they can make it with nothing. That's progress.

Last night I went to St. Anthony's. They had a big class reunion for my son John-John. I got two sons. John-John and Anthony. They had it downstairs in the church, so it was nice. They had a big spread, a big buffet. Oh, they had all kinds of spaghetti, all kinds of macaroni, stuffed shells, all kinds of lasagna, meats, cheese, eggs, quiche. Oh yeah, they had quiche. I had a small piece too. Me, I never make no quiche. The lady downstairs. She makes quiche. Hey! I'd like to know, what happened to all that food? They didn't have no band. They had tapes. You know, disco. Oh, I was sitting right next to that machine. My whole body was shaking with that noise. I danced with Anthony. My son. I got two sons! John-John an' Anthony! It was that exciting, exciting dancing. I like to dance exciting but I gotta be careful. Cuz my heart. It skips a beat. Hey! Whatta you want? I'm an old lady, I'm not good for nothing anymore! *Mangia L'vecchia!* Whatta you think? I'm gonna be seventy-eight April. Him? My brother? He's gonna be eighty February. Why? You wanna take him out an' give him a party? He don't look eighty? Whatta you mean? He don't walk eighty? He walks like he got the hunchback from Notre Dame! Oh, yeah! You worked! Now he's gonna start! All day long we don't hear boo from him an' now he's gonna start that only him worked. We all worked! Now he wants to play with himself! Oh! I worked in the Fulton Fish Market! So what! You wanna medal? Oh! I worked in the freezer! You wanna tell me he stood eight hours in the freezer? Since when? Since when? Hey! I don't wanna argue with you! We all worked! Not just you! Okay, so you went to work early but at twelve noon you would come home an' rest in the bed till four or five at night, and us gals, we worked in the factory an' when youse came home twelve noon, we was still working in the shop. Since when? Since when? We worked out and in! We still had to come home and cook and clean. We all worked, not just you. We all brought money home! We all worked! Since when? Since when? Hey! I don't wanna argue with you! Hey! Hey! All right, you went to work early but when you come home . . . Hey! When you come home, you would lay in the bed till four or five at night. Since when? I don't wanna listen to your bullshit talk! Yer bullshit. Go fuck yourself! [*Turning to audience*] Hey! He's bullshit. All right, he went to work early, I said he went to work early, but when he come home twelve noon, in those days we didn't have no pigeons to feed on the roof, he would go to bed and stay in the bed till four or five at night! We all worked! Not just him! We all brought the money home! The time was tough. My mother had it hard. She was janitor for the building and she worked in the laundry too. Most nights she'd come home, she was dead! I had to drag her in from the hall! I had to cook and clean. Hey! I went to work two years old. Two years old! You kids today, you don't wanna believe nothing! Six years old I knit socks for the whole family an' there were ten of us! I left school ten years old. I went to work in the big paper-box factory. My sister had kids an' I had to help her an' I was just a kid myself! What good times did I ever have? When did I ever go like my brother an' get a bat team together an' have a good time? What good times did I ever have? All right, one time I had a good time. One day, straight after school, my sister an' I got amongst girlfriends an' we started to jump rope. Now, this was a thing we never did. My mother came. She chased us in that school. She gave us such a beating with that rope! After all, there were things to be done! There was a house to be done.

Look, all my life I live in this neighborhood, we call this the Village. Used to be the people didn't want to come here. They was scared. Now up and down, up and down they got boutiques. You see that building across the street? That used to be a big paper-bag factory. Now over there they got a boutique. They call that boutique "If." If what? You should look in the windows of the stores! You should see the way the people dress! The girls? They got the dress long an' the hair up in the air. Or else the skirt short an' the hair in the eyes! An' the boys? The boys wear tights! That's it, just tights! With their thing an' everything showing. What's the matter? These people, they don't have one full-length mirror in the whole house? What? Everybody in the whole family is an enemy? They walk up an' down, up an' down. Monday through Friday you got a regular Forty-second Street. Saturday—Sunday? You got the Macy's Day Parade! They walk West Houston, West Broadway to Spring Street all day long. You wanna tell me all day they look at their reflection in the store window an' they don't see nothing? They don't say, "Oh, my God! I look like shit!" My son Anthony told me, "Hey,

Ma. They don't call this the Village no more. They call it SoHo!" I said to him, "SoHo, so what?"

Girl

My daughter! Why do you do these things? Know why, Mama? Cuz I'm a follower an' the devil, he wanted me to do wrong, Mama. So I got a bad disease, Mama, from sharing dirty needles an' that disease, Mama, that gave me AIDS, Mama. Please forgive me. It's a fault, Mama, that I never understood. That it could happen to me. But I'll tell you one thing. I wanna die the soft way, Mama. Not the hard way. Cuz I don't wanna feel no pain, Mama. I wanna feel good. Bo Bo Bo BoBo Bo Bo . . . I wanna be a singer. One day in the future. Yo! Brother! Gimme some change. Gimme fifty cents. Gimme twenty-five cents. Shit. Yo! Yo! Brother! I can tell a construction worker when I see one! Gimme some change. Come on! I know yer workin', brother, yer just lyin' to yerself. Hey, I'm goin' to the welfare line on Monday. Yo big brother! Big brother! Gimme some change! We are the world! We are the children! You are the ones who make a better day so let's start givin'!

Yo sister, pray for me. Pray for me, I'm in need. I ain't had nothin' to eat for three days 'cept for those nasty sandwiches from the Christian Friends. You know that white bread an' mayonnaise? An' then they come an' ask you if yer prayin'. I said, "Yeah, I'm prayin', I'm prayin' for ham an' cheese!" I'm gonna kneel, I'm gonna kneel down an' I'm gonna be yer follower an' then I'm gonna let you be my follower. Cuz I was hungry an' you gave me something to eat, I was thirsty an' you gave me something to drink, I was sick an' you comforted me. All right! This is me now. I'm gonna tell you what I'm feelin'. I have a child, that the CCS has taken from me. Not because I was an IV user, but because my sister, she put me in a mental hospital, she made me sick! Yo sister, give me some change! It's not for me, it's for my child. Dimes! Nickels! Quarters! Pennies! For me an' my child. *Yo tengo un nena* . . . I have a girl . . . *que me la gittaran* . . . they took her from me. *Yo suffro por ella* . . . I suffer for her . . . with all my soul. When the nighttime comes, after twelve an' I go to the moon an' I write my daughter's name. Her name is Naeesha, an' I would die for her . . . an' I would go through pain, just to see my Naeesha. I also suffer from a disease. I IV myself, for fourteen years. I also share dirty needles an' now I suffer from that disease called AIDS. If you don't believe me, I'll show you some papers, an' I also suffer from a heart murmur. I also suffer with asthma, asthma, you know when I breathe. Yo sister, yo sister, borrow me yer nail polish, yer nail polish! You don't carry that with you? I got to do something with my nails. They look like shit. Cuz I do drugs. You know, drugs? Crack cocaine, heroin. I ain't got high for three days. I met this guy, they call him Boy. He surrendered me. I been kickin' cold turkey. I wanna introduce you to Boy! They call me Girl. *Me gusta cantar! Me gusta balare! Me gusta gritar!* I love to sing Jamaican music an' my favorite color is red, black an' green. I wear perfume but that's expensive! I look the best when I got new dresses. I met this boy, his name is Boy. An' my name, my name is Girl, an' my father's name, he was Tarzan! An' he made me what I am today! I'm pregnant. Can you tell? Have it. It's mine. They say that baby's gonna get AIDS. That baby can't get AIDS! That baby never got high! Have it. Give it away. You ain't got the right thang to go with my fitness! Know why? Because I exercise myself, I do body building! Only my body building is like this [*she humps her hips in three directions*] an' sometimes like this. An' when I can't get enough, I get it like this . . . all the way around! You wanna help me out? With fifty cents or a buck? I can buy lunch with a buck! Shit. My name is Girl! An' I am homeless! But you ain't never seen no homeless person with no pair of New Balance! These jumpers cost my man thirty-nine dollars. An' some change. In a while, like Monday, I'm gonna be all right!

ELIA ARCE

Name: Elia Arce
Stage Name: Same
Birthdate/Birthplace: 9/14/61, Los Angeles, California
"Raised Up" Where: Costa Rica
Education:
1994 University of California, Los Angeles, B.A., Motion Picture and Television
1983 New York University, Intensive Film Workshop
1982 University of Costa Rica, Theater Arts and Dance
Honors/Grants:
1994 Rockefeller Foundation, Multi-Arts Production Grant
1993 J. Paul Getty Foundation, Individual Artist Award
1993 City of Los Angeles Cultural Affairs
Influences/Mentors/Heroes:
Influences: Emilia Prieto, Satyajit Ray, Maria Luisa Bemberg, Lina Wertmuller, Andy Warhol, Bresson, Wayne Wang, John Cassavetes. Mentors: Bread and Puppet Theater, Amy Trompeter, Tete Vasconcellos, Ana Maria Garcia, Tim Miller, the Hittite Empire, Los Angeles Poverty Department, Guillermo Gómez-Peña, Haskell Wexler, Hazel and Benjamin Berg, Helga Kollar, Barbara Zheutlin, Rev. Michael Beckwith, Fabian Wagmister, Ruben Martinez, Marcus Kuiland-Nazario, Mario Gardner
Places Performed: Countryside in Costa Rica, war zone in Nicaragua, Skid Row in Los Angeles; Highways Performance Space, LACE, Diverse Works in Houston, Blue Star Art Space in San Antonio, Texas; Boston Center for the Arts; Institute of Contemporary Art in London; Dance Theater Workshop, New York; Banff Center for the Performing Arts in Canada; Sushi, San Diego; Cultural Center, Tijuana; Macondo Espacio Cultural, Los Angeles; Barnsdall Theater, Los Angeles; Beyond Baroque, Venice; Los Angeles Photography Center; Capp Street Project, San Francisco, UCLA Dance Building; X-Teresa Arte Alternativo, Mexico City; and P.S. 122.
Pivotal Performances:
Improvised in front of my Catholic high school a comedic sketch about a single countryside pregnant teenager contemplating abortion. I was almost expelled from school. Watching *South of the Clouds* by the Los Angeles Poverty Department. It proved to me once more that good art and social issues do mix well together and restored my faith in performance art. I saw the piece three times and I fell in love. And a Keith Antar-Mason and Joel Talbert performance at the ICA in London confirmed that I was on the right track.
Favorite Performance Experiences:
Creating and directing *Maid Make Up Room/Please Do Not Disturb* with the housekeeping staff while in residency at Banff Center for the Performing Arts, Canada. Performing *I Have So Many Stitches That Sometimes I Dream That I'm Sick* in an outdoor installation setting on top of the ruins of Templo Mayor at X-Teresa Arte Alternativo, Mexico City.
Most Terrifying Performance Experiences:
After a performance at the border of Nicaragua and Honduras: Danced to a disco tune in English with armed Sandinistas while the bombs falling nearby were our only source of light. And while performing at a battered women's shelter in Houston I was told by a

fanatic religious social worker that Satan was speaking through my art. "Are you willing to accept Jesus Christ into your heart?" she asked me right then and there.

Favorite Prop or Costume:
Antique bathtubs, mirrors, pigeons, corroded metals, liquids, something mushy
Costumes? Naked bodies

Hobbies: Dancing salsa, eating Thai food, and having sex on the beach

Reading List:
The Lover by Marguerite Duras; Julio Cortazar; Impossible Vacation by Spalding Gray; Prof. Sukenick; Meditations by Karen Finley; English Is Broken Here by Coco Fusco; Warrior from Gringostroika by Guillermo Gómez-Peña; Twisted Sisters; Eileen Myles; bell hooks; Lynda Barry; Nancy Agabian

Favorite Music:
Liz Phair; P. J. Harvey; Bob Dylan; Jonathan Richman; Los Diamantes from Japan; Los Olvidados from Guadalajara; Los Divididos; Mano Negra from Spain; Tom Waits; Bonilia Prieto from Costa Rica; Bikini Kill; Leonard Cohen; That Dog; and performance band Cholita

Favorite Quote:
"Everything lasts until it is over."

Artist's Notes

Anything that I say onstage, I desperately need to say it. I write to relax my jaw. And I perform what I write to make sure that I listen to myself. Sometimes it takes me a year or more to realize what the piece was really about. I always trust that if I am honest with myself I will mean something meaningful. I like to work within the different layers of reality. Up and down the subconscious. My concept of time is that everything is happening at the same time. The past, the present, the future. I just become aware of it and sometimes can choose which one I want to be participating in at the moment. I used to say that the problem with reality was that there were too many of them. Now I am not so sure it is a problem. External stability can be a state of internal movement. And external movement can be a state of internal stability. Stability is a state of movement. Consciousness is the only type of control I aspire to have. I like to consciously go into the subconscious whenever I choose to. Consciousness is the safety belt that will bring me back. My work evolves at the edge of my limitations. I like to go deep down into whatever it is that is bothering me and write about it, improvise about it, draw about it. . . . I sit . . . and I breathe . . . I let my body relax and I notice that my legs are tight, that the insides of my thighs are pushing toward each other . . . and then an image pops into my head. . . . The tool that I choose to record my work with will usually determine the type of artistic language I will use to present the work. If I write on a computer, the text will have a different feeling to it than if I write on a typewriter, record it on a tape recorder, shoot it with a film or video camera, handwrite it, draw it on a piece of paper or just let my body remember it. I believe I am an artist who studies the mind and the spiritual world in psychological and sociological contexts. I got interested in the body because of the memory and secrets trapped in it.

. . . Sometimes I can't tell whether something is freezing or boiling . . . I open my hand and I feel my foot waking up. . . . Blood rushes into my fingers and I feel my foot wanting to take a step . . . open your hand . . . open your hand . . . I'm with you. . . . I fool my hand inside of the water, that can't tell whether it's too hot or whether it's too cold and I imagine the warm water getting right inside of my body . . . where all the pieces just float to the surface and there is no container that can keep the pieces together . . . and I am free . . . and I am free . . . to reinvent myself. . . . I dig into my muscles and dreams for images. I am grateful to the years that I could not express myself through the written or spoken language, because I developed a world of images that screamed louder than words. I believe that old limitation contributed to my artistic voice today. I am big on limitations. I like turning negatives into positives, limitations into artistic styles. I believe artistic styles change as one changes. My thing is to always be at the edge of limitations to ensure growth. I believe in continuity as a process I like to be committed to. I believe that my process changes as I change. And I continually look for ways of getting the material out of me. Each person should have their own methods of being disciplined with themselves. . . . "If you teach a person how to fish, don't complain when they don't want to buy your fish anymore. . . ." I believe each person can develop their own artistic language, if they listen carefully, observe with attention, taste with or without fear, experience with or without denial and trust with awareness. Sounds easy, very easy.

. . . around midnight I was floating upside down in the swimming pool, floating on my breath. The more I let go of my body, the more taken care of I felt. I started go deep, deep down. It was getting darker and darker. It was quiet. And I could only hear the sound of my heartbeat. It started to get louder and louder. Suddenly I felt the pounding outside of myself. The liquid around me started to get thicker and thicker. And all of a sudden I couldn't move, I couldn't breathe. There was all this pressure against my chest, there was all this pressure against my chest. I opened my eyes, and all I could see was all this pain around me, all this pain around me. It wasn't my pain, it wasn't my pain. It was pain that was coming from centuries and centuries ago, centuries and centuries ago. It was my great-great-grandmother's pain, it was my great-great-grandfather's pain, it was my great-grandmother's pain, it was my great-grandfather's pain, it was my grandmother's pain, it was my grandfather's pain, it was my father's pain, it was my . . . AAAAAGGHH . . . I say push me out of here, I've been in here for too long. . . . AAAAGGHHH. . . . If you don't push me out of here I'm gonna have to cling on to your ribs and chew them till my gums bleed, till my gums bleed. . . . I say push me out of here. . . . AAAGGGHH. . . . If you don't push me out of here, if you don't push me out of here I'm gonna have to kick your lungs against your heart till it stops beating, till it stops beating. . . . I said push. . . . I said push. . . . I said push. . . . If you don't push me out of here I'm gonna have to stretch that skin till I rip that wall out of my way, till I rip that wall out of my way. . . . I say push. . . . I say push. . . . That's it. . . . That's it. . . . Just keep pushing . . . just keep pushing. . . . AAAAAGGHHH. . . . That's it . . . that's it. . . . AAAAAAAGGGGGHHH!!!!!!!! (pause) . . . Breathe . . . breathe . . . just breathe. . . .

Some of the images that I work with are images that come out of a specific emotion. And some of them come out of external observation. I do not give myself rules about how to express them. Some concepts are better said in words, others in film images, or through the arrangement of objects. The more tools artists can have to express themselves the better. I believe in generalization rather than specialization. I like to take the audience on a roller-coaster ride through different realities, emotions, languages, voices and art mediums. Whoever wants to ride with me can, and whoever doesn't can watch from a distance. For me, it's about experiencing together as we study and reinvent ourselves and our surroundings. One is a representation of a universe. The simplest little thing could be transcendental if one treats it as such. I think that I am a simple little thing. I know that from the nothingness incredible things occur.

Leche Que Nutre—Leche Venenosa (Nutritious Milk—Poisonous Milk)

I sit naked on my couch, water still dripping from my body. I feel my head getting bigger and bigger in between my legs. And it was pushing, pushing through my mother's vagina. And that makes me feel very sexy . . . and that makes me feel very guilty. . . . *Leche que nutre, leche venenosa* . . . nutritious milk, poisonous milk. I sit . . . and I breathe. I don't want to feel all the things that I am feeling right now. I feel like I can't be sitting still one more minute. I am not supposed to be feeling what I am feeling. . . . I am not supposed to . . . Ohh . . . is coming . . . is coming . . . and I'm holding it in. . . . I don't want to go around scraping memories from my bones . . . but the accumulation of them hurt more . . . hurt more . . . Ohhh . . . Shhh . . . I open my chest, and I sit and I breathe. When I check my body to relax, I always notice that my legs are tight, that the insides of my thighs are pushing towards each other and then an image pops into my head. When my grandmother Helia and I went to Honduras, we were all crammed in this pickup truck. I wanted to ride in the opened back of the truck because it was sunny and it looked like fun. I was wearing a short green skirt that had hot pants underneath. And my cousin . . . you know, the one with the tongue in the ears . . . was looking at me through the back window of the truck. And then I started to feel this stare. . . . I started to feel this stare . . . it was my grandmother who was sitting next to my cousin and was motioning at me with her hand . . . to close my legs . . . to close my legs . . . she was furious because I was sitting in an Indian position. She thought it was a provoking position . . . an inviting position! I didn't understand what was the big deal at the time, but then I understood. I understood that even the way I sit now was decided by her twenty-five years ago . . . and that makes me feel like puking . . . and that makes me feel like PUKING . . . and that makes me feel like I just want to chew my roots and spit them out . . . CHEW MY ROOTS AND SPIT THEM OUT! And then I lay on my bed. I was touching my breasts in the dark, and that felt good . . . so I moved my hand to my crotch . . . and then this image popped into my head. I was six years old the day that my mother left me with Miguel de San Isidro de Acosta to take care of me while she went to the movies. Miguel, Miguel, you sonofabitch, Miguel. I hate you, I detest you, you marked my life forever, you marked my life forever, you sonofabitch. You are impregnated in my skin, in my muscles, in my bone . . . you sonofabitch. I have to expel you out of my hands, out of my thighs, out of my feet, out of my guts, out of my vagina, you sonofabitch, son-of-a-bitch, *la puta que te pario*. I have to sit, just sit in that Indian position . . . and give birth to you, mother-fucker. But no . . . instead I started to imagine that I wasn't a little girl anymore, I was a grown-up woman and I was with him . . . with Miguel . . . with Miguel . . . and I just wanted to fuck his head off, I just wanted to fuck his head off. So I pushed him against the wall. I looked at him straight into his eyes and I saw his burning desire to have me. And I just fucked him, and I just fucked him, and I just fucked him . . . and I left him there . . . aching and throbbing on the floor. I didn't even look back. I was satisfied. I guess sometimes you push your legs towards each other, but my grandmother never taught me that sometimes you open them instead. My Goddess would agree with that. Maybe this is a war of gods. I said, ". . . I don't want anything you have anyway!"

The following is an adapted version of an original Catholic rosary. It is sung as a liturgical chant.

Cordera de Diosas
  que quitas el pecado del mundo
  ten piedad de nosotras
Santa Virgen de las prostitutas
Madre de la Diosa
Madre sucisima
Madre promiscua
Madre puta
Madre con mancha
Madre corrupta
Madre insolente
Madre admirable
Madre del mal consejo
Madre destructora
Virgen imprudentisima
Virgen digna de compasion
Virgen digna de alabanza
Virgen poderosa
Virgen infiel
Ideal de ambiguedad
Morada de sabiduria
Honor de los pueblos
Modelo de contradiccion
Rosa despreciada
Fuerte como una torre
Hermosa como torre de marfil
Puerta del cielo
Estrella de la manana
Salud de las enfermos
Refugio de las pecadores
Consoladora de las afligidas
Auxilio de las paganas
Reina de las matriarcas
Reina de las profetas
Reina de las apostolas
Reina de las que no viven su fe
Reina de las no castas
Reina de todas las santas
Reina concebida con pecado
  original
Reina elevada al cielo y al infierno
Reina de la Santisima Rosaria

Reina de la paz

Cordera de Diosas que quitas el
  pecado del mundo
NO NOS DES PAZ

My Grandmother Never Passed Away

When my grandmother Helia died, I was in the middle of a puppet rehearsal. She had been in the hospital for a few days and I hadn't gone to see her because we were mad at each other. I can't really remember what the argument was about but she screamed at me from her bedside, "When I die I'm not going to leave you anything!" and I screamed right back, "I don't want anything you have anyway!" My grandmother was always in bed. She seemed to be very good with accidents, she had them all the time. The last one was in a coffee plantation. She loved to go and check on the coffee. If it was red, ready for picking, or if it was green, ready for waiting. She couldn't wait. She hated waiting. That's why she went that day with her cane, right after her doctor told her not to get out of bed. She went anyway, she slipped and broke the only part of her entire body she hadn't broken yet . . . her sacrum bone. This time they couldn't even put on a plaster cast, and she was supposed to stay in bed until it healed naturally. Well, she was in her sixties and her bones were already against natural healing, so I can't really remember her very well on her two feet. It seemed to me that she was only alive from her waist up. She looked like a pressure cooker ready to explode. And I would be terrified to go into her bedroom to comb her hair. . . . "When I die I'm not gonna leave you anything!" She was always screaming like that. That's why she had her house full of animals. She had a zoo in her house. She had chickens from different parts of the world. And I would love to check underneath them for a warm pinkish egg. She also had street dogs all over the place, and pigs in the back. I wouldn't visit the pig too much though, I didn't want to get emotionally attached. I always imagined a huge knife cutting its throat ". . . EEEEEeeeeeee . . ." She also had about a hundred doves that became pigeons with time. And she would feed them every day at six o'clock in the morning without delay. ". . . Palomitas, palomitas, palomitas! . . ." she would scream out of the upstairs window. And they would all come flying towards her. It looked like a huge white cloud, ". . . Prrr . . . prrr . . . prrr . . ." the pieces of old bread against the zinc roof. She wouldn't let me feed the doves though, she said I was too small to reach the window and I didn't have enough strength in my hands. So when my aunt asked me if I would throw one of the female cats into the river if she gave *cinco colones* . . . I considered it. See, my grandmother also had a room full of cats. There were about eighty-five cats in this room. This was the room nobody spoke of, only my aunt in secret. The room was dark and you could hardly see anything from the outside. I would sneak out the back door and put my face very hard against the window. And I could only see movement. Like rats, a lot of rats meowing all the time. My aunt wanted to get rid of the females because those were the ones reproducing, but my grandmother knew each cat by name and whenever one would disappear, she would get furious until the cat came back. They always came back. I guess when someone knows you by your name it is hard to resist. So, I gave the cat-drowning job to my cousin Patty. Patty loved the job. She figured she was getting richer and richer as my aunt was getting poorer and poorer. Besides, my cousin was always fighting me for one thing or another. She couldn't stand me being better than her in anything. I think it all started when her brother put his tongue in my ear when I was twelve. I didn't really want it . . . I thought . . . even though it felt good. But then I heard that he had been putting his tongue inside of all their maids' ears who kept getting fired. I didn't feel that special anymore and started to feel sorry about the maids. The last time I saw my cousin Patty was when I was twenty. I came into my boyfriend's house one morning and she and my boyfriend were having coffee. She had spent the night and they had been fucking all night long. It had been years since I had seen her. How and where she found out about him . . . I don't know. But I was happy to see her nevertheless. That was the last time I saw her, though, I guess she felt even after that. . . . "Palomitas . . . palomitas . . . palomitas . . ."

[*Plucking a dead chicken onstage*]

Garbage	Hungry
Broken pipes	No money, no time
Dirty dishes	Kentucky Fried
Clogged pipes	Rash
Dust	Itchy, scratch
Broken pieces	Growing mushroom
Dying plantas	Fungus on my foot
Emotionally clogged	Run out of toothpaste
Can't speak	Tar on my gums
Don't know what I'm feeling	Backaches
Can't breathe	Angry, angry, very angry
Smoke	God delusions
No toilet paper	FASCISM
No soup, no soap	And a dead leaf got caught in the
Papers, papers and more papers	second hand and time stopped
Saying yes to everything	And time stopped
Disappointing everybody	And time
Nowhere and everywhere	Ssstt. . . . Aaaaggghhhhh!
Needy friends, need	

Photo copyright © by Dona Ann McAdams

RON ATHEY

Name: Ron Athey
Stage Name: Ron Athey
Birthdate/Birthplace: 12/16/61; Groton, Connecticut
"Raised Up" Where: Pomona (suburb in L.A. County)
Education: High school
Honors/Grants: 1994 PEN Center West Award for HIV-positive writers; Art Matters Inc., 1994; ICA London Live Arts Commission, 1995; L.A. Department of Cultural Affairs Commission, 1996
Influences/Mentors/Heroes: Nervous Gender; Johanna Went; Vaginal Davis; Crass; Throbbing Gristle; James Baldwin; William Burroughs; Patti Smith; Jean Genet; Annie Sprinkle; Fakir Musafar; Bob Flanagan; Julie Tolentino; Reza Abdoh; The Voluptuous Horror of Karen Black
Places Performed: LACE, Highways, LATC, Fuck!, Sin-a-matic, in L.A.; P.S. 122, Tattoo Love Child, Meat, Jackie 60, LURE, in NY; Randolph Street Gallery, Cabaret Metro, in Chicago; Patrick's Cabaret, Minneapolis; ICA, Torture Garden, Fist, in London; CCA, Glasgow; Festival Atlantico, Lisbon; X-Teresa, Mexico City; Kananhallen, Copenhagen; Bordeaux; Green Room, Manchester
Pivotal Performance: *Martyrs and Saints* at LACE. To that point, I had been performing in nightclubs and group evening at art spaces. I had no idea that a full hour-long piece could have so much impact.
Favorite Performance Experience: Though low tech, nightclubs have the most energy. We did a performance at Sin-a-matic on a platform in the middle of six hundred people that was especially bloody. Everyone was screaming with us. Afterward, we found out so many people had passed out cold that security had laid them out in the rain on the sidewalk in front of the club.
Most Terrifying Performance Experience: In *Martyrs and Saints,* there's a scene where I am quartered out with ropes while dancing, and I have twenty-four thick needles through my head, making up a metal crown of thorns. One dagger pulled my ankle restraint too hard and I fell forward. I almost stuck the dagger in front of me with my HIV-infected crown.
Favorite Prop or Costume: The human printing press
Hobbies: Kink, gardening, and cooking
Reading List: *At Your Own Risk: A Saint's Testament,* Derek Jarman; *Memories That Smell Like Gasoline,* David Wojnarowicz; *Public Sex,* Pat Califia; *On Edge: Performance at the End of the Twentieth Century,* C. Carr; *One Arm,* Tennessee Williams; *Oranges Are Not the Only Fruit,* Jeanette Winterson; *Sister Aimee,* Aimee Semple McPherson biography
Favorite Music: Joy Division, Cabaret Voltaire, Swans, Diamanda Galas, The Germs, The Voluptuous Horror of Karen Black, Babes in Toyland, Afro Sisters, PME, Cholita, old Dusty Springfield, Xtra Fancy
Favorite Quote: "I be wanting his cruel club cock." (Vaginal Davis)

Artist's Notes

In my first "proper" performance piece, *Martyrs and Saints,* I attempted to convey the grandiosity involved in suffering from a martyr complex. The heart of my work has always been in bringing overdone gothic religious tableaus to life, using theatrical and kink, particularly medical-based s/m techniques. *Martyrs and Saints* starts out in an operating room, moves to a temple, then ends up in a Zen garden dripping blood. I used a cast that had pride in being marginalized (not only being s/m queers, but having hardcore physical appearances), and I dwelled in the holy suffering AIDS has brought, along with the helplessness we have over those dying premature deaths. It was everything that made me, all the images I'm possessed with, that constantly boil in my brain. This pageant of erotic torture and penance had to be seen, somewhere.

In *4 Scenes in a Harsh Life,* the concept is more all-over-the-place. In developing *4 Scenes,* I began to look at fetishes, kinks, and rituals as a rhythm. I wanted to communicate the absolute need for ritual and rites of passage, and how they have mutated, that there's a rhythm that makes us tick. I attempted to sandwich very different scenes together, from my own life and those I've observed. The characters: a holy woman, a dyke St. Sebastian, two spiffy altar boys, four steakhouse motherfuckers, two nude strippers, a big black drag queen doing a Gypsy Rose trick, a human printing press made up of three factory workers and three hundred pounds of human flesh, an intravenous drug user, three leather daddies, three boy slaves, a home-health-care worker, one sick leather fetishist with AIDS feeding an IV tube into his scrotum, a minister, three bulldagger brides, a modern-primitive altar boy, a shaman, and four drummers. Though some of the scenes were severe and depressing, if you looked without judgment, you could see the internal healings. But if you shut your head off, condemning: "religions damage," "that's sexist," "he's destroying his flesh," "heroin addiction is bad," "tattoos are just trendy," "this is self-destructive," "weddings are for straight people," you would never see past your own moral judgments and differences. This is how the wedding piece came about: I couldn't understand gays and lesbians being married exactly the same ways as straights, any more than I could understand teenage girls, dreaming of the day they walk down an aisle wearing white, while their family and friends fall to their knees, worshiping her beauty and her grandeur.

Of course, according to the media in the United States, what's more important than what these images mean juxtaposed together is the fact that my HIV status and the blood drawn in the performance were used to dismantle the NEA. It became a case of the hype threatening to become larger than the project, and I was forced to rise to the occasion.

Performing 4 Scenes in New York was the test. With almost no funding, I was forced to produce five shows in four nights (Saturday we had a late show). So busy meeting with the press, who were flying in from all over the country, trying to raise airfare and find housing for the cast, I worried about having some sort of a breakdown. Somehow we lived through it, and were truly stronger for it.

Afterwards I had to pose a question to myself: Am I enjoying this? Who am I doing this for? Have I become an entertainer? And the question I never wanted to think about: What is art and how do I fit in the current performance scene?

Fortunately, around this time, I found a following in the U.K. and Europe. The Ron Athey Company played art centers and nightclubs in London, Manchester, Glasgow, and Lisbon and received various profound responses, though not without problem: Operation Spanner in the U.K. caused me to work under censorship and risk of arrest. This left me with a bad taste in my mouth, but I let it all hang out in the fetish nightclubs, Fist and Torture Garden.

With all the media hype being around HIV-positive blood, I think many audiences have come to see a sort of AIDS-oriented Jim Rose sideshow. The opening tableau of 4 Scenes, "The Holy Woman," is not quite all that. I play the Holy Woman, she has been inspired by evangelists Aimee Semple McPherson and Kathryn Kuhlman crossed with an image from religious paintings, St. Irene pulling the arrows out of St. Sebastian. The monologue "Sister Linda's Stigmata" is a true story from my childhood, from a time when I was taken to strange Pentecostal churches to see or seek miracles. This strange child's story gives context for the many angles of bloodletting that occur in the piece. The story ends with me slicing stigmata into my younger sister and myself, my first act of holy defiance.

The text for "Suicide/Tattoo Salvation" is a voice-over, first describing the most suicidal day of my life, filled with self-mutilation and drug abuse. It concludes with a dream I had fifteen years ago, that I feel to this day not only saved my life, but made me equate my tattoo vision with spiritual wholeness.

"Sermon: There Is So Many Ways to Say Hallelujah" is a reinterpretation of false prophecies: that I was to be a minister for Christ, that if I'm not that I'm damned. This message is applied to a three-way lesbian wedding, where the dykes do a tribal dance for transcendence.

My third piece, Deliverance, is a term that also comes from a childhood prophecy; definition: to be freed or rescued. During my childhood, we prayed for deliverance: we believed that we were like Job, and the tests were to be finished one day, and that's when our chosenness would hook in. Deliverance is about shamanistic impulses; cleansing rituals and the need to see the filth; the temptation to abandon everyday life and go inhabit the psychic realm; and God's Chosen One's glamorization of the Apocalypse (Judgment Day).

Sister Linda's Stigmata

From the time I was a baby, my grandma and aunt Vena repeatedly informed me, "You've been born with the calling on your life, Ronnie Lee." I was just becoming aware of what that prophecy meant: that being chosen for a ministry made me different from everyone else. According to this message from the holiest of holies, I was to sacrifice the playthings of the world in order to fulfill the plans of God.

Throughout the course of my religious training, I encountered many great prophets, faith healers, mystics, and savers of souls. In church I would close my eyes and absorb the rambling vibrations given off from the gift of tongues, mixed in with the sounds of foot stomping and bodies hitting the floor hard as they went out in the spirit.

I would listen intently as people testified of physical healings, the exorcism of demons, and the detailed arrival of Armaggedon. My childhood was spent among adults who believed that their lives read like the Book of Job. It mystified me that as a mere test of faith, God unleashed hideous diseases and allowed actual demon possession. These could later then be removed, providing the laying on of hands was executed by a powerful reverend minister.

The rarest and least talked-about miracle is stigmata, wherein the gifted spontaneously bleed from the same parts of the body that Christ bled. As the only two living examples with stigmata were women, there seemed to be some indication that women were more open to receiving the gift. I believed with all my heart it could be given to me.

One day Aunt Vena had been given a promotional flyer announcing Sister Linda's Miraculous Gift of Stigmata: A Three-Day Visit to the Indio Area! It described how sometimes she bled pure blood, and other times she bled a clear, scented healing oil.

Putting the sweetest, holiest look on my face I could, I expressed my interest in attending.

"Aunt Vena, I'd like to see this miracle."

So my family drove into the desert to let me witness Linda bleed.

That first night, after sitting through an uninspiring sermon delivered by the local Pentecostal minister, it became apparent that Linda was not going to bleed. I was disappointed, but anxious to return.

On the second visit, the air was so still outside, I knew that she was going to bleed that night. Sister Linda had dark circles under her eyes, and her face was all shiny with sweat. She looked like she had the Holy Spirit rattling around inside of her. I joined in the hymn singing, a chorus of twangy hillbilly voices belting out, "When we all get to heaven, what a day of rejoicing that will be, when we allll see Jeeesus, we will sing and shout with victory." And again, I patiently listened to the minister try to, but not, achieve inspiration. Towards the end of the service, when she still had not bled, I wanted to have a temper tantrum. I thought, *She's just a big fat fucking scam artist.* I couldn't understand why everyone else was so patient with waiting for her "gift." All she had shown us were pictures; cheap snapshots of her bloody clothes, as if that were sufficient evidence of a miracle. And further, she shared with the congregation that impressions in blood would appear in her Bible: but I didn't want to hear stories of psychic phenomena, I wanted her to bleed. I had come there with a strong desire to be anointed in the blood seeping directly from her palms.

I had wondered if she would bleed from the place where the spear had been inserted in Christ's side. I pondered on whether or not she would expose the wound. Would she be modest like Aunt Vena, or was a stigmata hole different? I imagined what the blood would look like seeping through her clothes.

But she hadn't bled from anywhere on those first two nights.

Around the time of the stigmata, I found a brand-new razor blade, and took my li'l sister, Tina, into the backyard. I held her hand in mine, then sliced into the tips of all her fingers on that hand. Instinctively I knew that the clean slices would produce blood, and when it began to flow, Tina started to cry. I knew the cuts didn't hurt, that she was just frightened.

I then took the razor to my own hand, to show her how insignificant the wounds were, and to make her stop crying.

Ron Athey's Sermon: There Is So Many Ways to Say Hallelujah

Oh, there's so many ways to say Hallelujah

There's the dominant male evangelist Hallelujah
it's loud and commanding
[Hallelujah]

There's the prayer meeting Hallelujah,
it's a drawn out, drawled out Hallelujah,
yearning, pulling in the power
[Hallelujah]

and there's the "I've been cleansed in the fire of the Holy Spirit, washed in the blood of the Lamb" Hallelujah

it can be identified by its choppy phonetics
it sounds like an epileptic seizure
[oh-she-kun-der-a-mah-see-keyah hal-le-luh-jah mah-lay-leyah kun-deh-ruh
chris-tee-chris-to]

and of course there's the plain and simple churchgoer Hallelujah
it's a mildly inspirational expression of joy and praise
[Hallelujah]

Oh, there's so many ways you can say Hallelujah

Now, I know we all have a story with the church, but I had family members
blessed with the gift of prophecy
they discerned that I had the calling on my life
and throughout my entire early life,
a picture was painted before me of the most grandiose ministry that was to be
prepared for the honor of God through myself

But at age fifteen I had a change of heart,
and I turned away from that calling
I ran and ran and ran
and I rebuked the name of the Father
and I named false prophets
and I saw no way of ever saying Hallelujah again

But today, once again, I stand back up in a pulpit, Hallelujah

Now brothers and sisters, friends, family members, loved ones, today we
stand here in honor of a union for Pipgen, Cross, and Julie: three
passionate bulldaggers.

These daggers are of the belief that by their coming together in your
presence, by your witness, their union will be blessed, although not legally
binding. Let me hear a yearning Aimee Semple McPherson Hallelujah

Let me ask the daggers, what's this wedding really about? Is this about new
dyke politics, or is it that you've dreamed your whole little girl life of
wearing a big white dress down an embellished walkway? No? Then let me
ask some of you out there. . . .

Have you dreamed your whole little girl life? Then where are we to draw
our traditions from?

Suicide/Dream

In one of my earliest stunts I slashed my little sister's fingertips with a razor blade.

I then took the razor to my own fingertips to show her how insignificant the wounds were, and to make her stop crying.

That's just a creepy little kid's story, the chemical hell started with Valium when I was nine. By the time they cut my prescription six years later, I was long-term addicted. I suffered through a long summer of withdrawals.

I formerly tried to commit suicide with a Seconal overdose. I swallowed a hundred. It was a temper tantrum designed to reject the choices I saw for a life. I vomited for a day—did the failure mean I would be the type to take everyone down with me?

I shot dope for seven years and turned on anyone I could. Junkie life is a suspended state of being. Through some of it I hated myself—but mostly I was indifferent to anything humane. It was numbness interspersed with temper tantrums and a drive to stay well.

In my best drama-queen fashion I repeatedly tried to kill myself: intentional overdoses, wrist slashing, poison injections . . . I was never able to stop the picture going on. I was fucked up in my own private hell.

It irked me that I was a big baby-faced white boy. I wanted to be androgynous, dark and mysterious, exotic. Instead I was sweet like apple pie. I wanted to slash my face to spite my all-American wholesome good looks.

I tattooed Fuck You with a spider, cross, teardrops, and a crown of thorns on my forehead. "He Holy, He Holy, Forgive?" I couldn't shake the martyr complex. It got so bleak and a lot less easy.

If I could just sleep and never wake up.

If someone could put me out of my fucking misery.

Am I just a manifestation of my fucking self-destruction?

A suicide?

In the middle of my messy self-destruction came a dream. In that dream my tattoos were complete. My body was covered with massive black tribal designs.

In that dream that was to turn my life around, I stood strong, like a man. I faced a man who was tattooed as I, almost solid black, but the designs were stylized animals.

We stood the same size—we looked exactly alike. Slowly and simultaneously we began levitating. Elation washed over me.

That morning when I awoke, I felt the same, even though I was alone and my body was yet to become solid black.

After twelve years of getting tattooed, a tattoo artist told me a little saying about the power colors: "They wash in the black through the white and the red."

ERIC BOGOSIAN

Name: Eric Bogosian
Stage Name: Ricky Paul
Birthdate/Birthplace: Boston, Massachusetts
"Raised Up" Where: Boston suburbs
Education: University of Chicago (two years)
Oberlin College (B.A., Theater, 1976)
Honors/Grants: NEA Fellowship, 1982; Obie Awards for: *Drinking in America, Sex, Drugs, Rock & Roll, Pounding Nails in the Floor with My Forehead;* Drama Desk Award: *Drinking in America;* Silver Bear Award, Berlin Film Festival, for *Talk Radio*
Influences/Mentors/Heroes: Richard Foreman, Jeff Weiss, Richard Pryor, Jimi Hendrix, Bob Carroll, Bobcat Goldthwaite, Bill Hicks, Jack Nicholson, Frank Zappa, Lenny Bruce, Pete Townsend, Brother Theodore, Napoleon Solo
Places Performed: Everyplace
Pivotal Performance: Club 57, January 1982: *Men Inside/Voices of America*
Favorite Performance Experience: Berkeley, 1993: dog show
Most Terrifying Performance Experience: Performing at a literacy benefit, and Barbara Bush was in the audience
Favorite Prop or Costume: My hair
Hobbies: Gardening, trash metal
Reading List: Don DeLillo, Russell Banks, Robert Stone
Favorite Music: Led Zeppelin
Favorite Quote: "Blow me."

Artist's Notes

This group of monologues and essays first appeared in a book published by Wedge Press in 1983. The booklet was edited by myself and Brian Wallis. It's no longer in print.

Between 1977 and 1982 I wrote sixteen performance pieces—solos and ensemble. These were performed in places as diverse as the Mudd Club and the Kitchen. Some were huge plays with over a dozen characters each (*Sheer Heaven* and *The New World*), some were solos like *That Girl*, most were small ensemble pieces.

In 1983, I appeared off Broadway in the solo *FunHouse* (published by TCG: *The Essential Bogosian*). Since then, my work has gone in different directions, including "plays" of a more traditional sort, films, and books. I perform once a year at P.S. 122 using the more "raw" and unpolished stuff like what's included here.

This material comes from three pieces: *The Ricky Paul Show; Men in Dark Times* (named after the Hannah Arendt book of essays); and *Advocate*.

The Ricky Paul Show (1979) was a show in which I appeared onstage and insulted the audience in the guise of the comic "Ricky Paul." Usually I had a small band with me, fronted by Joe Hannan. Sometimes my "wife" would join me, played by Barbara Allen. It was fun. The point was to get a rise out of a complacent neohippie audience. (I was inspired by the punk/no wave music I was enjoying at the clubs.) This show toured a little bit and was often met by angry bottle throwing. In Berlin I goose-stepped around the stage and *Sieg heil*ed the audience. Today, the writing seems tame, but in 1979, it got me in trouble.

Men in Dark Times was an attempt to expand from my solo stuff to an ensemble in which I could appear. The show ran for four days at the Kitchen in New York City. (That was a "run" then.) With me appeared Marcellino Rosado and Jeff McMann. The high point of the show was when I did an exotic dance in minibriefs to the song "SuperFreak."

Advocate was an answer to critics who said my work was too dark. With the monologues came slides of child porn, concentration camps, and torture victims. I sat at a desk and simply recited the material. Some people left the room. "Our Gang" later appeared in *Drinking in America* completely rewritten.

I've also included a couple of short essays that I wrote for the Wedge book.

from The Ricky Paul Show

Joe D.

I mean wow, all right! New York City is a good time plus! It's got something for everybody, you just got to know what button to push, which dial to turn. It's a moving, grooving, twenty-four-hour-a-day flipped trip and I dig it! . . . "Yo, yo man, right here, joints and bags, joints and bags, coke and smoke, LSD, DMT, STP, PCP, and XTC! Yo man, yo, got a quarter, do you know what time it is? Gotta cigarette? What's a matter, yo deaf, man? Yo, I'm talking to you, man!" Love, Love, Love, Love, Love. Love makes the world go round! Who knows the meaning of love? Not many people . . . I knew one man who knew what love is . . . Joe D. Joe D. was in love with a stripper who used to work at a bar in New York called Diamond Lil's. Nice place, drinks were expensive, a little dark inside, but nice. Every night Joe D. would go to Diamond Lil's with his uniform on, stand by the bar, have a drink and watch the girls strip. He only wanted to see Sally, Sally with the appendix scar. He liked to see her take her clothes off, expose herself, get naked. Mmmmmmmm. One night he thought, *I love her, maybe she will come to my place and take her clothes off in my living room.* So he got all dressed up in his best clothes, aftershave, new shoes, and he came by the bar at four o'clock when Sally was done with work. He waited for her behind the bar, in the alley. Sure enough, four-fifteen, out comes Sally and there's Joe D. waiting for her. She takes one look at the guy in the alley, reaches into her purse, pulls out a .38 and blows his brains out! He never knew what hit him! Like the guy who walked when it said Don't Walk. Boom to the moon!

from Men in Dark Times

The Leader

It is with honor and great joy that I stand before you today. For today we mark a turning point in the history of our great nation. Today we can see very clearly the horizon of our destiny before us. As a people, we gather together to celebrate the defeat of a pernicious and dangerous threat to our individual freedom. Today we can say to ourselves: We have been challenged and we have met that challenge. As Martin Faust remarked on a similar occasion: "A people is judged by its greatest dangers. . . ."

We have met our greatest danger and we have defeated it. We have done what has been necessary. We have utilized the forces at our disposal. We have found the criminals and they will be punished. Once again we live in a land that is devoted to the law, to order, and to rule by the people for the people.

For the criminal, the treasonous, and the barbarous have no place in our society. Because a land without law is a land without boundaries. Without law we are no better than savages, without a framework to live by everything is chaos, without a strong leadership to guide us we are lost. When certain "elements" of our society are allowed to run rampant, to foster their own law, then all are endangered. [*Voice rising*] Those who wish to do things their own way, those who wish to declare themselves enemies of the people, enemies of our nation, must be taught the lessons of obedience. They must learn that the strong hand of discipline will come from above. We must act from strength, not weakness.

For the time has come. The time has come for our great nation to return to the glory it once knew. The time has come for our great nation to know the fruits of its labor. To savor the honey of its goodness and fairness. The time has come to eradicate the rot that has undermined us. To show that we are a nation undivided and strong. It is time that a once great people should return to their greatness, to conquer those who would have it another way.

We are gathered here today to celebrate a victory. A victory not only of our country against its enemies, but of good against evil. It is a moral victory. It is a victory of the spirit. And to the victor must go the spoils.

For it is destiny that it be so. It is the destiny of a great people. Destiny is shaped by history and the history of all mankind is from darkness and servitude to enlightenment and freedom. It is our task, no, our duty to seize the torch and carry it forward. [*Arm raised*] It is our duty to seize the power and carry it forward. It is our duty to seize history and carry it forward.

This is our duty and we will do our duty. No petty misfits can stand in the way of good men. No miserable and perverted terrorists and their terrorist leaders. No antisocial minorities who think they have the answers. No people of foreign blood who seek to contaminate our good earth and our good life.

Ours is a strong nation. Ours is a proud nation. Ours is a nation of upright men standing in God's illumination. We have the strength of the just, the will of the righteous. We are the chosen people. We must show the others the way, we must lead the others. We must rule the others.

There is only one road that can possibly be followed: our road, the right road. Those who stand in the way of the right road, in the way of history and progress, will be pushed aside. We cannot be hampered by the lame and the impotent. They have no chance of success, no future. We must have the courage to smash all resistance. The future belongs to the righteous. The future belongs to the strong.

The time has come. [*Pounds the podium*] The time has come to give a lesson to the world. For the good of all we must display our power. We must punish the errant at whatever sacrifice. We must be prepared to lose all, so that we may gain all. We must be prepared to destroy all, so that we may prevail over all. We must make the world understand what it means to reckon with absolute power.

All empty words must end and men everywhere must understand: *If necessary we will make the world shiver*. We will vanquish history. We will have the courage to do what is right. If forced, we will let loose the dogs. We will unsheathe the long knives. We must be satisfied, we will be satisfied. If we cannot know satisfaction, then none will know satisfaction. The lesson will be taught and darkness will reign. Our destiny calls us. We must show the way. The bells will toll, the time has come. *Let darkness reign.*

from Advocate

Our Gang

What? I said we were just standing around. Nothing. I dunno, don't get yourself all excited, wait a minute, let me think. Uh, we were looking at

Art's new engine. He had a new engine put into his Camaro. We were just talking. Just drinking beers. We weren't bothering anybody, we were in our part of the parking lot. Uh-uh, we weren't fighting. Uh, wait, yeh, that's Billy, Billy had blood on his shirt because . . . because of something with his girlfriend, I dunno, she punched him or something. We were just minding our own business, that's all. Wolf was fucking around with his car, 'cause some guys were playing cards in his headlights, you know, and so Wolf was doing that thing where you hold your foot on the brakes and gun the engine at the same time. You know, the tires burn and maybe there's a chance that he'll let go the brakes and run over the guys playing the cards. You know, that kind of shit. We weren't causing trouble. Nobody had any weapons or anything. We don't go in for that bullshit. . . . So then that chick comes over. Nobody asked her to come over, you know. She'd been to the parking lot before. Not when I was there, but they said that, I dunno, Larry, I guess, they said that, you know, she blew guys if they wanted. Why should they lie? There's girls like that. They just want attention, or they're upset because they broke up with their boyfriends. I dunno. Sometimes they're just crazy chicks. They come from other towns, like poorer towns or something and we're easy to find, you know. We're always here . . . I'm getting to that. So the next thing I knew everyone was crowded around Wolf's car. The guys playing cards just kept playing. I think maybe one of them, Chub, mighta got up because he never gets any, you know. He's one of those guys who collects every *Playboy* and still lives with his mother. I mean, for him it was a dream come true. His big chance to score. I don't think he got it up, though. . . . Yeh, I guess I did, I dunno, I was drunk. I just remember somebody pushing me over to the car and she was lying back, what? Yeh, I guess someone was holding her, but they said she was a whore. She looked like she was enjoying it, she was moving all over the place. I just kinda fell on top a' her and everyone was shouting. I just remember she smelled kinda funny and she had a shitload of eye makeup on. Boy, she was cheap. . . . Then somebody, I guess Larry, pulled me off and then everyone was moving for the cars real fast, they said there was an open house in the North End so we all took off for there and I don't remember what happened to her. I was too drunk. I musta passed out. . . . What? Yeh, of course I'm sorry. I wished I wasn't there in the first place.

Violence

Midnight. I'm in a porno store on Forty-second Street looking at a rack of magazines devoted to dominance and submission. On the sound system I hear Culture Club singing "Do You Really Want to Hurt Me?" I walk past the armed store guard with his billy club, out onto the sidewalk filled with black and Hispanic teenagers, clumped into ominous gangs. Down the block I find a movie theater with a TV outside playing clips from *Bad Boys,* a movie about teenagers who kill each other. On the subway platform, a man walks toward me and I keep my distance. I remember getting mugged at knife-point two months earlier. I get home and turn on the TV. My wife isn't home from work yet. I worry about something bad happening to her. I think about the terror of meeting a genuinely sadistic person, someone who delights in the screams and begging of his victim. I notice that I'm watching a cop show on TV and that a rape is in progress. The camera closes slowly on the woman's contorted face. . . .

The Poem

Black. A gooseneck lamp is switched on at a desk and we see the Narrator sitting there. The light shines on his face in spooky fashion. He speaks softly into a microphone, addressing the audience:

Light is such a wonderful thing. It warms us. It allows us to see. The light of knowledge. The flame of liberty. The illumination of civilization. All that sort of thing. Much better than darkness. In darkness we are lost. Befuddled. Fearful. Are you afraid of the dark? I'm sure you're not. [*Pauses*] The Dark Ages. The dark side of the moon. The dark side of the soul . . . The Dark One. [*Smiles*] We're not afraid of the dark, are we? We're not afraid of the dark because we know better. We know so much . . . we are . . . omniscient. Reach out [*He reaches for the switch on the lamp, but stops short*], flick a switch . . . "light." [*Pauses*] So let's all sit close together, here in the dark [*Matter-of-factly*] and I will read you a poem [*Brightly read, almost whimsical*]:

> And the little ones run in the streets. They run playfully and joyfully through the empty streets. They run hopefully through the dark ruined streets. Come here, my little children. Come here, small tender ones. Into my arms. Into my teeth of streets. Run into the midnight traffic. Fall against the hot drops of water from your mother's tears. Laughing into my teeth. With balloons trailing, kites flying, dresses all crisp and white and unspoiled by the oily rain of the midnight traffic. Run into the night, hopeful little children. Run into the streets and streets and streets and streets and streets. Little babes. Little babes in toyland. In magic-land. In gentle rolling green hills of azure blue skies and fluffy clouds and giggling phosphorescent soaring expectant wonder. Come here, little children. Open your eyes. Open your mouths. Open your arms. Run into the night. Hold it close to your tiny chests.

Let it into your veins of tiny power. Let the night into your hearts. Let your laughter echo through the dark ruined streets. Let the night into your hearts. Let the night into your hearts. Let the night into your hearts.

That wasn't so bad, was it? . . . I wrote it myself. I'm going to show you some pictures now. . . . Then, then we're going to have some real fun. . . .

Representation

Through the grimy glass of a New York City storefront I spy a man huddled over some dusty plants. Dark green, they sit in caked dirt in ceramic pots, chipped dishware, even a water glass stained where the water has evaporated. In this storefront darkness, the man moves, pouring a bit of water into each plant/receptacle. I have to wonder about these plants. They are neither vital nor aesthetic. And though the man is watering them, I can see they are completely neglected. Thousands of people in New York City have plants such as these: ugly, neglected, half-dead. I have plants like these in the window of my apartment. I guess if I could, I would have lush plants, beautiful and strong, charismatic and healthy. Until that time, I will have these other plants (actually repulsive) to represent the plants I would have.

Now I am in a teeming square in a northern European city. Everyone is well dressed, amiable, moving at an even shopper's pace. Everyone is basically happy, blond, pink cheeked. Even an old man who seems to act like a bum turns out to be wearing an expensive camel's hair coat and Bally shoes. People are crowding around a young man with a guitar. His long, thick hair blows in and out of his determined face. His singing voice is strong and clear like his expression. He is a minor deity descended among the shoppers to bring the message from Los Angeles: ". . . welcome to the Hotel California. . . ." I have to wonder about this young man and who he thinks he is with his perfected American accent at this moment in front of the massed shoppers, with his hair flowing, his eyes crystalline.

KATE BORNSTEIN

Name: Kate Bornstein (née Al Bornstein)
Stage Name: Kate Bornstein
Birthdate/Birthplace: March 15, 1948/Neptune, New Jersey
"Raised Up" Where: I was raised in Asbury Park, a sleepy li'l town on the Jersey Shore.
Education: Brown University, B.A. in Theater Arts. I was the first person to graduate from Brown with a concentration in theater, but that's only because I didn't have enough credits to graduate in anything *else,* and I don't think the dean wanted me around for another year [*Grin*].
Honors/Grants: None. Sigh.
Published Work: Author of *Gender Outlaw, On Men, Women, and the Rest of Us* (Routledge, 1994. Vintage paperback, 1995), includes the text of the play *Hidden: A Gender.* Co-author with Caitlin Sullivan of *Nearly Roadkill,* a novel (High Risk Books, 1996).
Influences/Mentors/Heroes: I was *big*-time influenced by Rootie Kazootie when I was around four or five years old. He was a puppet on television, a rival of the do-good Howdy Doody. Rootie was a mischief maker, and he had this great machine that could take him anywhere and anywhen he wanted to go. I also wanted to be Winky-Dink . . . a cartoon character of the same era. Wink was really cool. You'd send away for a piece of plastic that you'd put on your TV screen. During the show, these lines would appear, and you'd trace them with a crayon on this plastic sheet. By the end of the show, you'd have a message, or the way to save Wink from some horrible fate. It was interactive TV, *non*? But my grown-up mentors and heroes have got to be writer/performers Holly Hughes, Lois Weaver, Peggy Shaw, Deb Margolin, Annie Sprinkle, and Laurie Anderson. Author/playwright Caitlin Sullivan. Actors Jodie Foster, Gary Oldman, Sally Field, Vanessa Redgrave, Jack Lemmon. Comix writers/illustrators Diane DiMassa, Neil Gaiman, Alan Moore, Terry Moore, and Chris Bachalo. Filmmakers Bob Fosse, XXX, Charlie Chaplin, and Ingrid Wilhite. Comedians Kate Clinton, Bob Newhart, Jean Shepherd, Bill Cosby. My acting instructors John Emigh, Jim Barnhill, and Don Wilmeth. I'm also a *major* fan of Joan Rivers, Phil Donahue, [*Blush*] Geraldo Rivera, the Five Lesbian Brothers, and the Sacred Naked Nature Girls.
Places Performed: P.S. 122 (New York), Walker Art Center (Minneapolis), Josie's Cabaret and Juice Joint (San Francisco), Theatre Rhinoceros (San Francisco), Red Dora's, the Bearded Lady Café (San Francisco), the Marsh (San Francisco), Life on the Water (San Francisco), the Southern Theater (Minneapolis), the Green Room (Manchester, U.K.), Real Art Ways (Hartford), Alice B. Theatre (Seattle), ICA (London), Cleveland Performance Art Festival, Buddies in Bad Times Theater (Toronto), the Bulkhead (Santa Cruz), Sushi Gallery (San Diego), Highways Performance Space (Santa Monica), the Theater Offensive (Boston), the Climax Theater (Philadelphia), Capitol Theater (Windsor, Ont.), Seven Stages (Atlanta), the Clit Club (New York), Brown University, George Mason University, Stanford University, Brandeis University, Penn State University, MIT, Harvard University, Duke University, UC Santa Cruz, UC Riverside, U Mass Amherst, and Wesleyan College. Television appearances include the *Phil Donahue Show, Geraldo,* the *Joan Rivers Show,* the *Jane Whitney Show,* and *Real Personal* with Bob Berkowitz.
Pivotal Performance: Hadda be the first New York run of *The Opposite Sex Is Neither*

at P.S. 122. At the risk of sounding like Sally Field at the Oscars, it's basically when I really found out that people wanna hear and see the stuff I write and perform. I'd been bracing myself for rotten eggs.

Favorite Performance Experience: I played King Lear in my senior year of college. The last night of the run, I had a 102-degree fever, and I remember *that* was the night I finally grasped the mad scenes. My parents were in the audience that night. It was great.

Most Terrifying Performance Experience: I recently performed *The Opposite Sex Is Neither* at a convention of transgendered folks in Atlanta. The audience consisted of nearly two hundred T-folk, and I was scared to death at my own arrogance in presuming to speak so many transgendered voices in one piece. The tech was a wreck that night: the sound system didn't work at all, and the light cues came in and out at the wrong times. I felt mortified. But at the end of the show, at the last line, the audience got to its feet as one in a standing ovation. I just started crying.

Favorite Prop or Costume: The ankh I wore around my throat for the first time in the P.S. 122 run of *The Opposite Sex Is Neither.* I had just changed the whole costume of Maggie, the central character, and based it on Death in the comic by Neil Gaiman and Chris Bachalo: *Death: The High Cost of Living.* I still wear that ankh.

Hobbies: SM play, on-line *Star Trek* games, random net surfing/flirting, random Web crawling

Reading List: Novels: *House Rules* by Heather Lewis, Anne Rice's vampire series and Mayfair witches series, *Cry to Heaven, Geek Love, Housekeeping, The American Woman in the Chinese Hat.* Comic Series: *Hothead Paisan: Homicidal Lesbian Terrorist, The Sandman, Strangers in Paradise, Love and Rockets.* Graphic Novels: *V for Vendetta, The Complete Ballad of Halo Jones, The Watchmen, Arkham Asylum*

Favorite Movies: *All That Jazz, Nashville, Siesta, True Romance, Cabaret, Yankee Doodle Dandy, Breakfast at Tiffany's, Sister My Sister, Sweet Charity, Terminator Two, Housekeeping, Batman, Batman Returns, Camille, Thelma and Louise, Reservoir Dogs*

Favorite CD-ROMs: Myst, Puppet Motel, Freak Show, Gadget, *Star Trek* Omnipaedia

Favorite Music: Circus music, calliope music, merry-go-round and nickelodeon music, ragtime, twentieth-century Russian composers, Mahler, South African township music, Strauss waltzes and polkas, movie scores by Hans Zimmer, Elmer Bernstein, and Danny Elfman, Laurie Anderson, Astor Piazzolla, Ferron, Leonard Cohen, Mazzy Star, Dead Can Dance, Sophie B. Hawkins, the Penguin Café Orchestra, Chris Williamson, Sweet Honey in the Rock, Jelly Roll Morton, Art Tatum, Miles Davis, the Tom Tom Club, Lou Reed, Cecilia Bartoli, Marianne Faithfull, Spanky and Our Gang, Courtney Love, Laura Love

Favorite Quote: "All roads in life lead nowhere, really. So, you might as well choose the road that has the most heart, and is the most fun." (Anonymous Zen saying)

Artist's Notes

I've been consciously performing my life since I was about four years old, so it makes sense to me that part of my art includes performance. See, I went from male to female in this world (and then to neither, but that's another story entirely), so since the age of four, I've always been conscious of my performance. The way I see it, there's such a thin veil between life and art that this consciousness of performance carries over into my performance work.

Need to talk about the life/art thing. I'm still trying to figure out the difference. I keep assuming that what I get out of each is the expression of my unique experience of truth . . . whether that truth be beautiful and self-enhancing, or terrifying and utterly shameful. In order to tell the truth so that it can be heard, I constantly try to figure out: who's listening?

Who are you? that's what I want to know.

How can *you* best hear my truth?

The kinder that truth is to who I really am, or the more it contributes to my relative security, well, then the fewer filters I need to put between that truth and you. The more shameful or dangerous that truth is to who I am, the more filters I need to put between you and my telling of that truth. For example . . . I'd like Jesse Helms and Newt Gingrich to know about my truth, but it's fairly dangerous for me to lay myself on the line like that. So, I perform my truth for *you*, in hopes that through *you*, my truth may one day reach ol' Newt, if only by your vote for my rights.

Back to connection. I write or perform with an awareness of, and a need for, connection with my audience. Like right now. I know you're reading this. It's like I'm trying to peer up from these pages and grin at you. I'd write that in brackets, like this: [*Looking up and grinning*]. Maybe you're startled at my grin at first, but maybe you'll grin right back.

I like connecting with my audience in much the same way I like to connect with people in my life: I like to ask questions. I like finding out about people. My favorite questions are those without answers; the ones that make me think, fry my li'l brain cells to a crisp, and leave me with a wonder for the world. I have a lot of respect for folks who are willing to go that far with their own questions. [*Looking up from the page, quizzically*] Like you?

I'm a big fan of entertainment. I cut my acting teeth on musical comedy. So I always try to give my shows a bit of a zing.

I like the convention of the fourth wall. You know, where the actors pretend you're not there in the audience, and you have to be real quiet and pretend *you're* not there? But it's only one convention, and I think Western theater relies too heavily on it. I use it, like a spice, to lull my audience into thinking they're safe. [*Grin*] Then I collapse it for the bulk of the piece. I write in direct dialogue with my audience, and I always allow for the chance that someone in the audience will talk back. Scares me, but I love it when it happens.

The following piece is from my solo show, The Opposite Sex Is Neither. *I wanted to talk about having learned a lot about my gender(s) from advertisements. So I thought to myself: who would embody that? And in what kind of dramatic situation? I came up with Anaya. She's being channeled by the show's central character, a goddess-in-training named Maggie, who's trying to help seven souls achieve their next level of awareness. She's supposed to catch these souls in a moment of being "neither here nor there, neither one nor the other, and neither dead nor alive." As the scene opens, Anaya (who is currently being mugged and badly beaten) suddenly lands in Maggie's body, looking out through Maggie's eyes . . . directly at the audience.*

Anaya

I know my name. My name is Anaya.

Anaya is very badly hurt. Anaya is somewhere. And I am very badly . . .

Who are you? Are you even human?

I hear the bones in my face breaking.

Oh, God, I can just see the *National Enquirer* now: "Transsexual Saved by Space Aliens!"

I'm not transsexual!

Yes, I am. I know my name. No more hiding. Children could always spot me anyway. Are you a boy or a girl? they'd always ask.

I've played Anaya with several interpretations over the nearly four years that I've been performing this show. Currently, she's an uptown vogueing queen with a major attitude, and a flair for the dramatic. She loves her new body, and she's an outrageous flirt with the audience.

You look awfully hip to be aliens.

Is this a dream? No. If this were a dream, I'd be in a commercial. I know. I usually am. I know all the words. On my planet, we talk like this. We say: I've come a long way, baby. And I'm not even a model. We say what makes me different can make me beautiful, because some women are more ultra than others. And we say I'm worth it.

Are you real or are you Memorex?

The guys who're beating me up didn't know whether I was a real woman or not. As much as I'd buy, and as hard as I tried, they'd always spot me, and they'd always hurt me. Do you understand what I'm saying? Do you know what it's like to be hunted down, just because you're different. Of course you do. You're space aliens. You had to pass as earthlings, didn't you? It's very difficult to pass, isn't it? It takes so much energy, doesn't it? You have to be watching people's reactions to you, all the time. You have to . . . You have to read all the magazines to see how to do it.

On my planet, we talk like this. We say: I've come a long way, baby. Sometimes I need a little Finesse; sometimes I need a lot. Now I can have the body I've always wanted. Juicy mouth-watering color. And we say, take a bite.

I know all the ads. I bought all the products. If you lived on earth, you would too. Then the ads told me to be a flirt. So, I was. So they beat up on me.

They have knives, now. The sound of the blades cutting just under my ear sounds like meat being carved. You're not a dream, are you? Oh, god. I must be dying.

I know my name. My name is Anaya. On the day I was born, my grandparents gave me a television set. In 1948, this was a new and wonderful thing. It had a ten-inch screen embedded in a cherrywood box the size of my mother's large oven. My parents gave over an entire room to the television. It was the television room! And every day I watched it, it told me what was a man and what was a woman. And every day I watched it, it told me what to buy in order to be a real woman. And with everything I'd buy, I said to myself, I am a real woman. And I would never admit I was transsexual. Isn't that strange?

I am dying. Somewhere.

They say that blood tastes like copper. Mmmm. To me . . . to me, it tastes more like . . . blood.

After my surgery, I still never knew what was a man. Isn't that strange? I didn't know what was a woman. All that television. All those magazines.

I want to get down on my knees. I want to get down on my knees in front of you, and I want to ask you—what's it like to know? Can you tell me? I'm asking you because I've never gone to sleep one night of my life believing I was a man. I've never gone to sleep one night of my life believing I was a woman.

Can you tell me what it's like to be one or the other? Please?

Ha! Here's what earth people say when they're dying. They say, I've come . . . ha! I've come a long way, baby. I've come such a long, long . . .

Right . . . then she dies, and it's time for the next character.

The Opposite Sex Is Neither deals solely with transgendered characters. In the next solo piece I wrote, Virtually Yours: A Game for Solo Performer with Audience, *I ended up using nontransgendered characters to speak about what I thought was a rather unique transgendered experience: what happens to a person when their lover goes through a gender change?*

Allie, in Virtually Yours, *is the central character: a transsexual lesbian performance artist whose female lover is becoming a man. (Uh-huh, it's true . . . who could be that creative?) See, I wanted to describe all my fears around this, and I came up with the idea of a series of characters, each of whom embodies one of these fears. I didn't want it to be a loose string of monologues, though . . . I wanted to make it a coherent story in which the central character learns these lessons. What I settled*

on was the device of having Allie play a computer game (called Virtually
Yours) which allows her to invent personas for her own worst fears, and
then walk around in them for a while. The computer game (played, on
audiotape, by David Cale) has quite a bit to say on its own; its chief job
being talking Allie into becoming the next character.

ALLIE: All right, so I gave up being straight, boy, that's for sure; but if I
give up being lesbian, what's left for me?
COMPUTER: Dear Heart, the next fear is the fear of fantasy. Perhaps we'll
find an alternative in that?
ALLIE: Um, yeah, maybe.
COMPUTER: So glad to hear it! When it's all over, you'll look back and be
glad of this one. When the game is done, when the lights are out, when the
pain fades away to a dull throb.
ALLIE: Pain? What pain? What do you mean, when it's over? When the
game is done? When . . . when . . . when . . .

[*At this point, the computer starts throbbing, there's some great special*
effects, and Allie morphs into the next computer-generated character.
Over the sound system, a young girl's voice sings:]

When I am dead and in my grave and all my bones are rotten,
This little book will tell my name when I am quite forgotten.

[*This new character walks to center, swaying to the music of Lou Reed*
and the Velvet Underground. She smiles seductively at the audience,
reaches into a bag at her side, pulls out clothespins, and begins to attach
them to her arms, and to her bare skin above her breasts.]

One with No Name

The first thing my mistress took away from me when I bonded myself to
her, was my name; that was four years ago. And when she left me, she didn't
give me my name back. It's been nearly a year since she's gone, and I don't
know what to call myself. I don't know how to introduce myself to people. I
mean, people always want your name.

[*She's now got quite a collection of clothespins attached to her upper*
body. She looks up at the audience and grins.]

Hey, do you know about these? One of the first things I learned was that they don't hurt when you put 'em on. Really. See? Nothin'! The real pain happens when you take 'em off after you've left them on for a while. Isn't that great? The pain comes from the absence. See, the blood rushes to the spot that was pinched, that's what hurts, and if you've left them on long enough, the pain can be really intense.

Sometimes it feels like the blood is still rushing to my heart to fill the hole she left there when she said she didn't love me anymore . . . not as my owner.

When she took my name away from me, I learned to call myself "this one." Like, "May this one pour your tea, ma'am?" Or, "This one thanks her mistress for the sound caning." I need to tell you, I hated the canings. I mean, they really really really hurt, okay? But I let her cane me because . . . she liked to. And letting her do it, that just made me feel more giving. It made me feel more loving.

I play this character as relatively young: late teens or early twenties. She looks back down at the clothespins on her body.

You really have to have this done to you to do it right. Donna, she would make these patterns on my body when she did it. Donna would put me on display, and everyone would go ohhhhhh and ahhhhh, they would, and I was so proud to be her work of art. I always say if you can't be an artist, you can always be a work of art, huh?

I learned to put myself in bondage when I was fourteen. First I would tape my mouth shut, then I would tie my ankles together, and fasten my ankles to the bedposts. Then I'd tie another length of rope to the headboard, and with a slipknot I'd tie my wrists together. Then, lying on my belly, pressing myself to the bed, I would make myself come. Fourteen years old. Kids, huh? I never suspected someone would really want to do that to me. I always thought I'd have to do that to myself. Do you know what it's like to imagine your heart's desire, never really believing anyone would love you for who you really are? Not who you really are.

And then one day, she shows up. She shows up at the food co-op where you work the cash registers, and she makes sure she gets into your line every time. I know she saw my hands trembling as I'd ring up her stuff. It wasn't till later I found out she wasn't even vegetarian. . . . She just bought stuff at the co-op so she could check me out. "I usually eat burgers and wieners, ya know." That's what she told me a month after she first put a collar on me. I like thinking about that.

By the way, if you leave these on too long you can hurt yourself. Well, I mean seriously hurt yourself, okay?

The first time she touched me, she hurt me. It was right there at the checkout counter. She brought the palm of my hand up to her mouth and she bit me.

She has these small, sharp teeth, and she kept on biting till I bled right into her mouth. I felt like I was gonna come any second, but she left a second before I could. It was like she already knew my rhythms, ever meet a person like that? Oh! And then she left without giving me her name or her number. I know how to get ahold of you, that's all she said, and she walks out the door, laughing.

The next woman in line looked at my hand, and she asked me if I was all right. All right? All right? I'm fine. I'm fine, thank you. Wouldn't you be fine if your heart's desire had walked into your life not five minutes ago?

All I wanted to do was to belong to her. Not like her wife, I mean, ewwwwww! And not like her girlfriend. I've been girlfriend to enough people. Not like a one-night stand, either. I wanted her to *own* me, like property. I told her that on our third date, when she had me tied down to her bed. And by the way, the knot around my wrists wasn't a slipknot that night! I loved her completely. I trusted her completely. I knew her and she knew me. She asked me what I wanted more than anything else in the world and I said I wanna belong to you, and she smiled and said that can be arranged and I started crying and I couldn't stop. You never know how profoundly moving the fulfillment of your fantasy is gonna be until it actually finally really happens to you.

I've got marks, I got marks right here, it's her brand.

[*She touches a spot high on the inside of her right thigh.*]

Donna didn't do it, she had a friend of hers do it who knows how. They hafta heat the iron till it's white-hot. Any less hot than white-hot, and you have to hold it down to the skin longer, and that makes the skin crack and get all blistery, and ya really spoil the mark. So, she got someone to do it right, and there I was watching them heat up the brand. It went from cold metal gray to kinda green to cherry red to almost blinding white and they held my leg down to the table with four very tight leather straps. I couldn't move if I'd wanted to, but I didn't want to. I wanted her mark on me. I did. And when they touched the iron to the inside of my thigh, I felt like I was going to shoot right out of my body.

Some people remember how it smells, but I remember how it sounded. It was a bubbly sort of hissing sound. I was sick afterward, for a few days I had a fever and chills. I was embarrassed, but the woman who branded me said, eh, that happens a lot. Y'know, even now, at night, when I'm alone in bed, I like to trace my finger through the brand, it's really deep.

Okay. We were madly in love, the toast of the leather community. We were the perfect couple. We were the ones everyone looked to when they were so afraid ya couldn't find real love in sadomasochism. We got written up in all the leather journals. We even did *Oprah*: "Women Who Own Women, and the Women They Own." I was the latter. She had me, and we had it all.

Then she stopped coming by every day.

And I started to do this to myself more and more.

She started loaning me out to her friends more frequently.

She walks into the audience, and asks for audience members to help her to take the clothespins off her body. It's funny . . . I was always careful not to ask people who looked like they might be squeamish, but the fun part of it is that very few people looked squeamish, and most everyone enjoyed it. [Smiling] I know I did.

Could you help me with this, please? Just take it off me, okay? Thanks.

She started loaning me out to men. I didn't mind that, not really, I mean hey, I was doing it for her.

Thanks, this is nice. I usually have to do this myself. Thanks for doing this for me.

I said to her it doesn't matter about the men, as long as you love me. She didn't say anything.

About this time, I would kneel in front of one audience member . . . someone who'd been looking hungry for this. I'd have two clothespins left on my chest above my breasts. I'd kneel there, silent, offering. Sure enough, every performance, that audience member would lovingly re-move both clothespins.

This one thanks you *so* much.

[I'd walk back onto the stage, removing any remaining clothespins my-self to punctuate the next few lines.]

Four years we were together, and me without a name, and she came into my room one night and she said, "You're free to go now."

Free to go? Free to go where? I belong to you. What did I do?

You didn't do anything, she said to me. I just understand you.

You understand me? Do you understand that I have given you the most precious gift I can give anyone? I've given you me!

I just understand you, she said to me.

You understand me? Do you understand that who I am is that I live for your love. That is who I am. You understand me? What did I do?

You didn't do anything, she said to me. I just really understand you, and she unbuttons her jeans, and slides them down to her knees, and I see this fresh brand on the inside of her thigh. It was really clean.

Forgive me, she's sayin' to me. You've taught me so much, she's sayin' to me, and I understand you. You're free to go now, she says. Call it my parting act of cruelty.

So, it's been a year now since she's gone. Y'know, the old wizards and witches would never use their real names. They knew something we've forgotten. Whoever knows your real name holds the power of life and death over you. Whoever gets to name something gets to own it.

Okay, I told you a little lie before. I have a name now, sure I do, I mean whaddaya think? But I don't use it. I like it better, not using my name at all.

[*Over the sound system, a young girl's voice sings:*]

When I am dead and in my grave and all my bones are rotten
This little book will tell my name when I am quite forgotten.

To buy myself time to get back to the computer, and morph myself back into Allie, the central character, the following lines were spoken from audiotape, and are then followed by live interaction between Allie and the computer:

VOICE-OVER: This one is grateful for your kind attention to her pain. This one thanks you for permission to tell her story. This one hopes she has been pleasing to you. This one . . .
ALLIE: This one was really hard! What's the lesson here, mister? No pain, no gain?
COMPUTER: Pain in a virtual reality can indeed carry over to the world of flesh and blood, my little turtledove.
ALLIE: I'm not yer turtledove, and that was too close. I'll tell you what that one brought up for me—I just don't know if we're gonna be attracted to each other when he's done all his changing. And another thing! Even if that *is* my fantasy, I don't know if I'm ready to give up any of my power to a man. I've been a man, and I know what it's like!
COMPUTER: Well, you've certainly got my circuits working overtime, my dear. Care to press on?
ALLIE: What, after the clothespins? Oh, sure—let's keep going! I can't wait to see what's next. Probably pierce my toes. [*To the audience*] You okay? Want some popcorn?
COMPUTER: You'll just love what's next, my dear. The fear of Power it is!
ALLIE: Wait! I didn't mean that! Don't you know sarcasm when you hear it?!? This is getting too real! Life in the real world . . . life in the game . . . life in the flesh . . . life in virtual reality . . .

[*Lights flash, computer goes wild, and Allie morphs into the next character, based very loosely on Valerie Solanas, the woman who attempted to murder Andy Warhol in 1968. Solanas also wrote a tract called* The S.C.U.M. Manifesto, *and the text of this tract appears in voice-over throughout this monologue.*]

VALERIE V-O: *Life in this society being, at best, an utter bore and no aspect of society being at all relevant to women, there remains to civic-minded, responsible, thrill-seeking females only to overthrow the government, eliminate the money system, institute complete automation, and destroy the male sex.*

Valerie

Whaddaya do when the person you fall in love with is your worst nightmare? Whaddaya do when the kind of person you've been most afraid of all your life is suddenly sharing the same bed with you, and you like it? Let's talk about some irony here, okay? Let's talk about some kinda god with one funky sense of humor here, okay?

I play Valerie as a tough, young butch. Since I'm particularly fond of tough young butches, Valerie ends up being quite an engaging character. But I wanted to show the public and private sides of this woman. When she reads her own text, she's at a microphone, like she's addressing a rally. Otherwise, she's speaking very simply to the audience.

VALERIE V-O: *The male is completely egocentric, trapped inside himself, incapable of empathizing or identifying with others, of love, friendship, affection, or tenderness.*
VALERIE [At mike]: *He is a half-dead, unresponsive lump, incapable of giving or receiving pleasure or happiness; consequently, he is at best an utter bore, an inoffensive blob, since only those capable of absorption in others can be charming.*

His name was Brad, and he was a sailor. Don't look at me like that, I was fifteen, and I fell in love with him. What'd I know? He was nice to me. He was sweet. I liked the way he touched my hair, okay. He was sweet. He used to sing me to sleep with songs like: [*Singing*] Frog went acourtin' and he did go, uh-huh. Frog went acourtin' and he did go, uh-huh.

[At mike]: A true community consists of individuals—not mere species members, not couples—free spirits in free relation to each other. Traditionalists say the basic unit of "society" is the family; "hippies" say the tribe; no one says the individual.

I wasn't ever attracted to guys. I mean, maybe you figured that out from the stuff I write. But Brad was different. He came home one evening and he says, "Hey, Valerie, we're havin' a contest aboard the ship. A talent contest." Sort of a masquerade ball, the way he put it, and could I help him out with a costume.

Like what, I asked. I dunno, he said, do you have anything hanging around? Like what, I asked. I dunno, he said, maybe, I dunno, maybe one of your old dresses. Well, I just laughed my ass off on that one. And he laughed too. The two of us just sat there and we laughed and laughed, but then I could see that's what he wanted to do, he wanted to get into one of my dresses.

[*Singing*] He walked up to Miss Mousie's side, said, Mousie, would you be my bride, uh-huh. Uh-huh.

[*At mike*] *The farthest-out male is the drag queen, but he, although different from most men, has an identity—he is female. He conforms compulsively to the man-made feminine stereotype.*

I asked Natalie about this. She was my best girlfriend. She thought I was crazy for balling him at all, but she thought I was really crazy for letting him wear my dresses. She said if Senator McCarthy ever found out about us, that Brad would be thrown out of the navy, and I'd be put into a hospital because I was insane. Get outta here, I said to Natalie, he just wants to wear a dress! Get outta here! He ain't gonna get thrown out of the navy. I'm not goin' into some loony bin. Know what? That's exactly what happened to both of us. Isn't that funny?

What could I do, Cupid got me, zing! Boom! Right here!

That 'minds me of my favorite fairy tale from when I was a little girl. It's the one about Cupid and the cave of Death, right? Cupid is out there, flying around late at night. Ho hum, I'm Cupid and I'm so cute. And he's real sleepy, and he flies down and curls up to sleep in this cave, but he doesn't know it's the cave of Death, right? And he's sleeping and he's tossing and turning, and all Cupid's arrows spill out all over the floor, and they get all mixed up with all the arrows of Death, right? And when Cupid wakes up, Oh, my, he says, I am in the cave of Death! And he just scoops up all the mixed-up arrows he can—all of them—and puts them in his quiver, and so what happens? Ya never know if the arrow that hits ya is an arrow of Love or an arrow of Death. Isn't that bitchin'?

All right, so the night of the big contest comes, and there was Brad looking pretty, um, pretty. I mean really pretty. He was wearing my panties, he was wearing a girdle. He had on one of my bras, and we stuffed it with Kleenex and was he ever stacked! I was gettin' pretty excited, I can tell you that!

VALERIE V-O: *Sex is not part of a relationship; on the contrary, it is a solitary experience, noncreative, a gross waste of time. . . .*

VALERIE [At mike]: . . . *The female can easily—far more easily than she may think—condition away her sex drive . . .*

VALERIE V-O: . . . *leaving her completely cool and cerebral and free to pursue worthy relationships and activities.*

Gee, Brad, you look really good, I told him. You look like a real hot chick. Call me Pamela, he said, and I have to tell you he sounded like a chick when he said it. I laughed, but he said again, call me Pamela. Okay, "Pamela."

And you know what happened when I said that? He starts to whimper. You know, like a little girl? Pamela, I said, and his eyes start fillin' up with tears. Pamela, I said, and he starts shaking. Pamela, my sweet darling Pamela, and she starts to moan. Pamela, my little slut, Pamela, and she was shaking, and I laid that chickie down and I balled her, I balled her so good and that's when I had my first-ever orgasm, you see what I mean about irony? Perfect!

VALERIE V-O: *Sex is the refuge of the mindless. And the more mindless the woman, the more deeply embedded in the male "culture" she is—in short, the nicer she is, the more sexual she is.*

Pamela and I fucked each other silly for days, and it was just five weeks later she got herself stopped by the shore patrol. She was wearing a nice poodle skirt and a beaded sweater, and she got thrown in the brig dressed like that. They beat her up pretty bad, that's what I heard, but it wasn't till they told her they were gonna throw her outta the navy that she made a rope out of her poodle skirt and hung herself in her cell.

So thass why I write this shit. That's why I write. . . .

[At mike]: *The male is eaten up with tension, with frustration at not being female, at not being capable of ever achieving satisfaction or pleasure of any kind; eaten up with hate—not rational hate that is directed against those who abuse or insult you—but irrational, indiscriminate hate . . . hatred, at bottom, of his own worthless self.*

COMPUTER: Your time is nearly up. Please bring this character to a conclusion.

VALERIE: Fuck you! No man tells me my time is up, man. I say when my time is up!

Fifteen years later, I showed Andy this play I wrote about me and Pamela. It was brilliant. It was called *Up Your Ass. Up Your Ass* was gonna change the world, I have to tell you, it was. It was the real picture of the real male in the phony male world. I gave Andy the only copy of my script. Andy said he'd film it. He said to give him some time, and he'd film it.

Three months later, he says, Oh, Valerie, I've lost your script. I know for a fact he threw it away or burned it or maybe he ate it, I think maybe he might have eaten it, because that's what he did with other artists, he ate them up, especially women, because he was really afraid of women. Andy fought women. He fought artists. He shot my spirit full of holes, so I shot his body full of holes. It's the way of the world. Whatever you fight, you end up losing to. The way of the world.

They told me later it was a .32 I used. I didn't know, it was just a gun to me. I kinda wished I'da used a bow and arrow, you hear what I'm saying, that woulda been poetry.

I have to tell you the best part. The best part was when he begged me not to shoot him. Oh, god, don't shoot me, Valerie. Don't shoot me. And he pissed himself.

Blam! Blam! Blam, blam, blam blam!

He recovered, and the photographs of his wounds sold for tens of thousands of dollars. I made those goddamn wounds, I was the artist of that piece of work, and that little shit got the money for them. Know what I got? I got sent to an insane asylum for three goddamn years.

COMPUTER: And your advice to the traveler?

Leave her. Leave her fast, and leave her hard. You really wanna live with a woman who hates herself so much she wants to be a man? Didn't you cut off your own dick, man? She's throwing everything you worked for right in your face and she's saying fuck you, fuck you and all the women around you.

I'm not including you with the rest of the women, 'cause you know yer not a woman . . . you know that, right? But at least yer headed in the right direction. You cut off your dick. That's a good start. But yer not a woman.

I gotta tell you one more thing. Pamela, she would cry. She'd get all weepy, and when I'd ask her what was goin' on, some night when we were just lyin' in bed together, she'd look at me with her makeup runnin' 'cause of the tears and she'd say she wasn't used to bein' treated so good. She said I was tender, and she wasn't used to that. I hafta ask ya, what kind of world would be mean to a sweet thing like Pamela, huh?

VALERIE V-O: [*Singing*] Snake came in and made it clear that no one's gettin' married here, uh-huh. Uh-huh.

So that about wraps it. I try to get as many points of view into my shows as possible. Often they conflict, these points of view, and that raises questions, and that's what I love about performing: a good performance has the audience walking out with all these great questions they need to chew on. Kinda like this book . . . there's so many of us in here with different ways of doing things. Kinda like the world. Aw, shoot, I'm just an old hippie chick after all [Blushing, laughing].

Photo copyright © by Dona Ann McAdams

DAVID CALE

Name: David Cale
Stage Name: Same
Birthdate/Birthplace: 12/16/58/Luton, Bedfordshire, England
"Raised Up" Where: Luton, Bedfordshire
Education: Left school at sixteen
Honors/Grants: NEA Solo Performance Fellowship, 1992; NEA Interarts Grant, 1992; NYSCA Grants 1987 and 1993; NYFA Fellowship, 1987; New York Dance and Performance Bessie Award for Outstanding Creative Achievement 1987 and 1992; Sundance Writing Fellowship, 1990
Influences/Mentors/Heroes: Bette Midler, Samuel Beckett, Sherwood Anderson, Luis Buñuel, Joni Mitchell, Harold Pinter, Laurie Anderson, Alan Bennett, Sam Shepard, Neil Young, John Guare, Raymond Carver, Joseph Chaikin, Joseph Losey, Judy Garland, and Paul Lawrence
Places Performed: P.S. 122, Dixon Place, Museum of Modern Art, the Joseph Papp Public Theater, the Kitchen, Second Stage Theater, New York Theater Workshop, the Knitting Factory, New York; American Repertory Theater, Cambridge, MA; Yale Repertory Theater, New Haven, CT; The Studio Theater, Washington, D.C.; Life on the Water, San Francisco; Sushi Inc., San Diego; the Mark Taper Forum, Taper Too, Los Angeles; and the Goodman Theater, Chicago; etc.
Pivotal Performance: Having my own evening at Franklin Furnace, NYC, in 1985. It was the first opportunity I'd been given to put the pieces together into a show and it felt like I was onto something that was my own.
Favorite Performance Experience: Performing solo in Central Park at Summerstage in 1993 and the last week of *Deep in a Dream of You*'s run at Life on the Water in San Francisco
Most Terrifying Performance Experience: Performing solo in Central Park at Summerstage in 1993
Favorite Prop or Costume: The stool I bought for the Central Park show
Hobbies: None
Reading List: Grace Paley, *Enormous Changes at the Last Minute*
Favorite Music: Charles Mingus, Billie Holiday, John Coltrane, Joni Mitchell, Eric Dolphy, Abbey Lincoln, Leonard Cohen, Pet Shop Boys, Thelonious Monk, Duke Ellington, Neil Young, John Prine, Kurt Weill, Marianne Faithfull, Shirley Horn, Chet Baker, Laurie Anderson, Bob Dylan, Tom Waits, Miles Davis, David Bowie, Jimmy Scott, R.E.M., Deborah Harry and Blondie
Favorite Quote: "Only connect." (E. M. Forster)

Artist's Notes

> *When I die, they'll find intuition at the wheel*
> *(with probably fear still sitting in the back seat trying to bark out*
> *directions)*
> *but intuition at the wheel.*
> —*Lillian, from the show of the same name.*

All my work is personal, emotionally autobiographical and intuitive. However far away from me the pieces seem to get, there's always a strong emotional connection (though sometimes I'm the last one to realize it). I often can't explain, or justify why or what I am doing, beyond saying that it just feels right.

My background is in music, and I tend to relate more to singer-songwriters than other monologuists, seeing the shows more in terms of albums or concerts than solo plays. I write out loud and initially longhand, transferring what I come up with to a computer, to make editing easier. Writing aloud is important to me, as it is essential that the language be active. Theatre writing, or lyric writing for that matter, is leaner. The language has to be able to travel, you have to leave room for the performance, and the sound of the words matters. Like songwriting, some words sing and some don't, and you can't figure out which do in your head.

My writing generally falls into three categories, monologues that are written as portraits of people, lyrics, and theatricalized short stories. In the case of the character monologues I generally have a sense of the person whose point of view I am trying to write from, and assume their voice as I hear it, basically writing down what they say. I only try to portray people I feel an affinity for and affection towards, and try not to place any judgment or comment, either in the writing or the performance. The goal is simply to try to present portraits of people I feel moved or affected by, and their points of view. To present them as clearly and honestly as possible, and to let the audience respond as they will.

As soon as I have a first draft, I like to read it, or semiperform it, in front of an audience. It's only in the context of a live performance that I can gauge whether a monologue has a life, or is truthful, or what needs to change. This part of the process usually happens at Dixon Place in New York, which is set up exclusively as a venue to try out new work. I then start to refine and rewrite accordingly, eventually placing pieces alongside each other with a view of assembling a show.

So far I have written six shows: *Lillian, Deep in a Dream of You, Some-*

body Else's House, The Nature of Things, Smooch Music, and *The Redthroats.* Each has a different personality and three of them have music scores. I like simplicity in performance, so what they all have in common is the relative straightforwardness of the presentation. I don't use props, wigs, costumes, or makeup. Everything is conveyed through vocal nuance and physical gesture, and lighting.

I dislike analyzing what I do and have never watched a videotape of any of the shows, relying heavily on several perceptive and blunt friends to give me critiques, and occasionally working with a director.

"I Wish I'd Have Met You before He Did" is taken from my show *Deep in a Dream of You,* the loose theme of which was different men and women re-calling incidents or individuals from their past whom they're haunted by. The show had a lush string-based jazz score written by Roy Nathanson, and about three quarters of the monologues were performed with live musical accompaniment, consisting of two cellos, upright bass, percussion, and sax-ophone. The monologues were scored much like little films, and the music was precisely performed with the words; pieces occasionally opening up to allow for instrumental breaks or solos, much like songs. "I Wish I'd Have Met You before He Did" was probably the lightest section of the show and it served to set off some of the more dramatic pieces. It isn't really a character monologue, but for some reason I did adopt a voice that was not my own when performing it. (Probably as a means of distancing myself from the overtly autobiographical nature of the piece.) There was no particular rea-son for this change of voice, but it sounded right. There seems to be a run-ning motif in most of my shows of someone at some point being driven away from their life by a stranger. The real-life incident on which it is based happened in Pennsylvania and not North Carolina, and of that little es-capade let's just say, it was extremely romantic, for about forty-five minutes (at least I thought it was).

"The English Rose of Indiana" was an attempt to draw a portrait of my grandmother whose name is also Elsie and who only differs from the Elsie in "The English Rose" by the fact that she still lives in England and that her grandchildren reside in America, as opposed to Australia. A lot of the things that my Elsie says are direct quotes from the real Elsie. And I prob-ably shouldn't admit to this, even though it's more than likely obvious to anyone who's familiar with his work, but the monologue was heavily influ-enced by the English playwright Alan Bennett. I was particularly inspired by his brilliant *Talking Heads* collection of monologues. The piece was originally to be included in my show *Somebody Else's House,* but didn't quite fit. I was always very fond of the monologue, in part because it quotes my grandmother so accurately and liberally. So when it didn't work out to be included in *S.E.H.,* I performed it as part of a collaborative evening of one-act plays with writer/performer Roger Babb entitled *Promiscuous.* The original director of the show on our first and only discussion of how the piece should be performed thought I should be in full drag. "I want people to believe they're watching an eighty-year-old woman." Thankfully I listened to my instincts which were hollering, "Get out of this right now!" and performed the piece very simply, wearing my own clothes, sitting in a chair sipping tea, talking to the audience. On good nights I felt as if I was taken over by my grandmother, and the piece is lovingly dedicated to her, the real Elsie Arnold.

"A Trace of Panic" was written during rehearsals for the Goodman Theatre production of *Somebody Else's House.* After making extensive cuts in the script, I was short of material. Generally I write very slowly, but with the show's opening around the corner, and feeling the sheer terror of not having enough material to perform, I sped things up and wrote the monologue at, for me, breakneck speed, and in a whole lot more than just a trace of panic. Through the rewrites, the style of the piece changed quite dramatically, starting off realistic and becoming increasingly absurd, from draft to draft.

I Wish I'd Have Met You before He Did

In a stranger's house.
In the middle of North Carolina.
You move around the room cautious and a little wary.
Distrustful of the people around you.
Then as some surprise you take me to one side and say

"Let's go for a drive."

Your car is a long gray sports car.
I try to act blasé, like I get into sports cars all the time.

A ride in your car is reminiscent of heaven.

You turn up the Aretha Franklin/George Michael duet
while I look at your forearms.

"I knew you were waiting for me."

You tell me, it probably sounds foolish but you feel you like
animals more than people sometimes.

And all I wanna do is kiss you on the mouth and agree.

You tell me about your childhood.
It sounds like a car crash.
I try to keep my intentions underneath the conversation.

I don't want you to recognize the way I'm looking at you.

We have the top down on the car.

When I talk I'm looking at the side of your mouth.

Your speech is soft but somehow it gets into my stomach.

You're a kind person.
Every word that comes out of you has cushions round it.

We drive past the house where John Coltrane was born.
It's a blues bar now,
on the other side of the railroad tracks.
You say,
"My life's becoming this vague dream that I can hardly remember."
Neither of us notice that for a moment the car has left the ground
and both of us are swimming.

We get lost somewhere in the middle of North Carolina.
You can't remember the town we're staying in.
I say, "I can't remember either."
I'm lying.
I knew exactly where we were.
I just don't want to go back there again.

I just want us to keep driving.

I'll forget my occupation.

Leave the apartment behind.

I'll make you happy.

I'll wind down the windows.

I'll clean your clothes.

I'll punch holes in your darkness.

I'll crack jokes.

I wanna be the thing you discover, you didn't realize you were looking for.

And just as I'm running the list of what will be my new functions in life, you remember the town we're staying in.
Damn!
You ask a couple of people on bicycles for directions.
As they're explaining I start to feel contempt for children.

I hope they're lying.

So they'll send us further astray.

So we can be lost even more.

I want it to get dark so there's no choice but to stay out all night.

I wanna run out of gas.
I wanna check into a motel and roll around on your speech.

Being with you all past relations seem like hopeless mistakes.

Aretha Franklin starts to sing another tune.

This time she's left George Michael behind.

This time she's on her own.

The sky in North Carolina turns deep red.

The buildings we pass become familiar
and I realize we're nearly home.

As we get close to the house I can feel myself withdraw,

and there's only one thought that goes through my mind,

"I wish I'd have met you before he did."

The English Rose of Indiana

ELSIE ARNOLD, *a robust and healthy-looking English woman in her early eighties who came to America as a war bride. Her husband is deceased but she remains in the town in Indiana where they lived. When she speaks she affects a slightly posh English tone which occasionally gives way to a much truer working-class accent. She is seated in a chair in her house next to a window, which she occasionally glances out of. In front of her is a small table with a framed photograph. She is holding a cup of tea on a saucer. She sips.*

Mrs. Makepeace was quite right when she said to me today,

"We must be thankful for the Daughters of the American Revolution.
Without the DAR where would we old girls be?
We must keep active, Mrs. A, if we stop moving we
may find it hard to start up again."

What a soldier, Mrs. Makepeace. I don't think Mrs. White realizes
what a backbone Mrs. M. has become to the organization.
When Mrs. Taylor tried to take one of my shifts at the gift shop
at the hospital last week and stir up trouble, Mrs. M. was a
model of clarity.

"With all due respect, Mrs. Taylor, Mrs. Arnold is the Tuesday,
Wednesday and Friday shift. Ten to six. It's written on the sheet.
You know it's not our position to quibble with the sheet,
Mrs. Taylor. If the order is not complied with, the system
collapses."

But that dreadful Mrs. Taylor didn't let up.

"How can an English woman belong to the DAR?
Weren't the English the enemy?"

I've never seen Mrs. M. so angry.

"We're all pink ladies here, Mrs. Taylor.
Mrs. Arnold's late husband was American.
He served this country for fifty years.
She's as pink as you or I!"

That told her. Mrs. Taylor's only jealous of all the attention

I get. I don't know what she'd do if she found out that I'm only
a permanent resident alien. That I never actually became an American.
It's funny, I could never live in England again, but I can't seem to let it
go either.

That Mrs. Taylor. She may have been married to a big lawyer,
but I know which side of the tracks she's from and she knows
I know.

"You can wrap it in a mink," my father used to say,
"doesn't mean it's going to whistle a pretty tune."

Or something to that effect. Although with Mrs. Taylor the coat's
closer to rabbit than mink.

[*Clutching her hands*]

My rheumatism's getting so bad. Can't ignore it anymore.
Oh, Mrs. Makepeace.

[*Glancing out of the window*]

The lilac tree in the yard needs cutting back. Who's gonna do it?
Can't ask Alan next door. Not after he found out that I was the
one who complained to the town board about his nude sunbathing.
A man of nearly fifty walking around the garden naked!
He knew I was looking at him too. Parading himself.
Then that silly wife of his, Mary, banging on my door, in the nude,
asking if I want a cup of coffee. Acting like there was nothing
out of the ordinary. Silly naked woman. She knows I don't drink
coffee.

Least they're not trying to sell me Herbal Life anymore.
And I can't ask that ratty trumpet-playing boy of his. I wish
there was a council in this country I could write to. I'm just
worried it's going to fall over and do some real damage.

[*To the photograph*]

I do miss you, Barbara. Don't think of the children, Elsie.
You'll drive yourself to the waterworks. Oh, dear.

[*She begins to break down*]

Who would've ever thought I'd outlive my children?
I'd live to bury my children. Outlive everyone.

[*Fighting to compose herself*]

Elsie!

Mrs. Makepeace says this room is morbid.

"No use looking at photos of the dead," she says.

"But the dead are all I've got," I said.

"Put them in a drawer," she says.

"But what would I look at?"

"Then get a nice picture of the queen or something.
Someone you like. Get a picture of Perry Como."

"Where do I get a picture of Perry Como, Mrs. M.?" I said.

"You're not getting all helpless on me!" she says.

Oh, Mrs. Makepeace, what a backbone.

I know I'm well liked at the hospital. That young Dr. Butler,
lovely young man, I do enjoy having a laugh with him.
Calls me his English Rose. I must be three times his age.
Sometimes I slip him a Mars bar or a Kit Kat with his newspaper.
He says,
"Mrs. Arnold, you're a real tonic to the patients.
When you come round with the candy mobile,
You're a regular pick-me-up.
We ought to put you on prescription."

He wants me to call him Dennis. I can't do that.
He's a doctor. I couldn't bring myself to say it.

It's disrespectful. He took me to one side. Had his arm
around me.

"I thought we were friends, Elsie."

"We are, Doctor," I said.

"Well, my friends call me Dennis."

"All right, Dennis," I said, "if that's what you like."

But it didn't seem right. So I've decided not to call him anything. I'll just
leave a blank.

[*Glancing at the lilac tree outside the window*]

If Stan was alive he'd have that lilac as firewood. Elsie!

That new young ambulance driver is very nice. He gives us ladies
a ride home from the shop at the hospital in the back
of the ambulance. He's not supposed to. It's against the rules.
The ambulance is only to move the sick and the infirm.
So he says,
"So I don't get into trouble, ladies."
He always calls us ladies.
"So I don't get into trouble, would you mind, as you leave the
back of the ambulance when I drop you off home, would you mind
limping to your doors? So if anyone does see, I won't get into
trouble."

So all of us, as we get out of the back of the ambulance.
Mrs. Turner, Mrs. Makepeace. The dreadful Mrs. Taylor and me.
We all put on a fake limp, till we get to our doors, and are
safely inside.

Well, the other evening I couldn't stop doing the fake limp.
I was limping round the house. There was nothing wrong with my
leg. That was the same night that Alan and Mary next door decided
to go and play Bingo in the nude. They got as far as the railway
station when they got picked up. Calling me to identify them!
Well, they don't have any friends. It was all over the papers.
I had to laugh, sitting in the police car with the two of them,
wrapped in raincoats.

[She laughs to herself]

Maybe I should get a dog. I've already had a dog.
Butch. Outlived the dog. Get another dog. What about the training?

Never hear from my grandchildren. Elsie! Australia's a long way
away. The time difference. It's already tomorrow in Australia.
I'm still in yesterday as far as they're concerned. They don't
want to be bothered with an old lady.

Maybe I should get a lodger. I could put up a sign at the hospital.
What if a Mexican wanted the room? If I turned him down he
could take me to the race people and they'd make me live with him.
It's too much of a risk.

If he was like Hector at the hospital. Hector's different. He has
such beautiful manners. Somehow I don't think of Hector as Mexican.
Perfect manners.

I'd go out for a walk, but there's so much violence now.

Maybe I should go back to England. You don't know anyone there
anymore. It's changed so much. This is your home now, Elsie.
It's funny, I'm not really English anymore, and I'm not really
American.
What am I?

Sometimes I'll be in the house and the phone hasn't rung and I
hadn't seen or talked to anyone for days, and I'll feel like the
only person left in the entire world.

I could be the only one in the world when I'm in my house.

A Trace of Panic

A MAN WITHOUT A NAME, *he speaks in a voice that is a cross between
William Burroughs and the narration to a forties film noir. Nothing is his own.*

My mother's name was Paranoia. My father's name was Panic.
They lived in a place where gray was the color of choice.
On a windy day the preacher of the town decreed,

"I name these neuroses man and wife."

When I was born my mother's best friend, Chemical Dependency,
looked at me and cried,

"Oh, Paranoia, you must be so happy, he looks just like you,
but there's definitely a trace of Panic in his eyes.
And he's already wailing about something, and I bet he
doesn't know what it is he's wailing about. That's a good sign.
He'll fit right in 'round here."

My parents forgot to give me a name, so I was always referred
to as Paranoia's son, or the child of Panic.
And childhood for me was one long walk down a lonely lane.

As Paranoia got older she grew clouds around her head.
Till eventually all she could see were the clouds. So she started
growing eyes all over her body. At a certain point the eyes
started looking inward. Paranoia watched her every move all
the time, and she became like a truck whose alarms would go off
every time she got into her own driving seat. As she got older
she stopped moving at all, she just stood in one place with all her
eyes blinking, her alarms ready to go off, and the clouds drifting
slowly around the features on her face. Nothing got better for
Paranoia. From the day she was born it was all downhill.
Which was just the way she thought it would be. Panic spent
most of his time standing on the fence smoking cigarettes,
running away from views and muttering, "I can't deal with this.
I don't want to know."

One day they both just disappeared. The theory was, they'd canceled
each other out. All I inherited was the prison they lived in.
Well, one day I slipped through my own bars and made my getaway.

I was always drawn to the sky, so I spent most of my youth gazing
out of windows.
"You were a bird in a former life," a fortuneteller told me.

"What about this time around?" I cried.
"I don't see anything for you but your past. Your past stretches all the
way into where the future should be."

("Some accent, Madame Fong!")

"There must be some mistake," I cried.

"The cards don't lie," she said.

"Can we play another round?" I inquired. "Give me a chance to win back what I lost."

I started drifting. Anyplace I'd hang my hat was home.
I moved in with a little woman called Safety Net. Safety was drawn
to blank sheets like me. She got pleasure from coloring people in.
Safety had photographs of her parents all over her house. On one alarming
day I noticed she had cut up and glued a photo of her face over
the top of her mother's face, and a photo of my face was stuck on top
of her father's. Instinct told me it was time to be moving along.

But Safety's photo collage had planted an idea in me. You see, Panic
and Paranoia had neglected to give me any kind of character, so I
decided to use myself as a canvas and snip away the pieces of other
people's personalities that I was drawn to and stick them to me.

I soon became a well-balanced mixed platter, suitable for parties
or office functions, or just something to nibble on. I wasn't a real
meal, but I was happy. And Panic and Paranoia seemed like something
I'd made up. Something that had never happened to me.
Though occasionally I'd look up at the sky and wonder if they were
my mother's clouds.

Then I made a big mistake. The relationship with Safety was strictly
platonic. You see at this point I had no sexuality. Everyone said that
I should adopt one from the pound. There were all these unwanted
sexualities desperately looking for a home. So that's where I went.

Dima Dozen ran the pound. A recovering dominatrix, Dima was an expert
in drawing the line. She gave me the tour.

"If the sexualities are here for more than forty-eight hours,
they're put to sleep. All our sexualities are de-flead.
They've all had their shots. Oh, and choose carefully,
all sexualities are nonreturnable."

Initially I couldn't see anything I was drawn to. Then I noticed a big,
dark thing with needy eyes, separated from the rest.

"What's this one, Dima?" I inquired.

"Oh, that sexuality has no name."

I thought of myself, also drifting without a name, and a strange kind of bonding took place. At which point the sexuality jumped up and licked me on the face, and the look in its eyes told me the poor thing had been alone as long as I had.

"This is the one for me, Dima."

"Are you sure you can manage?" she asked. "This sexuality is very strong. Untrained. It'll need a substantial leash. And remember, it has to go everywhere with you."

"Dima, I'm alone in life. I've got nothing better to do than look after a big, uncontrollable sexuality," I naively replied.

I called my sexuality Scruffy. Scruffy and I left the pound with a sense of optimism. At last we'd both found constant companions. But reality was 'round the corner waiting to pounce on me and change all that.

I'd wake up every morning and Scruffy would be in my face.
It would get hyper. Walking the streets it wanted to jump up on everyone.
People backed away from me 'cause it was clear I wasn't walking the sexuality, but the sexuality was walking me. Dima's words echoed in my ears:

"All sexualities are nonreturnable, returnable, returnable. . . ."

Then I woke up one morning and looked down and there were little eyes growing all over me, and a subtle-looking cloud was passing my left eye. Mother! I had wondered where Paranoia had gone all those years, she was hiding out inside me. And I knew deep down, something was aggravating Scruffy. It was Panic.

There was no choice but to visit Init Forthemoney. Dr. Forthemoney was an ex-mercenary and onetime bounty hunter who now had a thriving Freudian practice. She had the word "Passive" tattooed on one knuckle and the word "Aggressive" tattooed on the other.
She'd clench the two and make a strange
growling noise. *Grrrr!*

"What does your mother look like, so I know what to look for?" she inquired.
"*Grrrr!*"

"Picture a cumulus cloud with bad shoes, Doc."

"And your father?"
"The Santa Ana winds with a cigarette."

A couple of days later she gave me her initial report.

"Inside you looks like bad weather. Take off your clothes, I need to look at your mother's eyes."

I obliged. There was something strangely calming about standing naked in front of such a total professional.

Scruffy, don't even consider it!

"What's all this?" the Doc asked.
"You have all these bits of personality attached to you.
This isn't your sense of humor.
These aren't your opinions.
That laugh isn't you.
And they have little labels with dates on them."

"That's when I got them, Doc."

"They're coming off!"

"Ow!"

She yanked at the pieces of personality.

"Ow, but I'm used to them now."

"This isn't you!"

"Ow!"

"And this here, is this you?"

"No, Doc. Ow!"

"I can't get to your mother and father without my assistant Seda Tive."

Suddenly the door flung open.

[*Wolf whistle*]

"Shut up, Scruffy!"

Seda Tive was a slinky little tablet with the vocal cords of a dove.

She was wearing a dress made out of clear water. It was love at first sight.
Seda threw her arms around me.
"Take me," she cooed.
"I'll get rid of Paranoia.
I'll get rid of Panic.
Take me."

How could I say no.

"Oh, Seda," I uttered, "I'm feeling better already.
What did you do with mother and father?"

"I'm not telling," she cooed, "take me again."

"Oh, you beautiful relaxant, you, I'm starting to find you irresistible"
were the last words I remember uttering.

When I came to I was wrapped in bandages, lying in the hospital.
Dr. Forthemoney had removed Mother's eyes. They were glaring at me
from the inside of a jar. I looked out the window and I noticed
the sky had a few extra clouds. And Father was blowing around outside.
The operation had been a success. I looked to my left and Seda Tive had
gone, and she'd taken Scruffy with her. *Such is life,* I thought to myself,
wiser but no more bitter.

Leaving the sanitarium, as we all must do, eventually, I waved at the elements
that once were my parents. The sky that day seemed particularly blue.

Now I'm a clean slate, I thought to myself, *a blank page. A new chapter.
Just waiting to be written.*

Photo copyright © by Dona Ann McAdams

LAURIE CARLOS

Name: Laurie Carlos Smith
Stage Name: Laurie Carlos
Birthdate/Birthplace: January 25, 1949/Queens, New York
"Raised Up" Where: Lower East Side
Education: Performing Arts High School
Honors/Grants: Two Bessie Awards for *Heat,* one for *White Chocolate;* Gregory Millard NYFA Fellowship and Obie Award for *For Colored Girls . . .*
Influences/Mentors/Heroes: Robbie McCauley; Greta Gunderson; Marion Lake; my mother, Louise Smith
Places Performed: P.S. 122; BACA Downtown; DTW; BAM; the Kitchen; Walker Art Center; Penumbra Theater; the Public Theater; the Guthrie Theater; MLK Center; Lincoln Center; Rodger Furman Theater; Aaron Davis Hall
Pivotal Performance: Doing the role of Dija in a play by Edgar White, in a park on the Upper West Side, I sang "Amazing Grace."
Favorite Performance Experience: *Teeny Town* with Robbie and Jessica Hagedorn, Thought-Music. *Talking Bones* by Shay Youngblood.
Most Terrifying Performance Experience: Doing *Two Times Less Than a Kiss* with Nicky Paraiso at DTW.
Favorite Prop or Costume: My costume in *Organdy Falsetto*—it had wings.
Hobbies: I paint and cook and I like to dye and make clothes.
Reading List: Everything that is in my hand
Favorite Music: Laura Nyro, Joni Mitchell, Prince, the Chieftains, Milton Nascimento
Favorite Quote: "Don't stop screaming."

Artist's Notes

Making a Recipe

Making the cooking show challenged me as the performer because although it is text based, most of the time it's improvisation. As an actor I take the words most times and stand them up. And as a recipe this work calls for all the senses to be active and activated. My work for the most part never deals with the audience as a component of the work. Here the pace of this piece is dependent often on audience reaction and confrontation. Using text music and movement in my kitchen mixing foodstuff together, going up against the rules of process all the time, asking where is the moon and how is the light on the other side of it. With all the elements of history and versions of the story. Somewhere there is a place where the light curves and gives and clears places for dancing. When the work connects to a music or the groan of memory of the simple pattern in an apron through text or movement I have to ask another question and then another. The questions are endless—pepper, bread, ice? The answers are always turning in on you.

I just cut up some onions and hope you don't vomit or spit them out or like them so much you eat them all.

During this work the aspects of current events are part of the improvisational component, and the written text changes around a lot to allow me access to materials that may apply. The dish so far over the last two years has been the same. Most of the time I work with other people on the stage. I hate solo. For the cooking show, though, my challenge has been to go solo. It's the only work I do solo. I've learned how to keep going when the top of my head is about to dry up and when to let the silence be real good while just letting the knife sing.

The Cooking Show & How the Monkey Dances

The stage is set with a chair on the far right diagonal. More center a table with as beautiful a cloth as casual will allow. The equipment needed to prepare a meal is placed there. A white candle, a photo of some relative or friend. A vase of flowers. For this recipe I have placed a large bowl and some canned goods predrained and washed. Fresh veggies and olive oil. Three kinds of vinegar. Wooden spoons, chopsticks, forks, and cutting board. Plastic bowls and spoons. Salt and pepper and fresh garlic, nine or ten bulbs of it.

The MONKEY *dancer enters singing in looped breath and high kicks broken gestures sweet and in the voice of her child light. She sings:*

> I'm going to jump down
> and turn around
> and pick a pail
> of cotton
> I'm going to jump down
> and turn around
> and pick a pail
> a day.

> [*Repeat two times*]

THE MONKEY:
My second-grade teacher taught us that song. In P.S. 97. The school I went to on the Lower East Side where I grew up. Before I went to P.S. 188 in the third grade on Houston Street. Before Joseph Bagarosa called me a nigger. Long before LaTanya taught me about the Negro systems of class. Mrs. Rodgers taught us the song. . . . I'm going to jump down and turn around and pick a pail of cotton. . . . Me and my friend Micky used to like to go to

the gym and do the dance that went with it when you sang it. Micky was the same color as me. I mean she had the same skin. So we were sisters. Mrs. Rodgers told us we were very wrong and should not say that anymore. 'Cause Micky was Jewish and I was a Negro. So we could not be sisters. Now, I knew that my great-grandmother was a Negro, and of course my father was a Negro and Uncle Bob and them. They couldn't drink from the white water spout in Virginia when we went down there and carried their own water and told me I was not up North, keep my mouth shut. They never told me it was 'cause I was a Negro. Mrs. Rodgers, though, made me understand. Micky could not be my sister. She was Jewish. Me? I was a Negro. Then the song she had taught us to sing I knew was all wrong. You see I knew now that my great-grandmother would sing it all of a sudden if I was a Negro then the song went like this . . . [*In the voice Deep Southern full of pain and woe, deep, colored, negroid:*]

I'm gwine to jump down
tern round
pick a bile
o' cotton
jump down,
tern round
pick a bale
a day.

[*Repeat two times*]

Donna Sears/Tedra/Ellia Rodriguez/Cynthia Ann Scott/Janice Valentine/George Johnson/Ellen Woodlon/Deborah Aikins/ Gladys Leon/Barbara Tepper/
These names are prayers/
Gentle ingredients/short recipes

[*The* MONKEY *steps up to the table*]

THE MONKEY:
Welcome to my kitchen world where the poems start sometime and all the problems get an airing and the possibility of dream walking with a casual visitor is dependent on how many of us eat garlic raw. And if you are here it's 'cause you want to be. Not like white boys want to just be any damn where they think it's all going on. But more like a true feeling for leaning long into the arms of a sister or a stranger who smells like wells of sadness sometime. Nothing academic to back up the story. Nothing to prove. No

way to prove it. This is where the memory of smell and furious tasting goes on. Don't try to write down the recipe. Listen to where you are going. This is not like stealing the sheet music off the stand after the colored composer has finished the gig.

Recipe now: Chickpea salad, oh, yeah.

I have here three cans of chickpeas & two of red beans. Oh yeah, I know I said chickpea salad. This is exactly what I meant when we started. When Rosa said she was packed and ready to go, she knew she could get a ticket at the airport. She knew she had it. Meanwhile they went calling around for confirmation to what Rosa knew. 'Cause she had not made a reservation they called her all kinds of liars. Even though Darden and all the rest know you need a credit card to confirm a reservation, and Darden knew that Rosa did not have one.

Darden knew the housekeeper from South America that came here to make money, to send home. To keep many members of her family from going hungry. Darden knew that in front of all the American people with her new hairdo. She could not say she didn't make a reservation 'cause she didn't have a credit card. He knew 'cause he was colored. Did his grandmother make a reservation to get to wherever north was for her? People just go to where they can always buy a ticket and get on whatever it is. Besides with what they pay women who cook, clean, watch their children, endure the insults, block out the arguments. They all knew she didn't have no credit card. Therefore no reservation for a flight back to home with a new hairdo. Darden being colored is why they put him on her like that. And they better be glad the jury didn't hear it. He knew he was wrong. Wonder why he cried so after they lost? After he whopped Rosa for the consumption of the viewing public? After he lost, Darden stood there like the nigger who saved the sheets from the burning house. When where he sleeps is on the ground. Chickpea salad, oh, yeah!

RECIPE

Empty cans into the bowl. All five of them.
Stir red beans and chickpeas to blend, give color, give flavor.
Crush six to ten cloves of garlic, in the mortar.
Crush to keep away the colds. Keep the love strong.

[*The* MONKEY *crushes the garlic. Gives breath. Kicks strong, an inside dance . . . Phosphorescent . . .*]

The dancers we are now
claw into businessmen's imaginations

Melancholy enters the bowels
Giving of phosphorescent lips, eyelids, earlobes.

They've arrived home at 7:30
With newsprint all over their palms
late for supper
Arrive with sweat on their lapels
and a scenario for the late night life disasters
The cocktail hour dancer allowed
him to kiss her heels with his numb pink tongue
The five dollars he slipped in her belt will never
be missed
it had no other destination

A dancer's mother weeps
&
all the time
Wampum real estate/Wampum real estate/
their hearts beat
Wampum real estate
And their tongues taste nothing in the
mouths of their lovers
Tongues with no dreams
no fire

Only solo voyages no pathways to forever

Wampum real estate

His tongue tasted the salt in the silver heels of
the dancer

The puddles of sweat where she works
are lakes of salt water.
She is not dead
########

Do you remember the man in the band
with the phosphorescent teeth?

I asked what happened to his wonderful smile.

They're all fallen out on the beach

pieces now of turquoise, stone, amber, jade.

I met him at the top of the stairs at the reunion
He took the onyx teeth from his pockets

Many people there had left them coming up the stairs

how fortunate some belonged to very close friends.
#########

My grandfather spoke of a Quadrille
and tap-danced on the grass
tap-danced on the grass

Tobacco Harvest Waltz . . . memory
Cotton Patch Tangos . . . new songs
Corn Shuck Hustle . . . new dances

Recipe for chitterlings
vomit for life my legacy
bitter herbs remembrance

memory . . . new songs . . . new dances

Tobacco Harvest Waltz . . . new songs, new dances

Cotton Patch Tangos . . . new songs, new dances

Corn Shuck Hustle . . . wampum, real estate

We've sold all the land in Virginia
to pay taxes

Nowhere to put the pot in the ground
wampum real estate
The hole will never be dug for pots of beans
wood, fire
drop the pot
beans
onions, tomatoes, five small pieces of pork

cover over
the way slaves did when they were trying to escape
Nowhere to vacation . . . plant black-eyed peas
the way slaves did living in the jungles of America

We're living in the jungles of America
we're living in the jungles of America
we're living in the jungles of America

[*The* MONKEY *gives the song to the dance. Each dance has its own gesture vocabulary.*]

RECIPE

To the garlic still in the mortar add some rice vinegar, and an equal amount white vinegar. The kind you douche with. This bottle is brand-new. It's a small one but it's brand-new, never opened till now. Pour this into the garlic. Add olive oil. My people don't use olive oil for this recipe. They would use peanut oil. That's so country. Due respect and all to Dr. Carver and all but olive oil taste better. Cousin Viola would ask me right about now if I thought I was better than everybody else. "Who the hell you think you are anyway!" All I said when I saw my cousin Lill babe's face messed up by Joe her husband was no man would ever hit me ever. "Who the hell you think you are anyway. What the hell makes you think you better than the rest of us?" That was 1962 and if I could have moved, Cousin Viola would have tried to kick my ass. I use olive oil in this recipe, extra virgin. And cilantro, lots of it. You chop it up rough or coarse depending on where you are from. The women in my family any side were strange war horses. Secrets and singing. A glance. The look put you in your place. If they had to talk to you in public about your behavior, you knew you were going to pay for their embarrassment. And shame ran deep to the roots of all those perfect curls and clean aprons. The look. It was your responsibility to watch for it. If you ever got so carried away that you didn't see it. That was worse than having seen and not cleaning up your act. Only a fool would do that. These secretive songbirds were all capable of beating you into submission with anything they could find. To beat the sass out you. The haughty. Thinking you were any better than the rest. My people came out of hard slavery. Mississippi, South Carolina, Memphis, Baltimore, Piney Swamp, Virginia. They came north and worked so hard to get here that seven days a week, two jobs, mostly three was nothing. We were all here eating canned food. Canned peas, asparagus, spinach, tamales, pickled okra. Until I was sixteen I never had a glass of orange juice that didn't come out of a can. Libby, Donald

Duck, Del Monte. Every single recipe called for some kind of meat. To sit down without it reminded them of poor. Plantin' poor. Pickin' poor. Meatless, barefoot. Five miles to work poor. Shiny pants, one good dress, meatless poor. Big thick pieces of ham, ham hocks, bacon, pigs' feet, salt pork and spare ribs. Hamburgers so thin on Wonder bread. Steak cooked hard, no blood. Pork chops, beef tongue, frankfurters, salami, boiled ham, Spam. Chicken necks, feet, wings, drumsticks, butts, livers, hearts and gizzards smothered in gravy. Fried boiled baked poached. Only my aunt Juanita poached chicken in white wine. Demonstrating for us her European strain. She carried her secrets to the grave. She visits me in dreams although the day she died we hadn't spoken in many years. Add to this mixture some sesame seed oil. The dark roasted one you used to only be able to get at the Asian markets. Cilantro, sesame and olive oil.

[*The recipe is a modification, an improvement, a memory without guilt. The* MONKEY *chews cilantro and hums. A way to the first memory. In the kitchen the monkey sings:*]

Borinque thru azure & rainstorms in ruffles, closed in fingers. An unknown listener of love and clear light playing guitar, answering questions about the origins of roaches and tears. Borinque clean washed linoleum raised against too much steam heat. High-rise 10 to 4 rooms and rice and rice and rice grateful for meat. Unable to find mangos in season or blue water. Loving everything American. Working New York brooms and Long Island gardens. Loving Ricky Nelson & Topo Gigio, Joselito on the *Sullivan Show.*

Calling Carmen! Carmen Morales Rodriguez Ortiz Aiyala Arroacho Perez Cruz Carmen Sanchez Dominques Pinero Rivera Santiago Sonja Clara Jose Manuelo Edgar Ellia Luz Anna Borinque. Crying *pleanas* in Pentecostal basements. Just good dancers. Villains cut in *brillante.* Singers leaning gorgeous in Woolworth powder. The Lord lives in us all! Borinque marching on the head of disaster. Declaring summer by congas and cheering loud for the Yankees. Parking DeSotos sideways on Columbia Street repairing nylons for the week. Borinque a world of pink rollers bringing stripes to florals orange to gold. Flirting loud on corners lined with garbage. Smelling summer in the eyes of Borinque thru azure eyelids lined in tragic black pencil.

[*The* MONKEY *sings open voice clean:*]

I am no one again
again I am no one
No one again am I
I am no one again.

I am Ethiopian again
again I am Ethiopian
Ethiopian again am I
I am Ethiopian again

I am not free again
again I am not free
Free again I am not
I am not free again

[*This song repeats three times with a different ethnic, racial nationality in the second verse. The* MONKEY *returns to the cutting board.*]

RECIPE
Combine everything together in the mortar. Mix it! Think multicultural! Add some of these capers and the paprika. Very important, paprika. Pour the dressing into the bowl and stir. Mix. Toss. Do not taste! Just smell! A person could get beat bad for that. Some ladies of the house didn't like it, so some of us are just smellers. I can tell if something needs salt or not just from the way it makes the back of my throat itch. You have to practice. You are in my kitchen. So do you want to talk? Got a thing you want to share? Is there someone in the room you would like to know better? I mean just 'cause I can't get a date doesn't mean someone else won't get lucky.
    [*Open up the floor to talk about movies TV music dates politics dance steps dreams. During this section the* MONKEY *cuts up tomatoes and green pepper.*]

RECIPE
Now we cut some onions. I would run the cold water if we were near a sink. A shortcoming with this performance-art stuff. Unless you're at that space on the Bowery where that woman gives shows in her house. Even there you have to turn upstage.
    [MONKEY *opens her eyes and the tears from the onions stream. Full of grief and unresolve. This is an opportunity to release, mourn loudly, slow then quick sobs. The old woman. The child left alone one time too many.*]

I survive the stampedes & a longing for
dangerous kisses. And all the longing is restricted, confined
to polite glances & a checklist of do not enter
I am living in the parking lot of my life.
Old movies, postcards with scenes from other wars.
Hattie does bars & poetry readings. Other people I know cook,
live with fibrous tumors & large boxes of condoms that don't cover

everything. At the sight of a new face that might interest me,
I become the FBI, the CIA, all desires require No. I live in the
melancholy of dangerous survival & longing for kisses.
my friends who remember fast moments, who are still hot, live in
forced monogamy, desire unchanged, with postcards & scenes from other
wars. If they were serious, if anyone was serious,
condoms would come in a size large enough to cover everyone from head
to toe. They'd cover the tongue & fingers & feet & penis & vaginas,
all the way up into the rectum. These condoms are chemically treated
so when tongues touch, you & your lover feel the chemically activated
saliva personal to yourself. Toes are covered for those people who do
things with them. Plastic fingers enter completely plastic covered
vaginas to release the liquids that come in flavors strawberry,
garlic, Heineken. And these condoms come with extra extensions of
width & length. And in six racial colors with three shades for
black Americans.
I survive the stampedes with a longing for dangerous kisses.

RECIPE
Add in tomatoes and green peppers. Put in them onions. Toss, sing, throw
your head back and enjoy the secret. Observe your own joy.

   [*Make way for the memory. The girl is dreaming aloud. The* MONKEY
makes way for this set of songs. The girl sings.]
Boxes were stacked for shipment and Rubio saw Roman the first day on the
job lifting. After hours of smelling Roman's sweat and hearing her laugh,
Rubio was struck with the fire of the ages. The kind that makes a man leave
Jesus or converts him to Catholicism. He married her six days later. They
worked together, still. Every other weekend or so, I'd go to visit their house.
Auntie Roman never cooked, so the food was bought from outside in bags.
They imported me every so often. When the cleaner's man, Mr. Meeban,
started seeing my mother, who they say hadn't had a man in five years,
since my father died suddenly in Canada looking for work. My brother and
I had his legs, and they grew all around my head when I sat down in grass. I
was thirteen when Mama started fucking Mr. Meeban, and Jimmy Baldwin
slept between my legs to keep the points of my knees from causing me so
much pain. Uncle Rubio never talked about books or history. Auntie
washed in Octagon soap and I read all the time. The long silences made me
desperate for food. Uncle Rubio washed the dishes sometime, first glasses,
then cups. In the kitchen drawer, under the aprons, he kept the gun. And I
watched him take it out long like a cowboy movie. He pointed it at Roman.
She stood slow. She headed for the door and threw the damn thing open.
Uncle Rubio ran her around the house. Both of them in silence around the

house running. I don't know how many times, around the outside of the house. Roman kept running even after Uncle Rubio returned to the kitchen. When she came inside, they pulled out the cards. No one said anything. I let go a stream of piss that now rolled down the side of the chair. Uncle Rubio took me upstairs in his arms, bathed me, and put me to bed. Jimmy Baldwin between my legs.

[*She sings:*]

[*Music*]

I'm just a girl the only one
I made my mind up to have you.
Don't care what nobody say
And I ain't got no daddy
Got lipstick these eyes
Put my sneakers in the garbage
Just for you.
Don't care what nobody say.
I'm just a girl the
only one
I made my mind up to have
You

Yes!
Can you imagine they thought nine black women did not understand the issues around domestic violence? Could not come deliberate this case fairly 'cause they did not/could not contend with the issues of domestic violence? Nine black women! My grandmother wouldn't talk about it. How when you worked in the white people's homes it was taken for granted that you would endure some touches. Endure kisses too friendly. They knew all about it. Although having to tell you all that was the same as trying to tell you that you were a Negro. Having to confess after they had made you understand. From then on always being suspect, always a doubt about how you got in the door. So I invite you to my kitchen. A pitched tent. The home of a refugee. Dinner is served!

[*A few bowls of salad are served by the smiling monkey. Then upon the exit the bowl is left, the people serve themselves and one another.*]

[*Exit*]

Photo copyright © by Dona Ann McAdams

RINDE ECKERT

Name: Rinde Eckert
Stage Name: same
Birthdate/Birthplace: Sept. 20, 1951/Mankato, Minnesota
"Raised Up" Where: Franklin Lakes, New Jersey, and Iowa City, Iowa
Education: Bachelor of Music, University of Iowa; Master of Music, Yale University
Honors/Grants: Like the Tin Man, I'm a little short on official testimonials.
Influences/Mentors/Heroes: Stan Laurel, Glenn Gould, Phyllis Curtin, Friedrich Dürrenmatt
Places Performed: Not everywhere yet
Pivotal Performance: Peter Rabbit in kindergarten. I played the title role. The audience laughed every time I dipped my head and the ears flopped over. That was a revelation.
Favorite Performance Experience: I sang a version of "Black Is the Color" for Dave Jenkins's birthday party. Margaret Jenkins danced while I sang. After I finished, an old sax player waiting to play again turned to me and said, "That was really in the pocket." And it was.
Most Terrifying Performance Experience: I performed *The Idiot Variations* in Czech for a Prague audience. It was terrifying and exhilarating.
Favorite Prop or Costume: I like objects that make sound: a piece of wire waved in the air or a hunk of pipe that one blows into. I like the white cotton skirt I wear in *The Idiot Variations*—easy to move and be moving in, I think.
Hobbies: I fashion small figures in clay. I play Bach on the piano a lot.
Reading List: Bohumil Hrabal's *Too Loud a Solitude,* also his *I Served the King of England.* Michael Ondaatje's *The English Patient.* Michael Palmer's great book of poems *At Passages*
Favorite Music: Glenn Gould playing anything, Bill Frissell, Paul Brady's more traditional stuff, Nino Ricardo played by Paco Peña, Carlos Paredes, and currently G. Love and Special Sauce
Favorite Quote: "The overestimation of estimable men leaves the people powerless." (Lao-tzu)

Artist's Notes

When I was about six, a couple of the neighborhood teenagers decided to play a little joke on me and a friend of mine. They stuffed us into a tool crate, tied the lid down, and talked casually about burying us alive. Since that terrifying experience, I suppose, I've been fiercely determined never to be boxed in again. This could seem like the governing metaphor of much of my work, since many of the characters I create find themselves at large and alone, at a kind of poetic remove from community and culture, and their attendant practices and protocols. But it's not.

The ideas behind *Dry Land Divine* developed from a simple question about the practice of water dowsing (or divining). I was fascinated by the conventional dowsing rod (a kind of Y made of willow or some other "thirsty" wood). I pictured myself with this green branch, walking across a field in a careful and attentive way. I saw myself stopped by the quivering of the stick drawn to the hidden source by a mysterious power. I thought this was a beautiful idea: a sexual metaphor subsumed and subverted by a spiritual metaphor.

A friend of mine had bought me a little accordion (another beautiful mystery). I was lugging it around, trying to learn how it worked. It had something Old World and otherworldly about it. It seemed to belong to the dowsing piece.

I think I'm my best when I'm trying to reconcile seemingly unrelated events or objects. The performance, then, becomes a kind of calculus or reckoning by the character of these disparate logics (for example: an accordion and a divining rod).

I began to imagine a dramatic context that would both accommodate these instruments (justify their use) and ramify their metaphoric values while giving me good reason to be out there in the first place.

After performing three different versions of the narrative I settled on the story of a water dowser who kills his brother, goes to prison, and is visited there by an angel who gives him a little red accordion, promising him redemption if he learns how to play all the old tunes. There's one sequence in which he kneels in front of a bucket of water, washes the red dust off his hands, gazes at his reflection, talks about his brother, baptizes himself, then beats on the bucket with a couple of wires, hums a little tune, and stirs the water. I think that's beautiful.

Dry Land Divine

[*He speaks in a blackout:*]

In 1952, in Ford, Wyoming, a man named John Fletcher killed his brother, an evangelical minister with the First Church of Christ Jesus. He pled guilty to voluntary manslaughter and was sentenced to fourteen years in prison. While in prison he wrote a short history of water dowsing and learned to play the accordion. He was paroled in 1962 and never heard from again.

Lights up on a man standing in the center of a sixteen-by-sixteen-foot white tarp with faded red stains. He is carrying a small red accordion. Just upstage of the tarp hangs a silver wire hanger from which drapes a black satin stole and a clerical collar. A gray bucket sits at the downstage left corner of the tarp. The man is operating the bellows of the accordion so it makes a breathing sound. He starts by playing a drone, then sings a plaintive vocalise in falsetto over it. At the end of this air he starts a waltz on the accordion. The voice begins doubling the melody. At the end of the waltz, the accordion and voice increase in pitch, intensity, and dissonance. Abruptly, he stops playing the accordion. His singing becomes a frantic and noisy breathing while he takes the instrument off. He lays the accordion down slowly, rises, then draws wads of crumpled newspaper clippings out of his pockets. The paper is covered with red dust that flies around as he unfolds it. Within the paper he discovers a harmonica in a small plastic bag. He begins to play the harmonica, then alternately plays and sings:

Down in the valley
The valley so low
Hang your head over
Hear the wind blow

Follow the fence line
Like a small dog
Run to the churchyard
You left long ago

[*He stops suddenly and backs up violently. While moving laterally in a programmed series of gestures, he speaks:*]

Sure I hit him
It was a dry year
Thought I was losing my touch
A guy gets nervous
Has a few too many
Timing's all wrong for a lecture on the gospel

Sure I hit him
The little prick has always been doggin' my ass

So I grab the book, see
Rip out the New Testament
Corinthians to Revelations
His face goes white
Jesus Christ, I say
You already know how it ends
All hell breaks loose
And you go down like a sack of dirt

[_He kneels before the bucket and begins to wash his hands._]

John at eighteen
Is the best around
He's got a way with a willow fork
Tap out the spring with a green sprig or a hanger wire
Forty feet or four hundred
Make no difference
Take him to water like a green-eyed duck
At eighteen . . .

[_He tips the bucket, then furiously and repeatedly anoints his head with water._]

John got a brother found Jesus at seventeen
His brother finds Jesus at seventeen
Jesus haul him off to Bible college
Drive him back in a big car
Say:
"Salvation look like a big car leaving sinners in the dust
Just like a big black car
A man of the cloth in the driver's seat"
Say:
"John, I'm gonna drag your well-witchin' ass to Jesus
Gonna drag your ass to Jesus, John, or die tryin' "

[_He starts pounding on the sides of the bucket with wires he's found beside the bucket. He stops, leans over the bucket and whispers:_]

One man makes the mistake of believing any man's pain is his own
The other man makes the mistake of remembering what he can't change

[_He pounds the sides with the wires again, then stops again to whisper:_]

One man was practicing to be a martyr
The other man will settle for redemption

You can bet your ass he'll settle for redemption

[_He uses the end of one of the wires to stir the water in the bucket while he sings wordlessly something that sounds like an old hymn. Suddenly, he stops singing, rubs the wire furiously on the lip of the bucket, and stands up. He_ *backs up, laughing strangely, the wires vibrating in his hands. Upon reaching the upstage edge of the tarp, he begins to cut the air with the wires and speaks:*]

Out of the alcoholic fog come something like an angel
Something like an old crusty angel got miraculous tattoos
Angel of the Lord look just like some old geezer with a shine on

[*As the monologue continues, he uses the wires to illustrate his point.*]

"Hell, I seen it done with a Barbie doll and a pipe cleaner
Forty feet straight down, bang, water till ten years from Wednesday
Get yourself a bucket the size of Germany
Cork it with a big red pump and buy yourself a lifetime supply of Tang

And don't tell me you got to be Jesus' special friend to make it work
God knows I'm hell on wheels . . . give me a hanger wire . . .
Oh, hell! Give me anything I can bend
I give you seven to one against any saint you can name

Put St. Peter out there with a sprig off the very cross and a half a day's
head start
I'll beat him to the water three sheets to the wind or dead drunk

A man got the gift he gets pulled to where the water's at

Or you can put your faith in some class A geologist from God-Only-Knows
University
Give him about a mile of extension cord
He'll still be mutterin' to himself three days later
When I come up along the rise on my coffee break
Stick my finger in the ground, come up wet as a happy whore

And you can bet your butt I ain't gonna tell him
I just took a pair of lineman's pliers to an old hanger wire
Blessed the whole mess with a little flat soda water and headed out the
back door
You can bet I ain't gonna tell him there's an ancient practice in it
He'll say,
"There ain't enough workin' parts"
Call it a coincidence
Write a paper on me says I just got lucky

No, sir! You got to cook up somethin' with numbers in it
Give the whole industrial world a hard-on
Imagining somethin' works every time no matter what
No mystery to it at all
Just start the engine, put any jackass behind the wheel

Well, sir, I'm here to tell you you got hands made for witchin'
No matter what the weather is

[*He takes out a red bandanna to wipe his face.*]

A man without ghosts, Johnny
Johnny, a man without ghosts is a dangerous man
And regrets, John
John, a man with no regrets, he's just plain crazy

Jesus, John
You can tell the church to go to hell
But you still got the Bible written all over you

[*He suddenly dives to the floor, snatching two short galvanized pipes from the ground and tumbling into a cross-legged position center stage. He rolls the pipes back and forth—they have hexagonal caps that make a ratchetlike sound on the floor. He sings:*]

Well, I never been to heaven, but I been told
Streets up there are paved with gold
Keep your hand on that plow, hold on
Hold on, hold on
Keep your hand on that plow, hold on

Matthew, Mark, Luke, and John
All the prophets are dead and gone
Keep your hand on that plow, hold on
Hold on, hold on
Keep your hand on that plow, hold on

[*He throws one pipe away, puts the other to his lips and blows into the end, improvising rhythmic variations on the note and its harmonics while a tape plays the following:*]

Stone church

Dog in the yard
Rusted wheelbarrow
No chickens
A dry year
A very dry year
Here comes a man of the cloth
Here stands a man with a length of pipe
No time for sermons
No time to think
Down he goes
All wet

[*Using the pipe as a mute, he intones an incomprehensible litany while walking to the upstage edge of the tarp where the clerical stole and collar hang on a silver wire hanger. He drops the pipe and puts on the stole and collar singing over the taped sound of churning water. Grasping the now empty hanger, he picks up a pair of linemen's pliers lying nearby, then cuts the hanger, twisting the wire into a forked divining rod. He holds the forked wire over his head in the semblance of a Gothic arch. His song swells. The rod comes alive in his hands, propelling him about the stage in a manic but graceful dance. He begins to laugh. He quiets down, drops the rod, takes out his red handkerchief, and mops the sweat off his face. He picks up his accordion and speaks:*]

"What we have here my friend
Is nothing less than the instrument of your redemption
What we have here is a goddamn angel with a little red accordion
Oh, hell, I could put you on the street
Give you the pig eyes of a missionary
You and all the other shouters
But this is off the record

"She's a real character
Won't play in tune no matter what you do
I give her to you
Find a street corner and learn how to play all the old tunes
You know, John
God hates a perfect thing
That's why he's head over heels in love with you"

[*He plays a slow version of the opening song underneath the following:*]

John got him an accordion
Carries it like a portable church
Cradles it in his arms like a breathing thing
Give him enough time he'll learn how to play the old tunes

What did the angel say?

"The art of dowsing, John, is the art of surrender
You're standing in the goddamn river"

That's how it ends, he hopes,
With something like a benediction

[*He stops playing and sings:*]

Amazing grace
How sweet the sound
That saved a wretch like me
I once was lost
But now am found
Was blind but now I see

[*He begins the final accordion accompaniment and sings:*]

Amen, amen, amen

[*The lights fade as he stops singing, laughs softly, and twists from side to side, continuing to play the accordion as the lights go out.*]

Photo copyright © by Dona Ann McAdams

ETHYL EICHELBERGER

Name: "I do have a common name but I never tell. Ethyl's been my name for over ten years." (Eichelberger quoted in Emily A. Kane's "Ethyl Eichelberger," *East Village Eye,* July 1985.)

Stage Name: Ethyl Eichelberger. "Only you have the right to decide what you are called. You can go along with what your parents name you, but ultimately, you decide who you are even down to your name." (Eichelberger quoted in Robert Chesley's "Ethyl Eichelberger," *Coming Up!* June 1983, p. 18.)

Birthdate/Birthplace: July 17, 1945/Pekin, Illinois

Died/Cause/Place: August 12, 1990/HIV-related suicide/Staten Island, New York City

Education: Attended Knox College in Galesburg, Illinois, 1963–1965. Graduated from American Academy of the Dramatic Arts, NYC, 1967.

Honors/Grants: Villager Award 1981, Obie Award 1983, Bessie Award 1987

Influences/Mentors/Heroes: Neil Bartlett: Who are your idols?

Ethyl Eichelberger: Charles Ludlam is the great genius of my life. He has influenced more people in this city, more artists, more theatre than anybody else.

I love Margaret Rutherford. She is one of my idols. I have millions of her movies. Well, I have several. Margaret Rutherford's son is a transsexual, that just happened a year or two before she died, and I read this quote, because you see I knew that she just had to be a wonderful woman, and she said, they asked her what she thought and she said "We loved him as a man and now we'll love her as a woman." And she was a great actress.

Zasu Pitts, she was a silent movie actress, a great beauty, she was in Stroheim's *Greed,* and then when talkies came she had this funny voice. But she didn't just drop down dead and die, she became a comedienne, playing these dotty crazy women. She did that in order to continue being an artist.

The drag performer I emulate is Lynn Carter, a great American drag, he did all the classic acts, Mae West, Marlene, all of that; and he owned his own club in Provincetown and another club in the winter in Puerto Rico, and he did the Jewel Box Review which toured all over the country. Besides being a great performer he was smart enough to keep his life together, he owned these clubs and put together this review and toured it. That's why I respect your Betty Bourne [one of the founders of Bloolips]. She's not only a great actress, she keeps that company together, she creates work for people. (Eichelberger quoted in Neil Bartlett's "Ethyl and Lily: Speaking Your Mind," *Performance,* July/August 1987, no. 48, pp. 26–27.)

"I learned how to act from Adrian Hall, I learned how to write from Charles Ludlam, and I learned how to put on a show from Larry Ree [founder of the Original Trockadero Gloxinia Ballet Company]." (Eichelberger quoted in Steven Oxman's "Marzipan upon a Birthday Cake: A Talk with Ethyl Eichelberger," *Theatre,* Summer/Fall 1990, vol. 21, no. 3, p. 71.)

Places Performed: Acted for seven years in over thirty productions with the Trinity Repertory Company as a character actor under direction of Adrian Hall, Providence, Rhode Island, 1967–1973; Edinburgh Festival with Trinity Repertory Company (first American company to perform there), 1968; numerous productions with Charles Ludlam and the Ridiculous Theatrical Company, 1975–1987; London International Festival of Theatre, *Leer* 1987; Serious Fun! Festival, Alice Tully Hall, Lincoln Center, *Leer* 1987 and *The Lincolns* 1988; Vivian Beaumont Theater, Lincoln Center, in Robert Woodruff's production of *The Comedy of Errors* with the Flying Karamazov Brothers, 1987; Belvoir Street Theatre, Various Grande Dames, Sydney, Australia, 1988; Rotterdam, Holland, in Mickery Theatre production of *The History of Theatre, Part II,* 1988; Joyce Theater, NYC, *Ariadne Obnoxious,* 1988; Lunt-Fontanne Theater, Broadway, in John Dexter's production of *Threepenny Opera* with Sting, 1989; Yale Repertory Theater in Andrei Belgrader's production of *Troilus and Cressida,* New Haven, Connecticut, 1990; active participant on East Village performance scene appearing regularly at such spaces as the Pyramid Club, s.n.a.f.u., 8 B.C., Dixon Place, and La MaMa. At time of death, P. S. 122's most produced performer.

Pivotal Performance Experiences: "When I was about twenty years old, I had just moved to New York and had just started going to acting school and had really committed myself to theatre. . . . Lincoln Center was new, it was 1965, and I used to walk down there and go to the theatrical library. One time they had this special exhibit. You'd walk through and there were things that moved and things that talked. I stopped at one display. Late in her life, Sarah Bernhardt had been touring, and [Thomas] Edison invited her to New Jersey on one of her days off, and she recorded scenes from Racine's *Phaedra.* So I pressed the button, I had the earphones on, and it was a long speech from *Phaedra* being done by Sarah Bernhardt. It changed my life. I listened to it over and over. Every time it stopped I pressed the button again." (Eichelberger quoted in Oxman, p. 68.)

"I'll never forget it; no one ever forgets their first meeting with Charles [Ludlam]. . . . [It was] in this beautiful loft on Great Jones Street. I didn't really know who anyone was, but it was fun. I just watched what was going on. This very short, balding man with long hair would jump up whenever it was his turn, do his rehearsing, and then, when he finished, just sit down. One time, however, he jumped up and said, 'Wait a minute.' He ran to this stuff piled at the back of the loft, picked out a piece of chintzy green satin, and wrapped it around himself. When he turned around, he was that great actress Norma Desmond. No makeup, nothing, just this piece of cheap material. It was incredible, a total transformation. It was one of the most amazing things I had ever seen. And it changed my life." (Eichelberger quoted in Ronn Smith's "Ethyl Eichelberger," *Theatre Crafts,* January 1989, p. 32.)

"On my fortieth birthday, I premiered *Leer."* (Eichelberger quoted in Oxman, pp. 68–69.)

"I'm looking at this point in my life for great man character parts. I've already done most of the great women's parts. I'm sure I'll do some more, but at this moment, I want to work toward being more like Jacob Adler or Morris Carnovsky. My dream is to be one of the great American actors." (Eichelberger quoted in William Harris's "Ethyl Eichelberger Cartwheels through History," *The New York Times,* August 7, 1988, sec. H, p. 5.)

Favorite Quote: "Art is something that isn't there before you create it, but would be missed if it was gone." (John Roebling, architect of the Brooklyn Bridge)

"I want to create something like the Brooklyn Bridge." (Eichelberger quoted in Michael Paller's "No Accident: A Profile of Ethyl Eichelberger," *Theatre Week,* September 7–13, 1987, p. 27.)

—Materials compiled by Joe E. Jeffreys

Notes on Chim-Lee

An artist of frantic energy and imagination, Ethyl Eichelberger (1945–1990) was a force in performance. Sadly, printed scripts fail to capture much that was unique to his art. These few notes hopefully illuminate some of his *The Tempest of Chim-Lee*'s contextual, thematic, and performative concerns.

Eichelberger is primarily remembered as a male performance artist who played female roles. Creator of a galaxy of such solo and group performance pieces as *Phedre* (1972), *Nefert-iti* (1976), *Medea* (1980), and *Lucrezia Borgia* (1982), Eichelberger plied his thirty-two works in wildly rotating repertory on any space that might pass as a stage in New York City and worldwide from 1977 until his HIV-related suicide in 1990. When he turned forty, however, he broke his strictly female chain of characters and began writing male roles for himself to play.

The fourth in a series of nine male characters that Eichelberger created including *Casanova* (1985), *Rip Van Winkle* (1986), and *Dilbert Dingle Dong* (1989), *The Tempest of Chim-Lee* premiered at P.S. 122 in August of 1987 and played three weekends in the large upstairs space. It was presented as the second half of a double bill which opened with a remounting of another Eichelberger monodrama, *St. Joan* (1987), featuring Black-Eyed Susan in the title role. The new work was performed on a small square platform of approximately three feet in height with footlights below creating a sideshowlike atmosphere for the chamber drama. Eichelberger was costumed in a floor-length black silk coolie ensemble and performed in a white chalky makeup with painted-on Fu Manchu mustache and arched eyebrows. Known for outrageous wigs, for this character Eichelberger sported a six-foot-long black ponytail secured to the back of his shaved head.

Chim-Lee is an extreme character. In the play, the boy Chan calls Chim-Lee an "unholy scoundrel of a jack-knave." *The New York Times* review of the production noted that "on his path to perdition, Chim-Lee snarls, sneers and thoroughly earns the label." Eichelberger, as the critic makes clear, was able to play and overact any gender role. Later in the review, his performance in the role is further characterized as having "a demonic intensity and a kind of self-willed momentum."[1]

As with most of Eichelberger's plays and those of the Ridiculous Theatrical Company genre from which he emerged, *The Tempest of Chim-Lee* looks to other and frequently recondite sources for inspiration. While the title most readily brings to mind Shakespeare's *The Tempest*, Eichelberger's play finds its most firm footing in Franco Leoni's one-act opera *The Oracle* (1905). Eichelberger's Chim-Lee, like his namesake Chim-Fin in the Leoni opera, is the villainous proprietor of an opium den on Hatchet Row in San

Francisco's Chinatown, circa 1906, or as Eichelberger ad-libbed in performance, "eighty-one years before the harmonic convergence." In this retelling of the Leoni work, Eichelberger cloverleafed many personal and idiosyncratic turns into the story including its Shakespearean twist. Employing elements of *The Tempest*'s Prospero character and his magical powers, the title character in Eichelberger's work uses his dark powers to summon up a storm in his scheme to capture the daughter of the prosperous Ding-Ling.

A close reading of the performance text also yields anachronistic resonances with the AIDS crisis. Chim-Lee states at the top of the work, "1906–1906 already, time marches on, Chim-Lee/ and leaves you far behind—/ Not like some people/ Teddy Roosevelt has it fine these days—/ I read the papers—/ Look at what surrounds me—/ Disgusting shadows of men that are no longer." Written shortly after the AIDS-related death of Ridiculous Theatrical Company founder Charles Ludlam, with whom Eichelberger had been intimately involved and highly impacted by, and during the last phase of the Reagan administration, the play, as with most of Eichelberger's works, draws apposite parallels between its historical source materials and the world in which Eichelberger found himself living and performing. As he explained to reporter John Karr shortly after the play's premiere concerning his shift from female to male characters, "When I play women, that comes out of joy. . . . It's very hard for me to write women's roles right now given the state of the world."[2]

Primarily remembered as a drag performer, Eichelberger's male performance works may at first seem "out of character." They are, however, rooted in his sense of political activism and range as a character actor.

At first glance, the play may seem to be written for several performers. In production, however, it was a solo performance work with Eichelberger playing all the roles. This performative tactic, like drag, is another common Eichelbergian device. For *The Tempest of Chim-Lee,* he maneuvered the challenge with the help of a few simple hand props and a battery of voices and postures. When speaking as Ah-Yoe, he placed a fan in one hand while holding a feathered headdress behind his head in the other. The double-headed baby brother, Chan, was represented by a small Asian doll which Chim-Lee eventually imprisons inside a small Lucite box.

Other common Eichelbergian devices were also present in production. Along with his ad-libs from the stage to audience members and comments about misplaced or malfunctioning props (an element which is not captured by this printed version), the production also included several traditional Eichelberger accordion-accompanied songs. What became a new trademark also emerged with the production of this work. For the first time Eichelberger presented his recently learned skill of fire-eating before an audience.[3]

At the time of his death in 1990, Eichelberger stood as the single most produced artist at P.S. 122. Through the uniqueness of his relationship to the space and his visibility there, his performance work impacted a democratic spectrum of artists as it articulated a performative voice that is as tied to the times of its production as it is classic and uncapturable in this printed script.

—Joe E. Jeffreys

[1]Mel Gussow, review of *The Tempest of Chim-Lee*, "Stage: Two Eichelberger 'Classics,' " *The New York Times*, August 18, 1987, sec. C., p. 3.

[2]Ethyl Eichelberger, interview by John Karr, tape recording, San Francisco, California, October 27, 1987.

[3]Eichelberger had learned fire-eating earlier that summer from a cast member of the Lincoln Center production of Shakespeare's *The Comedy of Errors* directed by Robert Woodruff and featuring the Flying Karamazov Brothers. In the production Eichelberger played both the Abbess and the Courtesan.

The Tempest of Chim-Lee

"Sewer-Rat," she calls me and hisses in my face
"Be off, madman," commands her father
As they toddle down Hatchet Row with that
Fat Brat between them—BAH
"Sewer-Rat," it rattles in my brain—
Why does she speak to me with contempt in her voice like that?
She drives me mad—
And yet I do love her
[*Pulls down cutout of Ah-Yoe*]
Ah-Yoe, my beloved, why do you love not me?
Every thought I have is of you
You possess my every waking hour
Ah-Yoe, Ah-Yoe, little Lotus Blossom
Chim-lee loves you
Could you not love me too? [*Gnash*]
Leave your father and brother
and live off the profits of Chim-Lee's
den of iniquity and pipe dreams [*Slobber*]
For a glimpse of one fair ankle I would give
to you my vast opium den and all I own—
Is it not enough?
Does it not fulfill your most feminine of desires?

Bah—Your father is rich whilst mine was but a coolie in a gold mine
Bah—Is that why you turn away and avert your eyes?
You spurn me because of my poverty, do you not,
cruel princess?
I wallow in a sea of debts and despair—
Yet, I ask, is it my fault?
No, no, I am blameless
Oh, poor Chim-Lee, can you not crawl out of your dungeon of debts
Which holds you down and keeps you mired
within the very gutters of San Francisco?
San Francisco—gateway to the world—Bah
I'd sooner be back in lovely Shanghai where I was a happy child
But, indeed, my work demands are such that I live here
where life is impossible and much too dear
1906–1906 already, time marches on, Chim-Lee
and leaves you far behind—
Not like some people
Teddy Roosevelt has it fine these days—
I read the papers—
Look at what surrounds me—
Disgusting shadows of men that are no longer—
And who were you before the drugs clicked in?
A good mother's son, no doubt, with hope in your Heart
Here, come kick the gong around and pay up pronto
—Oh, look at this, another soiled sodden laid out low
Oh, but of course, a drummer [*Pulls drumstick out of dummy's pockets*]—
they're all mad—
And what a beautiful timepiece to add to Chim-Lee's collection—
Be cautious, be prudent, be sly—
Remember, there are white men's prisons, Chim-Lee, beware—Bah
None of you worthless wretches is fit to lick
The tiniest of toes of my perfect Ah-Yoe
So wallow in your filth and come not near her
For soon she will be mine—
Ah-Yoe is rich and beautiful
Ah-Yoe is rich and young
Ah-Yoe is rich and gifted with a lovely voice
like unto the miraculous nightingale
Ah-Yoe is rich and has breasts like two ripe Chinese melons
She must marry me and her wealth will then be mine—Ha, Ha . . . [*Snorts*]
[*Kicks dummy*]
Filthy sot of an opium-eater, have you not had enough?

OHO—Aha—[*Rattrap snaps*]—OUUCH—
Are your pockets empty then? It's out the door with you
[*Throws dummy out*]
Begone, scum of Chinatown . . .
Misery, misery, scorn and abuse I pour down on your heads—I return but what the
gods have heaped upon my pate—Ah, Chim-Lee, this life is cruel—this world is
evil, filled with treachery and deceit
If I were loved, all would be different—
Life is hell
Without Ah-Yoe
Life is hell
Without the woman I desire
Obsession—I am possessed
Obsessed with desire for lovely Ah-Yoe
I want what I can't get
(it's a new tune, but an old song)
She dwells but just across the alley yet
She lives within another world
A world of wealth and reality
While Chim-Lee lives with his opium dreams and despair
This dank cellar will soon disappear and fade into memory
With my opium and schemes of possession, wealth, and beauty
Obsession of possession
It's Chim-Lee's bounden duty
To teach all Chinatown a lesson and laugh the loudest and the last
To follow his obsession
And possess Ah-Yoe
From her topknot to her toes
I'll dog her everywhere she goes [*Howls*]
Ah-Yoe, Ah-Yoe
I must possess the beauteous Ah-Yoe
The woman of my dreams
Loves me not
Hates me so
I love her still
I always will
My beautiful Ah-Yoe
My obsession, my Ah-Yoe
Will you turn away and sneer
My fawn, my doe, my deer?

I know it must sound queer
But I want to nibble on your ear
Whisper nothings, such sweet nothings sweet and clear
Then lock you fast away from the sight
of prying eyes
Then you'll be mine mine mine
The result will be so very fine
You'll be mine, all and only mine
Ah, you're so smart, Chim-Lee, you will surely succeed in your nefarious
plots
to acquire all you desire—Is not your business a success? Have you not
property
upon the Russian River?
Is not your cash a-flowing? Ha, Ha!
Consider now, Chim-Lee, what are the pathways open to
A clever conniver like yourself? Will you waste your
Life rotting in this rancid basement, or will you strike
Out against the odds and tame the storms about you?
Fortify yourself, Chim-Lee . . . [*Drinks opium tea*]
Conjure dreams of lust and longings satisfied—
Ha, ha, ha, snort, fart, belch . . . [*Lights incense and dims lights*]
Be not afraid of the dark ways, wise one
Fear not the netherworld inhabited
By the Old Gods . . . [*Lights sparkle*]
In the name of all that is wicked
Like unto the ole dam grown into a hoop
I conjure the fearfullest of forces from the mighty winds
May the dread deafening thunders clap and threaten
All who are awake to wonder and fear
Let the azured vault darken to a hooded cape
That covers all and chokes
[*Thunder*]
Oh dear, it seems to have worked—
Ha, ha, ha, the wind's a-howling
The lightning's lighting
The thunder rumbles and frightens Chim-Lee
BAH—
A southwester rises by my command
Unwholesome bogs give out their clouds
of fetid fen dew—
And red plague racks the beasts a-trembling
with bone aches and cramps—

The din is wicked indeed
"Hag-seed," she calls me and I love her still
"Wart-schnozzle," a poxo' that—
Whores and knaves, but I do love her—bat guano!!
I'll not be deterred by a weak and spoiled-rotten girl—
Drat her hide—*I'll make her mine*, by hook or by crook—
Or by fire [*Eats fire*]
Ahhh now—so be it
My opium works its magic
My magic cures my agonized soul
Pain, begone—I feel no pain
Ah me, the storm comes full force upon me
Misery acquaints me with strange bedfellows
Let me hie to bed with this odd-duck
Chim-Lee—tee-hee, 'tis me
Brother mine, let us sleep and dream of our love, Ah-Yoe
and how to win her
But first a trip to the loo—wheeoo—for my medicines are mighty
and my bowels are strong—[*Exits to loo*]
AH-YOE: Knock, knock
CHIM-LEE: Go 'way, go 'way
You heard me, go away
Today is Chinese New Year's day—February 18th
No work today, pass out the gate, go 'way
No opium, nope, nope, you're much too late
It's Chim-Lee's hour to play
So go away [*Flushes*]
AH-YOE: [*Enters*] Chim-Lee, let me in, let me in from the raging storm
without
Chim-Lee, it is Ah-Yoe, your nearby neighbor from the correct side of
the tracks on Hatchet Row—I am distraught and purple-plexed as you can see
Our Baby Chan is missing, my brother—have you seen him?
Is he hiding here in the silent chill of your parlors?
Does he play cat and mouse with his worried sister Ah-Yoe?
Baby Chan, Baby Chan—I call out to you, little one
Do not frighten me so
Let me see your sweet visage once again
Come, Baby Chan, it is the start of a new moon,
Let us go together without into the storm and purify
Ourselves with holy water—Let us pray to Samkai-Kong the king of
Three worlds who keep us safe—let us leave this stinking impure dwelling
of filth and infamy—come away with Ah-Yoe

Come with me to see the New Year Dragon, the king risen from the sea
Which is he who gives rain to our parched and troubled earth—
I fear this storm, I feel foreboding terrors
Do not hide from me, little one
Do not hide from Ah-Yoe—Aiyeah—Aiiiiee—Oh, excuse me—
CHIM-LEE: Shut the door, woman
AH-YOE: Cowardly Chim-Lee, I see you in your WC with your needles still
in your veins, are you hiding
my precious little brother in there with you? Unworthy blackguard, may
you die a hundred horrible deaths with a thousand wicked wrenching
spasms if it is true
CHIM-LEE: Ah, that melodious voice—can it be true, is it possible, at last
Is it really you, Ah-Yoe
Come to finally pay your proper respects to Chim-Lee?
Oh, good fortune smiles upon me
Make yourself comfortable, lovely one
I'll be right out
AH-YOE: What is it that frightens me? Should I turn heel and run or
Continue to seek here for my missing brother, my joy, my Chan?

An oracle came to me and told of a tempest
Such as this would be when the heavens would
Turn black
The winds they would crack
And torrents would fall from the sky
Oh, that would be a sad day
A day of misery and woe
Said the seer—"This I know"

I fear it—I fear it
That day has come to pass
A soul will leave the earth today
Oh, let it not be mine
And let it not be little Chan
For he is young
And has tasted none of the earth's many delights—
I fear the unknown
Specially at night when the winds groan
And tears are torn out of my eyes
I fear the unknown
The forbidding twilight zone
So I went to a seer and I saw

I fear it—I fear it
That day has come to pass
A soul will leave the earth today
Oh, let it not be mine
And let it not be little Chan
For he is young
And has tasted none of the earth's many delights—
I will waste my time here in this stinking cavern no longer
I must continue my quest and seek Baby Chan
Who is lost in this horrible deluge—
Big trap catches big rat
Sewer-Rat . . . [*Exits*]
CHIM-LEE: Ah, my beloved oriental pearl who fills my days with joy
Do you come finally to my door?
Ah-Yoe, my little chrysanthemum
Do you seek the wisdom and protection of Chim-Lee?
Ah, where is she? Her scent remains, herself has fled, unkind—
So she has left me—did not stay—ungrateful child
She has gone in search of her wandering ward—
But she will return—I will see to it that she does, for I have my
Evil ways, the ways of Chim-Lee
But first I must find that stupid child and claim Ah-Yoe as my reward—
I will conjure the brat
That's what I must do
I will find Baby Chan and claim Ah-Yoe . . .
[*Conjures Chan*]
So there you are, my little toothy monster
Hiding in my house now, are you?
Have you come to see how the other half lives?
Do you come to slum it in Hatchet Row?
Come here, little monkey
Do not run away
So you are afraid, are you?
Come to Chim-Lee
CHAN: I am not afraid of you, unholy scoundrel of a jack-knave
I have only come inside to escape the rain and thunder
I am lost and bewildered—I have wandered far away
But now I must run home
I hear Ah-Yoe call me—My father Ding-Ling too
Cries out for Baby Chan
I will seek help on my journey elsewhere
The kind olden cousinry of San Francisco

Will help me find my way back home
CHIM-LEE: Simpleton, it is not as easy as you make it seem to leave my humble dwelling—
Stay yet awhile, hateful infant—the calls you hear are but the groans of the drugged and dying dwellers in my opium den, no one at all misses you outside these doors—your father paid me to take you away from him—he wants you not, he loves you not—your room at home has been rented to strangers and your toys have all been burned—
CHAN: It cannot be true
CHIM-LEE: It is, child—Nobody wants you anymore—
You are now a homeless orphan with no place to go
CHAN: No, no, let me go to my home before my father and sister forget me
CHIM-LEE: Get into this box where you belong, child of a devil with two heads and no brain
CHAN: Help me, help me
Ah-Yoe, your little brother is abandoned and lost
Old Ding-Ling, your faithful son is held captive by a crazed lunatic
in Hatchet Row
AAAAAHHHHH . . .
I'm trapped in a box
And I've got to get out
Trapped in a box
And all I can do is shout
If I ever get out
I'll be happy till the end of my days
If I only get out
I'll thank the gods and never wander far away
from my home again
Oh, why did I ever leave home?
It was safe as safe can be
Nothing was out of joint at home
My teeth were always brushed, my hair was always combed
Breakfast was on time
We always ate at nine
And naptime could be counted on
The veggies were bottled, the logs they were sawn
The larder was full
The hearthfires were burning
The water was running
The plumbing was plumbed
The front door was guarded
The pit bulls were pitted

The windows were barred
Nothing ever marred our tranquillity
Oh, why did I ever leave home?
Ding-Ling, your baby calls to you
Ah-Yoe, please hear my plea
Don't leave me here
Come rescue me, my dears
I beg of you on bended knee
I miss my little playthings
I want to play with all my toys
I hate this den
What a filthy pigpen
Why can't I skip and hop and run with other little girls and boys?
CHIM-LEE: Get in that barrel-butt and stay there
Not a peep from you, monster child
Let your inscrutable father come rescue you
If he can, ha ha ha . . . [*Closes lid on Chan*]
DING-LING: Scurvy mandarin, do you hear me?
Are you here? Where is my son, my adored offspring?
Will you not tell me?
Witnesses have seen him enter here to escape the inclement weather
I say to you, open your mouth, wretch, and tell this anxious old man
whence and where is his beloved child—where is my Chan?
You do not speak—May you be struck dumb by thunderstroke forever
if you choose to remain speechless now
Do not let the fearful rumblings of the tempest
without still your voice a moment longer
Perfidious and drugged abomination I call out to
Thee—Where is my little Chan?
CHIM-LEE: Is there something amiss, old man—Hmmm?????
Your most humble servant has seen no one,
Not a soul has crossed my threshold today but you—It is too fearful
a stormy night for carefree traveling about the miserable streets and
alleyways
DING-LING: Infected worm, thou liest, where is my son, my light, my joy?
Why shouldst thou entice my innocent Baby Chan to
enter in this hole, this hell, this cave? Answer me quickly
that and more
CHIM-LEE: You wrong me, there is no one here but Chim-Lee
I weep that you should treat me so very base and cruel
and doubt my word—I should rather my tongue be split in two and
torn from my throat than to be doubted as I am

DING-LING: The flesh-fly blow thy cavernous hole, mooncow—
By sorcery and evil thoughts thou hast suborned the
most innocent of lovelies to follow thy behest
Do you think because I sit in luxury's lap across the
way that I see nothing of your carryings-on?
You are allowed your trafficking in pestilence and vice by the
tolerant powers that be, of which I am a part, only
because your foul business rids the chosen
of the riffraff that have quick minds and no morals,
and besides it's good for our economy—
A murrain upon your house and on your slanderous soul
CHIM-LEE: I never saw the child
DING-LING: Troll, mock turtle, tortoise, vampire bat, I will teach thee
to lie to an old reactionary—
I call down a curse on your head
'fore the moon disappears you'll be dead
The sky will turn bloodred
Then you'll belch in your dread
A sword is too good to remove your foul head—
Distemper and crippling remove you to bed
Canker sores, horse piss, foot licker, are thine
Trash bins for your dinner
And droopsy behind
I'll teach you to cross me
I'm rich and above the law
I have friends in high places
with teeth and sharp claws
First to die will be Chim-Lee
He disagrees with me
Does Chim-Lee have sympathizers?
Then let them die too
And if the timid do not curse your bones
Upon their brows my knife I'll hone
What good are you to Chinatown
or to the world indeed?
Neither soldier, nor father, nor husband are ye
No soldier, father, husband are you now nor ere shall be
To hang you from the tallest tree
Is much too good for three of the likes of thee
In my pessimistic view of things that are and possibly
can be . . .
CHIM-LEE: Curse me all you want, Grandpa

I don't mind, as long as I may still someday
claim Ah-Yoe
DING-LING: Never—This is monstrous . . . monstrous . . .
CHIM-LEE: In the name of all that is sacred and profane, do you
not wish to find your precious Baby Chan?
DING-LING: Yes, yes, in desperation I say yes . . .
CHIM-LEE: Good
Of course you do
Then I will find him for you
utilizing the ways of my ancestors
With my magic, my chicanery, my blackest of arts
with my evil eye will I spy out little Chan
DING-LING: Please, please find him for me
Quick, please do . . . please do
CHIM-LEE: On one small condition will I find the little tenacious bugger
DING-LING: Anything, anything you want, Chim-Lee
CHIM-LEE: Anything
DING-LING: Anything, on the honors of my ancestors, I swear . . . Anything
CHIM-LEE: In exchange for the two-headed infant Chan
I must be given the hand of Ah-Yoe in matrimony—
I want it in writing
DING-LING: Fiend—Greedy vexatious malabrand—foul unholy conspirator
Avoid, no more—over my dead body will I grant your wish
Ah-Yoe's virgin-knot is tied forever distant from your touch profane
By Hymen's torch well lit, I see thy plot most pernicious and foul
It is the dowry of Ah-Yoe that ye seek
It is filthy lucre, not the lure of love that drives thee on—
I would sooner my precious Ah-Yoe should go mad and drown herself
in the sea than for her pulchritude to be forfeit to you
CHIM-LEE: Have it your own way then
But I shall soon get Ah-Yoe and her dowry, mark my words, old crone. . . .
And don't be too surprised if I end up with Baby Chan's inheritance
too—I'll get my way now . . . I'm on a roll . . .
DING-LING: What do you know of my Baby Chan?
Speak, horror, or feel the wrath of my junta's torturers
CHIM-LEE: You will never see Baby Chan alive again
DING-LING: Where is he?
Answer me
CHIM-LEE: He has been harrowed by a trolley whilst being washed down
a San
Francisco hill in Chim-Lee's tempest

DING-LING: No, no, tell me it isn't so
Not my Baby Chan gone from me forever
Who will enjoy my riches, who will sit upon my wealth and sneer
at the poor passersby? Aiyeah
Henceforth, I here forswear my material possessions
They were acquired only to pass on to my seed, my Chan and Ah-Yoe's
husband someday . . . not to you, Chim-Lee . . .
I give everything to the gods
My many belongings shall herewith go to
the sacred shrine of Buddha in Marin County
where they tell me it is lovely
across the Bay . . .
I shall today take gold and jewels to the shrine myself—
May Ah-Yoe turn Catholic and remain a maiden all her days in a
southern nunnery.
Better that end than to be chained forever to your lowly unworthiness—
May little Chan have found his path to a rich man's heaven
How I do miss him
What impudence you manifest, Chim-Lee—Ah-Yoe belong to you—
Never . . . Never . . .
I journey now to find solitude up in the hills
Far away from Hatchet Row and its inhabitants . . . [*Exits*]
CHIM-LEE: This is your fault, little Chan
Feel the sting of a man much wronged and rejected
Take that . . . and that . . . and that
Pinch, pinch, tweak . . .
Ah, my mind is muddy and clouded o'er
More opium, set my mind at zero—give me clarity
Render me immobile with the curse of the pretty poppy—
Back in the box, boy . . . and keep still
AH-YOE: Where the beast trucks . . . there trucks I
I love rice and Szechuan flies
He is gone, he is gone
No more will my song
Entreat him to sleep
No more will his sweet smile
make me sigh and weep
'Tis false to believe he'll come to me again
Now 'tis my turn to die—
Daddy's gone, brother's gone
And I'll never know why . . .
Such is fate

I'll drown myself in this cup of rare old Chinese tea
I can go on no longer
I know it can be done, I read all about it once in the *Enquirer*
If I had only bound my nose like Papa wanted when I was young it
would fit in this cup like it should . . . darn, darn, darn
CHIM-LEE: Ah-Yoe, my beloved, stop, desist, cease
Are you jostled from out your senses
Be cheerful, lass, and look upon your rescuer Chim-Lee
Rack your weary brain no longer, for Baby Chan
is here—See for yourself—Aiyeah
He is dead, alas and alack—
What could have gone wrong?
Has the Baby Chan suffocated in my box? Oh, dear, oh, dear
is my face red
What have you done, villain?
AH-YOE: Whoop-de-shriek. What have you done, villain?
CHIM-LEE: Corraggio, Chim-Lee, there must be some way out of this
mess—
AH-YOE: Assassino, you have killed my tender Baby Chan and hid him in
this Lucite box
I have found my joy only to lose him a
second time encore
Chim-Lee, thou cretin, finalmente mio . . .
Taste thy own medicine . . . [*Garrotes Chim-Lee with his own queue*]
You were born into
A herd of buffalo, Chim-Lee
And now you have been trampled—
It's positive action that keeps the world spinning
positive action that makes life worth living
It's positive action that keeps us alive
Like bees in a hive
We flit to and fro
To drive ourselves crazy
or not—heaven knows
At least once in our lives
Let us take a step forward
To calm Chim-Lee's tempest
That swirls round our noses
Stop the wind
Stop the rain
Stop the hail and the snow
Stop this storm

Stop this tempest
Let the sun shine and glow
Happy endings are the rule, my foolish friend
Happy endings are the tool
To get me through to the end
Only money can ease the pain of losing a loved one
or so my lawyer tells me
So I'll take Baby Chan out on the road and exhibit his remains
to all the passersby
But he shall be mute to the world
and speak only to me late at night
That way I know he shall always be mine
Till the end of all time
and this is the end
come, Chan . . .
Happy New Year, Chim-Lee

Photo copyright © by Dona Ann McAdams

RICHARD ELOVICH

Name: Richard Elovich
Stage Name: same
Birthdate/Birthplace: Queens, New York
"Raised Up" Where: New York
Education: A little help from my friends . . .
Honors/Grants: New York Dance and Performance Award (Bessie), 1991; NEA
Fellowships; NYSCA Fellowships; Jerome Foundation Fellowship; Art Matters; New York
Foundation for the Arts; CAPS residency at the Sundance Institute
Influences/Mentors/Heroes: Jeff Weiss, Wallace Shawn, Isaac Bashevis Singer,
Joseph Chaikin, Gertrude Stein, Philip Roth, Kristin Linklater, Lenny Bruce, Art
Spiegelman
Places Performed: P.S. 122; Manhattan Theater Club; La MaMa, ETC.; the Performing
Garage; the Kitchen; the Whitney Museum; Art Institute, Chicago; LACE; Sushi; Beyond
Baroque; the Gate, London; the Green Room in Manchester, Birmingham, Liverpool, and
Nottingham as part of the first tour of *It's Queer Up North* organized by Gay Sweatshop in
London
Pivotal Performance: Performing with Jim Self in 1978 at NYU's Grey Art Gallery on a
bill with now quite accomplished dancers/choreographers Molissa Fenley and Karole
Armitage. I felt like Jerry Lewis singing with Dean. I was dressed in a cubist suit
designed by artist Frank Moore, and I was so nervous I forgot to take Jim's stool out of
my suitcase so he could dance around it. He chased after me around the stage, getting
madder and madder, and I couldn't understand why until he finally just grabbed the
suitcase out of my hand.
Favorite Performance Experience: Same
Most Terrifying Performance Experience: Performing one evening at Sundance
Institute's screenwriters workshop—in front of the Jewish writers from Hollywood I was
writing about
Favorite Prop or Costume: Frank Moore's costumes
Hobbies: Gardening
Reading List: *A Perfect Spy* by John LeCarré; *Counterlife* by Philip Roth; *Hindoo Holiday*
by J. R. Ackerly
Favorite Music: Carlos Santana, Temptations, Tina Turner, Aretha Franklin, Chris
Montez, Jimi Hendrix, Joe Cocker, Patti Smith, Kurt Weill, Bob Dylan
Favorite Quote: "It's madly ungay when the goldfish die."

Artist's Notes

In the solo works I have written and performed, I have attempted to find a
vernacular experience of theater, a "low" theater, in the same way that
comic-book artists have shown us how the "low" comic strip has the potential to function somewhere between the high arts of literature and painting.
Think of Krazy Kat, R. Crumb, Art Spiegelman's *Maus*, or Philip Guston's
late painting. Without props, costume, or scenery, I try to physicalize the

text through my performance. I am the cartoonist's black line. Inspired by two Jewish art forms—the stand-up comic and the psychoanalyst, I want people to see how, once performance is stripped down, language and timing are the essential ingredient. To become a performance it needs to turn into song and dance. To me, the abominable Jackie Mason is a master of making stand-up talk into a song and dance, and he is worthy of study.

From 1988–92, I shifted from writing and directing plays performed by an ensemble group to writing and performing solo plays, directed by an ensemble eye. I wasn't conscious at the time of what this change meant. I had taken a year off working as a nanny, cooking, sitting, walking, and diaper changing a friend's ten-month-old baby. I was also participating in a support network for a friend living with AIDS, and I was writing every day.

After about ten months, I had a draft of something called *A Man Cannot Jump over His Own Shadow*. It wasn't like anything I'd written before—I didn't know what it was, but I wanted to test it out, so I called people I didn't know well. Taking advantage of people's curiosity, accommodating nature, and fear of missing out on something weird, I asked them if I could come over and read them something. I promised it wouldn't take more than an hour. The hour came from something I thought Edgar Allan Poe said, that a story was something meant to be experienced in one sitting. I figured anything over an hour was pushing my luck.

I didn't know what to do with this story or as people in the performance art business say, this "piece"—but I thought something "interesting" was happening while I was reading it out loud, *trying it on* in front of people in their living room or kitchen. Reading it to someone, the communication actually felt two-way. I knew I was taking an hour of people's time, taking their space, I could feel them listening or not listening and I was listening to the text I was reading. In the experience of reading the text out loud, I discovered what every performer knows, how time opens up when you are performing. Nature hates a vacuum, so the performing space is filled with anxiety, choices, recriminations, and ideas. Listening to the reading as I was reading, I went home and rewrote. One person suggested that I'd already begun the process of making a performance, and that was all the encouragement I needed.

I coaxed a friend, Natsuko Ohama, a talented actress and a well-known teacher of Kristin Linklater's voice technique, to make her directorial debut with this work. We rehearsed first in her living room and then in rehearsal spaces until we finally moved into the performance space. In each solo play I have written and performed, I have worked very closely with a composer, Mark Bennett. Although he writes music, I asked him not to write a musical with me but begged him to be a brutal dramaturg and inspired editor with my text. He doesn't set the text I've written to music, but he tries. He

doesn't teach me to sing, but he tries. We argue, but I give up quickly because he is usually right and I know something useful is happening. Having
a musician join our performance team acknowledges a very necessary musical demand when you have so much talking. You see, the process of putting
the text into my head was very different from the process of talking to my
fingers as I typed into a computer. My head resisted a lot of what I wrote.
And later my voice resisted, mocking falseness in the writing. I think listening to the resistance is critical to making the performance, and in listening
to the resistance I hope I have learned to be a better writer. I don't know
how performance artists work without outside direction or an outside "eye."
Natsuko, and subsequent directors I have worked with, Cecil MacKinnen
and Itamar Kubovy, have played a very active role in the creation of my performances. Because the text I write is like "unsized canvas" the director and
the composer have to feel comfortable to get in there and direct the performance, and I have to trust them to be the "eyes," so I can close my eyes in
order to find a performance voice. Later, the director and the composer are
too busy with their own work and they stop showing up for performances
and I am alone with the text in front of a bunch of strangers.

I don't think that I really make solo performance. It just looks that way in
front of an audience. I like what looks like solo performance because it
looks like it is so mobile. It fits so flexibly into different settings. It looks
like it travels easy. I believe if it is to survive, some theater needs to be mobile. Culture that's going to survive is culture that you can carry around in
your head. I like culture that you can carry around in your head. I am always looking for connections: how the "laughing clarinet" in klezmer music
became the wacky laugh in Looney Tune cartoons. How Yiddish theater influenced vaudeville and how vaudeville influenced television, and where is
it now, what do we have in our hands? And where did Betty Boop come
from? Or Mary Richards on the Mary Tyler Moore show? Rocky and Bull-
winkle? Growing cultures must have something to do with how the miniature—something that actually happened somewhere, a local
gesture—becomes a universal, a broad stroke. Then by blowing it up or repeating it in sequence (as pop artists and minimalists discovered), you find
that the cartoonist's line is a gesture. Magnify the cartoonist's black line
and you see that it has burrs. It is a landscape. Joe Brainard's repetitive
studies of *Dagwood Losing His Temper* meant a lot to me.

Someone Else from Queens Is Queer

Someone Else from Queens Is Queer was first performed by Richard Elovich
in April of 1991 at Performance Space 122, New York. It was created in col-

laboration with Itamar Kubovy and Mark Bennett and directed by Itamar Kubovy.

Someone Else from Queens Is Queer is a composite of many stories, speeches, and confidences shared by friends. It is not autobiography, nor is it a piece of fiction. It has its roots in *This Is Not a Soapbox,* written with Gregg Bordowitz. This work is dedicated to him.

Someone Else from Queens Is Queer is to be performed by one person. All theatrical elements should be kept to a minimum, allowing the emphasis to be on the telling of the story and the relationship this telling creates between the audience and the performer.—R.E.

FELIX: One night, it's Friday night, 1976, I'm at—the Ninth Circle—and I recognize Gordie Benjamin. He still has these dark eyes that dart back and forth like a pinball, and this cleft chin like this. I didn't go over right away. He's hanging out with some people I knew. Finally he spotted me. He keeps staring at me and smiling. I look away—nonchalant. He squeezes in next to me:

"So now you know. I'm really a drag queen at heart."

"Me too. I'm relieved to know someone else from Queens is queer."

I left the bar with him and we walked for hours, not knowing how to get around to sex. When we were growing up, we weren't even friends, we were just from the same neighborhood, the same Hebrew school. But we had different friends from each other. The only time we spent together was once when we were practicing for this Purim talent show at Bayside Jewish Center. Gordie Benjamin was this skinny kid who could do great imitations. He wanted to be an impressionist, like Bill Cosby. He could do all of Cosby's characters from the Philadelphia ghetto like they were his own. The teachers loved Gordie's act: this scrawny little Jewish kid wanting to be this black comic. I was envious. I didn't have an act. I was supposed to be the MC.

And now as we're walking around, it's the same thing, I am mostly egging him on, listening to him do his act:

"The laughing clarinet in Eastern European klezmer music became the wacky laugh in Looney Tunes cartoons—smart Jewish guys writing situation comedy in Hollywood. These writers knew they were outsiders and as outsiders they were always sneaking in stories about themselves, just disguised. Think of the Addams Family and the Munster Family. The Addams Family, I mean who are these people?"

Finally we got to my building and I say to him:

"If you would like to spend the night with me, at my house I mean, I'd like that. I would be into the idea of you spending the night with me."

Gordie just looks at me:

"The Addams Family—you don't have a sense of them, where are they from? There is a mystery about the Addams Family, but all the people that come to their house always come as supplicants. They are always humoring the Addams Family, allowing them to continue their otherness. The world that they have is the world. The Addams Family is not weird. Gefilte fish is what everyone eats. Gomez Addams passes. They're like the Finzi-Contini: it's not just that they're rich, and it's not just that they have an Old World elegance, it's that they set a standard of a world consisting only of them. It's like that heartbreaking last line of the movie, the kind-of-middle-class Jew says as they are being herded together to be deported: 'The Finzi-Contini— you're here too.' "

I open the door and we go in. We sit on the couch. I put my hand—

"Now, on the other hand you have the Munsters. Herman and Lily Munster come from an entirely different class. They are like us, from Queens. Herman Munster is different from Gomez Addams. Herman is constantly seeking to assimilate. The happiest I have ever seen Herman is in the episode where he has won, in a TV contest, a month's free membership in the Mockingbird Heights Country Club! So he and Lily go to this country club and totally fuck up! Misunderstand everything!"

—Gordie's taking his clothes off!—

"See, no matter what Herman Munster does, no matter how much he tries to sound like *Father Knows Best,* he has that nose! That face! He always looks like Frankenstein!"

—I run for the pillows and the sheets.—

"The difference is Gomez Addams can pass, and that's all the more interesting because he doesn't know he's passing."

—I turn out the light.—

"The Jewish dream vision of aristocracy!"

—We get into bed.—

"Not ever remembering a time when one wasn't aristocracy!"

—We're both looking up at the ceiling. I'm wondering if he's ever gonna stop! I go to put my hand—

"So later in the same show, Herman is deeply invested in this contest he has entered—he goes to the TV."

—I take my hand back.—

"Now, this is a great moment of television: TV is watching TV. Herman goes to the TV and they're announcing the contest winners:

" 'The first prize is yadda yadda,' and it doesn't go to Herman. 'The second prize is yadda yadda,' and it doesn't go to Herman.

"After he doesn't get the third prize, Herman starts yelling back at the TV: 'Whydontja tell everybody that he's the nephew of the station manager—it's all a fix, it's all been fixed, fixed fixed fixed fixed fixed fixed fixed fixed fixed!'

"Herman starts pounding on the TV, screaming: 'It's a sham! It's a sham!'

"So here's this image of a Jewish man on a television show, Frankenstein, screaming back at the TV doing this yiddle yiddle yimmy dance around it, wrecking it, because it doesn't recognize him!"

—I pull Gordie's legs out from underneath him! He falls onto his back and I kiss him for the first time. Once he stopped talking he turned into an incredible lover.

I couldn't fall asleep that whole night next to him. I just watched him sleep.

I want to think there is something or someone watching everything—all-seeing, all-knowing—I dive off the high board: "Look at me! Just watch this one!"—living my life as if my father was my audience. I always regretted my father was not a romantic hero. You know, a patriarch, one of those pillars of society who would give you the possibility to rebel against him.

My father had a radio voice, very smooth and convincing—that was his job—light and easy to listen to. He was an announcer for NBC, most of the time you didn't see his face. He was station identification. Then my father got his big break: he replaced Al Kadabra on Kadabra and Klinch, an early morning radio show from six to ten in the morning. It was for motorists stuck in traffic on the L.I.E. and B.Q.E.—the Francis Lewis and Major Deegan. So it became Kat and Klinch: Dick Kat and Gene Klinch—Kat is short for Kater, that's our name.

My father was famous in Long Island, New Jersey, Connecticut, and Westchester, the whole tri-state area. Kat and Klinch had a big following. They played big band music and they worshiped the Chairman of the Board: "It's Frank Sinatra's world—we just live in it."

My father came to our seventh-grade class and talked about it, how he got rid of his Brooklyn accent after he was in the army and spent some time in the Midwest at a radio station. To the low-glamour, high-profit guys in auto parts, construction contracting, restaurant display who lived near us in Queens, my father was a big shot, somebody who rubbed elbows with people like Johnny Carson:

"You know, Dick Kat? WNBC? Yeah, Kat and Klinch. WNBC! He's joining us at La Vie En Rose for lunch."

In their heart of hearts, these business guys dreamed of being in the Rat Pack. You know, Rat Packers: Frank and Dino, Sammy, Joey—glamorous, and maybe a little crazy. Late at night at a party, away from their wives, loosening their ties, dangling a cigarette, picking up a glass of scotch, they'd sing,

"All of me . . . why not take all of me?"

At the business lunches and the parties, my father was a flashy dresser: colored handkerchief, sapphire pinky ring—Mr. Charisma, Mr. Show Business. But when he got canned, when he got replaced, when he got cut from Kat and Klinch by Kadabra—Al Kadabra was back—he didn't talk about it. He never explained to us what happened.

Most of the time I was in junior high, my father was telling us he had business trips. He didn't have business trips, he had this girlfriend named Maxine, who my mother called "Your bimbo!"

She was a lot younger than him. Most of the guys from Johnny Carson on down had girlfriends that were a lot younger than them, but my father couldn't make up his mind to leave my mother and marry Maxine, so he was always going into business with Maxine: "getting her started." One of the last of these businesses was a sixties boutique my father went into with Maxine. Now, my father is convincing, and to this day he won't even admit that Maxine ever existed:

"It's your imagination!"

That's what he was always telling my mother:

"It's your imagination. You're imagining everything."

So my mother kind of turned inward, thinking it was her. She took herself apart in therapy. You know, her arm is her father and her leg is her husband and she had her father and her leg talking to each other. Then it was talking to the child inside her. The child was writing her letters with her left hand and the grown-up was writing her back with her right hand. I come home, my mother's in pieces.

After my father's sixties boutique with Maxine went out of business, he drags home this giant giraffe made of wicker. Now, imagine someone mass-producing giant giraffes made of wicker. My mother takes one look at the giant giraffe and she's telling him: "This is not an antique. I collect antiques. And a six-foot giraffe from your bimbo's boutique is not an antique! It doesn't go with my Early American colonial. I collect colonial colonial colonial! The nerve, dragging your bimbo's boutique into my colonial!"

After that my mother joins this women's consciousness-raising group. And this group became legendary. See, my mother had this knack for bringing out the flamboyant side of people. So right away, in this group, she catches on to the analyzing, and she's immediately the ringleader of the analyzing. She's analyzing everything, analyzing their behavior at home:

"You cook, and bring the food to the table?! Baarbahrahh! You must make him get up and get his own soup! And if he won't, you pick it up and you throw it at him: 'Put that in your pipe and smoke it, Haaarryy!'"

She was great with slogans. I'd watch her pace back and forth on the phone while some woman told her story:

"Shirl, Shirl, wait. Shirl, Shirl, you can lead a horse to water, but you can't make him drink! Shirl—wait, what he needs, Shirl-eeee, what he needs, what he needs is a good kick in the pants!"

My mother decided, "Enough is enough! I have to bite the bullet by the horns and go back to work."

She went back to work! She became the executive manager of Party Box Catering.

FELIX [*In a hoarse, gravelly voice, like William Burroughs's, and puckering his lips like a fish*]: "Kim, if you had your choice, would you rather be a poisonous snake or a nonpoisonous snake?"

"Oh, poisonous, sir, like a green mamba, or a spitting cobra."

"Why?"

"I'd feel safer, sir."

"And that's your idea of heaven, Kim, feeling safer?"

"Yes, sir."

"Is a poisonous snake really safer?"

"Well, not really in the long run, but he must feel reeeal goooood after he bites someone. Safer."

"Young man, I think you're an assassin."

I was about fifteen years old. When my older brother, Eric, went away to college, his best friend, Mitchell, rented his bedroom from my parents. I was always sneaking into Mitchell's room to look at his things. One time I found this William Burroughs record. On the cover was a picture of this guy hanging with a hard-on. He was naked, undressed, so it was like a sex act. I was mesmerized. I played it and I hated it and I played it and I loved it. I stared at Burroughs's photograph on the cover, memorizing the way he held his cigarette. So right there, I developed this whole thing with William Burroughs. I read in a magazine about a Mexican restaurant in the Village where he hung out, Mexican Gardens, so I went down there. I must have looked weird, this kid dressed up in a suit and tie, I'm even wearing a hat—a fedora—pulled down over my eyeglasses like Burroughs. I go up to the bar: I *am* William Burroughs and this is Mexico City. I'm in a lot of trouble. I just shot my wife in the head, and I'm in love with this guy, Kells Elvans, who's straight and playing hard to get. We've been in the Yucatán together searching for this telepathic drug, Yaasshay. I had this letter I wrote to him, handwritten, it was like pages and pages—very uncool, but passionate. The bartender comes up to me:

"You lose something?"

I go through this routine with the cigarette, trying to look Hombre In-vee-SEE-blay.

"Hey, how old are you?"

I shrug and stare back at him, doing the fishy thing with my mouth.

"What's your name?"

"Felix Kater. Does William Burroughs come in here? I have a letter for him."

"My name is Giacometti and I'm going to see Bill tonight."

Giacometti gave me an address where I could meet him when he got off work. So I killed a couple of hours walking around acting In-vee-SEE-blay.

Giacometti takes me upstairs and we sit down on the couch. He rolls a joint. I take a couple of hits and I'm talking a blue streak. I start showing off all these routines I know from Burroughs:

"They are skinning the chief of police alive in some jerk-water place. Want to sit in?"

" 'Nah,' I said, 'only interested in my own skin.' "

"And I waltz out thinking who I would like to see skinned alive.

"Ta daaaaaa!"

[GIACOMETTI]: "Felix, you want to see something?"

Giacometti takes off his shirt, and unzips his pants. And it was huge! He was showing me this natural wonder, a phenomenon!

"Pants down, Felix. Keep your little socks on, it's sexy. Get the Vaseline, it's underneath."

He rubs Vaseline on his dick. I mean it wasn't like a human body part. It was huge! Like *this*. And I was so small, I had never done anything.

"Lay down, Felix."

And he slides two greased fingers up my ass. He jiggles them to a car horn I can hear on the street. He turns me over on my back.

"Here, take this pillow, Felix."

Now, I'm not even upset. I love the way he says "Felix," but I just don't believe this is happening. His dick is pushing through the path his fingers have made.

"Hey, can you stop a minute? Giacometti, you gotta stop—this is impossible."

He keeps going. Then I panic. I'm in incredible pain.

"You gotta stop! You're killing me! You're killing me!"

He looks at me for a second.

"Am I really hurting you?"

"You're killing me!"

"Then get up on your knees! Come on, Felix, relax. . . . Just give me your ass. Just give me your ass. Just give me your ass."

So, I did. I just gave up. Surrendered. That's when I learned how to do it. I started shoving my ass into his dick. I was good at it. I was really good at it. I was boogeying. After he came, I didn't want him to pull it out. We sat naked and passed a cigarette back and forth. Then he opens his legs and shows me he is stiff again.

"*Otra vez*, Felix."

So I got down on my hands and knees, feeling his finger inside me. My ass opened up like a flower and he was all the way in, his hot quick breath on my back. He gives me Vaseline for my dick and he rocks me. We shiver together and both finish in a few seconds. He turned me over on my side and folded up around me. We slept for an hour.

A couple of hours later he took me to see Burroughs, who was cooking this stew in a loft down on Broadway. Burroughs was preparing dinner, muttering in this voice like a creaking door, stirring an old carcass in a stew pot, absently dropping in cigarette ashes. Burroughs is telling us about this out-of-body experiment, so I ask him:

"William, do you believe in the afterlife? Do you believe in life after death?"

"What makes you think you're not already dead?"

Later Burroughs is sucking in a joint, his pale gray eyes staring deep into my eyes:

"Felix, were you ever youuuung?"

Giacometti points to me:

"He's memorized your books, Bill. And he's cute."

Burroughs just sneers:

"Pack up your ermines, Mary, he looks like Jeeeewwwwww."

Pause. Giacometti got me a job cooking at Mexican Gardens. He was the first adult to take me seriously, so I tried to be the person he could depend on. I hung around the kitchen all the time. I started off as a prep cook, I ended up on the hot line. It was a big deal the first time Giacometti left the restaurant early and let me close.

And every night after work, I went to the Ninth Circle to get picked up and every night it was a different story. Like this really cute guy comes over to me:

"What's your sign?"

"Capricorn."

"Good enough."

Boom! We're in his apartment. I look around. Clothes off. We're in bed. He turns me over on my stomach and fucks me really hard until he comes. The next morning we shower together and I watch while he dresses. I leave when he leaves. I liked waking up in other people's lives. Like I'm a shadow . . . like I'm a phantom . . .

Like Johnny Carson when the camera is off him, my father was a phantom too. He was a different person when he was off the air. You could talk at him but nothing came back. Nobody was home. It made me jumpy. My father started coming into the restaurant and I'd cook him a special plate of *mole poblano* and sit with him while he ate. For the first time my father liked having me around. We got together "father and son" on a regular basis.

One afternoon he comes into the restaurant:

"Felix, where you living?"

"Around."

"I've got an idea. Don't discuss it with your mother. I'm renting an apartment for this friend of mine, Bunny Kallman, a business associate. He has a wife and he has this mistress, he's no longer with the mistress and his wife makes him crazy, so until he finds someone else he needs another place to relax. So you see, we'll be renting it for him. Don't discuss it with your mother."

So I moved in and I'd tell all my tricks:

"This apartment really belongs to my father. He's living in Tangiers. He's a science fiction writer. He smokes a lot of pot. He shot my mother in the head and he can't come back into the country. Don't discuss this with anyone."

Me and my father didn't ask each other questions. We were discreet like spies, like businessmen on business trips. We didn't discuss our private lives. We didn't discuss. My mother discussed.

Officially, my father was still living with my mother in Bayside, so most of the time I had the apartment to myself. Some Saturdays though, my father came by dressed in this safari outfit, with epaulets, and his hair was combed one side real long, and pasted down across his head to cover what was missing:

"Felix getouttahereokay, I needda relax."

So on those days I would go on these walking meals. Anything, so long as I could eat and walk with it. Freezing my balls off, I'd go from one movie theater to another. I've seen *Midnight Cowboy* six times. So I get home after dark, my father's gone and the apartment's empty. But there's lipstick everywhere! A glass with lipstick, cigarette butts with lipstick, a wine bottle with lipstick—It's my imagination? I'm imagining everything?—Lipstick! Lipstick! Lipstiiiiick!

GORDIE: Cannibal! Criminal! Comedian! Lenny Bruce's only film I've seen has him doing his whole act in a raincoat because he'd been arrested a couple of nights before and he said, "I'm not going to freeze my balls off down at the police station anymore. I'm going to do my act in a raincoat. Let them come for me in a raincoat."

The Lenny Bruce *behind* Lenny Bruce was this aluminum-siding salesman, Joe Jitsu, lived with his parents in Bensonhurst. Joe loved black hookers and he liked hanging out with the comics, shpritzing for them. You know what shpritzing is? It's Jewish massage: Suddenly you get an inspiration, jump to your feet, shake the bottle vigorously and then shpritz it over everyone—Look at me!—pounding, pummeling the person listening to you like they're meat. Using words like karate chops, Jew-jitsu to the brain, using people like a trampoline. Now Joe Jitsu just shpritzed for friends. Once at some club, they made him get up and do some stuff, but Joe realized that getting up there meant you're up there to make them laugh and you could die in front of people. So Lenny Bruce takes what Joe does and develops it into classic Lenny Bruce, cannibalizing his best friend. For years, Lenny is afraid if someone hears Joe Jitsu do his shpritz while Lenny is in the room, they will put two and two together and Lenny Bruce won't look like such a genius anymore. To this day you can hear this siding salesman, Joe Jitsu, sitting around in remote places of the city, shpritzing his friends:

"Shit, you know it's weird. I'm trying to figure out the evolution of why people hate Jews. What did Jews ever do? How did they offend people? Initially, a country starts off, you know, they like the Jews, they love the Jews:

" 'Welcome, Jews! Hello, Jews! Hello, Jews! You bring books, you bring business, you bring good management! Sit down. Take off your hat. No? Okay. Whatever. Listen, Jews, why don't you stay for dinner, we're having cheeseburgers.'

" 'No, thank you. We like to prepare our own food.'

" 'Okay, so you can cook it. Here's the patties.'

" 'Well, no, thank you, we have our own way of slaughtering.'

" 'Okay, so you bring the meat, and we'll make dessert: apple pie à la mode. That's ice cream! Everybody loves ice cream. We've seen you eat ice cream.'

" 'Not with meat.'

" 'But it's your meat!'

" 'But it's dairy.'

" 'Fine. Have a holiday. Take Sundays.'

" 'We take off Saturdays, thank you.'

" 'Saturdays? That reminds me of a joke. Did you hear this joke?'

" 'We have our own sense of humor. We tell our own jokes.'

"So after a while the country turns around and says:

" 'Jews. You know you can't give them anything. You can't even tell them a good joke. You know what? Who invited you in the first place? Get the fuck ouddda here! Nowwww!' Paaadummm tssssach!"

Photo copyright © by Dona Ann McAdams

Name: John Fleck
Stage Name: Hey you
Birthdate/Birthplace: My birth certificate says May 7, 1951, but I think someone fucked up—I actually think it's May 7, 1958.
"Raised Up" Where: Mainly Cleveland, Ohio
Education: Cleveland State University; American Academy of Dramatic Arts; The Groundlings Improv; Rachel Rosenthal; Ned Mandarino
Honors/Grants: Three *L.A. Weekly* Awards; two Dramalogue Awards; one San Diego Critics Circle Award; L.A. Drama Critics Circle; two NEA Grants—one of which was denied in 1990, but was won in a lawsuit in 1994; one Rockefeller Grant
Influences/Mentors/Heroes: Rachel Rosenthal, Karen Finley, Johanna Went
Places Performed: P.S. 122, New York; the Public Theater, New York; ICA, Boston; Reality Ways, Hartford; Cleveland Public Theater; On-the-Boards, Seattle; Life on the Water, San Francisco; Artists for a Hate Free America, Portland; Diverse Works, Houston; UCLA; UC Santa Cruz; LACE; L.A. Highways, Los Angeles; Taper II, Los Angeles; Glaxa, Los Angeles; MOCA, Los Angeles
Pivotal Performance: This was a twenty-minute piece I did at a club called Olio in Los Angeles. The evening's theme was "Fish Night." At one point, I had a little goldfish in a glass bowl that I was shoving bread into. The audience started to chant, "Save the fish! Save the fish!" An irate man stormed up out of the audience, called me a mother-fucker, and saved the fish. I had to improv and I turned the tables on him. I said, "Oh, yeah, he's so good saving that fish . . . what about the ton of fish dying each week in Santa Monica Bay 'cause we're pumpin' your shit out there, oh, yeah . . . but as long as you don't see it, it's okay." This piece was later named "Blessed Are All the Little Fishes."
Favorite Performance Experience: This was my favorite, too.
Most Terrifying Performance Experience: Opening for Melissa Etheridge in Portland for two thousand lesbians. I was scared but ended up having a great time. They wanted Melissa real bad.
Favorite Prop or Costume: My tattered, rust-colored jumpsuit with blue fringe and blue platform shoes
Hobbies: Dancing, exercising, riding my bike, hiking
Reading List: *The Art of Eating* by M.F.K. Fisher
          Inviting the Muses by Marguerite Young
Favorite Music: Eclectic—I appreciate the best of all forms.
Favorite Quote: "The great majority of mankind are satisfied with appearances as though they were realities, and are often more influenced by the things that seem than by those that are." (N. Machiavelli)

Artist's Notes

My work has its beginnings in personal images and texts, and is not necessarily autobiographic, as much as a subconscious travelogue.

I find at least one song that hits me on a gut level and I gotta hit a high C falsetto somewhere, a moment of operatic relief. Other moments I strive for are moments that are both disgusting and beautiful, or doing beautiful things in ugly ways. Or a moment that makes people laugh while it's still painful, and also scary moments. I always try to incorporate at least a little movement or dance, primal sounds and anything that shows heart buried deep in the text.

I never know what my next piece is going to be about. I wish I could plan my pieces, outline them and just do them. But alas, my pieces seem to inform me.

As the deadline approaches, I usually develop insomnia. Days go by where I can't sleep. I feverishly read and listen to music that triggers something personal going on inside me. I call this deadline fever. This is when my dream state is on a conscious level. It's as if I am in a waking dream when I'm working on the performance. I record all my images, dialogue, or actions that bubble up. For example—I remember working on a "Snowball's Chance in Hell." I just couldn't figure out how to open the piece. That evening before going to bed, I listened to a particular Robert Ashley musical piece of gurgles, pops, and an incessant litany of names. At four in the morning I got this image of me wrapped up in toilet paper reading off a stream of words written on each sheet of the roll. It was a powerful image for me, like a snowball melting into words. When working on a new piece, I have a physical regimen that I do every day for at least five hours (usually beginning around 2 P.M. until about 7 or 8 P.M., my most creative time is before and after the sunset). I begin by vocalizing for about ten minutes before I start stretching, dancing, prancing like a mad Sufi trance dancer. I'm a big believer that breath can alter one's perspective and state of mind. This is when I start recording, talking into a microcassette. Talking, or rapping is what I call it, is a technique in Scott Kelman workshops. It's a state free of any mind control where body movement, sound, and dialogue are improvised. I liken it to the top of my head being opened and a jazz medley of words, song, and sound gushes forth in a total free form without any self-censorship present. You might say it's an ecstatic state. I'll do this for an hour at a time, making sure to take a break and play the tape back. If I'm lucky, maybe forty-five seconds of this rap really works. This is how I compile my text. I try to do it every day; trying to take it further, letting it break down, splinter, and evolve as it wants to. It takes me a while, but eventually, I sit myself down and type it all out in script form.

How I Built the Following Text Contribution:

"Snowball's Chance in Hell" was a response to all the labeling and media coverage that I received in 1990 as one of the NEA Four, i.e., "the man that pissed on Jesus Christ" by Congressman Dana Rohrabacher, "the artist who often urinates on his audience" by the *Washington Times*, "the artist who masturbates on stage" by *The New York Times,* and "Karen Finley and the three gay performance artists" by the *L.A. Times.* Deeply enraged by my work being taken out of context and labeled to serve other people's agenda, I finally emerged from being numb for two years to create "Snowball's Chance in Hell." The protagonist is a man who believes everything he reads. I appropriated texts (perhaps as an act of revenge) from fairy tales, *Hot Rod* magazine, *True Confessions,* the Bible, a Jim Thompson novel, R. D. Laing, Eric Fromm, *Cosmopolitan,* etc., etc., and interwove them into a cataclysmic text about searching desperately for an authentic voice and sense of authority in an information-driven society.

A Snowball's Chance in Hell

> *The great majority of mankind are satisfied with appearances, as though they were realities, and are often more influenced by the things that seem than by those that are.*
> —*Niccolò Machiavelli*

> *All I know is what I read in the papers.*
> —*Will Rogers*

Preshow music plays as audience enters—fifteen minutes later: Lights fade and [audiotape cue]—*sound of a snowball whirling through space that finally thuds to earth. "A Snowball" begins:*

Scene 1—Prologue

A white-robed character, on his knees, appears from offstage (monklike, dwarflike, amoebalike) hunched over, reading from a roll of toilet paper a litany of words
  [*Note: dialogue changes and evolves according to contemporary lingo.*]

Toilet Paper Rap

Rub-a-dub-dub, three men in a tub, the butcher, the baker, the candlestick maker, Albert Einstein, Baudelaire, Mark Twain—three blind mice, three blind mice, see how they run—da do run run run, da do run boys run Phil Gramm and Dianne Feinstein, I wish I were an Oscar Meyer wiener, then everyone would be in love with me Mia Farrow row row row your boat—Hickory dickory doc Doc Severinsen, Doctor Kildare, Ben Casey, When the red red robin comes ba ba baa baa black sheep ba ba ba Bob Hope and Kitty

Kelly—here Kitty, Here Kitty Kitty T T T T cell Mr T. T T for two and two for Tallulah Titilly too to be or not to be be bop a loo lop—Plop plop fizz zzz z z zza Zzza loves marzipan and I love Lucy and she loves me—she loves me not—she loves me Alice B. Toklas and Peter Sellers K-I-S-S-I-N-G g g gee gee whiz Cheez Whiz, a great new way to dress up a potato—one potato, two potato, three potato four for sure and for he's a jolly good fellow Bill Clinton and Barbara Bush in matters of premature ejaculation all around the mulberry bush Hark the Herald Angels Sing over the river and through James Woods to grandmother's house William F. Buckley, Patrick Buchanan—stump stump stump him—Mike Tyson pound her—pound her quarter pounder Big Mac and—Humpty Dumpty had a great fall and all of Rodney King's men couldn't put Chief Darryl Gates back together again— no pain—no gain Leona Helmsley—that's the way the monkey goes—pop goes the weasel sel sel sell it baby—baby baby baby prolife—prochoice, no choice prophylactics—everybody loves my baby but my baby don't love no- body but HIV-positive Jim van Tyne, Craig Lee, Act Up—Fight Back— Blessed be the meek for they shall inherit the wind—Beans, beans, the more you eat the more you Bart Simpson, Samson and Delilah, Just like Romeo and Jane Fonda and Ted Turner, man of the year C C C CNN CNN na na na na Nancy Sinatra picked a peck of pickled peppers, if Peter Frampton and Piper Laurie pi p p p p p playmate come out and play with me me me me Mylanta stuck a feather in his hat and called it macaroni and Cheez Whiz and Little Tommy Tittlemouse lived in a little house and Wolf Blitzer he huffed and he puffed and he blew General Custer—Cream puff Hostess Twinkies eenie meenie minie moe, catch a nigger by the toe—toe toto, Toto, there's no place like home, Auntie M. M&M—onomatopoeia— Pia Pia Zadora and George Burns back together again—Down in the Valley, the valley so low—sweet and low—swing low sweet chariot Our Father who art in Madonna, madonna, madonna and Michael Jackson—Beauty's only skin deep oh yeah and oh so far away I feel in love, soft as an easy chair— and Gary Coleman and I was a little boy. I had but little wit. 'Tis a long time ago and I have no more yet nor ever ever shall for the longer I live live, love, laugh and be happy—hap happy talk k k ka ka ka Kafka kung fu—Who? Wi- Willem Dafoe, hung like a horse, a horse is a horse of course they shoot horses 'cause they're cousins, identical cousins. They talk alike, they walk alike, you could lose your mind—Peter Peter pumpkin eater had a wife and couldn't keep her and old McDonald had a farm, e-i-e-i-o iou. 1.99, 2.99, 3.99 4 eggs, cheese, butter, barley and Manny, Moe and Jack, Ask not what your country can do for you you you and me against the world—we are the world we are the children and Eva Gabor and—Totie Fields in her muumuu, Moo, Moo, the cow jumped over the moon River Fatty Fatty, two times four, can't fit thru the kitchen door—Blow blow the fire, first you blow it gently, then you blow it rough, rough I am the eggman, I am the walrus, Coo coo ca chew

[*By this time, Fleck has ended rant and is lying in a heap of toilet paper onstage.*]

This was used for recording audio played softly under John's live rant:

A wise old owl sat in an oak—the more he heard, Who? the less he spoke, Who?—Lee Iacocca—See no evil, hear no evil. Ding dong bell, Pussy's in the well, The farmer's in the dell, the farmer's in the dell—What's good for the goose is good for the gander—Take it or leave it—What goes around comes around—and here's to good friends tonight is kinda spec-sh sh sh sh—Sally sells seashells—accentuate the HIV positive eliminate the negative and grand men and women Darryl Gates, Dana Rohrabacher—Polly wanna a cracker—Lindsay Wagner Have you driven a Ford lately?—Hickety pickety my black hen—she lays eggs for gentlemen—eggs, cheese, butter, barley, 1.99, 2.99, 3.99—4 Twittle de de, twittle de dum, I smell the blood of the Brady bunch buzzard family—Sing Sing? What shall I sing? the cat's run away with the pudding string, do do, what shall I do, and then I go and spoil it all by saying something stupid like Cock a doodle do, any cock will do—Goodness gracious—great balls of fire—the devil made me do it—Defense-Defense—Mum's the word—Dick Cheney and June Allyson says you can depend on Depends for bladder control problems Jesus Christ, Sally Jessup, and pussy cat ate the dumplings. Mama stood by and cried dear father, who art in hallowed Mary thy kingdom come—rats in the garden, catch 'em towser—cows in the cornfield—run, boys, run—Down in the valley, Fire on the mountain. Oh purple mountain majesty. Purple, purple, purple people eater—Passion Elizabeth Taylor Fortenski and Jack and Jill went up the hill to pat a cake—pat a cake baker's man—Rub-a-dub-dub—pat it and prick it and mark it was a T—t—t—t T cell—tea for two and the father, and the sun is very high and he that would thrive must rise at five and this is the key. This is the key of the kingdom. In that kingdom is a city. In that city is a town. In that town there is a street. In that street there winds a lane. In that lane there is a yard. In that yard, there is a house, in that house there waits a room. In that room there is a bed. On that bed, there is a basket, a basket of flowers. Flowers in the basket. Basket on the bed. Bed in the chamber, chamber in the house. House in the weedy yard. Yard in the winding lane, lane in the broad street, street in the high town, town in the city, city in the kingdom. This is the key—of the kingdom.

This dialogue continues as this creature crawls around the stage creating this spiral, toilet paper flying all over leaving a big trail (the end of the spiral, end of the journey ends up center stage (ya might say it's the cosmic umbilical cord of our collective unconscious—yeah, that's it). He finally crumbles to the ground, a spastic heap in the center of this hurricane of babble and discarded toilet paper strewn all over. He is born.

Scene 2

No more words are coming from his mouth, only his lips moving silently fran-
tically. Like a newborn bird or baby calf, he tries to lift himself up and out of
this nightmare before him. He stands, covers his eyes, slowly opens them. (Ya
might say this section is about psychic forces in this man battling for control—
metaphors for parental, religious, political, media control as he searches for
his identity.)

Action continues: He opens his eyes and hears a bird call—which he
makes—he notices his fingers, one of which catches a teardrop from his eye.
He sucks his finger, which becomes alive and like a bird takes flight carrying
him out of this debris downstage. He tries to get both his fingers back into his
mouth but his fingers avoid him. He finally succeeds in sucking frantically on
his fingers. The mood shifts. Lights above him go out. He's scared of the dark
and runs back center stage to the lit area he's familiar with. His fingers are
still alive, one of which is burrowing up his nostril digging for treasure—
which it finds—it's magical, it's alive, until he sees it for what it is—a
booger—he tries to get it off his finger, spit flying everywhere. We hear strange
helicopter noises coming from him—he's scared and bends down to wipe the
mess off the floor with toilet paper, but toilet paper, like the beanstalk, begins
to grow higher and higher. When he pulls toilet paper away, there's an apple
in his hand. He's scared. The apple descends slowly toward his chest, becom-
ing a pumping heart. He sings out in a high soprano falsetto. "Ma ma ma ma,
Da da da, Do re mi fa so, la ti do." The song becomes more and more pas-
sionate until he/she takes a bite of the apple—Ambrosia—until he grimaces,
as if he's tasted a poison apple, spits it out . . . and begins to walk around the
rug in a spiral becoming aware of where he is. (He's home.) The first words
this man speaks are "Don't bash my head in! Oh, God, don't bash my head
in [Running back and forth. Who/what is chasing him?] Oh, God, don't
bash my head in." He collapses and sees apple with big bite taken out and in
desperation he tries to eat the entire apple (the apple represents nurture-
ment/good, and he's so starved for it he tries to devour it—only it makes him
sick to his stomach and he pukes . . . and pukes the apple out . . . he slowly
rises, spit trailing out of his mouth into:

Scene 3—At home with Mom and Dad

[He backs up into chair, wiping spit off his mouth almost like a drunk coming
home after a binge, wheezing and coughing.]
DAD: Somebody pick that mess up. [(*He pulls light switch above him—*
lights come on him as he sits in easy chair, newspapers surrounding him on all
sides. Grabbing a front-page section of newspaper (important that audience

see each newspaper section)] Bunch of pigs. Slobs, no excuse for crap like that. [*Wheezing—he has asthma*] Bunch of filthy losers. Scum. What'sa matter with you? Make me sick to my stomach. Ain't good for nothing. You're all less than zero! No-good worthless losin' mother. [*He throws newspaper away and grabs another section.*]

MOM: There's no need for talk like that. Talk like that is cheap. Crude. Unrefined. Lacking an articulate point of view. It's true, Joyce Brothers says [*Reads*], "A positive attitude can make all the difference in the world." I mean, even Erma Bombeck says right here, "There's a place for garbage, don't dump it on me, thank you." Even Dear Abby says right here, "There is no need for talk like that—winners do not talk like that." [*Throws paper away*]

DAD: [*Grabs sports page*] Goddamn bunch of losers. Big zeros. Offensive, my ass. Knock 'em out. Strike 'em out. Shoot 'em. Hit 'em. Swing 'em. Sink 'em. Tackle 'em. Ram 'em. Slam 'em. No contest. Upset, my ass. [*Throws sports section away and grabs food section*] Cream 'em. Can 'em. Dice 'em up. Skin 'em. Cut 'em up. Clip 'em. Bunch of chicken-shit losin' mother . . .

MOM: [*Rips out a coupon*] Buy 7-UP and win. Six for a dollar forty-nine. Family savings. Carnation cottage cheese, fifty cents off.

DAD: [*Grabs other front-page news*] Goddamn Kurds. If I hear one more thing about another goddamn Kurd I'm gonna puke. I don't give a shit about no Shiites—Muslim this, Hindu that, shoulda bashed all them goddamn towel heads in when we had a chance.

MOM: [*Ripping out another coupon*] Hi-Dri paper towels two for one dollar. Save on savings. Ooo, Top Ramen noodle soup five for one dollar.

DAD: [*Holding up auto classified section*] Goddamn Japs. Bunch of yellow slant-eyed money suckers.

MOM: [*Grabs coupon*] USDA choice boneless rump roast a dollar forty-nine a pound.

DAD: [*Grabs other news*] Goddamn Serbs—Croats—Croat it out, you goddamn asses, buncha losing Slavs.

MOM: [*Grabs coupon*] Rosarita refried beans . . .

DAD: [*Holding up metro section*] Goddamn Mexican scum. You're all a bunch of scum.

MOM: [*Rips coupon*] Spic and Span changes the meaning of clean.

DAD: [*Starting to get more bombastic*] You're worse than a bunch of niggers.

MOM: [*Rips coupon*] White and porcelain bright. Polident . . .

DAD: [*Business section*] Don't try to Jew me, you bunch of money-suckin' Jew boys.

MOM: Get rich quick—Pillsbury snack cakes and brownies.

DAD: [*Arts section*] You're a bunch of fags, a bunch of sick cock-suckin' fags.

MOM: [*Coupon*] Shout detergent . . . Want a tough stain out, shout it out! [*The fight is raging and he's on the ground, papers flying everywhere.*]

DAD: You're all a bunch of . . .

MOM: Kelloggs frosted . . .

DAD: Flakes . . . What the . . .

MOM: Nuttin honey . . .

DAD: Bunch of . . .

MOM: Grape . . .

DAD: Nuts . . .

MOM: Coo coo for Cocoa Puffs . . .

DAD: Sick . . .

MOM: Bounty—the quicker picker-upper.

[*The fight continues on to the floor, newspapers flying. It's a cat/dog fight. John scampers out like a wounded puppy crawling downstage; lifting rug, he grabs* True Confessions *magazine into:*]

Scene 4 (True Confessions)

[*He's hyperventilating/sweating—wanting to escape—he becomes the characters in* True Confessions. *Reading headlines:*]

"A night of terror: He knows me—he wants me—but I don't know who he is." "I've waited all my life to ask: Are you my father?" It's a true experience. [*Holds up mag*] It's all true. [*Grabs* True Confessions *magazine*]

"Three men want me . . . but for love or murder?" It's a true confession. [*He's standing and begins to read a story from* True Confessions. *He becomes girl and guy*] "My split personality forced me to win a wet T-shirt contest. 'Go into the next room and put this on,' the man said gruffly, handing me a skimpy T-shirt. I stared at him. He had to be kidding. He was about forty, with a beard and hairy arms, and he looked bored. 'What?' I asked, confused.

"'If you get the job, you'll wear this T-shirt and jeans, you know.' He cupped his hands under imaginary breasts, made a jiggling motion, and laughed. 'Go in the washroom. Take your time.' [*He slowly walks downstage—lights come on downstage*] Like someone in a dream, I entered the bathroom, took off my blouse—and bra—and put on the T-shirt. Under the cartoon tiger on the shirt the legendary Striped Tiger Lounge was printed. I looked in the mirror over the sink and the face staring back looked vaguely familiar. But I couldn't believe it was really me—my breasts pressed tight, bulging out of the T-shirt. The face—fairly attractive, framed by long wavy hair—wore a puzzled expression, but did not look scared. Which surprised me. I should have been scared out of my wits. 'Who am I and what am I doing here?' I wondered. My mind was blank, as if my life had begun when I was handed that T-shirt. I couldn't even remember my own name! My body felt numb.

[*As if he were looking into a mirror—out to audience*]

"'Don't you know who you are? Who are you? [*Mimes wiping off mirror*] How are you feeling? Are you feeling anything?'

[*He backs up upstage*]

"'Cautiously, I emerged from the washroom, my breasts bulging under the skimpy T-shirt.'

"'Oh, yes,' the bearded man said. 'You'll do just fine, Chrissie.' 'Thanks,' I said. And for some reason, I felt almost happy." [*He/she throws magazine away and slowly walks over to the stereo like a wounded dog, humming. He grabs a record and shakily puts it on stereo.*]

Photo copyright © by Dona Ann McAdams

TERRY GALLOWAY

Name: Terry Galloway
Stage Name: Same
Birthdate/Birthplace: Halloween of 1950 in Stuttgart, Germany
"Raised Up" Where: Stuttgart and Berlin, Germany; Fort Hood and Austin, Texas
Education: BA with honors from University of Texas, Austin (I majored in American Studies with minors in English and Radio/TV/Film); a two-year combative relationship with Columbia University, NYC, where I got into periodic screaming matches with some professors and administrators while working towards a Master's in Theater Arts, never completed
Honors/Grants: Two Corporation for Public Broadcasting Awards for Best Script and Excellence in Writing; the Texas Institute of Letters/Ralph A. Johnson Foundation's J. Frank Dobie Paisano Fellowship; the Columbia University Heckscher Foundation Fellowship; Pew Charitable Trust; the 1983 Villager Theater Award for Outstanding Solo Performance; two Florida Council for the Arts Individual Artist Fellowships; a National Endowment for the Arts
Influences/Mentors/Heroes: The Brontës, Emily Dickinson, William Shakespeare, Abraham Lincoln, Eleanor Roosevelt, Malcolm X, Thomas Jefferson, FDR, Daffy Duck, Jerry Lewis, Fat Freddie's Cat, James B. Ayres, Julia Miles, Heiner Mueller, Peter Brook, Grotowski, Grace Paley, Mary Martin, Helen Keller, Gertrude Stein, Richard Pryor, Socrates, Mary Shelley, Virginia Woolf, the members of the Virginia Woolves, my friends, my lover, and my family
Places Performed: From A to Z? Okay. Alice B. Theater, American Place Theater, Arena Theater, Assembly Rooms, Bardavon, Betty Oliphant, California Institute of the Arts, Cameo Theater, Capitol City Playhouse, Chicago House, Dance Place, Dance Theater Workshop, Emerson University, Esther's Follies, Finborough, Florida State University, Green Room, Hallwalls, Highways, Horace Mann Theater, LACE, Liberty Lunch, Life on the Water, Limbo Lounge (mine was the inaugural performance), the Loft, Manhattan Theater Club, New Orleans Contemporary Arts Center, P.S. 122, Pyramid Club, Randolph Street Gallery, Roanoke Arts Center, Seven Stages, Shakespeare at Winedale, Southwest Missouri State, St. Lawrence, SUNY Purchase Performing Arts Center, Sushi, Tampa Bay Performing Arts Center, Tron, Tulsa University, University of North Florida, Vassar, Walker Arts, West Virginia University, WOW, X-Teresa, Zap.
Pivotal Performance: When I played Falstaff at University of Texas in Austin's Shakespeare at Winedale summer program in 1972. I loved the role but I was given to fits of improvisation that would sometimes get me into trouble with purists. But we hit the great tavern scene where Hal in effect banishes Falstaff. Now, I have always felt that reckless endangerment that comes with love and I loved Falstaff. I loved Shakespeare for creating him. And I loved Jim Ayres, the director of the program, for giving me that part. I felt that love and also an anger and protectiveness. I knew that Hal would triumph and go on to be king; and Falstaff and all the misfits would get left behind. And being as I am deaf and a woman and also at that time oh just poor as shit—I suddenly fell into the language. There was no division between what Shakespeare had written, what Falstaff had to say, what I was feeling at that moment. Falstaff's great defense of himself and his kind became my own defense of life, improvisation, fun; and of him; and of myself and all of us who were destined to be the comic relief, the dispossessed, those for whom

destiny had little to say . . . all of us really. And my friend Jan who was playing Hal, he felt the language turn real so he kept turning it—that is what we had aimed for when we rehearsed. And the audience felt it too. That is what they had come to experience. And there we all were, all of us caught in that moment. Everything turned stark still, the temperature dropped and we were all in that fictitious and real moment together, all of us—audience, performers, and whatever ghosts were in the rafters.

Favorite Performance Experience: I was doing a show with my group The Mickee Faust Club. I was doing a character called Jake Ratchett, Short Detective, one that was conceived way back in the seventies. I'm in detective drag, fake stubble, shoes on the wrong feet. My leading lady is Toni Denise, who usually holds court at the local gay bar. She's in the middle of the transsexual process, going from he to she. She looks like a million bucks plus and she's got a Southern drawl that makes me her sucker on stage and off. There are lots and lots of straight guys at this performance and these guys don't know the first thing about transsexualism, but they do smell sex and they have been wolfing Toni all night long because, well, she's the best-looking dame in the joint. Jake and Rose (me and Toni) are at the beginning of our scene together. In this scene there is some snappy talk, an exchange between the tough guy (me) and the treacherous babe (Toni). The talk is all about appearances. Here's how it goes:

TONI: I am what I am but I'm not what you think.

TERRY: What do you think I think you are?

TONI: I think you think I'm not quite what I say I am.

TERRY: Maybe. But I think you're pretty much what you seem to be.

TONI: [*Drops her voice about ten octaves and uses this deep, deep unmistakably he-male voice*] "Well, I'm not."

And whammo. The whole place is engulfed by that collective Hah that enlightens. A huge roar of shock and laughter. That audience had been taken. And in more ways than one.

Most Terrifying Performance Experience: Mexico City. The place was packed with non-English speakers and my piece is very, very language based and my Spanish is nada. I still had every belief in the transcendence of art and I thought *I'm miked so at least they'll be able to pick up my subtle changes of tone.* But right at the beginning the body mike shorted out. It was my subconscious fear of performing made manifest—just me screaming incomprehensibly for an hour.

Favorite Prop or Costume: The hairy rat ears I wear as Mickee Faust.

Hobbies: Like a million other people, I love to make lists. I bike. I read a lot. I play soccer. I color and paint. I play basketball. I go see a lot of films. I play tennis. I collect bones, skeletons, and stuffed and dried artifacts of natural history. I play racquetball. I smoke a pipe, which is a lot like having an electric train. I play a game called Squeak, which is extremely fast-paced group competitive solitaire. I belong to an arm-tickling club called the Loyal Order of the Lounging Lizards.

Reading List: I love to read and always keep a huge pile of books, comics, and magazines within easy reach of my bed. My favorite reads in all categories: Rebecca West's *The Fountain Overflows,* Michael Ondaatje's *The English Patient,* my sister Gail Adams's manuscript *The Notebooks of Madame Eye* and her book of short stories *The Purchase of Order,* Cormac McCarthy's *The Orchard Keeper,* Joyce Cary's *The Horse's Mouth,* George Eliot's *Mill on the Floss,* Zora Neale Hurston's *Their Eyes Were Watching*

God, Carl Hiaasen's *Tourist Season,* Euripides's *The Bacchae,* Alice Munro's *Friend of My Youth,* Wallace Stevens's *The Palm at the End of the Mind,* John Kennedy O'Toole's *A Confederacy of Dunces,* Joe Orton's *Complete Plays,* Henry Green's *Concluding,* Alfred Jarry's *Ubu Roi,* Yeats's *The Crazy Jane Poems,* Carolyn Forché's *Gathering the Tribes,* Chester Himes's *The Crazy Kill,* Dawn Raffel's *The Year of Long Division,* Marilynne Robinson's *Housekeeping, A Midsummer Night's Dream, A Wrinkle in Time, Orlando, A Canticle for Leibowitz, The Secret Garden, A Passage to India, Little Women, Jane Eyre, Wuthering Heights, Fawlty Towers, Gaudy Night, Enormous Changes at the Last Minute, The Sound and the Fury, A Long Day's Journey into Night, A High Wind in Jamaica, The Autobiography of Malcolm X, Kidnapped,* Roald Dahl's *The Enormous Crocodile, The Hunchback of Notre Dame,* Mabel Maney's *The Case of the Not So Nice Nurses,* Richard Dawkins's *The Selfish Gene,* and Oliver Sacks's *The Man Who Mistook His Wife for a Hat.* Jesus, I just realized I could keep listing my favorite books for the rest of my life. Sorry. I'll stop. But as far as comic books, I love Donald Duck, Superman, the Fabulous Fury Freak Brothers, Alf, Ren and Stimpy, St. Fury and His Howling Commandos, and I have a collection of Love Comic Books dating from the seventies. I subscribe to and/or buy at the stands *Mad, Spy, People, Alfred Hitchcock, Newsweek, Harper's, New Yorker, Monk, Out, Advocate, Reader's Digest, On Our Backs, Off Our Backs, Apalachee Quarterly, Women's Weekly, SHHHH, The American Voice, Women's Review of Books,* and the *Weekly World News.* I love to read.

Favorite Music: I'm deaf as a doornail but I do have favorite music: I can feel the blues from the soles of my feet so I love Lightnin' Hopkins, Muddy Waters, Washboard Sam, and Billie Holiday. I love Dan Del Santos's *Life in the Big City,* especially his song "You Make Me Sick . . . You Remind Me of Myself." Also, weirdly, Patsy Cline's voice goes right to my brain as do Hank Williams's and Janis Joplin's. And I don't remember who sang it but I love this song, "The Hungry Dog Blues." I can't perceive opera as well as blues but there is a part of *Der Rosenkavalier* that pierces my soul and *Einstein on the Beach* thrills me. And my mother has a deep bluesy voice that I could feel a thousand miles away.

Favorite Quote: I've got two: "To live in contradiction without shame." I don't know who wrote it but I recall it every hour of my life.
And this, from May Swenson:

> Body my house
> my horse my hound
> what will I do
> when you are fallen

Artist's Notes

In the early eighties when I was a graduate student at Columbia in New York, I was broke, deaf, queer, and feeling really put upon. I used to hang out at WOW, Limbo Lounge, the Women's Project, and P.S. 122 because that's where all my friends were. I loved theater but the only theater I could afford was, for the most part, performance art which was at that time plentiful and cheap. One night I saw a really shitty performance involving some woman I hope never to know writhing around on the floor yapping. It really sucked and it left me feeling elated. She stank! But even so, she had a space and an audience and for one solid hour the stage was hers. She was a true inspiration as only the worst of bad art can be.

I hated and still hate most of the roles foisted off on women—sluts in bathrobes who wait for the men to get home so life can start up again. But at that time, even though I'd been writing and performing pretty much all my life, it had not occurred to me I could write different roles for women all by myself. It's not that anyone ever told me no, it's just that I was afraid I didn't have what it took to write, to perform, to make the kind of "art" I wanted to make. I had it put into my mind that artists were guys—hard-driven, ugly-sexy guys hauled up into the stratosphere by their hair. But at the sight of that woman performing a piece she had (God help her) written herself, my heart leapt up. I knew I could do better. And that meant that I— a deaf, queer woman desperately in need of a better haircut and more inter-esting shoes—I, too, could have a stage, an audience, and an hour of time.

I was still not terribly certain what I would write. As an undergraduate at the University of Texas in Austin I had been deeply involved in UT's alterna-tive Shakespeare festival, Shakespeare at Winedale, and I'd been almost as deeply involved in the local poetry scene. After I graduated I had worked with one of my heroes, Heiner Mueller, on the American premiere of his play *Mauser*. And around the same time I helped start a very successful cabaret, Esther's Follies, with some other former UT students for which we performed material we wrote for ourselves. But in the eighties, I wasn't in Texas and I wasn't working with a group. I was in New York and on my own. What to do? I used the material I had on hand: the bad jokes I'd heard when I was bussing tables; the family stories told at holidays or funerals; the poems written when I was flat broke and eating nothing but Cream of Wheat; the physical bits I'd improvised when working with Mueller; the skits and characters I'd created performing with the cabaret. I put all this together in combinations which made sense to me. And when I started per-forming these combinations they seemed to make sense to everybody else in those cheap dives where my friends—queers and women and artists and po-ets and performers—were hanging out. And these guys took a personal in-terest in the art—they wanted to see it develop. The atmosphere was informal enough that strangers and friends felt they could say, "Hey, Terry, great line." But it was also weirdly rigorous. My friends (and strangers) thought nothing of telling me, "Terry that whole scene is a cheap bit of in-dulgence. You should be ashamed. Out it." What was so great about the at-mosphere was that if you could give your ideas form you had no problem finding yourself a space and an audience. I got to try combinations out in all sorts of spaces—at American Place Theater or the Women's Project it took on one form; at Limbo Lounge, WOW, or P.S. 122 it took on another.

By the time I had finished *Out All Night and Lost My Shoes* I felt I had created what I wanted, a piece about the life of a woman: a woman born deaf and hallucinatory because of a modern medical experiment gone awry; a woman who fought her way through the idiotic folly of the world that surrounded her, fought her own bouts of terror and madness; and if she didn't exactly triumph, she did save herself. I let that woman experience all those things I love about theater: the mystery and hilarity, the inexplicable connections and the sudden changes of emotion, the cathartic clarifying moments and the quiet denouements. I let her claim them as her own. And since it was my own life I was writing about I could claim those things as mine, too. Having claimed those things, I could finally imagine myself—within myself—an artist. A great excuse to keep on living.

[From the dark]

When my Granny Doris was a young woman, she lived in a place in Texas called Snake Canyon. It wasn't called Snake Canyon for nothing. She lived there way in the middle of nowhere with her husband and two children. One morning she got up to see her husband off to work as usual. And then she went in to check on the baby. My mother says she remembers waking up for some reason and seeing her mother standing in the doorway—barefoot, still in her nightgown, her hair still down. That little baby, he was just as still—a little, blue last-breath bubble coming out of his nose. My mother says her mother didn't say a word, didn't make a sound. She just picked that baby up and ran. She ran just as dawn was breaking. Barefoot. Through Snake Canyon.

Now when I was little that was the kind of bedtime story my mother always told me.

[Lights up full]

Hello. I'm Terry Galloway. Given the circumstances I thought it prudent to do the polite and safe thing and introduce myself to you before we got too much more involved. There is one thing you might like to know: I was born in Germany, in Stuttgart, and spent part of my childhood in Berlin. Nonetheless—as you can probably tell from that story—I am a Texan "and *[Texas drawl]* proud of it!" Unfortunately I share with other Texans a peculiar, sometimes fatal, flaw—I will presume an intimacy, and I'll do it most often when there is none.

There's a corny old joke about that. You've got three guys—a guy from Chicago, a guy from New York, and a Texan. They're shipwrecked. For days they're crawling across the hot island sands. They come across this magic lantern. Of course they rub it, and out pops a genie.

The genie looks 'em over and says, "Normally I grant one person three wishes, but there are three of you all so it's a wish apiece. What'll it be?"

The guy from Chicago says, "God! I miss the Windy City—I wish, I wish I was back in Chicago!"

Poof! He's gone.

The guy from New York says, "Hell, I miss da Big Apple. I wish, I wish ya'd send me back to New York!"

Poof! He's gone.

The Texan looks around and says, "Ah, gee, Genie, I sure do miss them two guys. I wish they was both back here!"

That's a Texan for you.

You know what this reminds me of? Being home with my mother's family. You know—everybody crowded into the one room that could hold all the chairs. We got to stay up late, and it was kind of an occasion. And we talked. We talked about who lived, who died, and what they wore. Important things. When I was a kid, the hot ticket was the comedy. Uncle Kenny was our favorite because he did this really great obscene Donald Duck. [*Donald Duck quacks, "Fuck you, shithead! Fuckfuckfuckfuck!"*]

Cheap. But we liked it. But what we loved were the mysteries. The mysteries usually involved Great-grandma and Great-auntie, Ava and Eva. They were twins and lived to be ninety-three years old and died within three months of each other. And they could foretell or just see something in the shadow of the future. They had been visiting my Granny Doris the day before that little baby died. But they'd left in the early evening and traveled by train through the night. When they got back home to Burkburnett in the wee hours of the next morning, they put their bags down in the hall and made themselves a pot of tea. And Great-grandma, looking at the tea leaves, said, "Eva, don't bother to unpack those bags. Somebody just died."

I had visions too. When I was nine, I could leave my body and fly with the demons. I'd be sitting on the back of the car looking up at the stars, and then all of a sudden I'd be six feet away looking at myself looking up at the stars. And the voice of God spoke to me. When I was nine, God said to me, "Little Terry, go forth and destroy the world!" [*Mimes upending the table and throwing the chair*] "Yes, God! Right away!" I did my damnedest.

But I wasn't obeying the true voice of God. Because I'm not just your usual Texan to whom God may conceivably speak. I'm a modern medical accident.

When my mother was six months pregnant with me, she developed a kidney infection. This was Germany in the fifties, the age of experimentation. And that's just what they did. They experimented on my mother. They pumped my mother with an experimental antibiotic and sat back and waited to see which one of us would die. Neither of us did. Whew. A few months later I was born. Everything was perfectly normal. The only glitch was that I was coming out a little early—I was coming out in the hallway on the way to the delivery room. And the doctors for some reason took this as a personal affront! They did not want me to be born in that hallway, no! They wanted me to be born in that delivery room where I should be born.

My mother is on that stretcher, and if you've ever been in labor, you know she was not up to protesting anything they did. I was here [*Hand at crotch*] making my appearance, right? And the doctors—in order to keep me contained just a little bit longer—took my mother's legs and crossed them on my face like this [*Legs in a tight and vicious wrap*]. So when I was born, I looked like this:

My nose was all swollen and purply. My poor daddy, who has a pretty big nose himself, went to look in on the baby. When he came out, he was weeping. "Oh, God, Edna! She looks just like me!" The swelling's gone down a bit.

Other than that, perfectly normal. And I was. Until I started having those visions. People suddenly developed double profiles. And when I looked away from them, they would start speaking in an alien tongue. I'm just a kid—it can't be me, so it's got to be the world. Unfortunately, I had just seen *The Invasion of the Body Snatchers*. I thought, "Of course! Pod people! I'm the last true human on Earth."

By this time my parents were getting worried because this was not normal childhood behavior. [*Child's voice*] "You are not my real family! Yes, God, I will destroy them all!" So they took me to a child psychologist who would ask me leading questions like, "Kid, are you a nut?" But children are very clever. I had rehearsed for this eventuality. [*Child's voice, incredulously*] "Me? I'm not crazy. Hahahaha. I'm not even creative!" [*Muttered undertone*] "You'll never trip me up, Pod People."

But they did. They found out, and I quote, "that a chemical imbalance caused by the introduction of drugs into the fetal nervous system" had left me not quite blind as a bat but definitely deaf as a doornail.

By the time I was twelve I was a freak. I had not yet had the years of speech therapy that allow me to speak this clearly. Or the miracle of contact lenses. Or the clever little behind-the-ear hearing aid like this one. No. My first hearing aid was a huge box the size of a Walkman that hung on my chest like a third breast. I had just gotten my breasts. I had just started my period. I had hairy legs and hairy underarms because my mother wouldn't let me shave. I had a dork-kid haircut, and I'd just broken my two front teeth playing a game of war. I was fat as a pig and wore these pink cat-eye glasses, always broken of course. And I desperately wanted to be normal, so I would hide my hearing aid box inside my blouse. But it's a microphone, so there's feedback—beep, beep. And every time I took a step everything moved along with me—and you'd better believe nothing was going to come along quietly. I would take a step and it was: Bounce Bounce! Beep Beep! Bleed Bleed! "I'm a monster, a monster!" BounceBounce! BeepBeep! BleedBleed! "Trapped in here forever!" BOUNCEBOUNCEBEEPBEEPBLEED-BLEED!! "Somebody save me! Save me!" BOUNCEBOUNCEBEEPBEEP-BLEEDBLEED! I froze. So they shipped me off to the Lions' Camp for Crippled Children.

That summer I won the swimming award because I was the only one who could do much more than float. Except for the blind girl who played a mean game of Marco Polo.

At the end of summer was award night. This was an equal opportunity camp. Everyone won something, sometimes twice over. You had this steady stream of kids going up to the stage to get their awards. But I really was the only kid who was mobile. So you had this steady stream of kids—but these were kids without legs, kids with artificial legs, kids on crutches, kids in braces, kids in wheelchairs, in wheeled beds, kids drawn up there by pulleys. So when it came time for me to accept my award, I limped all the way up to the stage.

As I limped back—on the other leg—I was thinking, even with all the paraphernalia making my handicaps visible—among those kids I'd just never be handicapped enough.

My best friend that year was a little girl who was a little older than I was. The age difference was so attractive. I was twelve. She was thirteen. She was paralyzed from the neck down. And she was beautiful. And she was sweet. And believe me, if that had been me, I would not have been sweet. I would have been going, [*Jerks violently from the neck*] "FUCK YOU FUCK YOU FUCK YOU!" But she was sweet. We were real tight. She liked for me to help her get ready for breakfast in the morning because you had to empty things. But we'd read *Mad Magazine* together, so who gave a shit, right? We'd get ready, and then I'd push her bed to breakfast. The counselors, they were suckered. "Those two little angels." But the real reason she liked me to push her to breakfast was that I loved her, so I was the only one she could bully into pushing her wheeled bed down the *verboten* hills. There were many of them. And they were very steep. So it was—*vavvvooomm!* Give her a little speed! Sometimes she fell out. [*To the imaginary heap*] "You asked for it."

I thought, *Oh, I'll love you forever.* But it was a summer romance. At the end of summer she went one way, I went the other, and I never thought about her again. Until years later when I was in New York. I auditioned for this live art group. At that time, among those people if you couldn't be mentally deranged, it helped if you could be physically deformed. "TaDaaa! I'm here!"

So I got to star in their production of Shakespeare's poem "The Phoenix and the Turtle." I wore my tortoiseshell glasses and set my hair on fire. Big hit. Of course, it was all unbearably ironic. Everything that had humiliated us as children was suddenly *woo-o-o-o,* hot stuff.

I wanted to get ahold of her and tell her this great, good news, but I couldn't remember her name. Besides, what could I say? What could anyone possibly say?

Dear Friend,
I know just how you feel.
But remember—
nobody's the real thing.
Look at me—no ears,
weak eyes, teeth broke,
fat butt, and these
legs.
No, I do not have beautiful
legs,
not even here in New York
City.
But remember this,
honey—when it all starts
getting you down—
people love their Freaks.
And, of course, it helps to
have a beautiful face.
Which I do.
And how are things in
Texas anyway, beautiful? I
can just imagine.
I mean my folks were
worried, too,
that I might not ever find
my rightful place.
You know, no ears, weak
eyes, teeth broke,
fat butt, and these
legs.
But it's different somehow
out here.
Here people love their
Freaks.
I know you'd find that
hard to believe, honey,
but—ever since I took up
the old trombone my
status changed:
suddenly this—no ears
weak eyes teeth broke
fat butt and these
legs!
Suddenly they are in
demand!
And of course it helps to be
a wizard
on the old trombone.
Which I am.
But I want you to
remember this, honey—
when it's just too much to
bear—
People love their Freaks.
Hey, aren't I speaking
from experience here?
People love their Freaks.
Well, the band's just
starting up, so I've got to
go.
But I'll write you,
sweetheart, real soon.
And no, I'll never forget
those beautiful afternoons
when I pushed your
wheeled bed
along the banks of the Rio
Grande
and moved your head
tenderly

to the side so you could
see across
to the Mexico of your
dreams.
Our kisses were the purest
love I've ever had.
And I'll never forget them
or you, my darling,
even though this busy life

pushes me even now
to the four corners.
No, I'll never forget them.
Or you. And I'll write.
I promise.
Real soon.

Ah. It wasn't all [*Makes the violin-playing motions of pathos*]. We were tough little cookies. That's how we survived. If we survived. And we could be so mean. None of us liked the little blind girl very much. She was kind of a snob. So that summer it was nothing but blind jokes. Our favorite was the one about the blind girl who goes into the china shop. You've heard that one.

The little blind girl goes into a china shop, and there's a table loaded down with expensive knickknacks, antique watches, priceless glassware. She picks up her cane and starts beating the living shit out of it all.

The proprietor comes running up, screaming, "What do you think you're doing?"

The blind girl says, "Ohhh, just looking."

JAMES GODWIN

Name: James Godwin
Stage Name: Same and/or Antlerman
Birthdate/Birthplace: March 22, 1966/Kingston, Pennsylvania
"Raised Up" Where: Wilkes-Barre, Pennsylvania; Walkerton, Indiana
Education: BFA, The Columbus College of Art and Design
Honors/Grants: National Gold Key Award; Scholastic Art Awards, 1984; Franklin Furnace Fund for Performance Art Grant, 1995; NYSCA Panelist
Influences/Mentors/Heroes: John Thomas, J. Gerald Godwin, Brother Jim Miller C.S.C., Bill Irwin, Jim Henson, Tom Murrin, David Leslie, Terence McKenna, Tom Waits, Kate Bush, Bill Baird, Joseph Campbell
Places Performed: Dixon Place, P.S. 122, La MaMa, Franklin Furnace, SoHo Repertory Theater, Cucaracha, Walker Art Center, Cleveland P.A.F., Lincoln Center, the Kitchen, Knitting Factory, Nell's, Pyramid, Surf Reality
Pivotal Performance: Doing "Antlerman" at Avant-Garde-Arama in 1990, big crowd, some beers, a big stage and some new equipment. I was *so* nervous, but the audience laughed and I felt like maybe I had something.
Favorite Performance Experience: Performing at the Henson Puppet Festival Cabaret using some new puppets I had built—the energy was amazing.
Most Terrifying Performance Experience: Was when I volunteered to come onstage during a Mimi Goese piece at P.S. 122. After [placing] a butcher knife in my lap, she strapped me to a chair and put Velveeta on my head and pushed me off a short platform. I pretended to be unconscious.
Favorite Prop or Costume: My Antlerman regalia and Rudy the Vegetable puppet
Hobbies: UFO research, paranormal phenomena, conspiracy theories, outdoorsy mountain-man wilderness survival
Reading List: *Riddley Walker* by Russell Hoban; *Urban Shaman* by Serge King; *Shaman's Drum* magazine; *Archaic Revival* and *True Hallucinations* by Terence McKenna; *Jitterbug Perfume* by Tom Robbins; *Schwa*
Favorite Music: Tom Waits, Latin Playboys, Soul Coughing, Stephen Sondheim, Alberta Hunter, Ella Fitzgerald, P. J. Harvey, Esquivel!
Favorite Quote: "Adopt, adapt, and improve!"

Artist's Notes

Most of my work begins with the construction of an object. If it is a mask or puppet or mitten, the process of constructing always triggers some connections within the ever-evolving mythology. I try to build upon previous experience, what works and what doesn't. I pay attention to images both popular and occult and try to formulate performances that can evoke a humorous response with an aftertaste of menace. Masks have an ancient history of myth and ritual. Shamans used them in ways that were both theatrical and medical. I aspire to their practice of myth building and performance. After using masks and building masks they seemed to provide instructions for "the piece." I let them live and we improvise upon the situation at hand; nightclub, theater, or sidewalk. Soon patterns emerge and I explore those pathways. My childhood interests are always reflected, playing spaceman or scuba diver now becomes a practice of shamanic interplay. Puppets become a natural avenue of expression. They are a challenge to build and operate. The tension between the operator and the operated helps to invite the audience to engage their imagination. We build the illusion together. To me imagination is the key, it opens a door that allows the subtle beings of other worlds to exist in our space. The fool lets them in and they can become aliens or angels. I like to be foolish, it usually starts with embarrassment and always results in inspiration, sometimes even astonishment.

Antlerman

[ANTLERMAN *enters playing a drum and chanting:*]

Hey yah hey, Hey yah Hoe!

Hi! My people . . . Good people, welcome, I am Antlerman! Spirit guide and master of metamorphosis from beyond the event horizon! Tonight I will be your guide, but not guru; your pal, but not patsy. Tonight I will teach you to become your own urban shaman-slash-performance artist-slash-alien abduction investigator! Yes, my people, tonight you will see the ancient connections that lie buried in the human undersoul. Tonight you will harness these energies and use them to shed the light of love on your love life, your shelf life, your career, your cancer.

These secrets can be revealed only after we have completed the ritual of unification! The ritual of unification requires a surrender of the ego-morph! A decision to involve our inner antlers in nothing less than transformation! But before we begin we must unify our groupthink! We must join our thoughts by performing the Antlerman Singalong! Repeat after me: Hey yah, Hey yoh . . . [*They repeat*] . . . Hey yah, Way oh . . . [*Again*] . . . Heyah Combah Lakka Chikka Manna Layah Kohna Vondala Mimba Kannah Vimbah Lahbba Leyoh . . . Ah, yes, the urge to follow is strong tonight! And now we have accessed the group dynamic. Now I must cleanse our mind of any errant or negative thoughtforms. I will cleanse by using my antlers!

My antlers are antennae fed by light. They will absorb the static cling of the psyche and deflect any and all demons of mundane reality until they become full. And when they are full and complete, they glow!

[*Lights out as antlers glow. Headlamp comes on . . .*]

It's a cheap trick but it works. . . . And to prove the efficiency of the antlers, I will now channel the conflict of the shadow mind!

[*The headlamp throws a circle of light on the wall and* ANTLERMAN's *hands are now two shadow puppets in that circle.*]

VOICE #1: What the hell is this guy doing? Y'know, I thought we would get to see some cute little puppets or maybe a visualization of gender politics, but this?

VOICE #2: Honey, please, this is performance art! Remember? I'm sure that any minute he's gonna take off all his clothes and start cutting himself or something!

VOICE #1: Well, I just hope it doesn't take him three hours to do it!

VOICE #2: Listen, honey, just give it a chance, you're blocking!

VOICE #1: Listen, I thought we could've gone to see the improv collective's deconstruction of *Baywatch,* but no, you had to drag me to this!

VOICE #2: Oh, fuck you!

VOICE #1: Fuck you! . . .

VOICE #2: Fuck you! . . .

etc., etc., etc. . . .

[*Back to* ANTLERMAN . . .]

Whew! It seems that the group dynamic is now cleansed. Those voices represent the left and right brain in conflict and that is what we need to achieve a strong unification ritual! [*He turns on lights*] As the Antlerman I must be prepared for any situation within the group dynamic. I must be open enough to heal the psychic scrapes of childhood. I must be able to adapt to the economic realities of life! In fact sometimes I make a little extra money during the Jewish holidays as Menorah-Man! But that's a different story, because now we must complete the ritual of unification! We begin with the first light of love on my right. Look into the light and visualize your first love, feel it. Remember how you had to cancel your prom date and how you ended up going with your stepsister, and then snuff it out! [*Lights out*] But then open your heart. . . . Rekindle the light of love, inhale the photonic memory and insert the strong metal base into the sacred nursing bra so that the light will reflect more brightly upon you. [*The lamp is now affixed to his chest via the sacred nursing bra*]

Now we move to the second light of love on my left [*Right light goes out, left light comes on*]. . . . Visualize your second great love, feel it, remember. . . . Remember that trip to Puerto Rico and how you ran out of money and how you had to borrow a hundred dollars and how she never let you forget it, and then snuff it out! [*Lights out*] But then open your heart. . . . Rekindle the light of love, inhale the photonic memory and insert the cold metal post against your already throbbing nipple. Set it securely within the sacred nursing bra so that the light will reflect more brightly upon you. . . . [*Both lights on*] Now you are a fully balanced Antlerman!

Photo by Linda Sue Scott

MARGA GOMEZ

Name: Marga Gomez
Stage Name: Whoopi Gomez
Birthplace: NYC
Birthdate: 1762 Bite me
"Raised Up" Where: Manhattan, San Francisco
Education: College dropout
Honors/Grants: 1. 1994 Theater L.A. Ovation Award Best Supporting Actress—*Carpa Clash*
2. 1993 Bay Area Critics Circle Award Outstanding Solo Performance—*Memory Tricks*
3. 1994 Co-Commission—Center Theater Group/Mark Taper Forum of Los Angeles, Gordon Davidson, Artistic Director; and New WORLD Theater, University of Massachusetts at Amherst, Massachusetts, Roberta Uno, Artistic Director
Influences/Mentors/Heroes: Lily Tomlin and Jane Wagner, Richard Pryor, Willy Chevalier, Ernie Kovacs
Places Performed: P.S. 122; New York Shakespeare Festival; Whitney Museum; Edinburgh Fringe Festival; Montreal Just for Laughs Festival; ICA, London; Highways, Santa Monica; Josie's and The Marsh, San Francisco
Pivotal Performance: The first time I workshopped *Marga Gomez Is Pretty, Witty & Gay* in San Francisco I placed cheat sheets onstage, hidden from the audience of fifteen. Midshow I accidentally kicked my notes out of order and admitted to the audience and God that I screwed up and proceeded to wing it. After the show, a charming lass named Lori E. Seid told me she'd like to book me at P.S. 122. She wrote her number down on a scrap of paper. Although I was dying to play New York I didn't call her for six months 'cause I thought she was bullshitting me. But she wasn't.
Favorite Performance Experience: Five minutes of stand-up comedy at the closing ceremonies of the 1994 Gay Games in Yankee Stadium, just a hop, skip, and a jump from my childhood home
Most Terrifying Performance Experience: I thought Cher was in the back row once at The Public and I was afraid I'd go up on my lines. It was just some guy who looked like Cher.
Favorite Prop or Costume: My pom-pom Carpa Babe outfit designed by Pattsi Valdez
Hobbies: Impure thoughts, meteorology
Reading List: Sandra Cisneros, George Orwell, *Bomb* magazine, *Curve* magazine
Favorite Music: Anything Latino from the forties, fifties, and sixties
Favorite Quote: As Mom used to say, "Walk like a lady. Eat like a man."

Artist's Notes

I was the only child of the marriage of a Cuban comedian-impresario to a Puerto Rican dancer and aspiring actress. I grew up in the sixties believing that my parents were big-time stars . . . and in the Latino community of Manhattan, they were. There was nothing more fun than tagging along with my parents to the *teatros* on the weekend and being a fly on the wall backstage while my parents and their show-biz colleagues (some very talented, others just well endowed) entertained the *familias,* from the grandparents to the babies, all dressed in their best. It looked like a church with a beat.

As I got older and saw my parents' grandeur dissipate into failure, I spent hours and hours reliving their heyday in my mind. I will always be a nostalgia queen even though I realize the present and future offer more for someone of my ethnic background and sexual orientation.

I do what I do because of my parents. Solo performance feels natural to me because I grew up as an only child and I was weird. As a stand-up comedian for eight years I used my personal experiences as material fodder but too often I had to simplify my ideas to get laughs. Since I was wanting to explore the complexities of assimilation and sexual identity, comedy clubs were becoming less appropriate venues.

In 1990 I got a call from someone who was involved in presenting a multicultural theater festival at the University of California at San Diego (UCSD). Her committee had been informed that I was a solo performance artist and they wanted to include my work in their festival. I said I would love to perform but I was in the process of changing the title of my piece and I would call her tomorrow with the new title. That's how I switched careers from stand-up comic to solo performance artist in one phone call.

For years I harbored the secret desire to write a play about my parents and make them famous for real and forever. After that was done I'd be free to create my own dramas. Unfortunately I had no idea how to write a play. I just knew how to tell a story and be all the characters. I knew how to be the play. I was already doing it in my stand-up act on a smaller scale.

Accepting the UCSD gig put a fire under me to quit procrastinating. Because my mother had been diagnosed the year before with Alzheimer's there was no question that my first theatrical monologue, *Memory Tricks,* would be about her life and our relationship. Writing and performing the piece and playing my mother has helped me discover the love that was there between us, and the resentment I had for her ceased to exist.

Five months after the UCSD festival I premiered a two-act version of *Memory Tricks* at San Francisco's The Marsh. The audiences were enthusiastic, the houses were full, but the piece needed something. After two years of touring, rewriting and almost killing it, I learned that what *Memory Tricks* needed was less. Thirty minutes were cut which included some very funny but unnecessary jokes, and my father's presence in the piece was greatly reduced. Since its premiere at the New York Shakespeare Festival it has been performed straight through without intermission and I'm always very thirsty at the end.

When *Memory Tricks* first played in my home base of San Francisco, my stock rose. I went from being a starving undervalued artist to a starving valued artist. But there were detractors in town saying *Memory Tricks* wasn't gay enough and accusing me of going mainstream—like it was that easy. At the same time a couple of my coolest friends were opening Josie's Cabaret and Juice Joint, a queer performance space in the Castro. I wanted to be involved right away so I booked four weeks in October of 1991 for *Marga Gomez Is Pretty, Witty & Gay*. I also wrote this second theatrical monologue to flaunt my queer credentials, and at the same time say "Fuck you" to those members of the mainstream, and my own community, who gave me grief. But the main reason I wrote *MGisPW&G* so soon after *Memory Tricks* was because I wanted to remind everyone that I can be very funny, and nothing but funny, from beginning to end. And then I asked myself, why is my self-worth dependent on making people laugh?

In October of 1993 I was invited by the Latino ensemble Culture Clash to work in a show they were developing for the Mark Taper Forum which focused, among other things, on the heritage of Latino performers. I began to write about my father. The vignette called *The Thirteen Minutes* was well received.

My father died in 1983 but he has appeared in my dreams regularly since then. I think he would want a piece written about him more than my mother would. If he were alive and healthy now he would probably do a one-man show about himself. He appeared in spectacular variety shows and later in half-empty dives but he always tried to maintain complete control over the productions. He was a very funny and charming man onstage, but moody and melancholy in private. Although a major theme of *Memory Tricks* is the fear and inevitability of becoming my mother, I still believe that I inherited more traits from my father. As I continue to remember and record his life I find good and bad parallels to my own experiences in relationships and as a performer. With these insights I can hopefully avoid making the same mistakes.

The three monologues have been referred to as a family trilogy, but I'm not so sure that *MGIsPW&G* is as revelatory as its companion pieces. It's a topical comedy I'm proud of, but my deeper truths are in between the lines of my parents' stories. Maybe I need to write a fourth piece about the real me. And I'll run my quartet indefinitely in rep off Broadway, Monday through Thursday, with a three-day weekend until I have a baby who will write my fifth monologue and add it to my pentagoria.

Memory Tricks

MARGA (MARGITA) *tells the following story on a stage that is bare except for a park bench.*

MARGITA

My mother complained whenever she made a deal with me so I wouldn't know that she got the better end. Like on the night of my seventh birthday. We were living on 169th Street in Manhattan. You could call that Harlem. We called it Washington Heights. We had the only house in the neighborhood. It was squished in by three big apartment buildings. And some of our neighbors would occasionally throw beer bottles and bags of trash into our yard. But my parents acted like we lived on a country estate and they would throw these high-class patio parties for their friends in Spanish show business and never invite those neighbors.

As WILLY, *her father*

I want to make a toast. Whiskey, please. *Para todos aquí—Bienvenidos y Salud.* [*Sound of beer bottle crashing.*]

MARGITA

But for my birthday they made an exception. I could invite kids from the neighborhood, although none of them could go because my party didn't start until ten on a school night.

[*Music and tiki lights come up.*]

So it was all adults. The first guest to arrive was Daisy the crazy dancer.

As DAISY

Margo, *mi amor. Besito. Pues,* I been workin'. Miami, Chicago, Union City. 'Cause who's better than us *tu sabes negra. Donde sta* Margita? No. That's your daughter? I didn't recognize her, she got so chubby. *Que gordita sta la nena.* God bless her. How do you do it, Margo?

MARGITA

And my mother bragged like she always bragged.

As MARGO

My daughter eats like a man.

[MARGO *and* DAISY *laugh.*]

As DAISY

Margita, I'm thirsty. Make me a Cuba libre.

MARGITA

And I said, "How do you make a Cuba libre?"

As DAISY

Well, first you *kill Castro.*

MARGITA

My parents had a lot of fascist friends like that and they were all there that night. Singers, actors, dancers, and they all had that grown-up Latino thing for pinching chubby children.

As RIVERA

So. This is Margita. Look at that face. Look at those cheeks. I have to pinch them. *Ven Aqua Pero, nena Ven Aqua.* [*Chases* MARGITA, *huffing and puffing and wiping his brow*] Margo, I don't think your daughter likes me.

MARGO

Margita, be nice to Rivera. He's going to do a story about me for *El Diario.*

As RIVERA

Si. Seguro. Margo is the number-one dancer in New York. Don't you agree, princess? Is your mother not a fantastic creature? *Claro que sí!* And you, little one. Monkey. *Ratoncito.* I got you a present but you have to guess which hand. Ahh. Ah. Got you. [*He pinches* MARGITA's *cheek.*]

MARGITA

After that my mother took me to her room for some deal making.
[*Music and tiki lights fade out.*]

MARGO

Margita, look at what Rivera gave you. An old torn twenty-dollar bill with Scotch tape. He must be drunk. What kind of present is that for a child? It looks like it was in the gutter. This is what he should have given you. Do you see how clean and crisp this five-dollar bill is? It's brand-new. I hate to do this but because it's your birthday, I'm going to trade my beautiful five-dollar bill for your disgusting twenty. Margita, it doesn't matter if it's twenty or one hundred dollars, when it's ripped no one will take it. It's no good. Okay, it's a deal. I don't know what I'm going to do with his old twenty. [*Stuffs it delicately into her cleavage*] You know, you are the most intelligent girl in the whole world. You're going to be just like me when you grow up.

Marga Gomez Is Pretty, Witty & Gay

The action takes place in MARGA's *bedroom the night before she is to appear on a national television talk show. There is a bed; a bedside table with a lamp; a radio; a clock; and some books.*

MARGA

. . . What are Sam Nunn and General Colin Powell and all the other colons so worried about? Why can't they lift the ban on gay men and lesbians in the military? Are they afraid that millions of us will enlist? I doubt it. Don't you have to get up early there? I'll do that one day a year—for the parade. We just want the right to enlist. Like my girlfriend and I want the right to have a legal wedding. But we don't want to get married. We're queer, not crazy. Are they afraid that if we could be out in the military we wouldn't obey orders? "Company, halt!" "No. We have to dance first." Or maybe they're afraid we won't salute anymore—just snap, "Yes, girl!"

Not that I'm pro-military, I'm anti-war. I just want to wear a sailor suit once in my life. Put a sailor suit on and go dancing for one night. White bell bottoms are hard to find. But this will be denied me because I'm considered a deviant.

My love is deeper than the ocean, wider than the sky, and too complex to be narrowly defined. But if you must apply a label—call me a dyke, maricona, queer, AC-DC, or an ice-pick-wielding lesbian . . . but not deviant. Because that implies I'm a superfreak in bed and I was raised Catholic. And I make love like a Catholic. Not good. With a lot of guilt. 'Cause we feel with enough guilt there's no sin. We're still pure in the eyes of the Lord. That's what I have to tell them tomorrow . . . the couch potatoes. The millions of Americans who will be watching me on television with that expression on their faces, the one they use to look at queers. [*Assumes homophobic expression*] This way no one will think that they're queer. "I'm normal, look at my face. This expression tells you that I have never met a homosexual and if I did meet one I would run because I am sure they would try to have sex with me."

I tried to get out of this. But there are so many of these homosexual talk shows. You dodge one and then there's: LESBIANS WITH LONG HAIR TOMORROW ON OPRAH. LESBIANS WHO HAVE NEVER BEEN ON OPRAH TOMORROW ON DONAHUE. GAY MEN WITH ORDINARY APARTMENTS . . . BISEXUAL, MONOGAMOUS GRANDPARENTS . . . How would . . . you know? And why are we being so unfair to straight people? Straight people can't get on talk shows anymore. No room! Straight people still have problems, don't they? HETEROSEXUAL MARRIAGES, WHY? AND WHAT ABOUT THE CHILDREN? It would be nice to share the limelight, because the demand for homosexual talk-show guests is exceeding our supply. Let's face it. We breed minimally, carefully, only after much thought and couples counseling. Contrary to popular belief we do not recruit. We can only impress.

And according to the Kinsey Report we are only ten percent of the population. Maybe it's a higher percentage in this room. But we're being used up by these talk shows. Squeezed . . . spent. I didn't ask to do this. This was not a choice for me. It was mandatory. They had my social security number. This is my lesbian jury duty. I'll serve my time to the best of my ability and who knows, I might make a difference. To just one person. Just one. That's not enough people for me to do this. I want *big* results. I want to be a role model to many lesbians, bisexuals, some gay men and even progressive heterosexuals of Latino descent. I can do it. I just need to change my personality.

I need to be more positive and perky. "Hello, America, I love a woman, yes!" A wonderful, wondrous, one-of-a-kind woman. Yes, I love a sister, a sensational, sensitive, sensuous sister. Not my sister, America! Just some woman, okay. We have a marriage just like your marriage, although ours is not legally recognized. No priest performed a ceremony. We received no avocado fondue sets from our relatives. Nobody tied tin cans to the back of our car and painted "Just Lesbians" on our windshield. But in every other way it's just like your marriage. We vowed to be together till death do us part. And we have been together for five years. Five years is a long time for any marriage. We live together. We sleep in the same bed. This bed America. [*Writhes on bed*] And you know this bed has seen a lot of action—until about four years ago. Just like your marriage. . . .

After, MARGA *has a confrontation with the cute young dykes, who live upstairs, and is left humiliated:*

When did I go from positive and perky to bitter and pathetic? I'm just like the first lesbians I ever saw. I was ten. I saw them on David Susskind's *Open End,* one of the first television talk shows. We were there. I never watched David Susskind back then, it was too dry, but my mom had it on that night. She turned down the volume very low. But I could hear David Susskind say, "Tonight's program might be offensive to people with certain religious beliefs and not suitable for children. I will be interviewing lady homosexuals." I could hear this upstairs, with my bedroom door closed and my radio blasting because by ten I had already developed *homosexual hearing.* I followed David Susskind's voice down the stairs into the living room and sat next to my mother on the sofa.

I made sure to put that homophobic expression on my face. So my mother wouldn't think I was mesmerized by the lady homosexuals and riveted to every word that came from their lesbian lips. They were very depressed, very gloomy. You don't get that blue unless you've broken up with Martina.

There were three of them. All disguised in raincoats, dark glasses, wigs. It was the wigs that made me want to be one.

[*Puffing on cigar, sitting with legs wide apart*]

"Mr. Susskind, I want to thank you for having the courage to present Cherene and Millie and me on your program. Cherene and Millie and me, those aren't our real names. She's not Cherene, she's not Millie, I'm not me. Those are just our, you know, our synonyms. We must cloak ourselves in a veil of secrecy or risk losing our employment as truck drivers."

[*Change to* SUSSKIND, *who is also smoking*]

"I only hope that everyone watching will realize that you are human beings who deserve to love whomever you choose. It's really nobody's business, is it? Yes, Cherene?"

As CHERENE, *smoking*

"It's just that when you live in a small Anytown, USA, then you better get used to people staring and whispering behind your back. Everybody from the bag boy at the A&P, to the Avon lady, she knows, to every neighbor in the neighborhood 'cause the Avon lady told them. Mr. Susskind. When you are in *The Life,* such as we, it's better to live in Greenwich Village or not to live at all! [*Breaks down and snaps out of it*]

"At this time we want to say hello to a new friend who is watching this at home with her mom on WNEW-TV in Massapequa, Long Island. Marga Gomez. Marga Gomez, welcome to the club, Cara Mia." [*Flicks her tongue lasciviously*]

My mother was in such denial she didn't pick up on Cherene's clue. Mr. Susskind and the lady homosexuals chain-smoked through the entire program. I think it was relaxing for them. I don't think they could have done it without the smokes. It was like they were in a smoky bar just before last call. And all that smoke curling up made *The Life* seem more mysterious.

The Life, that's what they called it back then when you were one of us. You were in *The Life!* It was short for The Hard and Painful *Life.* It sounded so dramatic. I loved drama. I was in the drama club in high school. I wanted to be in *The Life,* too. But I was too young. I asked my mother to buy me *Life* cereal and *Life* magazine. And for Christmas I got the game of *Life.*

[*Smoking*]

And as I moved the lonely game pieces around the board I pretended I was smoking *Life* cigarettes and living *The Life* life. But by the time I was old enough nobody called it *The Life* anymore. Because it sounded too isolating and politically incorrect. Now we say *The Community.* The Community is made up of all of us who twenty years ago would have been in *The Life.* And in *The Community* there is no smoking. [*Stamps out imaginary cigarette*]

Marga's incessant worrying leads her to her ex-Catholic schoolgirl's fear of eternal damnation for going on the talk show.

. . . God. God. God, this is Marga Gomez, a sinner. . . . God, please don't punish me. I've suffered enough. I'll do whatever you want. What do you want? Talk to me, God, talk to me. I'll be born again. I'll tell my girlfriend, "I cannot lay with you unless you're born again too. . . ." Okay, no girlfriend. I'll take unto me a husband. We'll have a Christian wedding. We'll never use birth control and I'll bear many Christian babies and they'll hate me and I'll hate them too. We'll be a typical Christian family, God, okay? And we'll leave San Francisco. We'll go someplace you like, God. What do you like? . . . Anaheim, Virginia. Just give me a sign, God.

[*The upstairs neighbors' stereo is heard loudly through the ceiling.*]

Excuse me, I'm talking to God. The nerve. And you know what? They're gay girls up there. They should have some consideration for me. But they're cute young dykes and they don't care what I think. They are very happy about their lives. They don't know what I know! Why do they have to have fun in the building? I don't. Why can't they go out to one of their trendy, hip, au courant clubs. They have so many clubs, why don't they use them? I know where they go. They go to the G Spot, Uranus, Club Snatch, Club Clit, Club Pussy! They go to all the body parts. When I was their age I went out every night. I was a regular at Club Rumors, The Hideaway, Don't Tell Mama's, The Incognito—places you could feel proud to be a lesbian. Sounds like they're starting their own club upstairs. Club Work My Nerves!

Oh, the dykes today, who can understand them? They buy expensive Italian black leather motorcycle jackets. You know, they're at least five hundred dollars a pop. Then they go and plaster political bumper stickers all over the back of these jackets. Labia Visibility. U.S. out of North America. Pete Wilson is an Asshole. Because our governor, Pete Wilson, vetoed the gay rights bill and also because he's an asshole. When we were twenty-one, we put bumper stickers on our cars, not on our jackets, because we wore down vests. Bumper stickers would pull out the feathers and then you'd have an asymmetrical down vest. Which was a fashion faux pas in the seventies. The only fashion faux pas there was in the seventies. But we expressed ourselves. We wore political buttons. Lots of them. We looked like refrigerators covered with magnets.

That's where they got the bumper sticker idea from, our confrontational, in-your-face buttons: How Dare You Presume I'm Heterosexual? Step back. And we thought this one was so funny, remember, Fesbian Leminist? Get it? Don't tell me we weren't cutting edge. We paved the way for you. Tell me we didn't pave the way for you. We wore the Frye boots so you could pierce your noses today! Oh, the dykes today with their piercings! So many earrings they wear! How can they hear with all those earrings? And the ones upstairs pierced their eyebrows. "Ow. Oww!" I can't even pluck my eyebrows. My girlfriend wanted us to pierce our noses so we can wear matching nose rings like all the other couples. But I couldn't take the pain. I said, "How about a clip-on, honey?" And now they're piercing nipples. Who started that? [*Fondling tits*]

Ooooo, this feels great. . . . Think I'll drive a spike through it! These girls are full of holes. They whistle while they work.

Photo copyright © by Dona Ann McAdams

SPALDING GRAY

Name: Spalding Gray
Stage Name: Spalding Gray
Birthdate/Birthplace: June 5, 1941/Providence, Rhode Island
"Raised Up" Where: Barrington, Rhode Island
Education: Emerson College, India, New York City!
Honors/Grants: Guggenheim and Obie
Influences/Mentors/Heroes: Helen Caldicott, Thomas Merton, Richard Schechner, Elizabeth LeCompte, Rambling Jack Elliot, Thomas Wolfe, Allen Ginsberg, Renee Shafransky
Places Performed: America, Europe, India, Great Britain, Australia, New York City
Pivotal Performance: *Rumstick Road* (1977)
Favorite Performance Experience: The night Shane Culkin threw up onstage during my long third-act monologue as the Stage Manager in the 1991 Broadway production of "Our Town."
Most Terrifying Performance Experience: The same
Favorite Prop or Costume: Plaid shirts; a glass of water
Hobbies: Downhill skiing
Reading List: Too long to list, a rainbow of books stretching between Becker's *Denial of Death* to *Zen Mind/Beginner's Mind*
Favorite Music: R.E.M. and Bach
Favorite Quote: "A voice whispered to me last night: 'There is no such thing as a voice whispering in the night.' " (Haidar Ansari)

Artist's Notes

This is how I work. I keep a journal, a Mead wide-ruled composition notebook. I only write in it when I feel the need. I rarely reread what I write. I think the simple act of writing leaves a sufficient memory trace to draw from. It's a way of engraving a memory in my memory bank. I don't type. I don't use a computer. My "five-pound universe" is all I work from. I also test out stories from my life with friends. I'm telling stories all the time. I like to talk a story, my mouth shaping the words. That feels good. I love all the elements in live performance: tone, silences, breath, presence, prana. Being there is everything.

So I start with my memory and begin to play with it and shape it. Memory, for all of us, is our first creative act. Everyone that remembers is creative, is *"re-membering."* Everyone that is remembering is always putting something together that is always not the original event. The origin is always lost to us forever. You can't eat the menu, but you can describe more than you can eat. And for me that's often more fun than eating.

I start by remembering sections of my life. It is like the ongoing soap opera of Spalding Gray. Then I begin to shape the memories around a particular high or low point in my life. I see these events as landmarks on the road from being to nonbeing. My monologue *Swimming to Cambodia* grew out of my experiences acting in the film *The Killing Fields*. *Terrors of Pleasure* grew out of stories about a disaster house I bought in the Catskills. *Monster in a Box* evolved around the struggle with writing my first novel and *Gray's Anatomy* dealt with the crisis of losing my sight in my left eye.

All my monologues are built with and in front of a live audience. Except for a pencil outline of key words there is no preperformance writing. I am doing a form of oral writing or improv. I prefer to call it oral composition because it is really headed toward being composed and set. Improv implies the desire to keep the monologue in a continuously open form. Of course, because it is a live performance each night, it is never finished and therefore always open to change. Although over the course of some two hundred performances, after a while the changes are minimal. But the opportunity for change is always there, which of course gives the monologue its spontaneous feeling. In fact I think that is one reason why the audience often feels I'm speaking the material for the first time. If this illusion does exist, I think it's because I am re-remembering each night. You see, because I have no prememorized text, when I sit down at my table, I am really in actual time doing or performing the act of recollection. This is a real event, an actual event that is not acted. It is a state of being. It's not a dramatic preconstruction. It is a fresh, in-the-moment event. On the other hand, a traditional actor in a more traditionally scripted play memorizes the text before the presentation and then employs methods to give the audience the illusion that he or she does not know what they will say next. They are pretending that they don't know the text. They're not trying to recollect it actually. For me where acting comes in, and this is where I need to single myself out as an "actor" rather than a "performance artist," where the acting comes in is when I begin over the course of the monologue's evolution to study myself and my behavior. I make audiotapes of all the early performances and then listen to them the following morning. Through studying my presentation, I begin to observe myself as a sort of character study.

I was trained to be a professional actor. I went through four years of traditional let's-pretend-scene-work at Emerson College as well as acting in over forty plays. It was this training that led me into being able to find the methods to play myself. Most performance artists are not trained in acting, although some are natural actors and find their way into it if in fact they want to go there. But when I first came to New York City in 1967, performance artists were rarely repeating themselves the way actors do. They would create and perform one event and then move on to an entirely new one. In my mind they were purists dedicating their lives to the exploration of an ongoing art form. Those were the days when art, for some of us, was like a state-supported religion. Now so many flounder with the new split of being a virgin in the day and a whore at night, or vice versa.

I am to some extent an inverted Method actor in the sense that I use autobiographic emotional memory to play myself rather than some other character. When it works, and it has for years, I'm able to transform what might be considered a psychopathology (divided or schizoid personality) into a creative act. The presentation of self in a theatrical setting.

There is of course a paradox here or at least two creative methods working together simultaneously. One is that I am present in the past. I am immediate and in the present in my act of remembering. And the other is that I am not only playing the remembered emotion of the past, but I am also sometimes playing that I am remembering it for the first time. This, of course, is all a very layered process depending on how developed the monologue is. When the monologue is at its freshest and most dynamic stage it is when these two paradoxes are in harmony together.

I think most of my fifteen autobiographic monologues go through three major stages: the raw, the restructured, and the lyrical. Of course, the always threatening fourth stage of "the overripe" is waiting for me at the end of a long run. The raw, or first stages of the monologue, are really me just talking to the audience trying with them to make sense of my life and therefore theirs. I in no way feel my work to be solipsistic or "navel gazing" as some critics have called it. I know my story is not far from your story, only the details are different. So in the beginning, I am finding my way with the audience. At that point in the work it is very much a dialogue as I begin to listen to tapes of the performance and become more aware of audience response and my own behavior, I become more self-conscious in a creative way. That is when the "art" begins to creep in. I begin to make creative choices, some minor and some more extreme. I will give you one example of what I consider an extreme choice, of what I would like to call creative editing or the rearrangement of my personal history.

My fourteenth monologue, *Gray's Anatomy*, grew out of one of the most traumatic events of my adult life, the loss of sight in my left eye. And of course one of the ways that I was dealing with this trauma was keeping a journal. Before I gave in to traditional surgery I was trying a number of alternative therapists including a visit to a Philippine psychic surgeon who had been brought to the United States from the Philippines. I was sure I was ready to give over completely to his on-hands manipulations including the fact that at some point his hands appeared to pass directly into the patients' flesh without any cutting or incision. But when I at last found myself lying on his operating table with his wife standing over me with a Bible in hand, I was too frightened to let him touch me. Not a very successful visit. So when it came time to include that episode in my new monologue, the poetic journalist surfaced in me thinking, wouldn't it make a much more dramatic story if I actually went to visit a psychic surgeon in the Philippines? Now, here is where what I referred to as my "poetic journalism" comes in. Any good fiction writer could take that first very dramatic visit to the psychic surgeon and without leaving the house shape it into a wonderfully rich and dramatic story.

I am not antifiction. Some of my favorite writers write fiction. I am just more comfortable with the experience of grounding myself in my actual personal history. Staying with the actual is not only a confirmation of my life but through the constant retelling of the story it is often a way into personal insight. I know I have lived when I have told you my story. By referring to the actual I bring it into the imaginary on its own terms.

So, well after I had experienced and collected all the material for my monologue, *Gray's Anatomy,* including having gone through surgery on my left eye, I began to feel that the story about the psychic surgeon didn't go far enough, was not dramatic enough. So at that point while working on the monologue I got *Traveler Magazine* to send me to the Philippines in order to research and visit six psychic surgeons. Then, after returning, I chose the most dramatic and flamboyant to become a new character and subject of my ongoing monologue. Was I living my life for the story? Was I creating the story? Yes and no. I was, I think, throwing myself into a structured unknown. I had no idea what would come out of it. I tried to be open. It was a very frightening experience.

Life is not a story, it's a life. It's a raw and unmediated thing-in-itself. We try to make sense of what happens to us and of who we are in terms of stories. For me, meaning only exists in a story.

I can remember riding beside the Barrington River on the back of my mother's bicycle and she was shouting out and celebrating because we had just dropped the bomb on the Japs in Hiroshima, and that meant that her two brothers were coming home. A lot of people died in World War II. I didn't know any.

The first death which occurred in *our* family was a cocker spaniel. Jill. Jealous Jill. We called her that because she was very jealous when my little brother was born. Jill died of distemper, which I thought meant bad temper because she was always jealous. But before she died, she bit me. Not *just* before she died, but some time before. I was harassing her with a rubber submarine, as I often did in the pantry of our house in Barrington, Rhode Island, and she turned on me and took a chunk out of my wrist; it looked like a bite out of an apple from my point of view. I guess it wasn't because I don't have a scar. I ran to my mother and she said, "You had it coming to you, dear, for harassing the dog with a rubber submarine."

When we were 14, a group of us used to try to knock ourselves out. Organically. By taking 20 deep breaths, head held between our legs, and then coming up real fast and blowing on our thumbs without letting out any air. Then all the blood would rush up or down, I don't know which, but it would rush somewhere, fast. And we would hope to pass out, but it never worked. Then we'd spin in circles until we all got so dizzy that we fell down. Then we went home.

So one day I was in the bathtub taking a very hot bath. It was a cold day and the radiator was going full blast. I got out of the tub and thought, well, this is a good time to knock myself out, I'm so dizzy, I'm halfway there. So I took 20 deep breaths and went right out, and on my way out I hit my head on the sink, which was kind of a double knockout. When I landed my arm fell against the radiator. I must have been out quite a long time because when I came to, I lifted my arm up and it was like this dripping-rare-red roast beef, third-degree burn. Actually it didn't hurt at all because I was in shock, a steam burn on my finger would have hurt more. I ran downstairs and showed it to my mother and she said, "Put some soap in it, dear, and wrap it in gauze." She was a Christian Scientist, so she had a distance on those things.

The next day when I got to school, the burn began to drip through the gauze. I went down to the infirmary, and when the nurse saw it she screamed, "What, you haven't been to a doctor with this? That's a third-degree burn. You've got to get to a doctor right away." So I went back home and told my mother what the nurse had said, and my mother said, "Well, it's your choice, dear. It's your choice."

Anyway, Jill died of distemper and I can remember I was wearing a tee shirt with a little red heart on it, and after the dog died I remember seeing the heart— my heart, the dog's heart, a heart—float up against a very clear blue sky. There was no pollution then in Barrington, Rhode Island. My mother told me that I stopped talking for a long time after that. She said they were thinking of taking me to a psychiatrist, but I don't know where they were going to find a psychiatrist in Barrington, Rhode Island, in 1946. Maybe they were thinking of Providence.

After Jill died, we got another dog, a beagle. We named the beagle Bugle because he made a sound like a bugle when he followed a scent. And Bugle would often get a scent in the fields behind our house where we used to play. We had a particular little grassy area we called "Hitler's hideout," inspired by World War II, where we would play Korean war games on weekends. My mother forbade them on Sundays and discouraged them on weekdays, so Saturdays were usually pretty intense.

We had toy rifles and used a galvanized metal garden bug sprayer for a flame thrower, which one of us would wear on his back. It was attached to a long hose which led to a little pump handle, and instead of DDT we would shoot water out of it. Also, Ralston Russell's father had brought back a German Luger from the war, as well as a German helmet, complete with swastikas. The Luger had had its firing pin removed, but it was very real. The helmet seemed even more real. You could almost smell the dead German's sweat on the leather band inside. I assumed someone had taken this helmet right off a dead soldier, but I couldn't imagine Mr. Russell doing that. He was a Christian Science practitioner during the war and I didn't think he'd seen much combat. I had always thought of him as a gray flannel mystic in his little office off their basement rec room where he went every day, dressed in a three-piece suit, to pray for sick people. They didn't even have to be there. He just sat and concentrated real hard on knowing "the truth" and sent out all his thoughts to wherever his patients were lying, waiting to get better. But maybe Mr. Russell did see action. Maybe he was in the field trying to bring dead GIs back to life. But the gun and helmet were very real. I was sure I could smell the enemy on them.

Judy Griggs was the only girl in the neighborhood and she lived next door to us. Her father was my father's boss at the screw-machine plant, and I remember that they had a very big yard with an apple orchard at the end of it. Judy played a game with us in her yard called "Ice Lady." The Griggses had a clothesline shaped like the Pentagon, and Mrs. Griggs would hang her sheets out to dry on it. Judy, who was the Ice Lady, would chase us through the rows of clean sheets until she touched one of us, and we had to freeze and stand still like a statue. Judy was queen of her backyard, but she wanted more. She wanted to be a member of our gang, which had only four of us in it, all boys. Judy tried to prove to us that she was a boy by putting a garden hose between her legs while her sister, Bethany, turned on the water. Once she used a turkey baster, but that still wasn't enough to convince us. We forced her to go into the fields with us and pull down her pants to show us that she really was a boy. Instead of a tinkler we saw her, well, I don't think we had a name for it actually, but I remember it as this very small, fleshy slit where her tinkler might have been if she had one. Then we took her into our chicken coop and tortured her mildly by tying her to a post and stirring up all the dust from the dirt floor with a broom. We'd leave her there until the dust settled, and she seemed to like it. At least she gave every sign of liking it.

The Griggses had hired an Italian yard man named Tony Pazzulo. Tony was lots of fun—he used to pick us up and swing us around and bury us under piles of raked leaves. The most fun was being thrown around by him. Our fathers, Dad and Mr. Griggs, never touched us in that rough, playful way, and we all loved it. One day Tony took the cover off the cesspool for some reason and we all looked down into it. It was a great dark pool of "grunts" and "doots" (we called the big ones "grunts" and the small ones "doots"), and suddenly the Griggses' yard took on a new dimension, even after Tony put the cesspool cover back on.

Shortly after Tony uncovered the cesspool, Mr. Griggs bought a whole bunch of chickens. One Saturday he cut off all their heads while we watched. He used the stump of a big tree for a chopping block and held the chickens' heads down on it while he cut them off with an ax. Then the chickens ran headless around the yard with blood spurting from their necks until they flopped down on the ground and died.

Soon after Judy Griggs pulled her pants down, houses began to grow in the back fields. We played in the foundations and among the electrical wires and saw wallboards go on and the houses get finished and the new neighbors move in. I can remember once being up on some scaffolding and seeing some boards lying against a house, and I just decided to push them down on my friend Tim Morton. I didn't think about it. I just pushed and they fell and crushed him. I thought I had killed him, not only because of the way he was lying down there, but also because of the way his father ran, jumping over the hedge, to pick up Tim's limp body in his arms. I was terrified. I ducked back in through the window of the unfinished house to hide, and my older brother, Rocky, who stayed out on the scaffolding, had to take the blame. Tony Morton just stood there with his son's broken body in his arms, yelling up at Rocky, "I'll be back to deal with you, my friend." I felt scared for Rocky. I felt scared for all of us.

Not long after that, Tim died of lung cancer. He was very young and no one seemed able to diagnose it. They thought it was what they called a lung fungus that had been brought back by American soldiers from the Korean War. Tim's death was a strange kind of relief because we'd always heard that one in four would have to die of something—cancer, tuberculosis, polio, whatever—so I always wondered who would be the *one* of the four of us who hung out together. That was often on my mind.

I call the woman in Idaho, and she gives me all the information. I actually called her—this is totally unlike me. I did it. I flew to the Philippines; I flew to Manila, without drinking once on the plane. I arrive, and I fly off to the north immediately to meet this healer named Pini Lopa, also known as the "Elvis Presley of psychic surgeons."

I find out why when I arrive.

I get there; I check into my hotel, and I go over to his place, which is called the Paramount Inn—it used to be the Red Monkey Disco—and he is there, not operating, as it turns out, because it's evening, but entertaining forty Japanese who are all there to be operated on. Actually, twenty have come for operations, and the other twenty have come to photograph the others while they're being operated on.

They're all there. There's no booze at all. It's a totally vegetarian gathering. There's Pini Lopa, and he's about fifty-seven years old. He's got gold chains around his neck; he's got powder-white hair that's cut in a Little Lord Fauntleroy style. He's in a powder-blue suit, wearing these Palm Beach–white lattice leisure shoes, and he's singing Frank Sinatra songs out of tune, with a band backup.

He's got a Desi Arnaz/Ricky Ricardo, babba-loo kind of energy, like a performer from Vegas. He's singing "I did it my way," chain-smoking cigarettes. He sounds like Leonard Cohen without the passion.

He's supposed to be the top psychic surgeon who operated on this woman! I'm saying to myself, No judgment! No judgment! I'm just going to hang in here, take it easy. I made it here without having any drinks on the plane. I'm just going to try to relax and maintain my diet and go through with this thing.

After he takes a little break, and the band takes a break, I introduce myself. He's smoking up a storm, and he's really a cocky little guy, just incredible. I start talking to him.

I tell him that I was sent by this woman; he remembers the woman. I tell him it is for an eye problem. Oh, he assures me that he's very good at eyes. In fact he's been known to pull an eye right out of the skull, lift it up, display it, wash it off, and put it back into the person's eye socket.

I said, "How do you reconnect the veins after that? How do they get all hitched up?"

He said, "We don't know. This is a mystery."

I can't believe this is going on. I go back to my hotel, and I get very little sleep that night.

The next morning, I'm supposed to go in for the operation. Nine-thirty is when I'm supposed to go in. And I have the choice to be operated on, or to observe the operations. So I have to see what I feel about it.

So I arrive, and first everyone's praying. There's a chapel. The Japanese have a Shinto shrine; I'm in front of Jesus. I don't know what to do with him. I'm mainly just sitting there thinking, What am I doing, what am I doing, what am I doing? After the praying is done, we go down this long corridor to enter the operation chamber. On the walls of the corridor are pictures of Pini Lopa performing operations. It's worse than the Mayo Family Clinic book. There are color photos of him, beginning to pull an eye out of the socket. Pictures of him pulling hemorrhoids out of someone's ass.

And at the end of this long corridor is a big crucifix. Some people are bowing and genuflecting to it. You have to realize that we're in the Philippines, where at Easter time they actually crucify themselves, nail themselves to crosses.

But what I was about to see—I was completely unprepared for. I couldn't believe my eyes. It was like a Halloween situation. Like when a kid is going into a Halloween funhouse? That's what I felt like. I felt like a frightened little kid when I walked into that room.

This operating room is divided in half, between the observation area—there are a lot of Japanese in there with videocameras set up—and the operating arena. There's a railing there, and there are about fifteen or twenty Japanese in just their underwear. The women are bare-breasted. There, under the fluorescent light, is a table with a plastic cover. Pini is standing there, with his eyes rolled up in his head, in a semi-trance, wearing a blue surgical gown, a butcher's apron, and white Palm Beach leisure shoes. A picture of Christ is behind him, and at the end of the table are two men with mops.

I decide I'm going to watch that day.

It begins. Here's what I saw. The Japanese who were there and who were ready to be operated on run up. The first woman lies down on the operating table. Pini puts his hand on her belly and his fingers seem to go right into her stomach. Blood shoots up into the air, six feet into the air, hitting the other naked Japanese. They're all shouting, "Woo! Oooh! Woooow!" like little children running under a bloody sprinkler in summertime. Pini's men are down on the floor with the mops, mopping the blood up. This woman jumps off the table and goes around to the other end of the line, getting ready to go again.

A man jumps up on the table. Pini seems to reach into his stomach and pull out what looks like a meatball the size of a cantaloupe. He hurls it into a plastic bucket. This man gets up and goes around to the other side of the table. A woman gets up the table, and Pini begins to work on her Adam's apple. What looks like this huge tongue of yellow and green pus comes out of her neck. He's catching it in a cup. She goes around the table and comes around the other side. Each one of them is paying three hundred dollars every time he touches them. And believe me, he's not going anywhere in the room to get stuff. It appears that his hands are empty, and that he is really pulling this stuff out of these people.

Another man gets up on the table, and Pini pulls out big bloody grapes this time and begins to handle them like a kid playing with his own shit. He hurls them down on the man's chest. Pini's wife comes over with gauze to sop them up, and throws them into a bucket. The man goes around again. A Japanese man walks up to the table, lies down on his stomach, pulls his pants down, exposes his firm, round rump, and Pini just starts reaching in and up. "Hold still, hold still, hold still," he says, and out comes what looks like spaghetti with red meat sauce. It's supposed to be hemorrhoids. *Thupp!* he hurls them into the bucket. That man goes around; everyone goes through one more time, has the exact same thing done to them, and then Pini says, "Finished!"

Pini crosses himself, he crosses everyone, blesses them, goes over and bows to the crucifix on the wall, blesses himself in front of it, bends over, wipes some blood off his white lattice leisure shoes, lights a cigarette, and leaves.

I go back to my hotel and have my first drink.

I have twelve of them in fact. Twelve San Miguel beers. I'm ripped, and I have no one to talk to. The Japanese aren't speaking any English. I'm thinking, Whoa, my God, what's going to happen to me? How could I spend all my money on coming to a place like this? Was I crazy? What a waste of money. I can't go through with this operation! I can't. "Ohhh, God. Give me another beer." The only people who speak English are the Filipino waiters, and I'm saying, "Oh my God, I went to Pini Lopa today. What a mess!"

One waiter looks at me and says, "Pini Lopa? Oh sir, if you go to Pini Lopa and you believe, you will be healed. But if you do not believe you must go home, because you must believe in order to get healed."

"Is belief a prerequisite? I didn't know that. I thought Pini was going to be like Jesus or E.T. One touch. No blood. God, God, God, help me, give me another drink."

"Sir, please, you must believe. You must believe in Pini Lopa."

"I don't believe in anything. Doubt is my bottom line. The only thing I don't doubt is my own doubt. And give me another beer."

"But sir, you have a Creator. Who is your Creator? Don't you believe in your Creator?"

"I don't know who my Creator was. I always thought I was idiopathic. You know. No known cause."

"But sir—"

"Oh God, God, what am I going to do? I wish I could get on the telephone. I don't know what time it is in the States. Oh God God God—"

"Sir, you are a very religious man, I can tell."

"Why do you say that?"

"You keep praying. All you say is, 'Oh God, oh God, oh God.' This is praying."

I go to bed, but I can't sleep. All I can see is meatballs flying through the air in my room. It's a nightmare. I finally get a little sleep and I wake up and realize what it is that I'm terrified of; I haven't faced it. It's AIDS! Of course, every American is blood phobic. My good God, the Japanese don't seem to be upset about it.

They say, "Oh, no AIDS in Tokyo, not really, no."

The Filipinos are telling me there's no AIDS in the Philippines either. They tell me that there has been no infection, ever, from psychic surgery. In the entire history of psychic surgery there's never been any known infection. They're like the people at Bondi Beach in Australia, who used to tell me that there hadn't been shark attacks in fifty years.

I said, "It's time. And I'm the one."

I was very paranoid. I knew that I had to speak to Pini before the operation. I ask for a private consultation. I can tell that he's really annoyed with me, the only American there, acting odd, hypochondriacal, frightened.

I ask him, "Please, can you work with me privately in my hotel room?"

"No."

"Please, just this once, look, if you could just wash your hands with alcohol and come over to my room—"

"No. No. We do only the group operation here. What is your problem?"

"I'm afraid of AIDS."

"No, no. Don't worry. I can't operate on people with the AIDS. I'd like to be able to, but—I tried, you see, one time, and the person didn't know he had the

AIDS, but my hands they know. They will not enter. They will not penetrate the body. So you have no fear, you see, for that.

"Also, if you are thinking of the AIDS all the time, and I'm sure you do, you will get it. You will manifest it through your thought, you see."

At this point, I tried to tell him the story about the man who was told that if he stirred a pot of water long enough without once thinking of elephants, it would turn into gold. . . .

But Pini didn't want to hear that story. He wanted to operate, and it was time. He left me; I went into the operation chamber, and I thought, I've got to get on that table. The only way I was going to get on that table was if I got right in with the Japanese—just got right in the middle of that kamikaze energy. The way they would jump on that table! It was incredible. I have never seen people move with such determination and lack of doubt. They were all laughing, having such a good time.

I stripped to my red underwear, I got in the middle, and the Japanese began to go up to the table. Out come the bloody grapes again! Out come the meatballs! My time comes, and I jump on. It's like jumping right into a Francis Bacon painting. Right into a Bosch painting. Right into a Catholic morgue. All this stuff is all on the floor, reeking of blood. I'm lying there quaking on the table, crying out, "It's my eye! Remember, my left eye! Please! Don't pull any meatballs out of me!"

Pini is looking down at me like I'm crazy.

First, he wipes his hands off. He's got short sleeves on. He rinses his hands off in what looks like a bucket of blood, really. His hands are a little pink, all right, but clear. He shows me his hands; there is nothing in them. Nothing in either one. His sleeves are rolled up.

He picks up some cotton gauze, and of course that's where the Amazing Randi and all the debunkers say the fakers hide the blood—in the gauze. But it's almost like he could read my mind. He opens the gauze to show me: nothing in that, either. You know: Disbeliever, Doubting Thomas, here you go.

He begins and heads right for my eye with his fingers. He is pushing in to either side of my eye, and at that moment, I really feel like my eye is a vagina and his two fingers are erect bloody penises coming at me. I'm having a shutdown virgin response here.

As soon as his fingers hit my eye, blood gushes out. Blood clots. Blood. Blood! It's pouring down and someone is sopping it off my face. It doesn't feel like it's coming out of my eye, but it's coming from somewhere! He pulls his fingers out, the blood stops, and I run—not to the end of the line, but to the men's room—immediately, to look at my eye. There's no blood there! There's no leftover blood, and the eye's not any better. But Pini tells me that he wants to do this to me again, and it's going to be fifty dollars each time he touches me. He wants to do it for seven days, twice a day—that's fourteen operations. That's what he wants to do to heal me.

I think, My God, my God! Why can't he be like E.T.? Come on! Fourteen operations! I thought this man had power. I couldn't do it; I couldn't feel comfortable. I couldn't force myself to be comfortable with this man.

I kept hearing my childhood friends from Barrington, Rhode Island—the ones who asked me what it would take to make me go to a doctor—saying, "What if you went to this guy who started pulling meatballs out of you the size of melons. Would you go to a doctor thennnnn?"

"YES!!!"

Photo copyright © by Dona Ann McAdams

DANNY HOCH

Name: Danny Hoch
Stage Name: Danny Hoch
Birthdate/Birthplace: November 23, 1970/Queens, New York City
"Raised Up" Where: Queens and Brooklyn
Education: High School of Performing Arts, New York City
North Carolina School of the Arts
British American Drama Academy, London
Honors/Grants: Obie Award, 1994; NEA Solo Theater Fellowship, 1994; *Village Voice*
Culture's Best and Brightest, 1993; Fringe First Award, 1995; Queens Teen Talent Show
Winner, 1985.
Influences/Mentors/Heroes: Rhodessa Jones, Roger Guenveur Smith, Nasty Nas,
TLA-Rock, Soulsonic Force, Ismael Miranda, Eddie Palmieri, Pato Banton, all peoples
locked down
Places Performed: Next Stage Company, Gas Station, NADA, One Dream Theatre, P.S.
122, Public Theater (NYC); Mark Taper II (Los Angeles); Baltimore Theatre Project; Organic
Theater (Chicago); Mixed Blood Theater, Walker Arts Center (Minneapolis); Solo Mio
Festival (San Francisco); Flying Solo Festival (Louisville); International Fringe Theatre
Festival (Edinburgh); International Theatre Festival (Havana)
Pivotal Performance: The first of many at C-74 Adolescent Reception Detention Center,
Riker's Island, with NYU's Creative Arts Team
Favorite Performance Experience: Doing theater five days a week in jails and high
schools
Most Terrifying Performance Experience: I opened for Gil Scott Heron in front of five
thousand people in Central Park. Never do theater for five thousand people in a park who
are drinking and expecting to see a band.
Favorite Prop or Costume: Black shirt, black pants
Hobbies: Going on missions to find a better roti than the last. Listening to radio and
watching TV in languages that I don't speak.
Reading List: *Black Looks* by bell hooks; *The Colonizer and the Colonized* by Albert
Memmi; *Wretched of the Earth* by Frantz Fanon
Favorite Music: Strictly NYC hip-hop, salsa, merengue
Favorite Quote: "There's a war goin on outside no one is safe from,
         You could run but you can't hide forever
         From these streets that we done took
         You walkin with your head down, scared to look
         You shook . . ."
         —Mobb Deep

Artist's Notes

Rarely will I sit down and actually write a character. To me the act of writing is about mental and visual literature and comes from a mental, intellectual place. Solo theater and solo performance in general should provoke *visceral* reactions in an audience. It's okay to have intellectual reactions from an audience, but if you start intellectually, you will end there and never arrive at a visceral place. I don't believe in tape-recording people or sitting with them and taking notes, with the intent of portraying them on-stage. This to me serves the purpose of documentary and not theater. My characters developed from doing what was natural to me, which was simply to speak what was in my head. My affinity towards oral language and di-alect can probably be attributed to my growing up with a speech pathologist as my mother. But rather than teaching me how to speak properly, she taught me how to listen.

The solo griots in ancient Africa, Asia, and the Americas never scripted their pieces. Everything is oral. The griot used pantomime, masks, accents, magic, dance, song, and possession to convey history, give moral teaching, and to entertain about social issues affecting the community. What inter-ests me is taking the stories and characters of my community in their oral form, and shaping them into cathartic entertainment. My community, how-ever, is a unique one.

I grew up during the birth of hip-hop culture in a towering brick-and-asphalt Queens neighborhood where there was no racial majority. My god-mother was Cuban, my neighbors African-American, West Indian, Puerto Rican, Israeli, Senegalese, and then some. I was a rapper, break-dancer, graffiti artist, and drug dealer by the time of my bar mitzvah. Given this childhood, my experience with language is chock-full of multiculture. My inner monologue has always been in nonstandard English, Spanish, and British West Indian patois. When I used to see Dan Rather on the news, I thought for a while that he was broadcasting from another country.

Having gone to theater school, I was trained in drama, comedy, and plain old acting. But I was also trained to drop all the language I grew up with so I could land a role in an empty sitcom, or a "traditional" interpretation of Shakespeare. As I became more politically and socially aware, this did not interest me at all. There were many "voices" in my head that used to come out when I was a child. Gradually they began to be accompanied by my po-litical one. I began to search for the roots of theater and the role of the solo actor in ancient cultures. This was very important to me because I knew I was supposed to perform for people, but if I had to degrade myself at an-other audition for some bullshit, I was gonna kill someone. I knew that I wasn't a stand-up comedian because although people were in hysterics when I would perform, there were moments of tense silence and some peo-ple would cry. By the time I was eighteen, I was frustrated with the capital-ist approach of my theater training and I left the conservatory. But before I did, the students had an opportunity to do whatever they wanted in front of the whole school for fifteen minutes. Some people did abstract dance to abstract music. Some people got naked and read Sam Shepard poems. I went onstage with an alarm clock and set it for fifteen minutes. I never rehearsed for this. I had four characters in my head. A Jamaican man from Brooklyn in search of a Nissan Maxima; a flaming Cuban methadone addict trying to put his life together; a sixteen-year-old crack dealer whose little brother gets killed in crossfire; a nineteen-year-old kid from the Bronx with severe brain disorder whose mother smoked cocaine when she was pregnant. I improvised all four, and let the oral language in my head take me on a riff, kind of like a jazz musician. People laughed and people cried. This was the beginning of my first show, *Pot Melting*.

Setups for Doris, Flex, and Message to the Bluntman

Doris

This piece is from *Some People*. She is the ninth character in the show. She's in her midsixties and lives in any of the outer boroughs of NYC. When she talks, it's as if she screams with no effort. Thus, when she screams, the earth shakes.

Flex

This piece is the tenth character in *Some People*. Flex is nineteen and lives in Brooklyn, New York. He and Doris come next to each other on purpose. See if you can figure out why. *"Cash rules everything around me, C.R.E.A.M., get the money, dolla dolla bill, yaw'll."* (Wu-Tang Clan, 1993)

Message to the Bluntman

I first performed this piece for a live audience at a taping for MTV's *Spoken Word Series*. I could feel the audience, which was very diverse in age, color, and sex. I could feel them sweating their lunch out. It was as if everybody had a reason to be very, very nervous. They had all heard Vanilla Ice and Snow before. But they never heard a white kid say some shit like this before, and were certainly not expecting it. I still catch beef over this piece, from people that say, "You shouldn't be sayin' that, you're white." In response I say, "If I was black, would you see me on MTV sayin' that? And who would really listen? The truth is brutal, kid."

Doris

[DORIS, *a mother of one in her midsixties, is in her kitchen, using her power tool, the phone, to communicate with some people*]

Will you shush! So shah! Martin, the guy is coming in five minutes. So leave the thing alone! In five minutes he'll be here and he'll fix the whole thing. . . . I know the phone is ringing, I'm letting it ring. . . . So let me let it ring! [*Answers phone*] Hello? Who is this? Who? Oh, hi! How are you? No, what are you interrupting? You're interrupting nothing. Oy, no, no. I'm sitting here, I'm . . . What wire, Martin? What wire? I'm supposed to know what wire you're talking about? Oh, that wire, sure. Keep futzing with the wire and blow yourself up. You're not blowing *me* up! . . . No, I'm fine. Martin's fine. David's fine. Yeah, in fact, I'm supposed to call my sonny boy in five minutes so I'll talk quick. No, no, he's fine. How's your daughter? Gonna marry to who? Not the same Nigerian guy? Does she love him? So, she loves him and she'll be happy and they'll be happy. Listen, did she make sure he's all tested with all whatever he needs with shots and everything? No, I'm just saying, because especially with he's from Africa, she should make sure, 'cause I saw in *The Times*. How terrible. Isn't it? He's a doctor, the guy? And he's from Nigeria? Eh, well, still. No, he doesn't see her anymore. Eh, Roz, to tell you the truth, I had a bad feeling about her when I first met her. She's a sweet girl, and she's attractive, but there was something creepy about her. She had a creepy aura. Anyway. Did I tell you what he's doing now, my son? Oh, Roz, he goes with this group of people and they go into all the bad neighborhoods, and I gotta tell ya, I am so . . . Yeah, I think it's like the Peace Corps, but in New York. Who? David? Hold on, let me ask. . . . Martin! Does David get insurance with the job? . . . David, your son. Does he get insurance with the job, the thing with the . . . Never mind, you're not understanding me. . . . You're not understanding me, never mind! Listen, I'll ask him when I call him. Listen, mamala, I gotta go, darling, okay? I'll call you back after. Okay, bye. [*She clicks the phone only to make another call*] Martin! How do I do the memory with the phone, I forgot? The memory, for David, I know I put for number one, but after I do the star button or before? . . . The pound button? There's no pound button, Martin. . . . There's no pound button, I'm looking at the phone! Uhh, I'm doing the star! . . . All right, shush, it's ringing! It's ringing and I can't hear! Will you keep with the wires, keep breaking the thing more, more break it! . . . Hello, David, sweetheart, it's your mommyface, listen . . . Hello? Hi, you're there? So what are you screening your phone calls, someone's after you? So pick up the phone, it's your mother calling, it's a secret that you're there? Uhh, you make me nervous with this machine, one day I'll call it'll say, 'Hi, this is David, I'm not here from they killed me on the train or wherever.' All right, I'm relaxed, I just worry with you in all these . . . uch. Yes, David, but not everyone takes the trains by theirself to the South Bronx or wherever. Sure, the people that live there, but they're different. . . . I mean not that they're different, they're the same as us, everyone is the same, but, all right, never mind, it's just diffcrent, you don't get it, forget it. You can't take a cab sometimes? So let everybody else take the train, you're not them, you have to do what they do? All right, I'm relaxed. Anyway, bubelah, what I wanna ask ya . . . Does your job, do they give you health insurance? So you'll pay the ten dollars and you'll have it. How much more? That's ridiculous, are you sure? All right, so I'll pay it. David, I'm not an extravagant person that I'm saving for a yacht, I'll be happy to pay for it. Or if you want you could go on the plan your father and I have, hold on. . . . Martin! What's the deductible on the insurance? What's that noise? *Now* you're drilling? What are you drilling? The guy is coming, Martin! . . . The deductible! On the Blue Cross, the Blue Cross! . . . That's what I'm asking you, how much! . . . Uh, forget it. Forget! It! . . . Listen, David, honey, we'll call the 1-800, wait, I'm on the phone with David! Hello . . . *which David?* Wait one second. Martin! When the guy comes for the thing, you're staying with him, right? . . . What do you mean, you're going for a walk? Martin, I'm not letting these people into my house, I don't know who they are, the minorities or whoever. Oy, you hear this from your father? Where is he walking? In front of a truck he'll walk. You're right, David, they could be anybody. They could be Jewish, whoever, I'm just saying I'm not staying here alone. While he'll be going for a walk they'll be drilling me in the head for the television. . . . All right. David. I said they didn't have to be minorities. Oy, you're such a mensch, you're a sweetheart, you're very caring, I'm very proud of you, *mmwa!* So listen, tatala, do you wanna do with the Blue Cross? What, no? Everyone has to have health insurance, David. So fine, thirty-six percent of the country doesn't have it, you're not thirty-six percent, you're my son. So David, let the thirty-six percent sit for ten hours waiting in some dirty emergency room somewhere bleeding to death with flies and urine and five hundred sick people with tuberculosis. My son . . . my son is not gonna sit waiting in some clinic full of people's phlegm all over the floor and everyone's coughing with no air. No, David. God forbid. David, God forbid I should be concerned already enough that my son doesn't get shot by some black kid, *or* white kid, in one of these places, but that he should go to a professional Jewish hospital? . . . I know white people shoot people with guns, David, but not on the train. David, look, I know I raised you to believe that everyone's equal, and not to be into materials, and to accept people no matter who they are, but David, I am your mother and I know you're an adult, but there are some things about reality that you're not understanding. I can't be concerned about my son? I'm not the one yelling, you're yelling! I just want you to be happy and not dead. David, don't hang up, I want to talk to you. I am proud of you. I brag to all my friends and they all can't believe it. They all say, 'I can't believe it.' Is it too much to ask for you to have health insurance? How do you know nothing'll happen? You have a crystal ball? . . . David, they'll have one of their riots, these people, and you'll be the first one they'll shoot. They shoot people, David, I read *The New York Times*, not the *Post*, the *Times*, and I see them. They shoot *each other*. And let me tell you something, David, I feel very bad. I wish these kids didn't have to grow up with all violence and uhh . . . a mess, and my heart goes out to them, it does, but let them shoot each other and not you, that's the way I feel. . . . I am not racist, David! Don't you dare call me racist! Because if you remember, I let you have all your black and Puerto Rican and Iranian friends at your bar mitzvah, and I treated them just like I treated your Jewish friends. You wanna see racist? Go read with this guy in the paper, bloodsuckers, he said. . . . I am not a *scared-liberal-complaining-reactionary*. What does that mean? When they'll wanna stick you in an oven you'll still defend this guy? You wanna be another martyr, David? You wanna be one of the Jewish kids in Mississippi with the voter registration and they killed them, them and some black guy? How is it possible for Jews to be prejudiced when everyone is prejudiced all the time against the Jews? David, we had lots of black neighbors before we moved and we got along fine. My friend Roz's daughter Cynthia is marrying a Nigerian guy and he's a doctor! . . . No, David, the difference is, did I call them bloodsuckers? I said they shoot people, I didn't call names. How am I guilty? I'm guilty of reading *The New York Times*? David, how come you'll never defend the Jews? You're Jewish but you'll never empathize with your own people. What is there to empathize? David, six million . . . The Jews are *still* victims. . . . How am I a victim in the suburbs in 1994? . . . Not because I have a juicer and an espresso machine makes me a vict—Black people have juicers and espresso makers too! What are you screaming? What bad thing did I do? I did something bad to them? David, I'm not crazy. You ask people if they'll be in these neighborhoods on the train . . . whatever people. You ask them if they'll defend this guy. The black kid who's in jail for murder I should defend? For what? Where do you get this from? Why are you so angry, you're not even black? Why are you angry at your own people? Why are you so angry at me, I'm your mother? . . . Oy, all right, calm down. Stop yelling! Listen to me. Are you still coming to the Seder on Thursday? Your aunt Barbara's coming and so is your cousin Mark. Mark, the high school principal, gay Mark. And I promise I won't start an argument with you, or Mark. Okay, stop yelling. Are you coming? Well, if you don't I'll be very upset. Fine, listen, I'm not angry at you. Are you angry at *me*? All right, well, it's all right, I'm your mother. Okay, I love you. Bye . . . Okay, stop screaming. Okay, bye, *mmwa!* [DORIS *hangs up the phone*] Martin . . . I'm going for a walk. [*She exits*]

Flex

[FLEX, *nineteen, pants saggin, timbos draggin, five beepers and a chewstick approaches a Chinese take-out restaurant rapping to a song on his Walkman and enters*] Hey yo, you on line? Aight then. [FLEX *looks up at the picture menus on the wall above his head*] . . . Hey yo I'm still lookin man. Damn man, niggas try to rush me man. . . . Hey yo Chinaman! Chinaman! Yo Chinese yo! Lemme get Number Seven yo. . . . Number Seven! Hey yo I ain't look on there yo, I'm lookin right there! Niggas got signs up, don't know what the fuck they got up. . . . Hah? Oh Vegetable Lo Mein? Oh I ain't see that right there, good lookin. Yo, Vegetable Lo Mein son, small. Small, you know what I'm sayin small? Small! . . . Hey yo my man, no mushrooms, no onions in that yo. Mushrooms, you know mushrooms? No mushrooms. And no onions . . . Onions! You know what a onion is? I don't eat that shit. I'ma tell you what, I find mushrooms and onions in that shit, you could take that shit back, word up. Hey yo son, how long yo? How long? How long? . . . Right, I'mo be back then. [FLEX *exits to street, rapping to another song and sees his boy*] Oh shit! Wasup kid? Oh my god! It's the god! It's the god right now. It's that nigga Al! Oh snap. Wasup with you man? Goddamn. I ain't seen you in the longest time. What you been up to? Word? I hear dat, I hear dat. . . . Nuttin man, I'm about to get some food in here right quick, go pick up my little brother from school. Hey yo it's good to see you man. Hey yo check this, I got five beepers kid, you think I'm lyin? Check them shits boy. One, two, three, four, Denent! What you wanna do bout that? These four are like regular, they go like, beep, beep. But this joint right here, this shit go like this, *ooh-ooh!* Shit's all disco style. You should hang out with me for a while and you could hear that shit go off. Hey yo so what you up to lately kid? What you gonna do next year though? . . . Get the fuck outta here! Scholarship? See that's cuz you all on that braniac tip. You thought I forgot. I don't forget shit boy. Remember we used to be in school, and we used to be in the library throwin shit and the teacher used to come by and we'd be like . . . But you was really readin that shit though right. So what you gonna study? You gonna study business right? My man gonna make mad loot in this piece! . . . Black history? My man said, black history yo. Tah ha. This nigga buggin yo! Oh shit, Harriet Tubman, Freedom Fighter, Denent! Your ass gonna be broke as hell beggin in the street and whatnot. Nah, I don't mean to break man, you get mad props for that shit, you get respect. Somebody gotta do that shit right? I'm sayin though, I gotta get that loot son, word is bond. I'm workin this job too, I'm makin bills boy. You want me to make a phone call, you need some extra cash before you take off to school, I could make that phone call for you. These niggas got me workin mad hard. Eight to eight every day, liftin mad concrete type shit. Cause they buildin this new jail right, so they need construction heads, seventeen a hour kid. I'm makin bank. . . . I don't know what I'mo do next year. I think I'mo start a Blunt factory. Nah I'm playin. I don't smoke that shit god. . . . I don't smoke nothin. My lungs is pure yo. This the god right here. I'm sayin how niggas goin buy into that? Let them white kids smoke them drugs man. They make that shit. Yeah right, crack also yo. How black people gonna smoke somethin that's white? You know mad white people be smokin it too, but you aint seen them on CNN gettin lifted though. . . . Right but see, you know what bother me? How one second niggas is like, oh yeah the white man this, white man that. Next second they smokin Phillies tryin to watch David Letterman. Explain that. I'm sayin, one second they like, yeah yeah yeah. Next second they like, yeah yeah yeah. You know what I'm sayin? I'ma tell you like this Al, it's already nuf white kids out here that's tryin to be black. Peep this, I had to go to Manhattan for this job interview in the Upper West Side. Dead up word to my moms I seen this white kid with Filas, Nautica, Philly Blunt shirt, this kid listenin to X-Clan walkin like this. . . . What the fuck is this? . . . Nigga look like a Weeble-Wabble and shit. That's that dumb shit. . . . Yeah yeah! But what you call them white people that don't wash theyself, but they be causin riots and shit? Yeah, them punk rock anarchy niggas right. I seen a bunch of them walkin, all raggedy clothes, rings stickin out they necks and lips. I seen this one black son in there. I said not the god yo. How a brother gonna be in that shit? Know what I'm sayin? I be seein wild shit! I see them on TV kid! How a sister gonna sing opera? How a black man gonna sing backup for some Kenny G . . . ? Kenny Rogers? Anyone of them Kenny motherfuckers. They all from Alabama and shit, Kentucky. . . . Oh that's where your school at? For real? I'mo see you at that school yo. I got a scholarship too son. Government type shit. They gave me five million dollars right. They gonna teach me how to make AIDS yo. I'ma make AIDS Two, AIDS Three, AIDS Four, up to ten. I'ma see how many niggas I could kill yo, boom! And then cause I'ma be rich right, I'ma buy a penthouse, BMWs, check this yo. . . . I'ma own McDonald's, Nike, Levi's, Sony, all that shit. I'ma own Red Lobster. I'ma own that company that make that bomb that we dropped on that nigga Saddam Hussein family. Pow! I'ma make bank! Then I'ma see your ass in the street beggin. You know what I'm sayin, you gonna be beggin! Talkin bout Frederick Douglass was a great man, lemme get ten cent. And I'ma be like, Oh whatup Al, remember me? Remember them college days, this and that? And I'ma hit you off with a twenty spot cause you my boy. I'ma get you a job sweepin up one of my Red Lobsters. Aha. What? . . . I'ma do what I want son, it's a free country right? . . . Oh, oh, you gonna tell a black woman she can't sing opera? . . . Aight then, aight then. He wanna talk garbage right now. This the land of opportunity son, I aint tryin to miss mine yo. This nigga tryin to keep me down now. You sound like this girl yo. I was tryin to talk to this girl, she wanna go see this art exhibit right. So you know me, I got a open mind right. We step up in this museum. Motherfuckers in suits. And it's this art piece on the wall, it got no frame, nails, glue and shit is on the wall. Motherfuckers is like, *'Mmm yeah, I like that shit.'* I said straight up, that's some bullshit right there. She go like this in my face son, *'Maybe if you was more educated you might understand that.'* I said, what? Hold up now. I'ma go to school so I could understand *that* shit? I'ma tell you what son . . . Nah, I'ma go to school, I'ma be president and I'ma blow niggas' whole countries up all over the earth and I'ma make bank! Understand *that* shit! . . . You see that Lexus right there? That Lexus fat boy. I'ma own Lexus, Jeep . . . Oh shit! I told you I'm gettin a Jeep? Word to god kid, Red, Cherokee, ninety-one. I'ma have the bomb system in that shit too. Bensi, equalizer . . . Cause I had saved up bills from that jail job. Hey yo, seven hundred cells we gonna build in that shit. We gonna lock niggas' heads up all day in that motherfucker right? So I'm sayin, already I got the Bensi, I got the equalizer. All I got to get is, um, the Jeep, and the insurance. Yo you should give me your beeper number, we should hang out. . . . You don't got a beeper? How somebody supposed to get in touch with you then? . . . The phone? Daha. This nigga livin like Fred Flintstone yo. On the reals though, I gotta pick up my little brother and get my food. I'ma call you then. . . . It's good to see you though right? Right. Hey yo Al, they still givin out applications for that shit that you doin? I'm sayin though. Oh next year? Yeah I might peep that shit out, definitely though. Aight then. I'mo call you then. Right. One love god. [FLEX *takes his time looking and thinking and re-enters the takeout*] Hey yo son. Yo son! Oh you don't see me now? I said you don't see me right now. You aint tryin to serve me now? Never mind son, my shit's ready? . . . My shit's ready though? . . . How you know that's mine though? It's in a bag, I can't see that shit. That could be my man's right there. Aight then, I'mo tell you what, lemme get extra duck sauce, hot sauce, napkins, all that shit kid. You know extra? Lemme get extra. . . . Three twenty-five? Three twenty-five. Don't be tryin to jerk me neither man. This nigga tryin to be slick, fuckin immigrant-ass motherfucker. . . . I said you a immigrant. You know what I'm sayin? You aint from here, I'm from here. Know that shit. . . . How I know what? How I know I'm from here? Nigga can't even talk English talkin bout how I know. What you know? You don't know shit! I'm American son. You aint shit! Gimme my shit yo. [FLEX *takes his food and motions to leave but then turns back*] Hey yo boy, you don't say thank you? . . . Yeah, you're welcome. [FLEX *exits*]

Message to the Bluntman

Forties, Blunts, Ho's. Glocks and Tecs
You got your X cap but I got you powerless
Forties, Blunts, Ho's. Glocks and Tecs
You got your X cap but I got you powerless

People be like shut the hell up when I talk
Like I shouldn't be talkin Black, even though I'm from New York

But what's that? A color, a race, or a state of mind?
A class of people? A culture, is it a rhyme?
If so, then what the hell am I you might be sayin?
Well see if you could follow this flow, cause I aint playin

Ya see I aint ya average twenty-somethin grunge type of slacker
I'm not your herb flavor-of-the-month, I aint no cracker
An actor? Come on now, you know you wanna ask me
I'll use my skin privileges to flag you down a taxi
But I could act mad type of rough to flex my muscle
I'm also from the seventies so I could do the Hustle
I been to Riker's Island, did crimes that was wrong
I smoked Blunts and drank Forties fore Kriss Kross was born
That's true. But so what. I know I aint Black to you

But I can take your culture, supe it up and sell it back to you
And I can sell crack to you and smack to you if you let me
I'm the president, the press and your paycheck, you sweat me
You never even met me or can fathom my derision
Try to buck my system son, I'll lock yo ass in prison
Cause that's my mission, profit in my pocket, I clock it
I got billions invested in jails, you can't stop it
I'm political, I laugh at all this anti-Semitical
It makes you look weak, when you try to be critical

And I laugh at all your rap videos with your guns and ho's
While you strike the roughneck pose, I pick my nose
And flick it on ya, ya gonner, no need to warn ya
I got mad seats in government from Bronx to California
And I got the National Guard and plus the Navy,
Army, Air Force, son I got *niggers* paid to save me

If it ever really gets to that but I doubt it
Cause the dollars that I print got your mind clouded

A kid steps on your sneakers and you beef with no hesitation
But you never got beef with my legislation or my TV station
This is my game, I can't lose
When I wanna see the score I just turn on my news
And see you got my Glock and my Tec, aimed at your man's neck
I got you in check and you still give me respect
Ha. That's real funny Mister Money

Mister Cash Loot Blunts Ho's, Mister Dummy
Mister Car Cellular Phone, Mister Junk
You think you got props, you got jack. You the punk
This revolution is just junk, and it sunk
With all the X caps that I sold you out my trunk

You bought my revolution and you wear it on your head
And then you be talkin bout, Yeah I'mo shoot you dead!
Who you supposed to be scarin, Brother?
You aint scarin me, but you scarin your mother
So keep buyin this fly revolution that I'm sellin
How much G's I'll make off you herbs, yo aint no tellin
Keep buyin my Philly Blunt Shirts and my Hats
Keep buyin my Forties, and keep buyin them Gats
And I'll keep buyin time with the cash that you spend
We could hang out, I'll even call you my friend
And we can watch this televised revolution that you're missin
On the commercials that's between Rush Limbaugh and the
    Simpsons.

What's the moral of this limerick that I kicked?
If you missed it, well maybe your head is thick
Or maybe your ass is too high from the Blunts
That's too bad, cause revolution only happens once.

Forties, Blunts, Ho's. Glocks and Tecs
You got your X cap but I got you power*less*
Forties, Blunts, Ho's. Glocks and Tecs
You got your X cap, what's next?

Photo copyright © by Dona Ann McAdams

ISHMAEL HOUSTON-JONES

Name: Ishmael Houston-Jones
Stage Name: Same
Birthdate/Birthplace: June 8, 1951/Harrisburg, Pennsylvania
"Raised Up" Where: Pennsylvania
Education: Classes with Joan Skinner, Yvonne Meier, Terry Fox, Helmut Gottschild, Brigitta Herrmann, Eva Gholson, Lisa Kraus, Stephen Petronio, Eva Karczag, Danny Lepkoff, Jim Tyler, Dana Reitz, Anna Dembska, Carol Swann, Steve Paxton, Minnie Moore
Honors: Shared Bessie Award with Fred Holland in 1984
Influences/Mentors/Heroes: Rena Rogoff (eleventh-grade English); and the usual suspects
Places Performed: New York City, New York, California, Alabama, Tennessee, District of Columbia, Massachusetts, Minnesota, Maine, New Mexico, Wisconsin, Illinois, Vermont, Pennsylvania, Ohio, Texas, Oregon, Washington, North Carolina, South Carolina, Georgia, Canada, Holland, Belgium, Italy, England, Scotland, France, Germany, Spain, Switzerland, Nicaragua, Venezuela
Pivotal Performance: Toss-up:
1. *Cowboys, Dreams and Ladders,* my favorite collaboration with Fred Holland. I got to ride a horse, meet a real cowboy in the Bronx, and share half the Bessie Award check with Fred.
2. *Them,* an intense piece. My first collaboration with Dennis Cooper and Chris Cochrane. Got to dance with a dead goat.
3. *f/i/s/s/i/o/n/i/n/g,* a solo that really synthesized my art and my politics plus pictures of me naked made the papers.
Favorite Performance Experience: The prologue to *Knife/Tape/Rope* with Jonathan Walker. I was blindfolded, tied up, and dancing to Kate Bush on the wrong speed.
Most Terrifying Performance Experience: Okay, sticking my head inside that goat carcass was no picnic.
Favorite Prop or Costume: Tie between the recurring cinder block and carrying my mom over my shoulder in *Relatives*
Hobbies: I have seventeen videotapes of films by the French pornographer Jean Daniel Cadinot.
Reading List: *A Herd* and *Safe* by Dennis Cooper; *Close to the Knives* by David Wojnarowicz; *Chelsea Girls* by Eileen Myles; *Story of the Eye* by Georges Bataille; *STH* issues 29–61, issues 31, 32, 33, 37, 38, 39, 55, 56 missing; hint, hint
Favorite Music: Bands live—the Spitters, Suck Pretty, HOLE
Bands recorded—HOLE, Magnetic Fields, The 6ths, Blur, Ween, Guided by Voices, Vintage Prince, and Aretha
Favorite Quote: "This is not a dream, this is really happening." (Rosemary as she's being fucked by the devil)

Score for Dead

DEAD *is a solo dance/performance piece created June 8, 1971, as part of a celebration of my thirtieth birthday.*

A. On the evening before performing the dance, prerecord a list of every death I can remember which has occurred during my lifetime. Allow pauses for memory lapses. Even if I am not sure a death happened in the last thirty years, if it seems like a real death in the moment, I must say it. Allow for people and pets I've known personally; relatives of people I've known; deaths of celebrities I've experienced through the news media; and fictional characters whose deaths seem real to me at the time.

B. On the day of performance play the tape.

C. For the first three or four names stand still and as I hear each name make the American Sign Language sign for *Dead*. (I.e., left hand open with palm facing downward and right hand open with palm facing upward. Turn both hands over so that they are in the opposite orientation from their starting positions.)

D. When I hear a name that has a particular resonance for me, fall down to the floor in some emblematic way and try to rise again before the next name is called. As the next and the next and then the next names are spoken, repeat the falling-to-the-floor-and-rising dance for each name.

E. Try not to anticipate a death. Try not to remember the death until I hear myself speak it on the tape. Try to respond to the death in the moment. Try to let go of the death as I rise from the floor.

F. Continue until there are no more names (about ten minutes). Allow myself to become exhausted with the effort. Don't stop until the dance is over.

Dead

JFK * RFK * Martin Luther King * Fred Hampton * Field Marshal Cinque * Jim Jones *************** Kitty Genovese ********************* Grandma Shadwick *** Grandpa Shadwick ************* Aunt Sister ***Uncle Son ****************************** Adrian ***** James ***** Charlie Jones *********** Jones, Charles H., USMC *************** Cathy Noland *** Nick Adams *** Monty *** Jean Seberg **********John XXIII *** Paul VI ***John Paul I ************************ LBJ *** Hubert Humphrey *** Martha Mitchell *** Judy Garland *** Hopalong Cassidy *** Jacques Brel *** Phil Ochs ******************************* Rango *** Nugget the First *** Nugget the Second *** Zincy ******** Roy Campanella *** Joe Louis *** Ezra Charles *** Emile Griffith ********************* Bob Crane *** Sal Mineo **** Clark Gable **** Marilyn ************* Patrice Lumumba ******* Joseph Kasavubu ********** All eight except Corazón Amuro

***************** Jack Ruby *** Joe Kennedy ****** Franco *** Eichmann ********** Gary Gilmore ***** Reza Pahlavi ******** Ike *** Mamie *********************** Warren's mother *** Warren's father *** Jeff's grandmother *** Kathy's sister *** Larry's dog *** Ginsberg's mother *** Ginsberg's father *********** Jim Morrison ******* Jimi Hendrix ******* Gus Grissom **** Janis Joplin **** Gracie Allen *********** Jack Benny ************ Spanky ***** Charlie Chaplin *** The man who used to sing on Jackie Gleason *** One of the Rolling Stones ***John Lennon ********* Maria Callas ********* Queen Fredericka **** King Paul *** The Duke of Windsor *** Duke Ellington ************************* John Wayne **** Superman **** Lassie ***** Ramon Novarro ********** Patsy Cline ***** Michael Bloomfield ******** Sharon Percy *** Sharon Tate *********** Inger Stevens ****** Jayne Mansfield ******************** Bess and Harry Truman ******** de Gaulle/ Piaf/ Malcolm X/ Helen Keller/ Sid Vicious ************************ Two at Jackson State ******************** Four at Kent State *** A lot at My Lai *******Less than a thousand at Jonestown ************************* Wil Jonnson *** Charles Geary ***** Manya Starkman*** Miss Kunkel ********* Wally Cox * James Dean * Ernie Kovacs * Joan Crawford * Khrushchev * Dag Hammarskjöld * Madam Nu's husband * Louis Armstrong * Golda Meir

    June 8, 1971

Photo copyright © by Dona Ann McAdams

HOLLY HUGHES

Name: Holly Hughes
Stage Name: Same
Birthdate/Birthplace: If I tell you I'll expect a present.
"Raised Up" Where: Saginaw, Michigan
Education: B.A., Kalamazoo College
Honors/Grants: Seven NEA Grants, NYSCA Fellowships, McKnight Fellowship, Obie Award
Influences/Mentors/Heroes: *Gilligan's Island* and WOW Café
Places Performed: All over lower Manhattan
Pivotal Performance: Lead vagina in seventies performance piece
Favorite Performance Experience: When Raquel Welch sat in the front row
Most Terrifying Performance Experience: When Ms. Welch walked out in the middle of my show
Favorite Prop or Costume: A La-Z-Boy and a diet Coke
Hobbies: Chasing girls (who don't look like girls)
Reading List: Anything by Martha Stewart
Favorite Music: Dusty Springfield, Petula Clark
Favorite Quote: "Holly Hughes is a lesbian and her work is heavily of that genre." (NEA Chairman, John Frohnmayer)

Artist's Notes

When I begin a piece of theater I have only one thing in mind, one objective that overshadows all others: Girls. It is my dream that there not be a dry seat in the house. Actually I'm interested in the kind of girls who most people don't see as girls; the girls I like look like boys. They're happy to let me be the girl.

Salon de la Mer

MEAT

I knew it was wrong, but goddamn it, I wanted pork chops.

And I was gonna have them, even if it did make my mother cry.

Meat did funny things to her. Once I made a meat loaf for her and she just about bawled her eyes out. But I knew why. The meat loaf reminded her of Daddy.

Daddy was her word, not mine. I called my father Mike. Or did. I didn't call him much of anything anymore because he was gone.

I didn't miss him. I missed meat.

So I was surprised when Mom said to me: "I could sure use some pork. How about you?"

It was funny because it wasn't the time of the year when you automatically think of pork. It was July when the hot sun sucks the color out of the sky until the sky lies limp on the tops of trees. Tomatoes bump and moan in the dirt. I've seen them press their fat faces against the aluminum siding and I've heard them call out for my mother at night, begging in their little green voices to get out of the hot dirt and back into her cool white bed. And weenies rear up on their hind legs, bucking on the hibachis till their skins split open and weenie blood sings on the briquettes.

Ladies can't keep their legs crossed, no matter how hard they tried. On the city buses, in the Big Boys, and in beauty parlors everywhere, ladies' legs fly open and fields of thighs bloom like pink and brown and yellow petunias.

I know these ladies are just trying to keep cool but it makes everyone else hotter.

Everyone forgets about the roses and the trumpet vines just about take over. The sound and smell of ladies' thighs shining with July sweat is honey from an impossible hive. Bees sting themselves silly, yellow dogs chase their shadows, trying to swallow their own tails, and men everywhere turn to Budweiser and Jesus to stay cool.

I bet I'm about the only person in a fifty-mile radius who thinks about pork this time of the year.

Still there was a breeze. A balsam smell out of Canada full of peninsulas and small springs. The breeze flirted with the kitchen curtains and kept us all from going the way of the backyard weenies.

"If we're going to eat meat let's not eat it alone," Mom said. And so I had Marcy over. Asking her was hard. I didn't know how she felt about meat of any kind, let alone pork. Some women get nervous around meat. Most of them like their meat creamed over a bed of something white, white rice, white toast. I didn't want to take a chance with Marcy so I didn't mention pork when I asked her over. But soon as she stepped in the door Mom said: "Marcy, how do you feel about pork chops?"

Marcy just smiled and said: "Sure."

Now, what did that mean? It could mean anything. Or nothing, because Marcy wore white underpants, but she had red hair.

It didn't add up.

I thought maybe Marcy was a bit of a spy. I knew that just because she said yes to pork didn't mean she was going to say yes to me, but I took it as a good sign.

What I liked about Marcy was she was the only girl that wore wool knee socks in July and, plus, *they always stayed up!* My shoes always ate my socks even though I had studied vacuums in science and played around with the Hoover some, you know, experimenting, still my socks were a problem.

I figured that Marcy must have some special sort of suction, some kind of force field that was stronger than the appetite of her Mary Janes. And I figured it was a secret she wanted to keep to herself because Marcy was the only girl in town that July who could keep her legs together, breeze or no breeze.

Supper was on the brink of being ready, the frozen peas in the pot were tapping out their vegetarian Morse code, canary Mississippis of Mazola flooded the red new potatoes and even the pork chops sounded happy, when the breeze stopped dead. The three of us felt it die. I was sure I heard the meat growl.

Outside the sky looked like it had been slugged. The sun was all bloody and sunken. Heat crashed through the windows, not the heat of the sun or of pork chops cooking or ladies trying to keep cool in July.

This was a heat as dark and serious as a motel Bible.

We all said our good-byes and we went down to the cellar. No need to say what was going on. I knew there was a tornado coming.

Personally, I could have used a tornado right about then.

I was hoping one would come, swoop down and take the whole house with it. It was just a house for crissakes. It was the house we lived in, but I didn't think of it as home. Mike had built the house for us. He dug the cellar we were hiding in by hand, he had done the electrical work, everything, himself. I knew because I helped. I held a light for him when he worked at night. My father built this house for my mother and me, but not for him. When the house was finished, we moved in and he moved to a trailer down the road.

No reason. I don't remember a fight. And sometimes he would visit, which was terrible, because the least people can do when they leave is to stay gone.

I asked my mother questions and she threw more questions back: "Can't you see how much Daddy loves us? Didn't he build this house for us?" And I knew I'd never get a reason. The most I could hope for is one good storm.

Down in the cellar we heard a rumbling we thought was thunder and growing closer, but I heard more dirt in the sound than water. Then we heard the kitchen door blow open but no dark wind followed. Footsteps came and a voice familiar.

I knew it. It was no tornado after all. It was just my father.

We came upstairs one by one, Mom first, then Marcy and me last. I saw him lit from behind, framed by the blue sky in the kitchen door. His hair moved and smelled of Canada. I knew he was watching me and smiling, even though he was just a shape. He was a man in a coloring book. Somebody was going to have to fill him in, but it wasn't going to be me. Let my mother do it. She was the one who called him Daddy.

She said: "Don't you have something for Daddy?"

And I said: "Who?" I could get away with saying those kinds of things because my parents had decided I was "at that age."

"Of course my girl's got something for me." Now it was the shape talking. "Doesn't my girl got pork chops for her daddy?"

"No," I said. "I got pork chops for Marcy." And under my breath I added: "Go away." It wasn't like I was afraid to say it louder. It just didn't do any good. He always came back, especially if there was any meat on the table.

"What did you say? Are you hiding from me? Is my girl afraid of me? Are you gonna keep all the pork chops for you and Marcy?"

That did it. I'd rather go up to the shape than have him come down to me and so I said: "No. I was *not* hiding." Loud and clear I said it, the way I do when I'm lying.

I came up the stairs and looked into his face, but I was careful to keep from coloring him in with my eyes. I said to him: "I was waiting for a storm."

And the shape laughed. He said: "You're going to have quite a wait. It's a beautiful day."

And he was right. It was sunny and hot but there was this breeze and I wanted to know what he had done with my storm. "Mom, tell him, it's not a beautiful day."

"Well, I'll tell him, honey, but I don't think he'll believe me." This is like some kind of joke for the two of them. They laugh and laugh and I notice they got martinis, too.

"If there wasn't a storm, why were you down in the cellar?"

"Honey, I went down to get applesauce for your pork chops. You're old enough to realize that pork is simply not digestible without applesauce." All of a sudden they're *my* pork chops, nobody else's, I think, as my mother holds up a jar of applesauce.

Marcy is my last chance. Maybe she remembers there was supposed to be a storm. But Mike gets to her first. "Marcy, did my daughter tell you that I built this house?"

Marcy says: "No." She turns to me and says: "I thought you said your father was dead."

"He is," I say, and Mike laughs. My mother joins in. I know it is never gonna rain.

Photo copyright © by Dona Ann McAdams

JEANNIE HUTCHINS

Name: Jeannie Hutchins
Stage Name: Same
Birthdate/Birthplace: Born in small town in Hudson River Valley, 1950s and 1960s
"Raised Up" Where: Hudson River Valley
Education: B.A., Sarah Lawrence College; Ed.M., Temple University; NYU—Madrid
Honors/Grants: 1986 Bessie; NEA (choreography 1987–1989); Fund for Performance Art; NYSCA commission; Peg Santvoord Foundation; Art Matters Inc.; MacDowell Colony Artist Residency; Temple University Alumna Achievement Award
Influences/Mentors/Heroes: Hudson Valley landscape; growing up with no television; solitude; travel; old people; visual arts of all cultures; Robert Anton
Places Performed: La MaMa, P.S. 122, Franklin Furnace, Dixon Place, Washington Square Church, Cathedral of St. John the Divine, Dance Theater Workshop, Merce Cunningham Studio, the Kitchen, Judson Church, BACA Downtown; in Miami; Key West; Rotterdam; Montreal; Barcelona; Florence
Pivotal Performance: The role of Emma in Ping Chong & Co.'s *Humboldt's Current.* It was my first opportunity to create and develop a character.
Favorite Performance Experience: Performing my solo *Slippery Little Devils* in Italy in Italian, never having spoken Italian before
Favorite Prop or Costume: Brown sackcloth shroud in *A Thing or Two About the Species*

Artist's Notes

Do Not Use If More Salty Than Tears is a piece about water, in which one performer plays the parts of three women, aspects of a single character.

I create a character in order to articulate the tricky layering of conscious and unconscious voices that make a person come alive. In the process, I hope to hit on something that rings true but that remains difficult to pinpoint—the murky mix of selves, both inner and outer, that occupy an individual. A character in one of my scripts, as much as she is a personality, is a hodgepodge of information. Some of that information is concrete, but most of it reveals her interior life. She is the repository of both an internalized external reality and an externalized inner one.

Each script is built around a theme that I treat in various ways, from various viewpoints. Usually, the theme is rooted in a natural phenomenon, and one of my obsessions is how a person takes in that larger reality—like a landscape that resurfaces for years in one's dreams. My pieces are not about me, but I draw most of my material from the unexpected overlaps and interruptions that I encounter in daily life. At any given moment a banal event and a metaphysical one may coincide; often, the mix is both poetic and absurd.

My work is short on narrative; what narrative there is emerges as if by accident. The script is more a dance around the theme than a linear progression of events. That "dance" is carefully crafted to appear spontaneous—words "just spill out" and events seem arbitrary and unplanned-for. The effect of this seemingly offhanded presentation is to allow easy access to territory that is usually well guarded. In the same way, I like to use straightforward delivery to get at abstruse ideas, so that a character appears to expose unwittingly her private workings. In my pieces, the sensuality and the veiled quality of language—its loopholes and delusions—are more important than any deliberate messages the words convey.

A person's actions are largely determined by the resolution of the push-pulls of opposing forces and desires. For me, tension is a source of tremendous richness within a character. I enjoy playing with different kinds of tension—tension between awareness and confusion, between the everyday and the otherworldly, between instinct and learned behavior. I offset tension with fluidity in the structure of a piece, in order to give the sense of a complete consciousness.

Each of my characters has a "daily life" persona, but the substrates of her personality repeatedly seep through or burst out of her consciousness. For me, what gives people vitality is this continual emergence, recession, and erosion of layers, some of which are specific to an individual and others of which are present in many of us. My solos are a vehicle for presenting the outcome of any one person's engagement with the unrelenting onslaught of experience.

Do Not Use If More Salty Than Tears

Do Not Use If More Salty Than Tears is a solo in three parts, performed without a break. The performer portrays three aspects of one woman, Agnes Porter. Part One reveals an indulgent, extravagant, sometimes overbearing grande dame; in Part Two, a down-to-earth Agnes chats as she executes a series of water-testing tasks; in Part Three she is stripped down, almost ageless, more essence than personality.

In a gray-walled room, in a shaft of blue-violet light, a woman lies on her back atop a high box upstage right. She is dressed in richly colored heavy silken garments and fancy pointed slippers with dainty heels; one shoe is black, the other white. She is wearing bright pink stockings, yellow elbow-length gloves, a purple silk jacket, gold-green shawl, and glittery orange hat. The effect is of a sacrificial bier; this box on which she reclines is draped in gray, the fabric also spilling out across the floor in billows, covering the entire playing area in an ocean of gray. Downstage left, near the edge of the fabric, is a mound of salt atop a small pedestal. The motionless figure merges in our view with the draped chamber that surrounds her. A single thin white line runs up the upstage wall to a height of four feet, along the wall and around the corner, and down again, framing the room to resemble an open book.

Lounge music is heard, as if from another room, punctuated by the intermittent howl of a distant animal. As the room becomes dim, the music fades; howl continues, off and on, throughout Part One.

Part One

[*She begins to stir, then wriggles herself into position to look out at audience, smiling slyly. She is jogged to alertness as animal howl breaks the silence.*]
I haven't the faintest idea *what* that sound might be! [*Laughing*] It could be anything—anything at all! Use your imagination!

[*She starts easily rocking, hands clasped around shins.*] Relax! You're all wound up! We'd be *so* much better off if we'd all simply relax. [*Laughing*] Heavens! We're all in the same boat! The same leaky, old rudderless boat, floating around God only knows where! Oceans of darkness. Hah! If you squint, maybe, *maybe* you can discern a shoreline—if you're lucky, or very very old! [*Laughing*] A shoreline! [*She props herself up on one elbow, stretching to a sidelong lounging position to address the audience directly.*]

Water plus earth equals . . . mud. Birthplace of the exquisite lotus! The magnificent phoenix, rising into the ether from the remains of a spent fire—oh, beauty is so horribly seductive! Creator and devourer of all we know! I confess to being dazzled, enthralled by her . . . him? Does beauty have a gender? . . . Relax! There's no answer to that question! [*Throws her head back and laughs heartily. Sits up abruptly, draws her skirts around her, faces audience, legs dangling off front of box, hands folded demurely in her lap.*]

—I never got what I wanted!
—Yes, you did. You always did. What are you talking about? You always did!
—No, no one ever asked me what I wanted, they didn't care what I wanted, and I never told them so they didn't know and I never got it.
—Oh, *please!* You always got exactly what you wanted.
—I did? You thought so? You never told me.

[*Sardonically*] What we want, what we want! . . . We want the voluptuous experience of life, don't we?

[*Tosses her hat dramatically into the sea of fabric; she rolls to her stomach and slides backward, wormlike, off the bier. As she descends to floor, it becomes washed in eerie gray-green lighting. Low-pitched drone, followed by rapid, rhythmically dense music. She kicks aside fabric to clear a space for herself.*

Movement segment, several minutes long, is cut off abruptly as she walks down to the feet of audience.]

[*With an air of patrician matter-of-factness*] I am hot—I am hot hot *hot* in these garments. And, I'm thirsty! I'm tremendously thirsty! Although I just drank *lots* of water. I do drink *lots* of water, yet I'm thirsty *lots* of the time. . . . I wouldn't say that I suffer from thirst, exactly. It's not usually a problem. If I'm thirsty, I simply ask for a drink of water; very often I get it myself. But then I find that very shortly after partaking of that water, I'm thirsty again—it's a cycle.

[*Retrieves her bag from top of box/bier, and sits down casually on platform at base. She removes from her bag an object which she unwraps. It is a jar of blue-green water. Opens jar and drinks with gusto.*] The magnificent and the slight, side by side. 'Tis ever thus. 'Tis ever thus.

[*Closing jar, methodically rewrapping it and returning it to pouch*] I'll be thirsty again very shortly.

[*Stroking her gold-green satin stole*] Isn't this lovely? This was once an *exquisite*—and I mean exquisitely beautiful—piece of deep green satin. Left out in the elements. Thank God I never let it get wet! No, it was bleached by the sun to this lovely bronze hue. But that, of course, comes as a surprise to no one—bleached from a leafy green to a golden brown. Fortunately, it maintained its suppleness and pliancy and never became dry or brittle.

[*Wandering upstage, as if lost in thought, then finding the words to express them*] Expression. We talk about self-expression. Express, to express, the word *express* . . . meaning to *squeeze* the liquid out of something, to extract the fluids. Ex-*press*. You squeeze a lemon, and the juice flows out. You express milk from a breast. Express express express. And then self-expression—to express our*selves*, which we do in so many ways—and, is our self-expression juicy or has it had all the juice expressed out of it? . . .

For instance, you might very well say, "The trees are swaying too much! The trees are swaying much too much!" And what would you be expressing by that? Not a mere fact about the flora, no! You would be expressing your own response to a phenomenon of nature. Fear, perhaps—dread, maybe even delight. Some kisses, for example, some kisses express affection, even love—oh, yes, some kisses express love! Some kisses express good breeding, politeness, hostility. . . . People often don't know *what* they are expressing by their kisses. And some kisses, with which we are all too familiar, some kisses express absolutely nothing! And we all know those kisses, don't we? Kisses that come nowhere near the mouth, kisses that are not even an exchange of breath—breathless kisses, not mutual kisses!

Some kisses land flat on your lips,
most are somewhat askew.
You can't comment on it, either—
a safe little peck, brushing past cheeks,
maybe too wet or a little bit of teeth.
Expressions of your own good taste. So casual

Some kisses go lips to lips,
more often they're off target.
A lipstick smudge could distract you for hours,
a pucker in the middle of nowhere—
intimations of intimacy.
Some kisses, strictly political;

Some kisses, some kisses, some kisses . . .

Some kisses cut right to the core,
carved out of complication
Polite hesitation is hard to ignore—
you're toying with the enemy.
Some kisses, barely kisses, reluctant kisses,
contemporary kisses, kisses . . .

A salute with the lips! An erotic invitation!

Some kisses land flat on your lips,
more often they're off target;
A safe little peck, turn the other cheek
maybe too wet or a little bit of teeth—
Expressions of your own good taste. So casual, so casual.
Some kisses, sometimes, intimations of intimacy,
some kisses, strictly political.

Some kisses, make-believe kisses, ordinary kisses,
so analytical.
Some kisses, some kisses, some kisses—
Reluctant kisses, dangerous kisses, ordinary kisses,

contemporary kisses,
Some kisses, some kisses, some kisses—*ciao*!

[*Movement segment, as music continues*]

Please, stop the music! [*Music is turned off*]

In an early dream, she pushes herself along on her back, through a subter-
ranean tube or tunnel. It's the only way she can get where she is going. She's
running out of air; it's damp and dark. Her nose . . . her nose nearly touches
the ceiling. Now, *that* is a creepy dream! In another episode, her prepubescent
self pleads in vain as her mother sells off the house. Then the family prepares
for an outing. It's nighttime, it's dark, she doesn't see where she is going.
They've left her behind, but she runs after. She trips, falls full face flat forward
into the mud. Triple humiliation! Ignored, abandoned, covered with muck.

Of course, in later years, that same darkness, and that mud, become images of
sensuality and pleasure. But that isn't for many years yet. Many, many years.

[*Closes her eyes, and begins to turn slowly as she speaks, as if in her dream:*]

Your eyes, your eyes and your hands.
Yes, your eyes and your hands. And your back, your brow. You could be
speaking to me still, after I've fallen asleep. Your words are not so desperate—to burrow in, pleading with sightless grasp—whatever.

The room is drenched in this nonsense!

The savored flesh will rot—the body will betray before it gets light.
    It is to this dark that I have built my shrine, aglow in a blackened room,
until our aging eyes extinguish it.
    . . . More! More sensations! More sensations, please, my friend! More,
more! . . .

I'm jealous. I'm jealous of the several species—humans not among them—
whose legacy from one generation to the next is a song, a complex, wordless
song. Who among us does not yearn for such limpid continuity, flowing like
an unharnessed river from the heretofore to the hereafter?

[*Drops recklessly to the floor, giggling and squirming and kicking playfully. Takes
off her shoes.*] I confess! . . . to the unpardonable luxury of long, perfumed baths,
imagining myself a sea mammal, celebrating the vastness of my ocean home,

blissfully ignorant of the giant hooks that will rip apart my flesh, of the saws and shovels and hardware that will desecrate my benign form after the massacre.

[*Standing up, regally*] Two swans gliding effortlessly around their pond; one to the other: "I feel graceful as all hell today!" And why not? Why the hell not?

[*Plunks down at base of bier/box, removes wrapped water jar from embroidered bag*] My bath! To complete my bath, after I have cupped my hands and burrowed my face into the warm water, now replete with the microscopic detritus of my sloughing body, and after I have squeezed that cloth above each shoulder, savoring the tickle of the rivulets as they trace the contours of my unseen back . . . *after* I have done all that, I take that same rough cloth and I wring the moisture out of it, and I scrub very briskly underneath each ear at the side of my neck, not, as might be expected, in anticipation of the desired kiss, but rather, an old wives' tale, to accelerate the flow of blood to the brain. . . . And then, I drink a glass of very cold water. [*Drinks*]

[*Closes and wraps jar, places it in bag; rambling agitatedly*] Six parts sugar, one part salt. Shouldn't be too salty. No plumbing anyway. Kids dropping like flies. Drought, famine. Can't all get the treatment. Shouldn't be too salty.

> She becomes a liquid,
> her breathing is so loud,
> the fluids roar inside her as she dives down.
>
> She keeps the cold at bay,
> smooth and dark like a seal,
> bursting from bedrock to dive and shout.
>
> (Chorus:) She's in the pungent place,
> we lumber along at some rate,
> we drone as if the sentence is not finished—
> we crave the dimness we say we fear,
> delicious descent without a lamp.
>
> . . . Smooth and dark like a seal,
> bursting from bedrock to dive and shout.
>
> Keeping the cold at bay,
> her breathing is so loud,
> a blizzard of color raging behind closed eyes.

The bony self/that moves/the flesh of us,
that gives us shape,
that self retreats and waits, that bony self,
a blizzard of color raging behind closed eyes.

(Chorus:) We're in the pungent place
we lumber along at some rate
we drone as if the sentence is not finished—
we crave the dimness we say we fear,
delicious descent without a lamp.

. . . Her breathing is so loud,
the fluids roar inside her as she dives down.

She becomes a liquid,
smooth and dark like a seal,
smooth and dark and boisterous like a seal.

The message on each cell
anticipates our actions—
we long to dream we dream it up ourselves.

(Chorus:) We're in the pungent place
we lumber along at some rate
we drone as if the sentence is not finished
we crave the dimness we say we fear
delicious descent without a lamp.

[*Segue into music, strong chords on organ. She disrobes, folding and arranging the garments carefully upon the gray fabric to again cover the cleared floor. She now wears a simple gingham shirt and work pants. Her hair, chignon undone, she draws back in a ponytail.*]

Part Two

[*Staggering barefoot on the gray cloth; demonstrating the actions she describes*] Air sucked in, air sucked out. Air sucked in, air sucked out. You can't really suck your own air out. . . . I'm sucking air in, sucking it in. Sucking in my stomach. It doesn't hurt. I'm sucking it in—it's not a problem. So far, it doesn't hurt at all. . . . Still doesn't hurt. . . . [*Exhaling finally, gasping*] Eventually, everyone has to let all the air out.

[*Turns to her tasks. Removes gray shroud along upstage wall to reveal a porcelain institutional drinking fountain; uncovers the bier/box, and it is now a bright white counter. Sets herself up for work behind the counter, with apron, pitcher, glasses, logbook, heavy rubber gloves. Talking as she works, much of what she does happens behind the counter and out of view. Glasses accumulate; she compares flavors of various colored solutions.*]

[*Attempts to attain a uniform water level*] I know it's antediluvian, but I just eyeball it.

I'm going to tell you about Florence Rideout. Florence Rideout was a neighbor who my sister Iris and I went to visit on summer afternoons to drink lemonade. Her idea of lemonade was the following: [*Demonstrating*] Fill a glass to here with ice water, half a lemon squeezed into it and left floating in the glass; next to it a bowl of sugar and a spoon. You could put in as much sugar as you wanted—no wagging finger. She knew we would put in too much sugar and make the lemonade too sweet. We'd be thirsty again right away, and we'd stay there drinking lemonade and talking to her which was what she wanted because she liked us.

Her son Gregory lives in a tent on a mesa now, because he developed an allergy to the world we live in.

[*Long silence, as she proceeds to the next set of glasses*]

The whole thing was animal life, animal behavior, animals' habits. Hands like paws, we wanted hands like paws; we wanted our hands to *be* paws, or at least hands that were mittenlike, furry, with long nails. Hands like paws. I wanted a tongue like a cat's—a sandpaper tongue.

Oh—eyes in another part of your body. An eye, or some eyes, anywhere else in your body than where they usually are. At least one eye, anywhere. Eyes in other parts of your body.

Emaciated, cringing beasts, their rib cages showing, [*Growls and snarls*] snarling and growling and shrinking away from me; like dogs that have eaten rat poison or something, really sickly and depraved, pathetic creatures! And something coming in the window, a medieval instrument of torture, maybe. Gigantic—everything tumbling down at odd angles, distorted and compressed. Grotesque animals, growling and slinking away and sick looking. This was not a dream. It was in the newspaper. I saw it in the paper—*our* paper. I think it was even a photograph.

And people, too—people like *things*. Piled up, heaped up, crawling all over each other, and groaning. Covered with muck, and carrying one another, people carrying other people like deadweight. Masses of people, like a pile of garbage. Emaciated beasts, and things tumbling, and sharp pointed— [*Snarling*] *Grrr!* All of these things I saw in the newspaper.

[*Pops third tape into the player. For final test, she blindfolds herself and selects glasses by smell.*]

We're standing at the edge of town,
we're near Exit 17B—
we're standing where you see the sky
sit thickly on the buildings.

But we're not really standing down there,
we're way high up in a building,
cars slowly creeping
on and off the cloverleaf.

(Chorus:) Let's take a trip,
Let's drive across the country;
Let's go to the edge of town,
Let's get out of town.

We used the access numbers
to enter the VIP lounge;
all the lights have been turned out
because it's after-hours.

Except the red fire exit,
shining off the stainless steel
of the ice-cold, spic-and-span
drinking water fountain.

(Chorus:) Let's take a trip,
Let's drive across the country,
Let's go to the edge of town,
Let's get out of town.

Everything's quiet up here,
just the hum of some vent,
we can't hear the traffic
inching homeward, or away.

Edging onto the main road,
flowing into the stream,
dots after glowing dots,
tiny red exit lights.

(Chorus:) Let's take a trip,
Let's drive across the country,
Let's go to the edge of town,
Let's get out of town.

[*Downs glass of tinted water; yanks off blindfold and gloves; stops music; steps out quickly from behind the counter to edge of platform on which it rests.*]

You're by yourself; it's dark. There's no light, no lamp, no moon. And you're looking, looking into the dark. It's black out there, and it's black in here [*Indicates eyes*]—your pupils are gigantic—the tiniest rim of an iris! You're looking, and you see . . . [*Scans imaginary horizon line*] . . . absolutely nothing! Forbidden thoughts creep in—what's out there, that I can't see, in that *sea* of darkness? You're being carried on the current of an unharnessed river, toward an unfathomable ocean of darkness. And you wish you were the navigator of those waters, you want to be the navigator, and you know you're not the navigator! You wish you were the navigator.

[*Returns to matter-of-fact*] But, you know something? That's human nature.

[*Music engulfs room. In darkness, she sheds another layer of clothing, emerging in a pale draped gown, hair loose. She staggers from behind the counter and gropes blindly. A shaft of pink light cuts into space from alcove stage left, casting long shadows on upstage wall. She speaks as if in a trance.*]

Part Three

Not long ago, I took a walk in the woods, and alongside the path was a stream. And I knelt down and I dipped my hand into it, and I drank a cupped-hand's-worth of water and it ran down my chin so it looked as if maybe I had been drooling. Later, I visited a friend and I drank a glass of water which I filled from her kitchen tap. Then she offered me a drink from the jar that she keeps in the refrigerator. She keeps a jar of water in the refrigerator at all times. And I noticed that all over her kitchen were jars and bottles and pans of water. She explained to me that this was in order to allow the chemicals, that they put in the water to purify it, this was in order to allow the chemicals to evaporate. And in a normal two-quart saucepan this evidently takes approximately twenty-four hours, although in a vessel with a smaller opening it would take longer, since it varies according to the surface area of water exposed to the air. And as I prefer room-temperature water, I dipped my cup into the pan with the greatest seniority and I drank it down, and it tasted delicious and also quite natural, having almost no flavor at all.

[*Walking along the upstage wall toward the stage-left light source, then down across the gray cloth, finally stepping up onto a small elevated "island" concealed beneath the fabric.*]

> She's an older female of her species.
> She's an aging animal, a decrepit vessel
> —though she'd never mope on the deck.
> She obeys no one, she prays not;
> she's hungry each day at two.
> —Her knees are stained!
>
> Her nose deceives her; she's beset by the weather
> she's . . . sloughing.
>
> A simple sip of water tastes more salty than tears.
>
> She is seated, gaping noiselessly into the dark,
> her tongue extended beyond the teeth.
> —The hands!
>
> She's an aging animal, asleep by nine.
> Fixed to her mooring, she avoids waving from the deck.
>
> She's an older female of her species, already. Already.
>
> An ancient beast sits staring at a wall,
> she's staring blindly at a wall;
> She knows there is a chasm just beyond it,
> and she gracefully anticipates the fall.
>
> Sometimes when we lose our footing,
> slip off a rock we've known,
> Sometimes when we lose our footing,
> that rush of blood reminds us what we've known.
>
> (Chorus:) How do we know what we know we know
> that no one ever could have taught us?

How we know what we know—
Do we even know it? Do we know?

An ancient beast stares blindly at a wall,
she's sightlessly retreating from the world,
She's slowing down, she's lying down,
and she'll keep her body warm until it's cold.

(Chorus:) How does she know what I know she knows
that no one ever could have taught her?
How does she know what she knows—
Does she really know it? . . .

Sometimes when you lose your footing,
slip off a trusted stone,
Sometimes when you lose your footing,
it's fear of losing shape that chills the bone.

An ancient beast sits staring at a wall,
she's staring blindly at a wall.
She knows there is a chasm just beyond it,
and she patiently permits herself to fall.

Sometimes when you lose your footing,
slip off a rock you've known,
Sometimes when you lose your footing,
that slip of a surrender chills the bone.

(Chorus:) How do you know what you know you know
that no one ever could have taught you—
How do we know what we know?
Do we even know it . . . I don't know.

[*Lights fade to black during last verse of song.*]

LISA KRON

Name: Lisa Kron
Stage Name: Lisa Kron
Birthdate/Birthplace: May 20, 1961/Ann Arbor, Michigan
"Raised Up" Where: LANSING, MICHIGAN!!!
Education: B.A. in Theater, Kalamazoo College, Kalamazoo, Michigan
Honors/Grants: 1992–93 Bessie Award as member of The Five Lesbian Brothers; 1994 NYFA playwriting fellowship; Robert Chesley Foundation 1994 Gay and Lesbian Playwriting Award; 1995 Drama Desk nomination for *101 Humiliating Stories;* 1994–95 Obie Award for *The Secretaries* as a member of the Brothers
Influences/Mentors/Heroes: My other four Lesbian Brothers; The Split Britches Company; Holly Hughes; Carmelita Tropicana; my college theater professor, Lowry Marshall; Rivka Lindenfeld, my Hebrew school teacher; Roseanne; Kathy Bates (really any actress over one hundred fifty pounds); my parents
Places Performed: Nearly every East Village club existing in the past ten years
Pivotal Performance: My first variety night performance at the WOW Café and my Serious Fun show at Lincoln Center
Favorite Performance Experience: Serious Fun
Most Terrifying Performance Experience: A few performances of *101 Humiliating Stories* at the New York Theater Workshop where no one laughed *throughout the whole show.*
Or, the performances of *101* in a rock-and-roll club in Chicago where I could not see the edge of the stage because the lights were hung on an I-beam five feet away from me at eye level so I was *completely blinded.*
Or, the show I did at the Pyramid Club many years ago with Holly and Carmelita which Holly had written that afternoon. Minutes before the show was to begin she handed me my lines typed on index cards. For some reason she had typed them in red and the lights at the Pyramid were also red so onstage the cards appeared to be blank. Oh, that was a fun performance, let me tell you.
Favorite Prop or Costume: My telephone in *101* and the psychedelic polyester floor-length dress I wear for my big dance number in the Brothers' play *Brave Smiles*
Hobbies: Crocheting, badminton, dressage, hot-tubbing and long walks in the woods with my fiancé, Bob
Reading List: *In Troubled Waters* by Beverly Coyle; *The Shipping News* by Annie Proulx; *During the Reign of the Queen of Persia* by Joan Chase; *The Dollmaker* by Harriet Arnow; *Song of Solomon* by Toni Morrison; Robert Graves; Isaac Bashevis Singer
Favorite Music: Nancy Wilson's album *Broadway My Way*
Favorite Quote: "I'm just going to go to that wedding and pretend I'm watching a *National Geographic* special on TV." (My mother describing her plan for attending my brother's wedding)

Artist's Notes

In sixth grade I had an epiphany. My teacher, *Ms.* Green, whom I adored, told me in so many words to sit down and shut up. I had inserted myself next to her while she was talking to another student to show her some bit of work that I considered particularly cunning. She cut me off. "Lisa, I'm talking to somebody else." I felt a flush of humiliation. I sat back down at my desk and it came to me. When I died the world would keep spinning and others would continue to walk the earth. In a flash I saw myself clearly in relation to others and realized that I had an obnoxiousness problem. At that time or shortly thereafter I began a conscious and concerted effort to learn comic agility—to always be on the right side of that fine line between funny and obnoxious. I developed the ability to tell a funny story and listen to my listeners—prepared to abandon the tale if interest seemed to be waning, or let someone else talk for a while. I learned that an embarrassing moment could be turned into humorous anecdote and the humiliation would go away.

101 Humiliating Stories is a series of stories, recollections of humiliating moments in my life. I interrupt the very first story to check in with the audience. I tell them that I'm aware that many of these stories can be resonant, particularly those dealing with junior high. Audience members are encouraged to raise their hands if they feel a need to share. Throughout the show I check in with the audience and acknowledge individuals if I sense they are reacting particularly strongly. One of my main strengths as a performer, I believe, is my direct communication with an audience. There is a dynamic theatrical moment when an audience realizes you are talking to *them* sitting *right now* in *this room.* It is my goal as a performer to be fluid enough to be able to take in anything that happens in the theater on a particular night and incorporate it into the world of the show. As I continue with my stories I am interrupted, first by a phone call from a woman named Debby Downs, who is calling from my high school in Lansing, Michigan, to ask me to perform at my high school reunion. I tell her no, that my work as a lesbian performance artist is not appropriate and suggest that she hire a magician. Throughout the rest of the show my lineup of stories is interrupted repeatedly by my inner conflicts over this invitation. I drop papers and forget my lines. I spontaneously erupt into a dance of joy and pain. I make a phone call to my girlfriend while the audience waits. And I deliver four imaginary speeches to my high school class—one in which I defiantly and repeatedly proclaim my lesbianism, one in which I remain in the closet and describe my life in lame euphemisms, one in which I brag shamelessly of many inflated theatrical accomplishments, and one in which I am a total

loser, trapped in the spotlight in front of a group of people who don't remember me.

There are two ever-present problems in autobiographical solo performance. One is that the story's material will be about *you* and not have that
oh-so-important universality. The other is that dramatic action is hard to
come by. I did not want a show that was a series of recollections. My girlfriend Peg Healey suggested the use of an invitation to a high school reunion and the first director of the piece, Jamie Leo, had the invaluable
insight that rather than just describe humiliating experiences, humiliations
would have to happen to me during the course of the show. Things would
have to fall apart. Although the show is very scripted and tight, the production and performing style are extremely naturalistic. It appears to be a conversation between me and the audience so when the "mistakes" happen the
audience is momentarily fooled by them.

I have included here three of the "stories." One of the things I wanted to
explore in the show is what makes a humiliating *story* funny. Often, after a
show, people from the audience tell me their humiliating stories and more
often than not they trail off into ". . . well, I guess you had to be there."
Jamie Leo pointed out to me the relation between the words "humiliation"
and "humility." Humiliating moments can serve to remind you that when-
you-die-the-world-will-continue-to-turn and I think it is that rude moment
when you are put back in your place, when your humility is forcibly restored to you, that can make a funny story.

Excerpts from 101 Humiliating Stories
Three Stories

You know, I worked as an office temp for many years and sometimes I came
out on my jobs but most of the time I didn't and I always felt really torn
about this. I felt like I should come out but it was always a little awkward. I
was never at these places for very long and who was I going to come out to
anyway? I wasn't working for those people, I was working for my agency. I
was out at my agency. They were all lesbians too. Anyway, I was always torn
about this and about a year and a half ago I got the first full-time job I had
had in a long time working as a word processor in a midtown corporate law
firm. And I got this job the same time some other things were happening in
the world. The Thomas-Hill hearings were happening and I went to a ten-
year memorial service for GMHC at St. John the Divine and these things all
happened the same time I took this job and reminded me that we don't
come out of the closet to make some esoteric political statement, we come
out of the closet for very concrete reasons, to protect ourselves and protect

our lovers and validate our relationships and . . . blah, blah, blah . . . you all know all this. . . . So I thought, you know, I have this opportunity on this job and I'm not going to mess around. I'm going to tell these people that I am a lesbian. I don't know what's going to happen but I'm just going to do this. And so, I wrote a memo. And these people were great. They were totally accepting of me. And they said, "No problem. You fit right in here." And when they said this something interesting happened to me and I realized that I don't really want to fit in at a corporate, midtown law firm. And I started to do little things to rebel. Although, rebellious is probably a little bit of a strong term for what I am. I'm more contrary, really. And I'd do things like when I answered the phone, sometimes instead of saying "Word Processing" I'd say "Food Processing" and no one ever really noticed, but then when I'd hang up I'd say, "Heh, heh, that was a good one." And the other thing I did was that I didn't dress appropriately for a corporate law firm and this turned out to be a problem. They could deal with the fact that I was a lesbian, but they couldn't deal with the clothes that I was wearing and so they called me in to talk to me about it. But they couldn't quite figure out what to say because it wasn't clear to them what the problem was. It was clear I wasn't buying my clothes at Chuckles or Strawberry but beyond that they couldn't quite pin it down. And they wanted to give me something specific so they said to me, "Lisa, we would prefer it if you didn't wear white socks to work . . . because that's important here." And so, you know, I started wearing pink socks to work and blue socks and gray socks, which obviously wasn't what they had in mind. Obviously they wanted me to wear panty hose to work but I nipped that right in the bud. I can't remember exactly what I said to them but it was something like, "If I have to wear panty hose to work every day my yeast infection will be on your head." Something like that. They backed off pretty quickly on that. In any case, we reached a sort of uneasy resolution. But I still always felt a little uncomfortable. When I left my house in the morning I'd feel fine. I was dressed like you'd dress for an office in the East Village . . . if there is such a thing. But when I'd get to work I'd always feel awkward. It was like that dream that you have where you go to work or you go to school and you're wearing your pajamas and I think that was part of the problem. I was just too comfortable. And here were all these women in their tight skirts and their high heels and I always looked like I could just take a nap at any time. And I think they resented that a little. Anyway, I always felt a little uncomfortable and so I really began to appreciate the things I do naturally that helped me to fit in with these very nice people that I worked with. And one of these things was wearing lipstick, because, as you know, I like to wear lipstick. And I began to make a daily ritual out of going into the bathroom and freshening up my lipstick. And this was a little bit of a double-edged sword too. Because, as any of you who've ever been in a women's room in a corporate office know, there is something about the way the lights are designed in these rooms that highlights the upper lip hair on a woman. They're all like this. I believe it's part of the patriarchal conspiracy. And so I'd freshen my lipstick and I'd think, *Good color, but you're looking a little like Gene Shalit.*

In any case, this one day in particular, I had freshened my lipstick, and I was feeling good. Like when I have a little moisturizing color on my lips I fit right in, I'm one of the girls. And I left the bathroom and I was walking back down the hall, back to word processing and I was taking my time and talking to all these very nice people that I worked with. I stopped and talked with a secretary. She asked about my lipstick. "Oh, do you like it? I'm an autumn! Prescriptives!" I chatted with a paralegal for a minute. "Nice blouse, Marcy. Where did you get it? Strawberry! It's cute!" I spoke with an attorney for a minute. He asked about his document. It wasn't ready yet. We had a nice chat. And I got to the door of word processing and one of the secretaries, Pat, came up to me and said, "Lisa, I have to tell you something." And I said, "Yeah?" [*Very excited, conspiratorial*] And she said, "I saw you coming down the hall here. . . ." And I said, "Yeah?" And she said, "And I saw you talking to all those people." And I said, "Yeah?" And she said, "And I just wanted to tell you that your skirt is tucked into your tights."

"Thanks, Pat."

And I had walked all the way down the long hall sashaying my exposed butt to everyone in the office.

But when I got back into word processing I had an epiphany. And I had an almost uncontrollable urge to tuck my skirt back into my tights and take a long walk around the law office. Hello, law office! This is my butt! You don't get a butt like this eating Slim-Fast for lunch. You have to eat a real lunch to get a butt like this. Welcome to my butt, everyone! Hello, Buttville!

I come from the Midwest and we don't believe in whining in the Midwest. We don't believe in whining, we don't believe in therapy, we don't believe in depression. If you feel bad, it's because of the weather. It's because there's a big barometric pressure zone coming in and when it's gone you'll be fine. And as a result of being raised in this environment I don't have any patience for people who whine. For instance, the other day I was in the subway, standing on the platform waiting for the train, and there was another woman standing near me on the platform near the stairs, and a man ran down the stairs and as he ran by her he stepped on her foot. And when he did, she did this [*Looks down at foot and then looks up accusingly*] "OW!" I hate that. And the worst thing was that it didn't have anything to do with her foot, right? She didn't go [*Looks down at foot and whimpers*] "Ow!" She went [*Looks down at foot and then up accusingly at audience*] "*OW!*" I hate that! That's the worst kind of whining. Accusatory whining!

And I try to hold myself to this same standard and I try to never be in a position where I will be caught whining. A few years ago I was working at another one of my many temp jobs and on this job, in addition to my usual word processing, one of the things I had to do was to cut pictures out of magazines. This was a design firm and they had had a lot of their work published in design magazines and I was supposed to cut these pictures out with an Exacto knife. And this was making me feel really artistic to use this Exacto knife. And I'd cut out the pictures and put them in portfolios and I was loving this, with the Exacto knife and the portfolios I felt like I was really being creative, like I was really exploiting my creative potential and I had been doing this for a few days and I was getting really efficient and whipping down these pages and one day . . . I cut into my finger.

And as soon as I did I went [*Grasps finger with other hand*] and I thought, all right, I'm going to have to talk to someone about this. And I was working for very nice people in a one-room office and they were in a client meeting and I didn't want to interrupt them but I thought, well, I should check this out, so I went over to them and I said, "Excuse me, I'm really sorry to interrupt. This will just take a quick sec. But I was wondering if you could take a quick peek and tell me . . . have I cut the tip of my finger off?"

And, of course, they were very concerned and they said, "Let's see."
And I went like this. [*Holds out finger with other hand wrapped around it*]
And they said, "Okay, you're going to have to take that other hand away."
And I said, "Okay."

And they looked and they determined that I should go to the emergency room and they asked if I was ready, and I said, "Yes, I'm ready. I'm all ready. There's just one thing. I'm just going to need to lie down here on the floor for a few minutes."

And so I lay on the floor and I put my hand up in the air and they bandaged it up and then I was fine and I got in a cab and went to the hospital, I went to St. Vincent's.

And when I got there I felt so stupid. Because here I was with my little cut finger and I looked around this room and there's somebody over here with a big bandage on their head, somebody over here with their arm in a sling, somebody over here with something in a . . . stained bag. And I felt so stupid with my little cut finger and I thought, I'm just going to go. But then I thought, no, I'm here, I'll just let the doctor look at it. So finally the doctor came and she unwrapped the finger. And she wanted to see how deep the cut was. And so she took a little stick—[*Breaks narrative to check with audience*] Is everybody all right? If you need we can just take a minute and all put our heads down between our legs. [*Demonstrates*] I just have to tell you, it's going to get a little worse before it gets better so if you need a minute, just say so. Okay? Okay. We'll just go on.

She wanted to see how deep the cut was so she took a little wooden stick and went . . . poke-ety, poke-ety, poke-ety, poke-ety, poke; poke-ety, poke-ety, poke-ety, poke-ety, poke; poke-ety, poke-ety, poke-ety, poke-ety, poke. And I said, "Excuse me. I'm just going to need to lie down here on the floor for just a minute." And she said, "Could you please wait just one second! . . ." Poke-ety, poke-ety, poke-ety, poke-ety, poke; poke-ety, poke-ety, poke-ety, poke-ety, poke; poke-ety, poke-ety, poke-ety, poke-ety, poke. And I said, "No, you know, I'm going to have to lie down here on the floor right now." And she said, "Okay." And she got up and she went to the other side of the room. Because next to me was a gurney from which they had just removed some trauma patient, and I think she was going to get a clean sheet for the gurney. But at that point I didn't really care what was on the gurney, I just knew I had to get up onto the gurney. And I went over to it and I had one leg up, about to get on the gurney when she saw me from across the room and screamed at me, "*Can you please wait just one minute!*"

And I went back to my chair. [*Returns to chair*]

And I sat on my chair. [*Sits on chair*]

And I then slid off my chair, onto the floor. [*Slides off chair*]

And from out of my mouth I could hear this sound [*Crawls across floor toward audience*]: "*Oh, my God! Somebody help me! Can't you people see how sick I am? Can't you see I'm going to die? Haven't you people seen my finger? What the hell is wrong with you people? Somebody help me! OW!*"

One day I was walking down the hall and there was a sanitary napkin lying in the hall by the Vo-tech wing.

It was a big one, the way they used to be big in 1979—like a Depends diaper is now—which makes you wonder how big Depends diapers were in 1979.

That pristine pad of cotton was lying in the hall in the morning when I got off the bus and at the end of the day it was in the exact same place. It lay in the main artery of the Dwight Rich Junior High School and was passed throughout the day by approximately two thousand people.

And of course, the issue is not that no one noticed. And it's not what you might think, that people saw it through their peripheral vision but pretended not to. There was a lot of screaming and pointing going on. That's how I first noticed it. A crowd had gathered around what I assumed from the hysteria must be a severed limb.

And the most interesting thing to me about all this is that no one picked it up all day. None of the kids picked it up which wasn't too surprising.

These were junior high school students with a very low gross-out threshold. But none of the teachers picked it up. None of the administrators would touch it. And most revealing to me, none of the guidance counselors would be seen touching an unused sanitary pad in front of other people. The cooties on a sanitary pad are that strong—actually cross-generational.

Is everyone all right?

Okay, then let's move on to the fulcrum of this story—fraught with humiliation, i.e., the moment when some girl—we'll call her Cheryl—the moment when Cheryl reaches into her junior high purse for a Jolly Rancher, or some Juicy Fruit gum, or some change to buy a jumbo, double chocolate chip cookie for breakfast in the cafeteria—and as she pulls out her hand, out with it *explodes the sanitary pad!*

There must have been a frozen moment where everyone felt implicated. Until, slowly, everyone else realizes that this happened to Cheryl, not to them. You can just see them starting to quietly comment and laugh and point just to make sure everyone knew that they were just standing there when—*pow!* "Cheryl's sanitary napkin flew right out of her underpants right on us!" That's not what happened, of course. But that's how Cheryl feels. And her face flattens into a white plate and she tries to make her body nonchalant which only makes it stiffen more, and she walks on down the hall, as if nothing happened. Nothing happened.

And what's even worse is that all day, every time Cheryl walks down that hall she thinks, *Surely it's gone by now.* And all day, it's always there. And Cheryl begins to realize that that sanitary pad will be in the hall for the rest of her life, and that eventually they'll just build a big glass case around it with a brass plaque on it with her name on it—"Cheryl." And so later in the day, when she has to pass that infamous spot in the hall, in spite of the fact that she knows everyone knows it was her that dropped it, Cheryl adopts the who-did-that attitude, well known to anyone who ever passed gas in elementary school. And when she has to pass that spot in the hall, Cheryl points and laughs too and asks her friends if they have any idea who the idiot was who dropped a sanitary napkin in the hall.

Photo by Glen Jussen

DENIS LEARY

Name: Denis Leary
Stage Name: Denis Leary
Birthdate/Birthplace: Worcester, Massachusetts
"Raised Up" Where: Worcester/Boston, Massachusetts
Education: BFA, Writing/Acting, Emerson College, Boston, MA
Honors/Grants: From age seventeen on lived eighteen years of my life with no credit cards, no car, no possessions, and nothing legally in my own name
Influences/Mentors/Heroes: Richard Pryor, Eric Bogosian, Carl Yastrzemski, Albert Brooks
Places Performed: Actors' Playhouse, Village Vanguard, P.S. 122
Pivotal Performance: Age thirteen: Patrick Dennis, "Mame," St. Peter's High School
Favorite Performance Experience: Age thirteen: Patrick Dennis, "Mame," St. Peter's High School
Most Terrifying Performance Experience: Age thirteen: Patrick Dennis, "Mame," St. Peter's High School
Favorite Prop or Costume: Elvis Presley's powder-blue jewel-encrusted jumpsuit, waist size 53
Hobbies: Both Kennedy assassinations, stalking Liza Minnelli, etc.
Reading List: *I Gotta Be Me* by Derek Sanderson; *Logic of Images* by Wim Wenders
Favorite Music: Stones, Clash, Dexter Gordon, Ray Charles, Adam Roth
Favorite Quote: "Write what you know." (Jesus to apostle)

Artist's Notes

No Cure for Cancer started out as a reaction to my past and present circa 1990. Having worked in the theater since the age of thirteen—in everything from musicals to dramatic one-acts to scene workshops and original productions I found myself at age thirty-three with no money, no job, and no access to the stage. Stand-up comedy was not a viable route, since my particular point of view worked well only in New York's downtown clubs and a few spaces up in Boston. So I decided to write a one-man show incorporating all the anger, humor, and pathos I could muster under one tent. A lot of the material came from bullet points I had in my head. A lot of it came from full-blown monologues I'd kept in a separate notebook. Still more came from getting up on stage and flying by the seat of my pants. Ideas would tumble together. Trains of thought would collide. The good thing about rage is that once you start venting it, the emotion will carry you further than you intended it to go. I put this formula to work in performances all over London, England, where I happened to be at the time. Theaters, clubs, pubs, auditoriums—wherever I could get an audience. Then I honed the material by playing "NO CURE" at the Edinburgh Festival in Scotland for three weeks. Once we opened off Broadway at the Actors' Playhouse in the fall of 1991, the show was pretty much set in stone. I would improvise around certain parts of the monologue nightly, but seven performances a week means keeping enough structure for the audience to follow the through line and come out the other side understanding the point. My director, Chris Phillips, would watch the show's development and suggest certain ways to lean it out and/or fatten it up. Chris helped to keep a balance between the all-out anger, the softer dark side, and the over-the-edge aspects of it. By the time we came to film the show (seven or eight months after the Actors' Playhouse run, due to film commitments) I had to reacquaint myself with all of the material and emotions. Strangely enough, due to theater's natural "in-the-moment" requirements—that sense of all-nerves-on-edge, every-pore-open energy—it was then that I ended up improvising a few key moments that Chris and I had spent a year and a half and almost 300 performances looking for, even up to the final night of shooting—when the piece about Irish men being unable to cry ultimately came together. In retrospect, "NO CURE" was like every other theatrical and filmed production I have ever been involved with: tons of exciting preparation, terrible dress rehearsals, nerve-wracking anxiety, promising opening night, a blur of several performing weeks, tiredness, creeping desire for it to be over, hatred for it, final-week excitement, renewal of love, and then a sad and empty end. Would I do it all again? Can't wait. Every time out you end up creating something new and testing your limitations until you've taken a risk you otherwise would never pursue.

More Drugs

[*Lights cigarette. Drags deeply. Inhales. Chugs beer. Exhales.*]

I have the solution to the drug problem. Nobody asked me for it but here it is: not *less* drugs—*more* drugs. Get more drugs and give 'em to the right people. Because every time you read about some famous guy overdosing on drugs, it's always some really talented guy. It's always like Len Bias or Janis Joplin or Jimi Hendrix or John Belushi, you know what I mean?

The people you want to overdose on drugs never would. Mötley Crüe would never overdose! You could put them in a room with two tons of crack and they would come out a half hour later screaming, "Rock on!"

"Shit, they're still alive."

Unfortunately bands like the Crüe and the New Kids on the Block would never overdose.

I take music pretty seriously. [*Pulling up left sleeve*] You see that scar on my wrist? Do you know what that's from? I heard the Bee Gees were getting back together again. I couldn't take it, okay? That was the only good thing about the eighties—we got rid of one of the Bee Gees. One down, three to go. That's what I say, folks. Here's ten bucks, bring me the head of Barry Manilow. I want to drink beer out of his empty head. I want to have a Barry Manilow skull-keg party in my apartment, okay? You write the songs, we'll drink the beer out of your head. Barry Manilow—that's the U.S. contribution to world culture? You know how he made it? Overweight Catholic girls love Barry. He had a record-signing party in New York last year; there were one thousand overweight Catholic girls outside the record store going, "We love Barry Manilow. He's so cute. He's so sweet. I just want to meet him because I know he'll fall in love with me like I fell in love with him."

We live in the country where John Lennon takes six bullets in the chest and Yoko Ono—who's standing *right* next to him—doesn't get one bullet. Explain that to me, God. [*Banging on the floor*] I want it explained to me now! Now we've got twenty-five more years of "Yayayayayayayayaya!" I'm real happy, God. I'm wearing a huge happy hat. Jesus, give me a sign about this one.

Stevie Ray Vaughn is dead and we can't get Milli Vanilli on a helicopter? C'mon, folks. "Get on the 'copter, boys. There's free gum. Get on the 'copter. Get on that 'copter, c'mon. Vic Morrow's in there. He's the one without the head. Get on the 'copter!!" One of the boys in Milli Vanilli tried to commit suicide. I guess he finally listened to the album, huh?

What was that thing about heavy metal bands on trial a couple of years ago because kids were committing suicide? Judas Priest was on trial because [*Whining*] "My kid bought the record and he listened to the lyrics and then he got into Satan and blah blah blah blah!" Well, that's great. That sets a legal precedent. Does that mean I can sue Dan Fogelberg for making me into a pussy in the mid-seventies? Is that possible? "Your Honor, between him and James Taylor, I didn't have oral sex until I was thirty-one years old. I was in Colorado, wearing hiking boots and eating granola. I want some money right now."

Let me make sure I'm crystal clear on this issue. Heavy metal fans are buying heavy metal records, taking the records home, listening to the records and then blowing their heads off with shotguns? Where's the problem? That's an unemployment solution right there. It's called natural selection. It's the bottom of the food chain. Okay?

I don't go for this whole new thing that's happening to rock 'n' roll. You know, this new MTV movement with these new bands that are trying to start a late sixties, early seventies retro thing again? Bands wearing bell-bottoms again? No. Trying to start a sixties revival? No. Oliver Stone is the leader of this trend, isn't he? Every movie he makes is mired in the sixties. He made a two-hour movie about the Doors. Do we *need* a two-hour movie about the Doors? No. I can sum it up for you in five seconds: I'm drunk; I'm nobody. I'm drunk; I'm famous. I'm drunk; I'm dead. There's the whole movie. Okay? *Big Fat Dead Guy in a Bathtub.* There's the title for you! "It seems like an awful short script, Oliver. I don't know if we can shoot this or not."

[*Lights up cigarette. Inhales. Exhales.*]

And what about these rock bands that don't want to just be bands anymore? It's not enough to have a pop song that becomes a hit, or a dance number that people like to dance to. They want to be more than that. They want to tell us how to vote and how to feel about the environment. You know what I'm talking about? Like R.E.M. [*Singing*] "Shiny happy people . . ." "Hey, pull that bus over to the side of the Pretentiousness Turnpike, all right? I want everybody off the bus. I want the shiny people over here and the happy people over here. I represent angry-gun-toting-meat-eating people, okay? So sit down and shut up!"

I got two words for Michael Stipe: Stevie Tyler. Okay? Don Henley's gonna tell people how to feel about the environment? I don't think so. A former member of the Eagles? I don't think so. I've got two words for Don Henley: Joe Walsh. Okay? Take off your ponytail and prepare to die. All right, Donny boy?

They should have shot all rock stars after Lennon was killed. They should have lined them up; we should have gotten on the Partridge Family bus and driven around shooting them one by one.

Elvis Presley should have been shot in the head back in 1957 at close range with a .44 magnum. Just plant it right behind his brain stem. Sneak up from behind while he's sucking down a bowl of potatoes and BLAM! So you could remember him in a nice way. Wouldn't it be nice to remember Elvis thin with a big head of hair and that gold lamé suit? Wouldn't that have been nice? Sure it would. Because how do you remember Elvis? You know how you remember Elvis. He was found in the toilet with his pants around his ankles and his big, fat, hairy, sweaty, king of rock 'n' roll ass exposed to the world and his final piece of kingly evidence floating in the toilet behind him. Creepy! One of his aides had to walk in and go, "Dang, Elvis is dead. I better flush the toilet. [*Flush*] Oh, man, I should have saved that. I could have made some money off of that. Dang! Ding dang!" That's how you knew one of Elvis's guys was pissed, when he said "Ding dang!" instead of "Dang!"

So I'm glad Jesus died when he did. You know, if he'd lived to be forty he would have ended up like Elvis. C'mon. He had that big entourage—twelve guys willing to do anything he wanted to do. He was already famous at that point. If he had lived to be forty, he'd be walking around Jerusalem with a big fat beer gut and big black sideburns going, "Damn, I'm the son of God—give me a cheeseburger and french fries." "But, Lord, you're overweight." "Fuck you. I'll turn you into a leper. Now give me a cheeseburger and fries right now. Where's Mary Magdalene? I'm gettin' horny now. C'mon now."

I'm going to hell for that bit—and you're all coming with me! Don't try to get out of it. "We didn't laugh at that joke. Please, Jesus. Please don't make us go to hell." "Get on the bus with Leary and Scorsese. You're goin' right to hell! Say 'Hi' to Andy Gibb for me when you get there." That's what hell is, folks. It's Andy Gibb singing "Shadow Dancing" for eons and eons. "Oh, my God. He's singing it again." And you have to wear huge bell-bottoms with orange polka dots and Hitler has all the coke.

Jesus was a great guy. He must have been incredibly patient. He didn't know he was the son of God until he was in his twenties, so as a teenager he had these incredible powers. And he never abused them. Not once. Not like you and I would. Oh, come on. If I had those powers at age seventeen, I'd be walking on water backward—naked—with a thirteen-inch erection— at the CYO picnic. [*Walking backward*] "Hey, girls! Look at this! Free wine for everybody!"

Jesus carried his cross through the streets for miles—with people spitting on his face. At the end of the journey they stripped him down and nailed him up. They stuck a lance in his side. Wow. I get tired carrying a bag of groceries two blocks. [*Out of breath*] "Shit . . . I shoulda had these delivered."

I'm sure he must be real happy about that Easter thing. He hangs on a piece of wood in the desert—hands and feet bleeding—he gives his life for our sins. Then three days later he comes back from the dead to forgive us. And how do we celebrate? By eating chocolate eggs. Yeah. Great. [*Hanging on the cross*] "Eggs, huh? Yeah, that's just fine. Why don't you get a bunny involved while you're at it? And some of those little pink marshmallow candies. Sure. Why not have a parade? Get some really expensive hats, hide the chocolate eggs and then look for them. What a tribute. Me? I'm fine. One of the great things about being a human is that you go into shock about half an hour into the agony. Get me something to drink, will ya? Sure—vinegar would be great. Just throw some vinegar on a rag and stick it into my mouth."

You would be hard-pressed to get Jesus' name across in any of the messages we send to kids at Easter or Christmas. It's all eggs and bunnies and presents and reindeer. It's great when you're a kid. Until you hit the end of that first decade. When you're eight or nine or ten years old. When your parents tell you the truth. What a brick wall to run into, huh? Everything's going great and then one day—"Oh, by the way. Santa Claus and the Easter Bunny don't exist. The Tooth Fairy? Bullshit. And Big Bird isn't even remotely funny. Okay? Life's pretty good until you hit twenty-one, and then it's taxes and student payments and death and disease—if you live long enough to actually get one. Okay? Now run outside and play. And don't get hit by a car. We want you to live at least long enough to feel guilty about all the money we spent on the presents."

If Jesus came back now, he'd have to do a tour. A rock tour. Get a band together. The Apostles. Do a video. Get it in heavy rotation on MTV. Just to get his message across. And it would have to be a great show. All the promoters are complaining about high ticket prices and unsatisfied customers. It would have to be an outstanding show. [*High*] "Saw Jesus and the Apostles. Excellent, man. He played for three hours. Fed us all—bread, fish, wine. It was unfuckingbelievable. And for the encore? Awesome. He brought Jimi Hendrix back from the grave—Buddy Holly, Big Bopper, Janis, Lennon—and they did this all-star jam thing—they did a twenty-minute cover of 'Stairway to Heaven.' I almost puked—it was that intense."

I saw the Pope on his last American tour. I love the Pope. I think he's the best Pope we ever had—John Paul George—the Beatle Pope. And he was such a regular guy. When you're the Pope, you can wear that ten-gallon Pope hat whenever you want to wear it. It's up to you—you are the Pope. But when he came to America on that big tour he didn't wear the giant Pope hat. He wore the tiny little Pope beanie. I admire that. He's trying to send a common-man image. I like a Pope who steps off the plane wearing a pair of Zebra jams and a White Sox cap—sucking down a Budweiser. [*Waving beer*] "God bless ya! What time's the show start? Let's rock!" [*Makes sign of the cross with beer can*]

Opening night for the Pope at his gig in Los Angeles was this Mexican kid. You must have seen the highlights on CNN. This kid was born with no arms. He taught himself how to play the guitar with his feet. The triumph of human nature. I was watching it on TV—he's playing some old spiritual—I can't even remember the song, I was so taken aback—he's taking solos—his toes are moving up and down the frets. And I just thought, "Man, what a miracle. This kid's born with no arms and now he's playing the guitar with his feet!" I couldn't play the guitar that well if I had been born with *ten* arms. But then again—I can blow my nose if I have to. God giveth and He taketh, you know what I'm saying? I'm sure the Pope found out pretty quick backstage after the show. "That was truly inspirational, Julio." "Thanks a lot. Hey, could you grab a Kleenex for me? I got a booger in my left nostril that's been whistling all night."

[*Chugs more beer. Inhales deeply. Exhales with a loud spitting sound.*]

I'm sick of these new rock stars. I'm fed up with the health kick rock 'n' roll's been on for the last decade. Bruce Springsteen, Madonna, and even Mick Jagger. They're all pumped up and worked out—Jagger's jogging fifteen miles a day. I like my rock stars the old-fashioned way. Skin and bones. Wasted away from drugs and drink. Tortured by their working-class origins and the wretched battle with early success. Open sores on their arms and scabs on their necks. Bad teeth. Bad sleep. Big chip on the left shoulder. The most exercise I want my rock stars to get every morning is when they pull the vomit out of their throats from the night before. [*Choking and pulling something out of mouth*] "Uh . . . oh—pizza!" [*Places it back in mouth*] "Tastes even better the second time around."

I shouldn't even mention Madonna in the same breath with rock 'n' roll. Or Cher. This is a whole different genre. Rock slash pop slash movie star slash disco diva slash, buy me some old riffs with new lyrics aerobicizers. Cher has a perfume, a workout tape and a diet book on the market. I saw her on TV pushing the sugar substitute Equal. She said—and I quote— "You care more about what you put in your car than you do about what you put in your body." Thanks, Cher. But I never put silicone breast implants in my car. And I never blew Sonny Bono, either. Two words: Gregg Allman. Okay?

I went to see Jerry Lee Lewis in concert last year. Unbelievable. Sixty-something years old and he played for two and a half hours without a break. And he's been married twenty times. He gets married on a Tuesday, they find his wife dead in a swimming pool on Thursday. The cops show up: "What happened, Jerry?" [*Shrugging*] "Ah dunno. Guess she drowned." Maybe if you married someone who's old enough to swim next time, okay, Jerry? Maybe that's the problem. Between you and Bill Wyman, there aren't any fourteen-year-olds left.

Bill Wyman's leaving the Rolling Stones. He's unhappy. Jesus, what does it take? Millions of dollars. Hundreds of millions of dollars. I read his book and he claims to have slept with five thousand women. Hey, Bill. I got news for you. You leave the band—it's over. You think you were getting laid off your looks or your dynamic onstage persona? Yeah, right. You were getting the women who couldn't get to Mick or Keith. Or Ron or Charlie. Or Brian Jones for that matter. [*Disappointed girl*] "You're sure he's really dead? Shit. And you can't dig him up? Guess I'll have to sleep with the bass player again."

Count your blessings, Bill. Morley Safer could get laid if he was the bass player for the Stones. Leonid Brezhnev. Richard Nixon. Quasimodo. Wake up and smell the set list, pal.

I thought rap was going to kick rock's ass with some street credibility, some gritty blood-soaked footsteps. NWA was at the top of the charts. Run

DMC. Then. BANG! Vanilla Ice. Elvis Presley all over again. Colonel Tom Parker must've been sitting in his suite in Vegas going, "Get me a nahce young whaht boy ta sing this nigger music an' all them little whaht suburban girls'll be shakin' their little titties at 'im."

Vanilla Ice. If I was a black urban rap guy I would've been on a roof with a box of Tech 10s shooting every white pumps and red sweatpants. "There he is!" BLAM! "No—*there* he is!" BLAM!

Just like everything else, rap has been eaten up and poured into the mainstream. McDonald's commercials have rap beats. Everybody's rapping. Comedians. Morning FM radio zoos. The Pillsbury Doughboy is doing a rap commercial. Every time you turn on the TV it's "Ba dumpth—thump-dumpth—Ba-dumpth-thum-dumpth." My dog is rapping: "B-b-ba-ba-bow wow. B-b-ba-bow wow." The cat's in the other room scratching. [*Running fingernails down box*] "Reow-reow-reow-reow." I don't want to see my dog rapping, okay? I'm pretty sure that's a sign of the apocalypse. "Honey—start the car. The dog is rapping."

I was reading a magazine recently with a Keith Richards interview in it. I'm flipping through because I like Keith and in the interview Keith Richards intimates that kids should *not* do drugs. But, Keith, we *can't* do any more drugs because you already did them all. There's none left. We have to wait till you die and smoke your ashes.

Of all the people to come down off the antidrug mountain and give us a seminar, Keith Richards—a guy with his own private blood and heroin supply. I don't think so. People marvel at Keith. "Hey, man. He did hard drugs and drinking for the last thirty-five years and I saw the last Stones tour and he looks pretty good." "Pretty good" is a relative term when it comes to Keith. It's one of those "pretty goods" you apply to a friend who's been through chemotherapy for the last six months and has just begun seeing visitors. You thought he was gonna be dead, but instead he just lost 125 pounds and has two hairs left on his head. "Well . . . I *guess* he looks pretty good . . . I mean, considering . . ." Take a good look at a photograph of Keith Richards's face. He's turned into leather. He's a giant suitcase. He has a handle on his head. That's how they move him around at the concerts. [*Lifting Keith up*] "Stand over here, Keith. No, stand over here. No . . ." He's got entire cities of miniature people driving around in those crevices on his cheeks. [*Waving*] "We get into the concerts for free!"

See, the rock stars told us to do the drugs back in the sixties and the seventics, so now they feel guilty. "Do the drugs. Wear the bell-bottoms—we are! Stare at the album covers, there's messages in there!" Now they're trying to tell us to get off because they've quit. Hey, I don't need 'em to tell me. I quit it all, folks. I quit it all.

Photo by David Hughes

JOHN LEGUIZAMO

Name: Johnny Alberto Leguizamo
Stage Name: John Leguizamo
Birthdate/Birthplace: July 22, 1964/Bogota, Colombia
"Raised Up" Where: Jackson Heights, Queens, New York
Education: C. W. Post (four semesters), transferred to NYU Tisch School of the Arts
Honors/Grants: Obie; Outer Critics Circle; Vanguardia; 1992 Lucille Lortel for Best Actor; 1992 Dramatists Guild Hull-Warner Award for Best Play; two Cable Ace Awards: Best Comedy Special Writing/Acting
Influences/Mentors/Heroes: Lily Tomlin, Richard Pryor, Whoopi Goldberg
Places Performed: Gas Station, Nuyorican Poets Café, Knitting Factory, Home for Contemporary Theater and Art, P.S. 122, Dixon Place, Gusto House, American Place Subplot, American Place main stage, Orpheum, the Goodman Theater, Westside Arts Theater
Pivotal Performance: American Place Subplot. During the entire run, I really saw my work improving, the characters becoming clearer to me.
Favorite Performance Experience: It's always what I am currently working on.
Most Terrifying Performance Experience: Opening nights (any opening night) I'm always most nervous right before I get on. Then I get on and the terror is over.
Favorite Prop or Costume: Manny the Fanny's wig
Hobbies: Basketball, classic movies, spending time with my pets, dancing, trying new exotic foods
Reading List: Anything by Woody Allen, nonfiction books on Latin culture, *Creative Visualization* by Shakti Gawain, *1001 Jokes They Haven't Heard* (and any joke books) or comedy books by comics or writers of comedy
Favorite Music: Old school jams, classic soul, rap, grunge rock, and Latin
Favorite Quote: "Olive skin makes good kin." (M*A*S*H)

John Leguizamo Interviewed by Yelba Osorio

I've sat down with John Leguizamo to ask him about his process—he seems a little uneasy about this interview and starts off by characteristically joking. I start, "I think a lot of people reading this book are probably going to want some insight into how a solo performer gets his job done—" He cuts me off with a, "Why are you coming to me?" I know he knows why I'm coming to him, so I state the obvious. "Because you've done it!" and with that we get to it.

YO: So, we want some insight. So, how do you do it?

JL: [*Feigning pretension*] It's a very involved, nah . . . I think it's something that, first of all, you really got to want to do, because it takes a lot of work, and a lot of . . . solo performance is exactly that—it's solo. You're very alone when you're creating it. And you have to have a really strong vision. And I think, you know, a lot of people do them for the wrong reasons. People do them to show off their talents and skills, but I think a really good one [solo show] has a lot to say. It's an opportunity to be political, socially aware, and to really sharpen your opinions, and your satire of society and art. It's a great forum for attacking issues and things that bother you and to channel your rage against society. You can still do it in a funny way or in a very serious way. I like Eric Bogosian and Whoopi Goldberg and Lily Tomlin. I like the comedic human revelation that they get to, or come from.

YO: That's something I want to talk about, the comedic. I saw both *Mambo Mouth* and *Spic-O-Rama* [live] and it was clear to me that I was seeing an extremely talented actor. I mean actor as opposed to stand-up comic. But I've read a lot about you, and people have used the term "stand-up comedy" to describe your work, which I think is really inaccurate.

JL: But labels are foolish, labels are for food, like Mcfud from R.E.M. says, but it's ridiculous because some people say it's performance art, others say it's stand-up, or others say theater piece and others say comedic one-man show. Everybody labels it differently. What I tried to do was a theater piece that was very funny. I labeled *Mambo Mouth* "A savage comedy" and *Spic-O-Rama* "a dysfunctional comedy." And that's basically the theme of it. *Mambo Mouth* was attacking the fact that Latin people are marginalized in a lot of ways, and these are the media types that we're all aware of and our image of ourselves, and Latin images. And that's what I did in that one. *Spic-O-Rama* was a family situation, so it's a kind of a pseudo-quasi-demi spoof of my family in a way. My growing up.

YO: So you take stuff that's meaningful to you.

JL: I always take stuff that's meaningful to me. To me art, and I try to do art, not always, you know there's been plenty of times, like *Mario Brothers* and other movies that, well, what I'm doing is not art. But I always try to do art. And to me art is something that is meaningful to you, it's an experience that has a lot of value for you, that has a reason for being, and that challenges you and excites you. I'm from the school of thinking that theater is like a church, a church of sorts, you know, and when you were there it's sort of a religious experience.

YO: What differentiates your shows *Mambo Mouth* and *Spic-O-Rama* from stand-up?

JL: It's very different, the thing is I do want to do a stand-up type of show next. That's my goal, I want to do my next project, *Full Frontal Nudity,* as more of a concert in the Richard Pryor *Live on Sunset Strip,* or Eddie Murphy's *Raw* and *Delirious* vein. The one-man theatrical piece that I did in the tradition of Lily Tomlin, Whoopi Goldberg, and Eric Bogosian is much more about pieces that are funny through character. And they reveal character. And talk about humanity. They all have stories. They're all about storytelling, but you tell it by becoming a character. You create their whole world. Stand-up, you usually find a persona for yourself, and then from there you tell a lot of JPMs [jokes per minute] and they're all stream-of-consciousness, and they all don't have to relate to each other. You tell little bites, little riffs, they can tell stories, but it's not as theatrical. Richard Pryor was the only unique one in the sense that he had pieces within his concert in which he would become a full-fledged character and tell a story within that character, which is really unusual for a stand-up performer. I guess that's why it was so revolutionary. And Lenny Bruce in his would become different characters and tell a whole story. Jonathan Winters as well, but that's different.

YO: Is that your next goal—to do a stand-up show?

JL: I admire that work. It's harder for me, because it's not something I was ever really going after, I was always after a more theatrical, acting point of view, and that's so much more about jokes—it's quick, quick bits. I want to do a stand-up show, because I feel that it challenges me as my own personality, it challenges me in terms of creating jokes and just making them quicker and sharper. It's like haiku. It's an exciting challenge because I've never written that way. I've always written much more respecting the character, and the story. *Spic-O-Rama* for me was a step from *Mambo Mouth*, in terms that it was a whole play, not only monologues, but each monologue led to a conclusion. It became a play and I found that exciting. I'd like to do, maybe someday, like a *Rashomon*, I don't know how many more of these I'll do—but where each character tells a point of view of the same incident, but it's from their point of view. I tried to do it with *Spic-O-Rama*, but it came out with a lot of forward movement, as opposed to replaying that same moment over and over.

YO: That would be more of a solo performance?

JL: Yeah, that would be going back to solo performing.

YO: How does your process start?

JL: Either playing around. Goofing around, I come up with a character I really like or I see someone in the street that I really enjoy, or something in my family sparks. And I see these characters, these mannerisms, this way of talking, and all of a sudden like I want to create this character, give it a life, a body, a voice. A story and to highlight it, make it sort of a sculpture—a verbal sculpture—verbal and physical sculpture. Then after I create them in separate chunks, then sometimes they spawn other characters, other stories within those stories—like spin-offs in sitcoms. If I have enough of a story like *Spic-O-Rama*, it became a whole concept. But I write very free-form, very different then . . . I don't structure the whole thing and then it comes through, I create each character and then that brings another idea, and another, and it starts snowballing.

YO: You mean you don't sit down and write *Spic-O-Rama* from beginning to end, learn the lines, and then perform it?

JL: I created one character, and this one gave me a whole bunch of ideas for other characters and then I discovered they were all related. So I had all these family characters, and with Peter Askin, my director, we tried to make it have forward momentum, having each monologue relate to an event. Then we came up with an event. Then I'd improvise, then I write it, then I improvise and write some more, then I reimprovise and rewrite. Constantly, constantly rewriting, because to me it always seems like it can be better. Editing is the hardest thing, because a lot of times I fall in love with things that I'm writing. I guess that's my weakness—that I like so much what I'm doing that I find it hard to pull back—to kill my darlings.

YO: So your process of writing includes a lot of improvisation, you don't just sit at your computer?

JL: It depends. With some characters I put on my garb and walk around the house and then I get the idea and then I write it. It just comes out different—sometimes I just sit down and write it 'cause it's been inside my imagination as I'm walking. But I'll always improvise.

YO: You talked about it being a lonely process, but you also mentioned your director, Peter Askin. How important is collaboration with the director, or with another writer?

JL: Any piece of great work is always a good collaboration. Just because it's a solo performance doesn't mean it's completely done by one person. But before you bring in someone else to help shape it, you got to have done the groundwork yourself. Because it's your point of view, your story that they will help you shape. Then after you have that, your point of view, it's important to bring in someone else, so they can give you an objective point of view. It's hard at that point to be objective.

YO: How were you able to make this commercially successful for yourself, in other words how did you go about getting your shows produced?

JL: I was performing in avant-garde spaces for a long time, as a comedy team, and doing solo stuff. I did it in these avant-garde spaces, because regular comedy clubs weren't comfortable with someone talking that long—and doing things that take too long to develop—they want quick, quick jokes, so I left the stand-up spaces and went to the avant-garde clubs which were really comfortable and really nurturing to performers trying things out. Then people saw it there and they were liking it, so I got confidence. Then I heard about Wynn Handman, who produced a lot of one-man shows, and I just shopped it around to a lot of places, until it hit. Until somebody liked it, and Wynn Handman liked it, and then he wanted to do it.

YO: So, Wynn Handman took it from a workshop situation to actually putting it up and getting people to pay for tickets?

JL: Well, he did do that, but I had performed it in other spaces. The H.O.M.E. Theater put it up. I did it there for eight performances, and then for *Spic-O-*

Rama producers from the Goodman Theater in Chicago who came to see me perform at the H.O.M.E. space, and they put it up as a workshop in their theater.
YO: It's really about getting your work seen. Performing in all these spaces—anywhere, anyplace that will let you do your performance.
JL: The thing about creating performance type of stuff is that you have to do it, and I wanted to do it. And what I was doing was just sharpening it and honing it, and people do come and see you, and things happen. If you have your idea you just got to put it up wherever you can. And when you have quality material people will come and ask to do it.
YO: When in the process do you start performing in front of an audience?
JL: I shape it a lot at home first, as best as I can, and then I do readings of the material, but just for my closest friends and family. I do it for them a couple of times, and then I do it for another extended group of friends. So I do hone it somewhat before I take it out to an audience. At that point I start doing it in little performance spaces. And I go back to the drawing board. People give me comments. They like some characters, others they don't understand or they don't get, so I have to go back and do my work. Because if they're not understanding what I want to communicate then it's up to me to fix it. I don't blame my audience. I don't treat them like they're stupid. I always take their comments.
YO: It sounds as if performing is part of the process.
JL: Yes, I just go out and perform it wherever I can.

Silhouette

Comes out with clothes in his hands, a headset, and a wig and fake breasts. The scrim goes up

[*To actor*] My cue, my cue. What about your cue? You completely missed that. I hit my mark right on cue.

[*To stage manager on headset*] I had the jacket ready but His *Omnipotenceness* kept on dancing. You should talk to him, he's dancing way too much. . . . Yeah, he's throwing my timing off.

[*Beat*] What's wrong with my dancing? [*Demonstrates*] I'm doing what you told me—the spin?! I'm not doing any spins, I'm not a ballerino. All right, there, happy? [*Demonstrates a sloppy turn. Freezes suddenly*] I'm just doing what you told me—make up your mind. You want me to dance, you want me to pick up his clothes, you want me—[*Interrupted*] Don't tell me how to do this job, buddy. I don't need to be here. I could be out doing something stupider and it would still be better than catering to the whims of this egomaniacal black hole that sucks the life out of everyone and everything. [*Still frozen*] Can I move now? Fuck you very much.

I don't care he's my brother. But this is the last time I get involved with this show. I don't care the girl got mono. It's not my fault. I do feel sorry for her, but hey, she should be more careful about who she . . . exchanges fluids with.

For your information I have always been there for him. I've always bailed him out. I'm not his wardrobe slave. I don't even like the way he dresses.

And the last time at the other theater—they treated me with much more respect. Yeah, much nicer. You can't fire me, I quit. Who's gonna change him for the next scene? Not me. How would you like that? He comes back and there's no one to change him?! Is there a way out back here? I bet I could find a way out. [*Starts down aisle*] Butts will be kicked, faces will be slapped, heads will roll. I'm just sporting with you!

Yeah, yeah, I'll wait. Don't worry, I know what I'm doing. I know this show inside out. John used to do these characters in the living room when we were kids. Yeah, same ones, they haven't changed. [*Acts out one of the characters*]

You know, if you ask me, there are too many sexual references in this show. I can't believe people find this entertaining and pay for it too.

My wife thinks he's a sexist. You think she's got a point? She won't talk to me because I'm aiding and abetting a sexual deviant. I'm not kidding, we have heated yelling debates about this at home. I only defend him because it reflects on me. And she's not even a feminist. I mean she's liberal and all that, but she's educated.

And all that Latino bellyaching—his girlfriend played by a white girl. Give back to the community. After he takes what's left to give back. Secondhand leftovers.

He also relies too heavily on props and costumes for dramatic effect. I like Eric Bogosian, myself. He is so minimal. It's not that I dislike theater. I just like opera better. Now, me an' my wife, we go to the theater a lot, not this kind of theater. But my real passion is opera. I am what you might call opera smart. Tell you what, you name any opera and I'll sing you the first verse of the tenor's most climactic aria in the original language. Opera has nothing to do with manhood. I was in Nam . . . No, not the war, the seminar. New-Age Male Seminar. To get in touch with the Robert Bly "wild man" in all of us. Didn't you read *Iron John*? [*Air of superiority*] Don't you know anything?

He was never this way. I remember when we were kids and our parents split up. All we had was each other, and now . . . all he has is himself. For God sakes, we were latchkey kids. He's older by five minutes. None of our family is together. We're all separated. Still, he is the family this, the family that . . . Well, where was he come Christmas, come Thanksgiving? I'll tell you where. In some orgy, that's where.

He is getting mileage out of our family friction. You know, whenever my parents argued or didn't want us to understand something they would speak Spanish so we wouldn't understand . . . but we spoke Spanish too.

And nothing in our house was ever done on purpose. Everything was always an accident. When they forgot to take us on vacation with them—it was an accident. When they didn't buy us good clothes it was an accident. Only thing on purpose was when Mom fell out of the window. That wasn't an accident. Life became too much for her. Dad always wanted her to be perfect and she wanted to be perfect for him. But perfect can't be. Changed our lives. We all blamed ourselves for everything from then on. Oh, she's okay. Now. She wore a body cast for six months. But you'd never know.

Damn, gotta go . . . next cue!! [*Cue—he runs back, holds up costume as if to wait for actor/brother. While the real silhouette comes to the scrim like Agamemnon, both freeze. Blackout.*]

May his testicles desiccate.

I am only one individual on a small planet in a small solar system, part of the same galaxy, and I have to do all the work.

Photo copyright © by Dona Ann McAdams

DEB MARGOLIN

Name: Deborah Margolin
Stage Name: Deb Margolin
Birthdate/Birthplace: September 8, 1953/Manhattan, New York
"Raised Up" Where: New York City suburbs
Education: B.A., New York University
Honors/Grants: NYU Honors Scholar; NYFA Fellow 1990–1991; Obie Award for *Split Britches*
Influences/Mentors/Heroes: Spider Woman Theater Company; Peggy Shaw; Lois Weaver
Places Performed: United States; Holland; Denmark; Germany; Scotland; London; Manhattan, Kansas
Pivotal Performance: First solo performance at Dixon Place on First Street, gussied up in a bathing suit and high heels doing the "To be or not to be" speech from *Hamlet* in a Deep Southern accent
Favorite Performance Experience: Giving the keynote commencement speech at Hampshire College, May 1990, after a ritual shot of Jack Daniel's.
Most Terrifying Performance Experience: Performing new material, days after having given birth, with baby in my arms, both of us about to barf
Favorite Prop or Costume: Hideous pink-and-orange silk dress with sentimental lacing on bodice and tendentious ruffle at bottom
Hobbies: Swimming, writing plays, making phony phone calls, playing the ocean game with my kid
Reading List: Rilke, Neruda, Henry Miller, Gabriel García Marquez, Doris Lessing, Margaret Drabble
Favorite Music: Jazz: John Coltrane, Miles Davis, Kip Hanrahan
Favorite Quote: "Wagner's music isn't as bad as it sounds." (Mark Twain)

Artist's Notes

I found theater through a love of language, and performance art through a love of theater and a very practical need to make theater by myself. Having begun writing and performing solo shows, I remember feeling marginalized by the term *performance artist* which was being imposed on me; I thought of myself as a playwright for one. It wasn't long before I came to embrace both the term *performance artist* and the crucial distinction it implied from conventional theater. This distinction between performance art and theater inheres, I think, in the very things that engendered performance art in the first place, beginning with the shedding of certain conventions that attend conventional theater: curtains, proscenia, fancy costumes and makeup, and all the trappings that make an actor invisible beneath his or her character. Such things were out of reach for a lot of us, and performance art allowed us a kind of postmodern license to perform anywhere and without such conceits, making it immediately into a kind of poor folks' theater. Secondly, performance offered us license to work from personal material; as opposed to conventional Broadway scripts, where there's a rape, a murder, or a car chase, or there are songs and dances to compensate for the lack of those, performance art accredited the intimate image, the autobiographical stories, the moments between moments, and the accidentally political and extremely powerful presumption of personal significance that such scripting is predicated upon. Thirdly, and most delicious of all, is the way the performance artist creates a translucent layer between the character and the self, allowing the audience to see right through the character to the actor, right through the writing to the writer; and to pay attention not just to what the actor says but to the actor's unyielding desire to say it. This latter creates an instant dialectic between the character and the actor, and has a way of politicizing and expanding the simplest theatrical moment.

Of Mice, Bugs and Women is the avatar of my belief in the power of all these things. Two of the three character monologues are delivered by fictional characters, and the writer who wrote them separates them in the sequence, although she is treated no differently by me, the actor, for her "realness." The entire triptych sprang out of a single image: once, when I was twenty-seven, I went swimming, swam a hundred laps, came home and sat down at a table by a window, sank into the high summer, and somehow realized that I was at the peak of my form both physically and spiritually. There was a bee trapped in the window shade, buzzing furiously for its life, and I'm afraid of bees, and so I shared my greatest still moment in pity towards and terror of a dying insect.

The Exterminator

[*Sound of insect buzzing*]

Hello! Exterminator! Exterminator!

[*Enters*]

I got it! I got it! [*Pulls out flyswatter, looks for insect, swats. Sound of buzzing off.*]

Hello, exterminator! Tell me about your problem! And yes, I'm still the exterminator! Still on the job! You know, people think because it's ex-terminator that I no longer have the job, but I'm still on the job! See, it's Latin!

Ex is Latin! Anybody here take Latin? Anybody! Anybody! See, *ex* is Latin for out! It means out! Like *ex-it* means you go *out* of *it*! Or like Ex-Lax means it gets the shit *out*! Or like *exterminator*! *Out* of people like me, they make a *terminator*! Exterminator! Now! Tell me about your problem!

Now! A woman I service on the East Side got them big thick roaches! Waterbugs! You know she actually tried to kill them by stomping on them, covering 'em up with oaktag! She'd herd 'em all up, put oaktag cardboard over 'em, and jump! Took two hours a shot! Now! Tell me about your problem! You know, bugs! I'm a bugs man and a mouse man! Bugs and mice are different! Okay! What's the difference between a bug and a mouse? Right! A mouse is a little bit bigger than a bug but there's another important difference! What is it? What is it? It's . . . *motivation*! *Motivation*! Because a bug just tries to survive, whereas a mouse is burdened with an actual *will to live*! Will to live! Separates the bugs from the mice! Will to live! See a bug . . . all right, now what is a bug? Okay, it's an insect . . . maybe it has wings or whatever, but it's no falcon! And you, Senator, are no Jack Kennedy! Haha! That was very good when he said that! Whereas a mouse has no wings, but flight is its middle name! It flees! It flees! Silently! Okay, what's the most devastating thing about a mousetrap? Anybody! Anybody! It's the *noise* it makes! Because it's *attention*! Mice don't want no attention! Bugs don't mind! I saw a mouse once, brown. Lived at the apartment of one of my clients. Lived there so long it was listed in the phone book! Tried everything. Tried everything with this mouse! One day, my client was going to work, fumbling with her keys. The mouse ran out of her house and under the door into her neighbor's house. Moved out all at once, just like that. Gal called me up the next day, said she missed the mouse! Didn't have no closure with the mouse! Made me come back and look for it! Crazy gal! Crazy gal!

And now the bugs won't move when they've got it good! Now! Tell me about your problem. Now, bugs swarm around the dead! Mice don't swarm around the dead! Saw a frog once, dead! Looked like a bearskin rug! Dead before it had a chance, flattened by a guy walking to the swimpool! It looked like a fossil! Fossils are funny! Okay, what is a fossil? Anybody! Anybody! Fossil's an impression! You know, not the creature itself, but the impression it makes on a soft surface! Impressions of the dead last for years! Centuries! Impressions of the dead! Anybody! Impressions of the dead! So there's this dead frog, you know, and it's like Tavern on the Green for the flies! Now, this young frog's mother did not intend for her baby to be squashed under a bunch of bugs like the buffet table at a bar mitzvah! But you take a mouse! A mouse won't do that! Mouse won't get all gussied up to come out and eat barbecue from the dead! Why? Because it's publicity, see! Publicity! A mouse don't want no publicity! Like a criminal, or a celebrity on vacation! Mouse is private! Quiet! Good neighbor, you see!

Saddest mouse I ever seen in Port Authority! They beep me, tell me Port Authority! I go over there, second floor up the escalator, there's a mouse in the candy corn! Plowing with its feet in the candy corn, like trying to walk on a mountain of balloons, it can't even eat 'cause it can't walk, can't walk 'cause it can't get no traction, like a treadmill! Treadmill of death in the candy corn! Couldn't breathe too good in there either! Flailing its legs, wagging its tail, trying to move, scared. I get it out for them, they reopen the store, don't clean up or nothin', little kid come in, what does he want, he wants candy corn, mother buys him candy corn, he's eating it. I show him the mouse, he falls in love with it. Had little orange crumbs on it. Killed it with the spray gun.

Tell me about your problem! See! I know a lady got porcupines! Porcupines, they eat houses! Lady's got porcupines lunching on her house, see! She buys a gun, right? She puts on a hat, lies down on the ground near the floorboards, starts shooting! But she shot a bunch of mice! The porcupines, they loaded their guts with wood, laid down, waited it out, like at McDonald's! Kid hid in the dishwasher till it was all over, see! Twenty-three people dead, kid hid in the dishwasher! Kid hid in the dishwasher! Wouldn't come out! Didn't know it was over, wouldn't come out! Wouldn't come out till the cops drug him out!

It's against company policy! See, I'm not allowed to kill anything myself, see! With my own hands, see! It's against company policy, see! I just create an atmosphere, see, where they just drop dead! But I don't do it myself, see! I'm an operative! And I got a radio, see! A radio! Someone got bugs, they can reach me! Call the front office, they send me right out! To the exact place and everything!

One lady calls me up for a bee! Christ, I got stories! She calls me up for a bee! See, she's sitting there in a bathing suit with a cup of coffee, and there's a bee caught between the screen and the blinds! Buzzing deep! She's aging! I see her, a young woman! This is the best moment of her life, see, she's been swimming, she's got coffee, she's strong, see, but she's listening to this bee! She's at the top of the V! See your life is an upside-down V! Everyone's is! You reach the top of the V at, let's say, twenty-nine! And you perch up there in a little outfit with a cup of coffee, see! And you know that's the best it's gonna get! See! And how long it goes on like that depends on how long you can sit with your ass perched on a spike that sharp. Anybody! Anybody!

So she's listening to the bee! See, it was gonna die anyway! The buzz was low! See, when the buzz is high it's got a will to live! Well, not a will to live, but it's trying to survive! It's conserving energy, which is a bee's form of hope, see! But when the buzz is low, it's weak and angry! And that's a bad combination, weak and angry! Can't conserve! Can't conserve! It's death in a matter of minutes, see! So here was this beautiful gal! And her life was at its best moment! See, I could tell! I could tell! Swimming! Coffee! Summer! Bathing suit! Enough money to call a man to kill a bee! Listening to a bee trying to die at four o'clock in the afternoon! So I said, tell me about your problem! And while she was telling me, the bee died. I'm like a psychiatrist or something! That's what they do!

One guy's got ants! He lays on the windowsill 'cause he got nowhere else to sleep! And red ants ate him alive, so he calls me. See, psychologically she knew! She knew! She knew she was at the top of the V, she was balanced at the top, and the bee was on the way down! That's what was upsetting her! They were heading in opposite directions, and she couldn't take it! See that's I-ronny! See, when something is sitting over here, and the other thing's going in the opposite direction, it's I-ronical! Got to have a stomach for it! Like doctors, military men! They got a stomach for it! She got no stomach for it!

See, then you got lightning bugs! They're nice, right, everyone likes 'em, right? Little kids and so forth, right? But they're not all they're cracked up to be! What is a lightning bug? Anybody! Little flashes of light all night! What mosquitoes do with sound they do with light! They whine all night *with light*! Meaio, Meaio!

[*Sound of insect buzzing*]

Okay, I got it! I got it!

The Novelist

Planes and flies. All night long, I've got these planes and flies. Well, they've got us right on the flight pattern here, so I'm sorry about the flies, the planes I can't do anything about. Well, I can't do anything about the flies either, but people don't know that, my friends all say: Spray this! Spray that! Well, I'm not going to spray these things, I mean God knows what they have in them! You know, I read about this ultrasonic device that emits a sound above the level of human perception, and this sound supposedly gets rid of all your bugs and rodents. They all just march to the front door of your home with their things in a little scarf tied to a stick, and try to emigrate as quickly as possible to a better life, that's what they lead you to believe, I read about it in one of these catalogues. So you buy one, you plug it in, you think it's okay; your mice and bugs leave; your house looks great, you're throwing dinner parties left and right, and the next thing you know you're jumping out the window! And you think to yourself: Now why am I doing this? And it's from listening for three months to the shrieking of this machine you didn't even think you heard!

You know they have us right on the flight pattern here. I'm not even going to go to the airport anymore, I'll just take my luggage and go up to the roof, they can pick me up there, it's right on the way. All night, those planes. It's like having your ear to a huge stomach in the throes of a terrible hunger. They sound like pangs to me, these planes. No wonder I can't sleep. Plus alcohol. I always think if I have a glass or two of wine it'll help me sleep, but it never does. Oh, I fall asleep! But then I wake up like a dog on a leash on a sidewalk in the summer whose master just jerked him to attention. I've got sweat in a circle around my lips.

Anyway, that's just the way I write. It's just that way, always has been. I'm having a fuck of a time.

Writing's so hard, it's amazing I get anything done. Terribly hard. Terribly hard to get anything done. I wake up, and out the curtains through the window I see the mountain, and that draws me outside onto the porch, and then I smoke a cigarette, and after I smoke I get hungry, so I come inside and eat; then after I eat I need to go back out and have a cigarette, then after I have a cigarette I feel like lying down, and once I'm lying down I go back to sleep again. And this palindromic series of events follows me in cycles many times throughout a day; it's terribly hard to get anything done at all.

You know, thirty-four years ago I sat down and wrote the first industrial novel since the postindustrial era. And I thought it was really hard because it was my first novel, but every novel has come equally hard, and hard in the same way.

See, I'm not an intellectual, I'm just a good listener. I don't sleep well. I get up at night and I hear people talking; sometimes it's my neighbors, sometimes it's people in my head. And I listen and I write down what I hear, that's all. Plots invent themselves out of voices. And I insist on politeness from my characters. I want to get to know them. I don't like it when real or imaginary people tell me their whole life story when I don't even know them. It's false intimacy, I hate it. I once moved into a building and said hello to a good-looking young lawyer type who lived in the apartment below me. Next day we happened to get on the same subway car and he ended up telling me about his sixteen-year-old daughter, you know he's divorced of course, and how he took her with him on a Club Med vacation, and how she walked in on him screwing a girl about her own age. Now, did I need to hear that? Did I? Now every time I think about the American Bar Association I think of statutory rape at the Club Med.

Same with my characters. I need to get to know them, need to chat with them for months before I'm ready for stories like that. I had one gal who wouldn't wait. Young college gal from the Jersey Shore. Not only wanted to *tell* me everything about herself that first night I imagined her, but also demanded to know everything about me: why I dye my hair, how my boobs got the way they are, why I always write about dissatisfied men instead of dissatisfied women. My politics. Why I fantasize about being a teenager when I have sex . . . the whole works.

Well, none of her beeswax. It's interesting . . . I wanted to know all that stuff about my mother . . . that must be why she ran away from me so much and hated me so often. . . . It's like some natural principle . . . whatever you did to drive your parents crazy, there's someone waiting in the wings to do that to *you* . . . even if you have to invent them. I had a dream about this college girl. Let's see . . . she was a lit major with a minor in theater, by the way. [*Munching*] Mmm. These are delicious! And it says here: No cholesterol. Oh, but there's fat! Eighty grams of fat! Imagine that! No cholesterol but a thousand blobs of fat! Fat and cholesterol are like Sacco and Vanzetti, everybody knows that. So this little lit major said:

I spin with my planet in deft, senseless earnest

She was quoting a poem. I thought the line was vacuous and stupid, I'm opinionated, I admit that. She defended the line, thought it was resonant and meaningful. When I woke up I realized maybe there's something to it; I mean, we are all spinning all the time, and that's probably very debilitating in its way: our TV dinners are spinning, our books, our papers, our clothes, our literary agents. I mean, when you get on a plane and fly across the country, you get off the plane and you're very tired when all you did was sit there; the involuntary movement was exhausting. Maybe that's why we're all so inexplicably blank and tired all the time.

I couldn't stand that college gal. She was smarter than I am and I don't suffer geniuses gladly . . . so I cut her from the novel. Couldn't enjoy her, didn't want to listen anymore. It's so funny . . . that's what my mother did to me, only she wasn't a writer, she was my mother. Although in a way, a point could be made that we write our kids . . . you use DNA instead of ink, but the channeling aspect is the same. [*Munching*] These things are delicious!

[*Eating*] You know what these things remind me of? Those Bongos or Condos . . . Conchos . . . no, Combos! Those pretzels that have the cheese stuffed up 'em! Those say no cholesterol too! I was in the library working, and there were these two boys eating them. . . . I adored these little boys! They were about fourteen or fifteen, wearing hats . . . one of them had a baseball cap on backwards, the other had a rag tied around his head . . . these headdresses were acts of rebellion, intelligent, friendly rebellion . . . and they were laughing and laughing . . . so I started eavesdropping . . . one of them was talking about how when the atom bomb fell, it landed on this one particular girl! He said: 'The atom bomb landed on this one girl! It was really funny! She went splat! Parts of her body were spread out for ten miles! Her hands were all cut off and everything! It was gross!' And they laughed hysterically. So then the other boy said: 'I heard when you get shot in the head you don't even know it! I bet she didn't even know it!'

And they laughed again, but different. Then the first boy said: 'My sister has never cut her hair and it's four feet long, and there's a little triangle missing from her nose! My dad was giving her the beat and she chipped a part of her nose! If you look you can see a triangle missing!' And they laughed again.

I love those boys . . . I love the way they take the gruesome things they hear about . . . merge them with details of daily life, and then laugh! That's adolescent humor! Mythic humor! Like that story I grew up with about a girl with a beehive hairdo, and one day she put honey in it and a thousand bees came and stung her to death! Mythic humor. It's that humor whose purpose is to try to understand horror, act real casual about it, and establish a big distance from it, all at the same time . . . it was so cute, that gruesome story about the bomb falling on this one girl . . . what a nerd she must have felt like that day at the high school! . . . and then combining it so casually with that story about the sister with the Medusan hair and the Bermuda triangle missing from her nose. . . . I loved those boys!

I wrote nonfiction . . . it was beautiful, my nonfiction . . . it was beautiful the way novels are beautiful, because I used images from my own life . . . images I'd saved up from all places: here, there, little chips of poetry I'd been collecting all my life. These images make me think of sea glass . . . you know, that's what they call those pieces of smooth, not quite but almost transparent slices of shell you find on the beach . . . they're clear colored, or nearly green, from who knows what years of compression and abrasiveness at the whims of the tide . . . sea glass. I collected that too, sea glass, found hundreds of pieces on thousands of sleazy beaches up and down the world, saved them up and finally put the pieces in a glass jar with water. I loved the sound the pieces made as they clicked, they looked like trash, beautiful pieces of a shattered something, only smooth from centuries of abrasion . . . or like the glass windows people put up in the bathroom to keep people from looking in. That's what these images were like, but now I don't have any more images. They're all gone, I used them up, tossed them into fountains of other purposes, gave them away . . . people wondered why my work was beautiful. I'm out of images now, all I do is listen. So as you're leaving please speak extra loudly. I've got my notebook and pen out; this is how I make my living now.

Photo copyright © by Dona Ann McAdams

ROBBIE MCCAULEY

Name: Robbie McCauley
Stage Name: Same
Birthdate/Birthplace: July 14, 1942/Norfolk, Virginia
"Raised Up" Where: Columbus, Georgia; Washington, D.C.
Education: B.A. Howard University, History/Theater
M.A. New York University, Educational Theater
Honors/Grants: Obie Award, 1992; Bessie Award, 1990 for *Sally's Rape;* AUDELCO
Award, 1974, for Best Supporting Actress; Franklin Furnace Fund for Performance; NEA,
Rockefeller, and NYSCA grants; 1993 Biennial Performance/Theater Artist of the Whitney
Museum of American Art
Influences/Mentors/Heroes: Joseph Chaikin, Gylan Kain, Bob Carroll, Bimbo Rivas,
Kristin Linklater
Places Performed: Franklin Furnace, St. Marks's Danspace, P.S. 122, Dixon Place, La
MaMa, Nuyorican Poets Café, Context, DTW, Davis Center for the Performing Arts
(CCNY), New Federal Theater, Public Theater, and numerous places outside of New York
Pivotal Performance: Chorus Leader in *Medea* at Howard University. I got an award for
"Best Walk-on."
Favorite Performance Experience: Creating "Clara" in Adrienne Kennedy's *A Movie
Star Has to Star in Black and White* directed by Joseph Chaikin
Most Terrifying Performance Experience: The first improvisational performance of
Persimmon Peel at La MaMa with Laurie Carlos. No script, no rehearsal, and Laurie was
being true to the bone.
Favorite Prop or Costume: My homemade notebook, wrapped in rope with pencil
attached in *A Movie Star . . .*
Hobbies: Reading mysteries, watching television, and bike riding
Reading List: Martin Bernal's *Black Athena,* Stuart M. Kaminsky mysteries, *Jazz* by Toni
Morrison, *Z Magazine*
Favorite Music: Rhythm and blues and modern jazz (James Brown, Otis Redding, Aretha
Franklin, Janis Joplin, Miles Davis, Cecil Taylor), and Joan Baez
Favorite Quote: "Kindness eases change." (Octavia B. Butler)

Artist's Notes

In *Mother Worked* I am talking about my mother. Most of the words are
hers. I am pleased with its comic nature. It comes years after the pieces
that emphasized the father parts of my family stories. This piece was written and performed in 1995.

The musical and movement references are designed to inform performers and directors about rhythm and style. Whatever musical composition or
choreography they suggest is welcome. I like for the musical and movement
references to be in the atmosphere of the creative time, but not to be
strictly adhered to. The point of these works has been to get the work done,
trusting the imagination of the workers involved.

Outside influences have largely affected my identity. My fight for individuality involves recognizing that. From there I am able to change when necessary. I can't be the only one. In theater people can engage with others on how so many different people are connected to the same events. The colors and textures are infinite. The content is the aesthetic.

Performance theater pieces that I conceptualized and presented from 1985 to the present (1995) were consciously created from thoughts about how personal issues are connected to social ones. *My Father and the Wars*, *Indian Blood*, and *Sally's Rape* were largely self-produced and performed throughout the United States. The Buffalo Project was curated by Ron Ehmke at Hallwalls; the Primary Sources series (*Mississippi Freedom* in Jackson and other sites in western Mississippi, *Turf* in four neighborhoods of Boston, Massachusetts, and *The Other Weapon* in four neighborhoods of Los Angeles, California), produced by the Arts Company, all involved performers in those various communities. Currently (1995) I am working on the Stories Exchange Project in Prague, the Czech Republic, produced by the Fund for New Performance/Video and the Underground Project with the Walker Arts Institute and Penumbra Theater Company.

In these works the actor involves herself in the subject matter to reveal an aspect of her persona that can play the "characters" who speak. Character in fact is not so important, but the actor's involvement in the text is. Character, then, evolves through that. In *Mother Worked*, I was surprised how much my mother's character was revealed through my involvement with the world of her work.

I move material from one work to another carefully, the idea that one can enter the story at any point, that the stories of ordinary people are primary sources for history, the idea of continuousness. References from *My Father and the Wars* appear in *Sally's Rape* and in *Mother Worked*.

The survival of black people in the United States is the subject matter I concentrate on. This subject resonates in many areas. It involves issues of sex, class, and power. It is full of war stories, real war stories, not just the official ones.

Mother Worked

A Telling

by Robbie McCauley
composed for
Jon Spelman's
Tall Tales, White Lies, Local Color and Monumental Views: Stories from the Nation's Capital.

Prelude

A sculpture of cubes arranged on different levels. DAUGHTER *sits on lower level and rattles off matter-of-factly.*

I told y'all already how Great-great-grandma Sally brought her daughters up to be ladies, and how my mother got her name from one of those fine daughters who used to sit on the porch with organdy dresses on. . . . Now, I told everybody the father parts—about the contradictions of violence and possibilities—and how Mother said, "If you talk about me like that after I die, I'll come back and haunt yo' ass." So I'ma do her part now while she's alive and well.

I. Ballad [*She moves to another step.*]

Mother said: When I first came to Washington in 1937 to get married, most people I knew were going to churches downtown or living up on the hill or down near U Street someplace. When I came back in 1946, after World War Two, the city was more crowded, a lot of people were working and people had moved farther out . . . far northeast . . . even far northwest. [*Pause*] Black people. That's what I'm speaking about.

[*Conversational music*]
Before then far northeast where we later lived wadn't developed, it was more rural-like. Most of those churches—even when we moved out there in the early fifties—the Episcopal, Methodist, Lutheran, Church of God, the big Catholic church on East Capitol were just being built. More and more black people were being hired in the government.

[*Movement. Slight plié.*]
Low-paying jobs, most of 'em . . . but still considered a pretty good job even if you were a Two. Some people went in as a Grade One. That was the lowest. And then there was another . . . set of ratings . . . like, charwomen and maintenance men . . . didn't have to pass the clerical test like I did . . . but they were rated and some had very good jobs—especially drivers like

your daddy did once—paid by the hour. We got paid every two weeks. Some of them made very good money—especially if they worked overtime.

[DAUGHTER *stands behind a cube and cuts up, randomly passes to audience, and munches on pieces of cheese and whole wheat bread.*]

Mother always made good sandwiches. She had experience. The family down South had had a café and they were going to expand but Grandpa Tugg died . . . then the Depression . . . and one thing and another. . . . Mother's first job up here wasn't even a government rating. But I thought it must have been mighty fine because when she came home from work, she looked so beautiful. My mother always loved pretty clothes. . . . She actually worked in a little snack bar attached to the Senate dining room in the Capitol Building . . . where they served salads and sandwiches and little quick-ups.

II. Blues

All day long, you know, she said, the senators were sending their secretaries and messengers down . . . while the senators were up there beating on the table [*Two beats on the cube*] . . . talking 'bout the niggers [*Third beat*] And the niggers [*Beat*] this . . . and the niggers [*Beat*] that. That's what the messengers said, say they up there fussing now, say they would [*Beat*] say, We not, we not . . . the niggers [*Beat*] . . . Everything they would say they would hit [*Beat*] . . . especially that Storm Thurmon—or whatever his name is from South Carolina.

That's what the messenger told me. But the messenger just ignored it because . . . well . . . the messenger was black and it didn't mean he was a nigger, didn't mean he wadn't gon' get his paycheck. The messenger was almost immune . . . because that was the way it was.

[*Conversational bop*]

But I just worked behind the counter in the snack bar. I worked with a beautiful white gal from Hungary who had the same name as mine—Alice . . . uh-huh . . . and she worked behind the counter with me. And then there was a white woman on the cash register. I forget her name . . . but, oh she was so liberal, so crazy 'bout black people. And a beautiful black gal worked in the kitchen . . . very rough speaking though . . . Gertie. And this white woman tried to be buddy with Gertie and everything.

So one day . . . you know how visitors always come in the Capitol . . . and walk around? . . . *Tour*. So a bunch of kids came from New Jersey on a tour. About a quarter of those kids were black. And as they got in line to come through—the head people over this little snack bar, and the nice white woman got a-mumbling an' whisperin' and carrying on. . . . Then they told us they couldn't serve those black kids, but they couldn't take 'em outta line, so they told us to stop servin' 'em and they just closed. [*Pause*]

So, I told them, if you intend not to serve them, why don't you make a big sign, like they did in Georgia. Say, For Whites Only, so everybody'll know. After I said my piece, I went home and never came back there to that job.

[DAUGHTER *clears up foodstuff and steps up one level*]

So Mother took a test for Grade Two—messenger or clerk or whatever . . . made a good grade, got her rating, got that call and went on to work in the government.

Bridge

She said, See, I had got calls during the war when they were hiring a lot of black women, but I didn't want to come up here with two children and pay somebody to baby-sit, and pay rent and blah blah blah while my husband was in the war, so I stayed down in Georgia with my family where I was comfortable. And people said, Well, you missed your opportunity. [*Blues finish*]

So when I got this, it was like heaven. I was elated. And the job was interesting to a certain degree. They gave me my job description . . . which was something that if you didn't know what it was, you wouldn't know what it was . . . but I asked questions and realized it was a simple job any ordinary high school graduate could do.

III. Staccato

[*Moderate rhythmic gestures*]

Filing and matching. Invoices with contracts. Naval Regional Accounts Office, NRAO . . . We paid bills, for places all over the United States and some other places like Guam . . . the Philippines . . . wherever sailors or naval activities would be . . . even ships. . . . We had bills from one of the ships your daddy was on once . . . a big ship . . . I forgot its name.

[*Rhythm accelerates*]

Sometimes just small purchase orders, like from a commissary, just a list of things. Then there would be a purchase for a big . . . big . . . big something, like a torpedo plant! When the invoice or bill would come in for payment, it would have a contract number and I would match the bill with the contract. We had a file and I would set it in order—numerical or alphabetical—somebody wanted something, they could go put their hands on it. So that's how it was called Match and File Clerk. [*Release*]

IV. Plantation Rap

[*She sits on a higher level*]

Miss Malone was the overseer. She would sit like this . . . leaning over checking everybody out. Somebody asked her what was her job, and she said she didn't have to work, her job was to watch us. They would have meetings and talk to us like we were in kindergarten . . . and we had to sign in and out. . . . And the master, Miss Roberts, you surely didn't mess with her. They talked down to you all the time back then. Supervisor and chief. And, yeah, both were white.

And I mean you had to sit still and do your work, or act like you were doing it, or else you get beat. I don't mean they whipped. No, we didn't get whipped, but it felt like if you misbehaved you would.

I called it the Lookdown. Everybody had to look down no matter what they were doing. I'd look up and see everybody looking down. One lady I called Miss Lookdown wouldn't even hold her head up when she went to the ladies' room. On the thirtieth of June, at the end of the fiscal year, every year, they would give us ice cream and cookies.

Miss Pepper was a black supervisor, a Grade Six. I thought she was not relaxed in her position. She would tell us what the white people told her to tell us whether she agreed with it or not. She had to dance by their music. Many people didn't like her for that, but it was understandable and I thought she was a very nice person.

So, they sent for her on a temporary basis to come to the Office of Economic Opportunity, OEO, to help set up and pay those bills over there. After getting her in there, they decided they wanted to keep her. So they sent a letter to the navy saying that OEO came directly under the office of the president and had authority over Navy Finance Center, so they were gonna keep Miss Pepper . . . and never let her come back to the plantation.

[*Stands, goes up to different level*]

Okay, when the letter came, I'm a correspondence clerk now, Grade Four, and my desk was right here . . . [*Indicates diagonal relationship*] . . . and Miss Roberts's office there . . . so they could really keep an eye on me. So she said, [*Both voices sickeningly sweet*] "Alice . . . go make me a copy of this letter. . . ." "Sure, Miss Roberts. . . ." I was glad to be going 'cause otherwise we couldn't leave our desks. That meant we could talk to people in another section or something. I was glad to do that nigger work sometimes.

Anyway, going down there . . . I said, God, this is . . . I had already heard about OEO . . . and had already applied but that letter had just gone in a pile, I guess. . . . I said, O my Lord! Then I knew they were keeping Miss Pepper, and had an opening . . . for a voucher examiner. . . . I'd done that!

When I made Miss Roberts a copy [*To audience*] guess who else I made a copy for? . . . *Alice.* I gave Miss Roberts her copy. When she said thank you, I said to myself, thank *you.*

I got the letter, made out an application and went straight to OEO . . . just like they'd sent for me. And what made it so pitiful, I went on my lunch hour. And they were very strict. They gave us just a half hour. I was lucky enough to get a cab and ran up to Nineteenth and M to leave my application . . . get back to work. Coming back . . . ran out the building . . . had to get a cab. A white guy right here . . . and I'm standing right there on the corner . . . and I said "Taxi" and I slapped that man right ka-dap in his face, and I got so scared . . . I *am* from Georgia. He said, "Ma'am, you slapped me and you don't even know me." I almost peed on myself. When I got back to work I was out of breath. [*Release*]

V. Finale

I got the job, but my supervisor at OEO was not Miss Pepper. His name was Mr. Kick. He seemed very nice but no! He was prejudiced and didn't know it. One thing about him was he was Jewish and Irish. He said he did not want his Jewishness emphasized.

She said, They'd give me more work, but not the grade or the salary. More and more people would come in—usually younger white women who I would train to do the work—and they were passed over me. I had pulled myself up to a GS Six. [*Gesture of pulling up by bootstraps*] Then they gave me a Seven. Eventually I decided that I wanted to write up the job so I could improve on the process and make the job easier. It was referred to as a "beneficial suggestion." It was accepted and in March 1972, I got a Performance Award . . . but still no promotion.

In 1975 I filed an antidiscrimination action against Mr. Kick. I had to get my promotion so I could have three years in a higher grade to get full benefits in that grade. He knew, but thought I wadn't gon' do it. He called it hot air. Uh-huh, well, the hot air turned cold. I filed. I won. I got my promotion. See, I'd started in government service as a Two . . . and in 1979, I retired after thirty-one years as a GS Eleven.

Coda

[*She moves to the highest level*]
    She said, Oh, yeah, I liked the government.

Photo copyright © by Dona Ann McAdams

TIM MILLER

Name: Tim Miller
Stage Name: Same
Birthdate/Birthplace: Pasadena, California
"Raised Up" Where: In Whittier, California, just down the street from Nixon's brother's seafood restaurant
Education: Moved to New York City when I was nineteen and did not end up headless floating down the Hudson
Honors/Grants: American Choreographer Award, numerous NEA Grants, and an arrest record with Act Up
Influences: Jeff Weiss performing on East Tenth Street doing a wild dance and singing, "Do you think I got lips like this from sucking doorknobs?"
Places Performed: Yale Repertory Theater; Actors Theater of Louisville; P.S. 122; Walker Art Center; the Hollywood Bowl; Citizens Theater, Glasgow
Pivotal Performance: A mad dash from being beat up by the police in San Francisco at the Sixth International AIDS Conference to a show in Minneapolis at the Walker Art Center. I felt all these forces surround me during the show. This messed-up society. The wonderful queer audience in Minneapolis. I flew and felt the performance so strong inside me.
Favorite Performance Experience: One really hot sweaty hoot & holler performance during the peak of the NEA Tour stuff where I got a coupla audience members to take off their clothes while I did my piece *My Queer Body.*
Most Terrifying Performance Experience: In one of my first performances at P.S. 122 in 1980 I was stuffed in a locker with a bunch of burning newspapers. This is why there is one big burned spot on the floor at 122.
Favorite Prop/Costume: My sacred seed pod from Walt Whitman's grave that I use in *My Queer Body.* My skin and sweat are my favorite costume.
Hobbies: I look after my fruit trees and like to touch sweet men.
Reading List: Reynolds Price, *The Promise of Rest*, and, of course, *Franny and Zooey* at least twice a year
Favorite Music: Pansy Division, Mary Chapin Carpenter, Michael Callen's incredible voice which I miss dearly
Favorite Quote: "Live these days!/Love well—value every kiss!/Savor your body's blink—/Between being born and dying!"

Artist's Notes

I generally take about the same amount of time creating a new performance work as it takes for a pregnant elephant to come to term: approximately twenty-two months. For me, and perhaps for the elephant, this is a crazy time of filtering through my most intense dreams, fantasies, obsessions, and personal stuff to arrive at exactly the piece that I need to do *right now.* I especially try to tune in to my reality as a queer man in relation to my community to locate that place of urgency in the work. What is the material

that most desperately needs to find expression in a new performance? So
desperate in its need to be told, that if I didn't, my head would explode.
Yikes!

For this piece, "The Maw of Death," which was part of a full evening
work called *Some Golden States,* I was keen to remember the incredible
voltage of arriving in New York at the age of nineteen. This Homo-Boy-
Adventure-in-the-Big-City is contrasted with the parallel journey towards
the arrival of AIDS and the first loss of a lover to this fucked-up plague.
This was an essential topic for me to explore in 1987 when I created this
work. Meeting the enormous challenge of placing the mounting losses to
AIDS through some kind of performance structure was necessary for my
wholeness as an artist and person. Somehow to craft my own little divine
comedy, my own journey into the underworld, became vital to me. I needed
to acknowledge that I had gone to a scary place (the Maw of Death, no
less!) and come back. But something is lost whether this faggot-Orpheus
looks over his shoulder or not. You can't bring all your friends and lovers
back with you. The weight of these losses continues to haunt me. In my
performances, I need to allow the full mythic potential of the forces that
surround us to work on all cylinders. The more metaphors the merrier! It is
a chance to fuck with the history of our time through the story of our lives.

In "The Maw of Death" as I recount the pleasures of a great love affair,
and the terrible moment of knowing that a man I'd loved was dead, it's my
opportunity to really claim the importance of this story in my life. To claim
its smells and tastes: from the smack of the V-8 juice to the whiff of that
boy's butthole. But I also want to place these experiences in the community
of the audience, to name the importance of these moments in *all our lives.* I
think somehow this is the starting point for the potential communion to
happen in a theater or performance space, the naked acknowledgment of
the good stuff *and* the shit we are all going through. For me, both as an
artist and a man, I can't imagine a more interesting alchemy to try to make
happen in my performances.

The Maw of Death

X marks the spot. Right here! In 1978, I arrived on a nonstop flight from
LAX to JFK. I dragged my nineteen-year-old ass (and my avocado green polished plastic suitcase stuffed with rantings and poems) into Manhattan on
the Carey Bus. I spent my first three nights in NYC at the International
Ladies' Garment Workers' Union Building at Twenty-third and Eighth Avenue. I repeatedly listened to Joan Baez's song "Farewell, Angelina" and
stared through the Chelsea night at the glowing Empire State Building pok-

ing through July's thunderclouds. I lay in a sexless bed with a metalworker who was a kindly friend of a friend of my friend Rachel in Seattle. She had sensibly looked after her goyische Tim from California and had assigned me a string of her Long Island Jewish pals to look after me these first days. Their job, should they decide to accept it, was to make sure I didn't end up floating in pieces down the Hudson.

I had three days in that bed with the metalworker. Then, I quickly met someone on the street. What a clever nineteen-year-old was I! I moved to Second Avenue and Tenth Street. This was the Siberian Express of railroad flats! The smell of a thousand years of Ukrainian borscht from the Second Avenue Deli dripped on the walls. I spent the next five nights bouncing up and down on this Irishman's dick from New Jersey. Each rise and fall of my body brought the sight of the Deli Man carving the lox so thin you could read through it. Things got too tight here. So, off I went.

I got a roommate from a bulletin board and I moved to 13 St. Mark's Place. I moved in with an insane novelist cab driver just out of Harvard. He was desperate for Puerto Rican boys. He drove them around New York in his cab with the meter off. Shuttling them from Jerome Avenue to Atlantic Avenue on their mysterious pursuits. He was always being cited by the Taxi and Limousine Commission for giving these boys blow jobs on his breaks in the back of his cab. The day I moved in, Con Ed turned off the electricity. (He hadn't paid the bill in five months.) For fiscal security, I decided to move downtown.

All the way downtown. I moved to 393 Broadway. *Oh, beautiful Broadway!* Broadway was there before me! Right over here was White Street. I lived kitty-corner to what will soon be the mondo hipoid club, the Mudd Club, later that year of 1978. I moved into a loft with two thousand square feet of hovering nineteenth-century sweatshop ghosts. Five hundred dollars a month divided four ways with the three painters that I lived with here. We built rooms out of ripped-up packing crates from Chinatown and a bunch of fabric we found on Lispenard Street. The Talking Heads song "Living in Wartime" played on the turntable nonstop while the coffee and beer poured down our throats. I dragged a phalanx of men down Broadway, up four flights and finally into my loft-bed perch (more on that later). It is here that I began to learn how to love the men of New York City. I even, in one Devo-inspired moment, have a threesome with my girlfriend from Chelsea and the new man in my life as we too discovered that we can't get no satisfaction. During this time, I was also bringing home cats, dogs, and Chilean refugees!

I was also spending my nights basically with my boyfriend of that time at 64 Wooster Street trying to make this guy love me. The plot thickens. He wanted to move in with me at . . . 393 Broadway! But there were already twelve people living there. He drove my housemates mad. They said, "He has to go!" I said, "If he goes, I go!" I go.

In fact, I went all the way back to California never to return to New York again. But then this same boyfriend snapped his finger via a postcard and I went running back. Oh, Foolish Youth!

I moved into 153 Norfolk Street. Three rooms. Two hundred fifty dollars a month with a view of the Empire State Building and clumsily drawn swastikas appearing in the incinerator room. But no heat or hot water all winter. That same boyfriend finally asked me to move in with him right up the block at . . .

One hundred eighty-four Norfolk Street! And I thought, "Oh, thank God, at last. Living together! Victory is Mine!" But it didn't work out. We almost killed each other. He went to Poland. I·didn't have anywhere to go. I got a new boyfriend and spent some time at 306 East Sixth Street. Then I fucked up in a big way, but that, as they say, is a different story.

A friend is out of town and I moved in to 309 East Fifth Street. This was the perfect apartment. Three rooms. Five windows on the street. Corner of Second Avenue. On a block with a police station. For one hundred forty dollars a month!!! I could be happy here. I could make a life. Was I in heaven? But I couldn't stay here. It was a sublet.

So, I moved to 234 East Fourth Street, at the corner of Avenue B, which from now on I will refer to only as "The Maw of Death!" The huge metal doors of the Maw of Death clanged behind me as I walked down the dark boric-acid festooned hallway with that polished avocado green suitcase. The walls were filthy and smelled of paleolithic piss from a Times Square toilet. Abandon Soap All Ye Who Enter Here!

This building was equipped with an array of drug dealers, armed people lurking in the hallways, and a particularly active Santeria chapter. Which at the time seemed to me to be the Lower East Side version of voodoo meets the Virgin Mary. This Santeria chapter was very big on blood ritual. Often, I would come home and find the headless bodies or severed heads of chickens, goats, and the occasional unfortunate piglet.

My friend Dona was gonna move in to 234 East Fourth Street, but then someone carved a death's head on her door and hung a piece of that piglet's entrails from her doorknob. Dona was smart. She didn't move in! I am embarrassed to say, *I signed a lease for the Maw of Death!*

There was a family of twelve next door and a punk rock band above. A trendy boy named Martin lived to my left. He was blond. With a vengeance. Martin would prove to be the one good thing I would find in the Maw of Death.

The day I moved in, there was a terrible fire in the tenement next door. It was an abandoned building, but it was being used by junkies as a shooting gallery. As the fire got worse, those junkies started throwing themselves out the windows, scampering down the red-hot fire escapes. They looked like roaches jumping out of a toaster when you turn it on or shake it. I looked out my window and thought to myself, "Gee, at last, a home of my own."

There was a knock at the door. Who could it be? Well, of course, it was this guy Martin. That's who the story is about! He wanted to welcome me to the building. He was cute. Beefy muscles. Lotsa earrings. Great smile. And truly the most extreme and ambitious haircut I had ever seen in my life. He invited me into his apartment. It was done in what I think I would call . . . Latish Nuevo Wavo Junkshop: aqua walls, twinkly lights, a stuffed tattered marlin fish hanging over the bed next to the bas relief of the Flintstones. We looked at his paintings, for he was of course an artist, and we did a large but not unreasonable amount of cocaine. Now, clearly, we could have kissed right then via the usual neck-rub strategy. But we didn't. We just talked . . . and watched the fire burn the building down next door. Then we listened to our favorite song of that time, The Human League singing "These Are the Things That Dreams Are Made Of."

And that's how we met. And that's how we became friends. I would live next door to Martin at the Maw of Death for almost two years and during that time many terrible things would happen. Three people would kill themselves by jumping into the central airshaft of our building. Once a week, Hector, our super, would run through the hallways pounding on our metal doors with his machete cursing us in Spanish. Martin had to fight off a bunch of junkies in the stairwell by kicking them in the faces with his newly fashionable pirate boots. Finally, most horrible of all, I went out on the stairwell one morning and saw finger trails of blood going all the way from the fourth floor to the first. This blood ended in a more decisive pool by the torn-out mailboxes going *Drip drip drip.* There was something wrong with this building. Something terribly wrong. Have any of you ever seen the movie *Rosemary's Baby?* Well, it was a lot like that, but without parquet floors, Mia Farrow, or million-dollar Central Park West views. Finally, I couldn't take it anymore. I put my stuff in storage and left the country. I just counted myself lucky that I had broken my lease with the Maw of Death.

When I came back to New York, I found a new apartment. It was only eight feet wide. But it was on a good block, Mulberry between Prince and Spring in Little Italy. No light or cross-ventilation. But only two hundred fifty-five dollars a month. I have it still, these many years later. Also, at the same time I got a new boyfriend. This guy Doug. And I still have him, these many years later.

But I keep going back. I keep thinking back to 234 East Fourth Street and my friend Martin, the one good thing I found there. We didn't become good friends while we lived there. It was like we were already practically roommates, so we kept a kind of neighborly distance. It was only once we had both moved out of the Maw of Death that it felt like we could become better friends. And begin to flirt in earnest.

I met Martin again the next summer after we had moved out of the Maw of Death. We ran into each other as we rode our bikes on lower Broadway. We were so happy to see each other. We hugged, kissed, bought each other an icy cold V-8 juice, and we sat down and talked.

Now, it was August. August is a very strange time in New York. It is so hot. It is so humid. In August, it feels like life and time have stood still. You can get carried away from who you think you are by the hot breath of the subway as it rises from those grates under our feet. It feels like everything is up for grabs. All the rules can be broken. And you can spend the entire month of August doing nothing but riding your bike with no hands down Park Avenue South in the middle of the night as you chase after a lunatic blond doof with a great butt as you race through the lower twenties. I was twenty-three then. I was racing through my lower twenties too. And I was glad to be on my bike this August in New York.

One night, we got on our bikes to catch a midnight showing of the movie *The Draughtsman's Contract* on the Upper East Side. We raced around Grand Central Station. Past the Pan Am Building. Through the Helmsley-Spear tunnel. Impervious to cab and cop alike as we raced through every red light and got there with just enough time for an icy cold V-8 juice. And to make out a little bit on the stoop of a building at Sixty-first and Second Avenue. Now, we didn't sleep together that night. I'm not sure why. Idiots.

But the next day I called my friend Dennis to ask him what he thought safe sex was. We were all sort of new at this then . . . in 1983. He said, "Oh, yeah . . . hmmm . . . safe sex. Well, I think, basically, you can do whatever you want. But whatever you do, don't suck, fuck, rim, or kiss him." The icy tidal wave of this information washed over me. It was, and is still, a complicated time. But it was complicated for other reasons too. See, I was already seeing my friend Doug. It was nothing definite yet, but it was definitely on the verge. But Doug was off in Boston with an "X-boyfriend." ("X," but not so "X" that he wouldn't still accept free trips to Jamaica from him.) So I was alone in New York in August. And I was much taken with my friend Martin and our wild rides uptown. Because we were Martin and Tim: The Two Who Had Escaped the Maw of Death!!!

The next day, it was even hotter. So we got on the subway and went out to Brighton Beach. I had recently purchased on Fourteenth Street a handsome blue-and-yellow inflatable surf rider. When we got to Brighton Beach, we blew up that surf rider, got on it together and floated way out beyond everybody else. We just bobbed there, told stupid jokes, kissed a little bit, showed each other our dicks underwater, and waved to people far, far away back on the shore. It felt so private. It felt like we were on our own little surf rider island floating there off the coast of America. It felt like we might never have to go back. We could just stay there on our surf rider island for the rest of our lives.

But we did have to go back. It was getting dark. So we paddled towards the shore and lay kissing on the deflating surf rider as it hissed out its salty breath all around us. Then, we got on the F train and headed back to Manhattan.

When we got back to Little Italy, it was still so incredibly hot that we headed straight for my apartment, took off our clothes, and got in the shower together with only the cold water on. Finally, we began making out in a serious way. Now, this was very nice. Martin was a big blond guy, what today I would call a dude. Martin had more yummy body than I knew what to do with. We sucked and nibbled and supped at each other's table. The shower's spray sharp on my back as we sucked each other's dicks. I started to weird out. The water began to feel too wet. I started to think, *Oh, Douglas is coming back to New York tonight.* I began to feel a little guilty. I'm like that sometimes, Mr. Guilt.

So I told Martin I thought we should stop. I think Martin knew what was going on in my head. He just looked at me sweetly and smiled, shrugged his shoulders, and said, "Rub-a-dub-dub." (Three Men in a Tub), my cartoon thought balloon said.

We got out of the shower and dried each other off. We regretted having to put on our clothes in this heat. If only we could walk naked hand in hand out onto Mulberry Street and buy an Italian ice at the corner. Instead, Martin and I went out in our black cutoffs into the hot wet Mulberry Street night and had one last freezing cold V-8 juice.

Later that night, Doug came over after his train got in from Boston and we made out like nuts on the floor of 241 Mulberry Street.

Later that year, Doug and I moved in together.

Later that year, I ran into Martin at Rockefeller Center and we had a very good talk.

The next year, I put Martin in a videotape I was doing.

The next year, I just caught a glimpse of Martin. On a new bike. Racing down Broadway with an even more ambitious haircut.

The next year, Martin was dead. Of you-know-what.

I had been out of New York a lot. I had moved back home to California. So I didn't hear about it when it happened. Didn't do the hospital time with Martin. Didn't see the *Enquirer* shove toward his hospital room to flash Madonna's photo. It was only later a friend told me and I sat down on the street and said, "Oh, shit." Martin's big blond body. His paintings for album covers. Our bike rides together. The life between us. It's like all nothing now.

"Oh, shit."

See, I had actually thought we both had escaped the Maw of Death.

Ha ha.

Photo copyright © by Dona Ann McAdams

JOHN O'KEEFE

Name: John O'Keefe
Stage Name: John O'Keefe
Birthdate/Birthplace: October 6, 1940/Waterloo, Iowa
"Raised Up" Where: All over the place
Education: B.A., Philosophy; M.F.A., Theater
Honors/Grants: Shubert Grant (playwriting); Rockefeller Grant in Playwriting; New York Dance & Performance Award (Bessie); Bay Area Critics Award; Glickman Award (dramalogue); *L.A. Weekly* Award; Sundance Institute (cinema); Equinox Film Institute, France
Influences/Mentors/Heroes: German expressionism, Artaud, Ionesco
Places Performed: Japan/America Center (Los Angeles); Lincoln Center (New York); La Jolla Museum of Contemporary Art; ICA (London); Statsgabaugh (Amsterdam); Third Eye Center (Glasgow); Cowel Theater (San Francisco); Berkeley Rep (Berkeley)
Pivotal Performance: *Shimmer*—P.S. 122 introduced my most known piece.
Favorite Performance Experience: Playing Bob Ernst's insane wife in my play *Mimzabim* at Club Foot in San Francisco. I was a very ugly woman, he was a very short man. He hung himself with an elastic dollar bill while unzipping his fly, and I threw my baby against the wall.
Most Terrifying Performance Experience: Playing Volpone at the Berkeley Rep—the rape scene—my victim, a beautiful Afro-American actress, before five hundred teenagers from an Oakland ghetto
Favorite Prop or Costume: A lighted room with a swinging door which I wore on my head
Hobbies: Biking, bird watching, TV watching, basketball, mushroom hunting
Reading List: C. G. Jung, Thomas Merton, Teilhard de Chardin, Greek classics, Stephen King
Favorite Music: Hard, hard rock; John Cage; Hildegard von Bingen
Favorite Quote: "Suddenly we start to worry about nothing."

Artist's Notes

Vid was commissioned by P.S. 122 in New York and Life on the Water in San Francisco. At the time I wanted to experiment with narrative. I wanted to find out what would happen if I combined two lines of narrative that seemed to have nothing in common and have them meet up and become one in the last five minutes of the show. I've always liked video games and the commission gave me the chance to indulge digital cravings. I would create an interactive video game, the kind that puts you into dangerous situations which must be solved by choosing the right object. My protagonist was a little fellow in a green suit, a kind of Peter Pan gone porn. I named him Gig. The antagonist was a treelike creature, a kind of Gumby gone wrong. I called him Bog Pie. Gig's job was to get through all of the pitfalls and traps, run Bog Pie down and take the prize he was carrying. That was the first narrative line.

The second narrative line was an abbreviated autobiography of the two years I spent living in my VW camper in a parking lot back in the mid-1970s. I came to Berkeley to direct an original play of mine at the Magic Theater. The play caused a near riot. The theater shut down and so did I. I met some very funny and strange people to say the least. In this crazy once-in-a-life-time world of mid-1970s Berkeley I met a brilliant painter and her child. During the piece I alternate between the video game and the autobiography. In the last five minutes of the piece, the artist's boy (four years old) tells me about a video game he's invented called Vid. He tells me that there is a monster named Bog Pie that scares him. I counter his fears by telling him that I know a guy that can beat Bog Pie. I think a moment and come up with his name, "Gig." Later that night the boy falls off the loft and goes into a coma. It is at that moment that the two stories meet and turn into one. I know the prize Bog Pie is holding. It is the life of the injured child. The entire piece has been happening in my head while waiting for the boy to come out of the coma. I return to the video game and as Gig I chase after Bog Pie. As I do I begin to transform into myself and the two stories become one. Leaves begin tearing away from Bog Pie. I realize that they are the souls of the children in the trauma ward who, like Magic Dee, are in a state of coma. They entreat me to take them but I am here only for one. Finally, that one is left. It too flies from Bog Pie. I dive for it and it transforms in my hands into Magic Dee. "I got you! I got you!" I cry. I feel someone touch my shoulder. I turn around and it is Jen-Ann. She tells me that Dee has come out of the coma. We had been in the hospital for thirty-six hours.

Vid

"*Yes!*" I hear my voice crying, much to my surprise. And "*yes!*" I find myself kneeling in samurai posture before the dwindling void, a vortex of darkness forming before me and although I cannot see it, I can sense a tunnel within, leading out from me.

Eeeeee! There's a high-blood-pressure siren. Then the onset of the Vid music theme, "Bom bom bom bom bom bom" . . . A face appears in the dark with synthesized neon eyes, one red, one yellow.

"Come on, soldier, let's tussle!"

"I'm ready," I shout, gripping the sudden sword at my side made of wood carved from the rudder of an old ship sheathed in a scabbard of leather, the faint tracings of a map etched on its side.

I trot through the darkness, sparks like Fourth of July whirligigs spiking from my feet. I'm in full loin gear like Peter Pan gone porn. A steely spear of tensile alloy is strapped to my back. My eyes goggle in the darkness like blue dream babies painted by Minnie Mouse. My nose twitches accompanied by an eruption of elfish thoughts. I am the apprentice, Gig, at the threshold of Vid's first level.

"I'm ready!"

The music has become a rainfall.

"Oh hoh nae eo coe eee . . ."

Ping! Ping! There's a stinging sensation in my left hand and the smell of smoke. Smoke! There are two small black wounds.

Punk! Something's hit my head.

There's a hole in my head!

Pong! There's a stinging in the center of my right hand and yes, there's a hole in it.

The top of the cave is dripping video acid.

"What can I cover myself with?"

I look in the bag suddenly hanging from my shoulder. There's a big pill in there. I push it aside, a box of wooden matches with the name "Night Light," two dog biscuits, a razor Frisbee with the words "Dee Finder" written on it, a big Life Saver the size of a steering wheel, there's an old crow's head, I eat it, it crunches between my teeth like thin dry fish bones, it tastes salty. *Vvvwzzzzz!* two blue beams of light break from my eyes. I look in my shoulder bag. There's a plate in there. I put the plate on my head. *Plink!* The acid drops burn through it. The bag is beginning to melt, video acid has broken through my back!

"Too late, bye-bye!"

I cast my blue eye beams into my melting shoulder bag. There's a tube of underarm deodorant, the word "Shield" written on it.

"Do you wish to continue?"

Children in bandages and hospital gowns are gathered near Dragon Smasher. A few are maneuvering through Gory's Hole, the rest are scattered among the old machines, lazily plucking at the electronic images. Plastic tubes are coming from their noses and out of their arms, black boxes with beeping graphs are over their heads. Attendants in white are giving them quarters to put in the machines.

There is a beep. My hair rises. It's a countdown!

"Do you wish to try again where you left off? You have ten seconds to decide. Ten, nine, eight, seven, six, five . . ."

I . . .

"four,"

reach . . .

"three,"

for the . . .

"two,"

quarter in my pocket and pop it in the slot.

Djeep!

Again I'm Gig, admiring my spear. I grab the bag, then the crow's head, ram it into my mouth.

Vvvwwwzzzz, blue beams break from my eyes!

Pip! Pang! Poom!

Splatter drops spank my heel and pain ekes out.

Ping!

My cheek burns as an acid bead eats its way into my face. I uncap the deodorant stick and rub it on the hole. *Djreet!* A gritty scab rises.

Pop!

Another, this time just above my elbow.

"God!"

I swing toward the pain, a strip of leather stretches in the space in front of me.

"Aha, it's Liquid Shield!"

I scribble in the air. [*Triumphant blast*] A shield appears. Drops of video acid sparkle in the blue light of my eye beams like gay rain. Holding the shield over my head, I inch forward. . . .

A few weeks after the "opening" of Jimmy Beam, John Lion invited me to join him at a national conference on Buddhism and the Theater in Boulder, Colorado, hosted by Chogyam Trungpa, a guru who was one of the major spiritual leaders from Tibet on the run from the Red Chinese. John joked about eating brown rice and sleeping on a straw mat. The major theaters and performers from around the country were to attend. It seemed like perfect timing to get out of the Berkeley storm.

When we arrived at the airport we were greeted by a famous playwright, Claude Vanatalli. At last, I thought, I'm going to meet some famous people. I could use some spiritual grounding too. Things were looking up.

When we got to the ashram we were welcomed by a good two hundred fifty avid Buddhists. We were treated to a huge feast of Tibetan delicacies. I was gratified to find wine, beer, and whiskey in abundance. In no time at all we were becoming inebriated. But still, no guru. People were getting "zealous" about each other when I heard someone whisper, "He's coming!" Two young women came in, one carrying a cushion, the other, a small table with a large bottle of sake and a glass. I was seated in the front. Everyone went quiet. A short man with a jack-o'-lantern face entered. He had a shriveled arm that dangled lifelessly from him. He sat down on the cushion, the two lovely Buddhist nymphets on either side. One of the girls poured a glass of sake, handed it to him. Trungpa sipped his sake and smiled at us. He welcomed us in a strangely high and innocuous voice.

It seemed everything he said had a double meaning. He was welcoming us and yet he was challenging us; he was gracious almost to the point of servility and yet he was our judge. He introduced several members of his "staff," they had a kind of gung-ho casualness. Suddenly he said, "Now—go and dance!"

Trungpa retired, followed by his handmaidens. The lights were dimmed, the doors in the hall were opened and rock-and-roll music was sent over the speakers. Instantly the acolytes were dancing. The theater people almost immediately followed suit as if they had read some itinerary that had slipped my attention.

I was too drunk to remember much of what followed. There was a lot of making out and screaming and finally several fistfights. The art luminaries seemed enchanted and perplexed with it all, as if perhaps what they were witnessing was some kind of secret Buddhist ritual. The next morning I didn't wake up on a straw mat. It was a mattress thrown on the floor.

Later that afternoon, several theaters displayed their wares. Robert Wilson took an hour to walk across the room while a teenaged girl counted from one to ten. The Open Theater performed American Indian chants shaking big Indian rattles and intoning things in English like, "We are separate from each other. We should be one!" Jerzy Grotowski was supposed to come but he was delayed in Europe, having his blood changed. André Gregory filled in his slot by taking members of the audience and whispering instructions in their ears, creating a kind of personal mystery play between him and the performers. I was falling asleep when a group from California came and "improv"ed people's dreams. It all ended with a two-hour critique in which they slam-dunked each other unmercifully.

Later that night Trungpa gave a lecture. I heard during the dinner break that he had bunged up his arm in a fit of intoxicated inspiration. He thought he could drive his car through a mountain. He tried. After that he switched from Seagram's Seven to sake.

The guru appeared an hour late, accompanied by two new nymphets. Everyone was church-silent. The tape recorders were rolling. One of the female staff, a higher-up, severely cheerful, performed Tibetan yoga positions while Trungpa made commentary and sipped bottles of sake. It started out normally enough but when a disciple, a drunk boy of twenty, began to tease Trungpa, the Bodhisattva started stabbing the boy in the arm with a pencil, and things began to break down. Suddenly, half-slobbering, Trungpa pointed at the woman and shouted, "You're doing it wrong!"

The woman abruptly stopped, stood up, quelled her tears, and started to leave. Trungpa shouted at her.

"Stop! Come back! Do it right!"

She returned to the area.

"Get down! Put your thing up! Your thing!"

She didn't know what "thing" he meant so Trungpa stood up, staggered to her, and smacked her on the rump.

"That thing!"

She got on her hands and knees and stuck her butt in the air. The crowd laughed.

She batted her tears back and laughed too.

Trungpa said, "No, no, that's all wrong. I'll show you."

He went to the floor on his two good knees and his one good arm and tried to stick his "thing" in the air. After several attempts amidst the howling of the crowd he was able to stick it up there. He crowned the moment with a loud fart. The crowd cheered.

The night before we were to leave we were each graced with a private three-minute audience with the guru. I spent my three minutes simply looking at him in silence, hoping somehow he might suddenly wink at me and break out in a belly laugh but he didn't.

It wasn't long after the construction of the primal screaming room and the acquisition of a small black-and-white television set that the Pit moved into full swing. Besides Russ and me and the screamers, there was Lynn, a poetess from Iowa, moody, intelligent, not quite sure what sex she was. And there was Alma.

Alma was an American with two passports. He was born in Texas but raised in Mexico. His mother lost his passports and through some American version of a Kafka story he could never get them back again. At that time he was in his midtwenties and beautiful, Christ, was he beautiful. He had long silken chestnut hair that hung about his shoulders like the mane of a horse. His face was chiseled yet soft and erotic. He looked like an offering for the Aztec gods. And he loved women. And they really loved him, not just because of his beauty but because he really loved them, not lecherously, but fully and all of them. "I j'ohst loaf they'm," he'd say, and his face would melt like hot fudge on ice cream.

One night after a long spell of growing depression and poverty about five of us huddled around the just-cooling TV set. Doug, one of the screamers, sat with us cooling out before a "session." There was Russell and me, Lynn and Alma. There was a roughening edge to the atmosphere. I had dirty clothes on and I smelled. "Jesus Christ, I'm a bum." I wanted to say it, I wanted to belch it out.

"What would you do, if you had to spend a million dollars in one night?"

"Oh, Christ, Russell," Lynn groaned and turned toward the dead TV set.

"You couldn't show anything for it?" Doug asked.

"Exactly."

"I'd buy a church and set it on fire," Lynn said.

"That would be tough," Doug said.

"I'd throw a party," said Russell, "I'd hire a few jets, about twenty operators, and I'd have them call people at random in the middle of the night and have them picked up in limos, I'd buy a few tons of drugs, an army of whores for both sexes, and I'd fly them all to Rio where we'd gamble all the money away."

"That's possible," Doug said, crossing to the blackboard which had been confiscated from a dumpster behind the hospital. He started writing figures. "A jet would cost, say, two hundred thousand to rent."

As he went through the figures and I shouted out my desires I could feel money flowing from my fingers. I was on a sugar high and for a brief time I really felt rich until the money was all gone and we were sitting in the room again, lower than before, a spray of insane figures written on the blackboard. We sat in silence.

"I think there's flying saucers," said Alma.

We all looked at him in spite of our gloom. It was very rare for Alma to speak out.

"I think they come as a result of our wishes. I think that's how you talk to spacemen. You just wish for them."

"You sound like Bambi," Lynn hissed.

"Man, I think tonight the flying saucers are out."

"I'm going home." She sighed, gathered her things, and left.

"I've seen them," Alma persisted. "In Hawaii. They have a big port there in a volcano. Seven of them in the night, going too fast to be jets. Zapped into that big smoking mountain. Just before I saw them I got this feeling, like I wanted to go hide from something big. And then I looked up and saw them. I got that feeling now. I bet you if I went up on the roof right now I'd see one of them. Anybody want to come?"

"I can't, I got to scream," Doug said.

Of course there weren't any flying saucers. But what the fuck, who was I to dismiss such a possibility when I had considered all the others?

"Yes, I'll go up with you."

"What about you, Russ?"

"Nah, I'm gonna paint."

Alma looked at me with a satisfied smile.

"Come on, John."

We stood out on the roof. The night was crystal clear and balmy. The hills sparkled with lights. It looked like Italy on a festival day. The stars twinkled down on us despite the city glare.

"It feels like a spaceport," Alma said, smiling.

I pulled out a beer I had stuffed in my pocket. I was just about to pop the top when he put his hand over the can.

"We don't need that kind of stuff, we're going on a trip and we aren't coming back."

"We aren't coming back?"

"No, man, that's the price of the trip."

I stuffed the beer back in my pocket.

"Will you go with them when they come?" he asked.

"Sure."

"I wouldn't say it so quickly, you aren't ever coming back."

"I don't care."

"You aren't ever going to see your friends again. You aren't ever going to see a tree or a girl, or even the same colors. Sometimes you're going to be very homesick."

"For this?"

"Yes."

"Would you go?"

"Yes, in a second." He looked at me, his soft animal eyes unblinking. "I don't care about any place. I have no place."

I thought about it.

"What the fuck, me either."

Just then his eyes became violent.

"I feel them, man, I feel them."

He turned away from me and searched the sky.

"Look!" he shouted.

I looked but I didn't see anything.

"There!" he shouted, and pointed toward the eastern horizon.

A light was coming toward us.

Alma looked at me savagely, "I told you, John, I told you!"

I squinted at the light trying to filter it with my eyelashes. There was no doubt about it, it was coming toward us.

"It's a jet," I said.

"Yeah? Then where is the sound?"

I listened. It was silent. *It couldn't be,* I thought, *it just couldn't be.* But involuntarily I felt my hairs prickle.

"Do you feel that energy, John?"

"No, Alma, it's a jet, it's got to be."

"It's no jet. Look at the light."

The light had a piercing quality. I felt a strange thrill. The air around me became alien, magnetized. The light was coming closer and still there was no sound. Alma looked at me transformed as if standing on a mountain, his hair whipping in the wind.

"It's coming, John, do you want to go?" he shouted.

I stared at him.

"Are you coming or not?"

We started jumping up and down waving at the approaching light.

"Hey! Hey! We're here! We're down here!"

There was a roaring around us. My heart felt like it was going to break out of my chest. I screamed. The sound smothered it. We threw our hands in the air toward the light, both of us screaming, eyes streaming with tears.

"Take me home! Take me home!" we shouted.

The thunder rolled over us. We turned and watched it pass, its taillight blinking a mocking red as the jet liner flew over us. We stared at it as it banked around to the east on its way to the Oakland airport.

I gazed at Alma, his face was transfixed with pain and bliss. "That was something, wasn't it?" he whispered.

I wanted to feel let down, cynical, but I couldn't. I looked at the Berkeley hills, the amber strand of Shattuck Avenue streetlights, the peeling top of my camper, the rough gutted asphalt of the parking lot, the bamboo violently breaking out between the buildings, and finally at the black shadow of the Bay with its light-beaded bridges and I was glad that I was still here.

"Yes," I whispered back.

Below us, in the middle of the night we could hear a soft mewing. It was Doug screaming in the screaming room.

I find myself standing before a cereal-box landscape, rolling hills with a lollipop sun. The air is sweet with a slight tinge of strawberry Kool-Aid, the trees are asparagus green, the meadows of corn-cob yellow hay roll down to chocolate-colored trails, the sky is isotope blue.

I check a map now suddenly in my hand and see a little elf representing me and my position.

"This is the map of my journey," I utter, my voice strangely high in the helium air.

A sparrow flies across the sky, stops, stuck there as if someone had cut the frame loose from the film and left the world in frozen photography.

"Can I move?"

"Yes," I hear a voice within me whisper, "if you make the world move with you."

And I do. I don't move my feet over the path, I move the path under my feet. The bird unsticks and flies east.

Tl-tl-tl-tl-tl! There's this tinkling. *Tl-tl-tl-tl-tl!* A cloud of birds is rushing at me. Suddenly my face is covered with hundreds of chickadees. *Fl-fl-fl-fl-fl!* They scatter and land in a tree. My face is moist. It's blood! They've made hundreds of perforations in my face and scalp. From the sun a cloud appears with the high lisping calls of cedar waxwings. Suddenly they're on my body, their shining eyes ablur, their lovely crests moving like tiny, delicate hammers. *Fl-fl-fl-fl-fl!* Once again, like the chickadees, they're gone. My body is damp. It's blood, but like my face, it quickly dries. I brush the blood away. My arms and fingers are aswirl with vines and alien insignia. I figure my face is covered with them too. Tattoos.

I hurry the path along, the lollipop sun melting like a hot orange oyster. As I walk the sky grows dimmer. So that's the way it works; the faster I walk, the darker the sky. I walk faster and darkness surrounds me.

Photo by Roya Photography

DAEL ORLANDERSMITH

Name: Donna Dael Brown
Stage Name: Dael Orlandersmith
Birthdate/Birthplace: New York, New York
"Raised Up" Where: Harlem/South Bronx, primarily Harlem
Education: Washington Irving High School; three years of Hunter College
Honors/Grants: Received an Obie in 1995
Influences/Mentors/Heroes: Toni Morrison, James Baldwin, Diamanda Galas, Marianne Faithfull, Marlon Brando, Gogol, James Dean, Nina Simone, Velvet Underground
Places Performed: American Place Theater, Roundabout Theater, Nuyorican Poets Café, Bessie Awards, Obie Awards, the Kitchen, Whitney Museum
Pivotal Performance: Second week of *Beauty's Daughter* when everything just "came together"
Favorite Performance Experience: With *Beauty's Daughter* at the American Place Theater
Most Terrifying Performance Experience: Performing work at the Actors Studio and having famous actors sitting in the front row and being extremely nervous, then thinking, *Fuck all o' you*
Favorite Prop or Costume: Black Danskin with a long leather coat on top
Hobbies: Reading, listening to music, cooking
Reading List: *To Kill a Mockingbird, Dead Souls, Satanic Litanies, The Bluest Eye*
Favorite Music: Old blues/R&B, rock and roll, old salsa, zydeco
Favorite Quote: "What interests me is to get at the bottom of experience. I am interested in the basement of emotion." (Carl Jung)

Artist's Notes

My first initial approach is to language, speech, accents. I listen for a certain quality . . . of a voice and what mood it creates. The mood of course reflects a meaning. What is this character saying without actually saying it? Obviously there is the text (what the character is physically saying) versus the subtext (what the character really means), i.e., Maryann and Richard have been married for twenty years. Richard was a promising architect but over the years sells real estate. He has made many promises to Maryann about them living a life of luxury. Over the years, Maryann has heard his promises and has turned a deaf ear. Maryann gave up her career as an actor because Richard made these promises and wanted her to stay home. Maryann at twenty-three wanted nothing more than to please him. Twenty years later she is dismayed. Richard is still in love with Maryann and does not want to look at the possibility that she may not love him anymore:

RICHARD: Honey, I love you so much. [*He goes to embrace her*] You know we haven't made love in a while.

MARYANN: [*Moving away from him*] I've been busy with the house, Richard, I'm also getting back into acting. I've been taking a few classes.
RICHARD: Honey, that's great. [*Beat*] Hey, maybe we can go away on a weekend real soon. We haven't been out of the city for a while.
MARYANN: [*Attempting to hide her disgust*] Like I said, Richard, I'm busy.

Obviously the subtext is that Maryann really wants out of the marriage and uses excuses to keep Richard away. She may be afraid to leave.

This is what I look for in characters. I also am heavily influenced by music. Often when I look at people or hear conversations I'm aware whether music (and specifically what kind of music) is playing in the background or not. I am a major rock-and-roll and blues fan, and specifically those genres kick me into the heart of characters everywhere. For instance with the above scenario I would probably set the scene from Richard's point of view and play the Stones' version of "I Don't Know Why I Love You."

Music has always helped me approach characters. I'll choose music that I think the character would like, listen to it incessantly, and imagine what would I do if I were in this character's circumstances. It usually takes off from there.

An Excerpt from "Beauty's Daughter"

DIANE: I've always done the slide. Like you never, never show your heart! [*She smiles*] I mean you can kiss and fuck, but show your heart? Naw! A love thing? That's TV and records and books but there's always somebody looking for it, right? And I have seen some tough-assed broads go down on account of it, but they say, man, that you haven't lived until you felt it. [*Pause*] It's more than just a grind/groin thing, and me? Well, me, I could never see me doin' that—goin' down like that.

That's what I thought, but then, right? I'm in a car and I see him—this man, and he's six three with long black hair and blue eyes and a mouth like a girl's—a pretty girl mouth, and he's the most beautiful man I've ever seen, and as I watch him walk, I'm wondering how his voice sounds. I wanna hear how his voice sounds, what kind of sounds come from your sweet mouth? I wanna say [*She pauses*] I hate feeling this way! [*She smiles*] But I love it! [*Beat*] I can't be a punk-assed bitch going soft over a love thing? What's that—love! [*She stops*] It feels so nice. [*Beat*]

This one night I'm across town and I'm in this bar and there's some woman on her last legs trying to pick up young boys and she's singing along to Van Morrison, slurring—a terminal blues, right? And he walks in and she wants to talk to him, wants to hold him tight, but he's in his head and doesn't want her, and I say to the woman, "You can't do that. Can't suck someone's youth and try to make it your own." And she laughs and walks to another part of the bar and him—Cal—he looks at me and smiles and I'm excited, right? Fidgeting in my seat—like Elvis. See, when I'm mad or excited I begin to move—right leg, right hand move like half-anarchistic boogie, half Elvis, and I feel the King. The King is reaching for me now, 'cause I'm excited, right? Elvis is rippin' through me now or is it Bessie Smith comin' down in double time screaming a ball-'n'-chain chant? And Cal sits next to me and he's got a Celtic/mystic eye and he says soft 'n' slow, "I'm from Dublin. You?" "Harlem," I say. And when he makes a point he touches my leg and cocks his head to the side and the vodka and beer is slidin' down our throats and somebody called "Closing time" but I swear I didn't hear them, didn't want to hear them.

I walk the streets and I see him, could be two in the morning, could be two in the afternoon—it doesn't matter 'cause Harlem and Dublin are rolled up into one. [*Beat*] We had dinner in my house and I read him some of my poetry.

I could have given birth at sixteen
But I was too busy dodging bullets
I was harnessed in rhythm
Muscles taut
Thighs bent
Blocking blows
Praying for kisses

And he calls me a powerhouse. I fuckin' loved it—being called a power-house! 'Cause it's a boy thing, a ballsy dick thing, boy thing, man, and we just keep trading black/Celtic/rock-'n'-roll dreams and happy dancin' to spastic operas of our own design. James Brown. Sam the Sham. Catch us if you can! [*Sheepishly*] Don't I sound like a punk bitch? Shit! I really hate this. [*She smiles broadly*] Bullshit, I love it.

Me and Cal walk Dublin's streets full of music and noise. There's no difference between Grafton Street and 125th Street and Lenox Avenue. It's a Mick/nigger blues. People trying to hustle you the same way they do in Harlem. Chicks with babies trying to cop some change. [*She pauses*] This kid comes up to me and said, [*Irish accent*] "I need some fookin' money. Yer rich, yer American, I'll take yours." [*She pauses and smiles slightly*] I looked at him and said, "Now, boy, if you try and I do mean *try* to take my money, as God is my witness, I'll snatch you out of your pants and disconnect you from your asshole." Powerhouse!! [*She laughs*]

We go to Francis Street to check on a friend who was on the dole. We drink Harlem/Black Guinness in Grogan's pub and one night we sleep together. Don't make love. Just sleep together and he rubs my stomach and between my breasts and I don't move because I can't go down like that. It wouldn't have been right like that had I done it—had I loved him that night. I just knew it'd be incomplete, going down like that. Cal looks at me and smiles and strokes my face. I run my hands through his hair. Touching, we're always touching. We're surrounded by people in pubs. When I make that decision—I say, "I love you." 'Cause I do. This one night the thought police invade his brain and he's had a lotta vodka and ale and he's slack-jawed and talking loud, judging himself, judging others, and he thinks everything becomes crystal clear through muddy Guinness. He talks about people he no longer wants in his life and how he wants to get rid of them or shoot them down to the ground and I say, "What about me?" And he looks through me, blue eyes glassy, and says, "I don't love you. Don't even know you." And here comes the King (does Elvis Presley physicalization), I can feel the King coming. He's ripping through me now. So I get up and walk out, walk cool—a cool take-no-shit Harlem walk through Dublin but there's something crashing inside me/crashing to the ground. I'm on the floor crying like a bitch, like the punk-ass bitch I swear I'd never be. He's got my back now. I'm doing the slide.

Papo's Move

So there's this little boy, Papo?
and he's got merengue and
a little desperation in his
move and he bops and
drops to the side
both to be cool and to
avoid his father's blows and
in his walk when he
dips to the ground—
talking streettalk/walkin' talkin' Spanish,
this boy, Papo, man
Got
Salsa Shoes
Got
Mambo Blues
And when he rises from his
bop, he dreams of things
like fine oak desks and open
spaces where voices don't echo
like in housing project bathroom

walls and there's gotta be
a place where ideas are
written on luxurious white sheets
of paper and
ain't life a bitch
when the cuchifrito grease hits you
in the nose?
And Mommy got a black eye
and Mommy, she got a black eye again
And Latin boys wanna be Latin Kings
And Latin boys wanna be Spanish Kings
And when Latin boys don't get shot
they get lost
Goin' down
Goin' down the block
Goin' down the block
again

Papo

Aged seventeen, Puerto Rican male from Lower East Side. He has come to Diane's house pleading with her to do his term paper, which is due in two days.

Yo, Diane—how you doin', sis? Yo, I know it's late, y'know, but like yo, I needed to see you—know what I'm sayin'? [*Beat, looks around*] Boy, you got a dope house, man. Look at all this shit! Yo, Diane, look at this chair—this is fly! It's gotta be an antique, right? See, I know good quality when I see it! Also, before I forget, you look exceptionally beautiful tonight. [*Beat*] Oh, shit, that's a picture of Rimbaud. [*Beat*] See, I remember what he looks like from his picture on the *Illuminations* cover. "I alone have the key to this savage sideshow." See, I remember. [*Beat*]

Yo, Diane, like I know it's late, y'know, but like I gotta ask a favor, Diane? I really feel bad, y'know, showin' up at your house like this and it bein' late and whatnot, but . . . [*His voice trails off. Beat. Suddenly:*] Diane, you wanna make some money? Yo, I know you said that when you weren't performin' you worked in an art gallery, right? Man, that ain't no real money—so check this out, okay? I got a proposition for you to think about, okay? I really . . . [*He takes a deep breath*] Okay. I'll pay you ten dollars a page if you write my term paper for me. [*Slight pause*] Don't say no yet! [*Beat*] See, my paper, right? It's due in two days, sis! Two days, man. I can't do the paper in two days.

Porque? Porque it's just impossible! See, y'know I had to hustle four days this week, right? 'Cause you know, like, the bills were comin' in real fast, right? And yo, Diane, [*Crosses himself*] I swear, my pop is drinkin' all the time now, right? And that's where the money is goin' and shit and—now, Diane, think about it, it's not like I'm dealin' blow or heroin. It's only weed, right, and I know it ain't right but yo, I gotta look out for my moms and sisters—you gotta understand. I ain't tryin' to cop a plea, but yo, I need money! [*Beat*]

Anyway, this paper, right? It's for my English Lit College Prep course and the teacher—yo, man, she ain't no joke! Her name is Mrs. Marks—Mrs. Naomi Marks and she's real strict. [*Beat*] Diane, I had told you about her. She's the one that helped me get into Bowling Green State College, remember? Check this out, the thing is, even though I'm technically accepted, I still gotta have a certain amount of credits, right, and yo, I'm only three credits short, sis, so c'mon, now! [*Beat*]

It's not like I'm stupid—you read my stories! You know the story about what it's like growing up on Avenue D? You said it was good, remember? [*Beat*] Know what Mrs. Marks said? She said, "Papo, you have the potential to be a great novelist. You've got light, you got perception." I wouldn't make that shit up. That's what she said, Diane, and she sent my stories to the head of the English Department at Bowling Green College and he wrote back personally to say I was accepted. [*Slight pause*]

What? [*Sheepish*] Well, I had three months to do the paper. [*Beat*] Diane, check this out, though. I keep tellin' you that things are bad at home now—see, you oughta know 'cause your mother drinks too, right? So I know you understand. Also, it's not like I smoke reefer all the time. I smoke maybe twice a week. And shit! Like I sell it, but yo, I'm about takin' care of my moms and shit. Yo, I gotta make that money, yo. [*Beat*]

Maybe you don't understand 'cause you're a female. Man, it's hard bein' a guy—specially if you're Spanish or black 'cause, y'know, it's a double thing of sex and race. Know what I'm sayin'? Oh, shit! Okay, okay! Women got it rougher than men—I'm sorry, Diane—I was wrong—damn! Don't kill me! [*Beat*] In fact that's what my paper is about. The effect of black and Hispanic male writers on American literature. I chose Piri Thomas and James Baldwin but I can't read two or three books in one day. [*Sheepish*] I didn't get a chance to get my books yet. [*Defensively*]

Man, see, I was gonna get them but like anytime I go to Barnes and Noble, right? There's this homo who works there, but he's nasty to me, right? I checked out his name and it's Allan. I call him Allan the Butthole. So right, like the last time I was in there, he was all snotty and shit. [*Beat*] See, I had to do this book report on *Les Misérables* for Mrs. Marks, right? And I went to ask him for the book but I fucked up the pronunciation and said "Lez

Miserables" [*Pronounces it "Mis-ur-a-bulls"*], right? So him, he's behind the cash register and he's writing something down and this faggot, man, don't even look at me, man [*Imitates him*], "First of all, it's pronounced *Les Misérables* and it's in the classical section but of course you wouldn't know that." [*He shifts, cocky*]

Now, I had to be chill, right? 'Cause yo, Diane, I wanted to hit this three-dollar bitch homo, and I told him, "Yo, anytime I walk in here you're scopin' like I'm stealin' somethin', and I know it, 'cause I'm Puerto Rican. Well, understand this. I'm Puerto Rican, not a spic. Treat me like a Puerto Rican the same way I'll treat you like a gay man and not like a faggot." Then I walked out. Hells naw, I wasn't goin' back for the books.

[*Beat*] See, Diane, I let that motherfucker know I ain't no punk *porque yo soy Boricua*. See what I'm saying? The double thing about being Puerto Rican and a guy. See, if you were there maybe he wouldn't have done that to you. [*Beat*]

Tell you what, the next time I have a term paper I have to do, yo, I'll bring you in there with me well in advance and you can check this homo out and if he says bullshit to me you tell the motherfucker off, that's dope, right? Diane—mommy, please, please, you gotta write my paper for me. [*Beat*] Listen, I told you what Mrs. Marks said. Yo. You wouldn't want to ruin the potential of a future genius? [*Beat*] See, I know you can write that shit and hook it up, so it'll be real dope. [*Beat*] What you writin' here—let me see. Check it out. [*Bends over as if reading something on her desk*] "I touched the shoes of Mary Magdalene on Avenue D." Yo, Diane, that shit is fly! See, c'mon, mommy, write my paper for me. See, if you bring that kinda poetic justice, yo, my shit will be hooked up, and I promise, yo, not to do this shit again 'cause I know the only person I'm cheatin' is myself. [*Beat*] See, next time, I'll hook it up, so that I have saved enough loot and I can quit scramblin' and just do my schoolwork. 'Cause yo, I care about my future. [*Beat*] See, let me tell you what I plan on doin'—check this out, I'll attend college in about a year, a year and a half, no later. See, after I graduate high school, 'cause even though I wanna cut back on dealin', yo, I gotta be realistic, yo, I gotta scramble like twice a week 'cause like I said, my pops is buggin' out on Bacardi all the time now! And also before I go away I gotta make sure he don't hit my moms and sisters no more. See, I can't be selfish, Diane, y'know. [*Pause*] Sometimes, right, like even though somethin' may be wrong —like I know dealin' weed is wrong—like you gotta realize that the money I make is helpin' out, y'know? See, Diane, sometimes you gotta do certain things 'cause you know eventually it may pay off and help somebody in the long run, right? [*Beat*] Like you refusin' to do my paper—yo, like that, right? I mean, how many times can I tell you, that although I fucked up—unintentionally—that my future is in your hands.

Say what? I know you ain't callin' me a punk. [*Pause*] Diane, *de que?* Lissen, Diane—I don't let nobody call me that. Know what I'm saying? Yo, I don't like that shit. [*Pause*] I'm a punk 'cause I can't leave? That's my family. Yo, I can't turn my back on my family like that. [*Pause*] Yo, no matter how bad they are, they're still my blood—you don't turn your back on your own, man. Yo, I'm not you. I can't do that! The last time he beat her, man, he kicked her like she was a dog. I grabbed that motherfucker and said, "Hit her again, and I'll ram my shank up your ass."

Diane, man, I'm beggin' you please, yo, please. Yo, I'll never ask you to do this again. [*Crosses his heart*] I swear to God! Diane, remember, what did you say to me? You said, "Papo, you got to make your life better and ain't nobody gonna give you shit. If you don't create a life for yourself, on your own terms, your life is not gonna amount to anything." [*Pause*] Huh? You're disappointed in me? Yo, you're disappointed in me? Well, I'm pretty disappointed in you too! Like you and me supposed to be friends and yo, you give me back when I need you. How do you think that makes me feel? Well, dat's what I'm trying to do, Diane. Mommy, please. So what do you say? I fucked up? Lissen, you know what? I'm leavin' your house. Yo, I already know I can't be all that anyway—writing books? Yo, that's bullshit—I'm leavin', okay? Sorry to bother you. Fuck it, I'm gone. [*He exits*]

Thirteen 'n' Bleeding

I am thirteen 'n' bleeding
'N' there are bloodstains in my
Panties
And the Catholic school
Uniform itches my skin and
I'm
Told that I gotta watch
Myself now
'Cause
I'm a girl now
And
I gotta get my hair
Pressed 'n' curled 'cause I'm
A girl now
And
If I wanna go to Randall's
Island to shoot dice and
Play stickball with a gang
Of boys, I can't
'Cause I'm a girl now
And
If I dream of
Touching boys differently it's
Because I'm becoming
A young woman now and
If I dream of lipstick
Traces, it's because
I'm becoming a young woman

Now . . . but I think
"What about my leather jacket
And how I wanna wear it
With one earring, with the
Bold/cold air of a
Reinvented female?"
And I'm thirteen 'n' bleeding
With blood
Gushing from between
My legs, for the
Next forty years
And
The woman I'm supposed to
Emulate is standing
Before me caught up in
Some inebriated spent
Perception
And
I can't believe I sucked
Milk from those defeated
Breasts or
Whispered childhood secrets
In those withered ears and
I don't want to have babies
Give life from red—gore—
Blood.
I'm thirteen 'n' bleeding
In a Harlem living room
Left to flick switchblades
In the dark

NICKY PARAISO

Name: Nicasio Ver Paraiso
Stage Name: Nicky Paraiso
Birthdate/Birthplace: October 14, 1951/Flushing, Queens, New York City
"Raised Up" Where: Flushing, Queens (we lived a short time in Brooklyn until I was five)
Education: St. Andrew Avellino, parochial school, Flushing; Stuyvesant High School, New York City; Oberlin College/Conservatory of Music, B.A., B.M.; New York University School of the Arts, M.F.A. (theater program)
Honors/Grants: Villager Award (for performance in Jeff Weiss's *Dark Twist*); NY Dance and Performance Award (Bessie); Art Matters Grant; NYSCA Performance Art Initiative Grant, Member NYSCA theater panel
Influences/Mentors/Heroes: Oberlin College: Herbert Blau (theater), Jack Radunsky (piano performance); NYU theater program: Peter Kass, Olympia Dukakis, Omar Shapli, Ron Van Lieu; Heroes: Bill Hart, Jeff Weiss, Meredith Monk, Patti Smith, Ron Vawter, Jessica Hagedorn, Neil Young, Mickey Mantle, James Brown
Places Performed: La MaMa, Dixon Place, P.S. 122, Dance Theater Workshop, Westbeth Theater Center, Artists Space, Exit Art, the Alternative Museum, St. Mark's Church Poetry Project/Danspace, HOME for Contemporary Theater and Art, Yale Cabaret, Biblio's Bookshop
Pivotal Performance: For my third-year project at NYU, I acted the lead character in Ronald Tavel's *Boy in the Straight-backed Chair;* it was the part of a psycho/serial killer. Both my parents were in the audience, and as I was killing people onstage my dad yelled out, "That's my son! He's the star!"
Favorite Performance Experience: Performing with Jeff Weiss in *And That's How the Rent Gets Paid, Part III* at La MaMa, the Performing Garage, and at Muhlenberg College in Allentown, PA, Jeff's hometown. I was in blackface wearing a tuxedo, a hired killer named Guapo who played piano and sang.
Most Terrifying Performance Experience: Performing in Bluefields, Nicaragua, with my friends Ruth Fuglistaller and Eva Gasteazoro at the local high school before an audience of three hundred local townsfolk during a deafening tropical rainstorm
Favorite Prop or Costume: Playing Ethyl Eichelberger's grand piano at P.S. 122's First Floor Theater
Hobbies: None
Reading List: Dostoyevsky's *Crime and Punishment, The Idiot;* Jessica Hagedorn's *Dogeaters;* Patti Smith's early work; read most recently: Scott Heim's *Mysterious Skin*
Favorite Music: I'm a fan of great musicians and a lover of music. This is an impossible category to adequately respond to but I do have some personal obsessions: Van Morrison, Neil Young, Joni Mitchell, Patti Smith, early Streisand, Laura Nyro on *New York Tendaberry,* Al Green, Jackie Wilson on *Lonely Teardrops,* Tracy Nelson singing "Down So Low"
Favorite Quote: "You got to use what you got to get what you want!" James Brown, "Hot Pants"

Artist's Notes

So I had all this training (from Oberlin and NYU) and then I met Jeff Weiss and Carlos Ricardo Martinez at their apartment on East Tenth Street in the East Village—cooking dinner, serving wine, singing, and regaling us with true stories and tall tales. I was laughing so hard I thought my side would split. It was only later I realized how scared shitless and astonished I was all at the same time. Jeff Weiss was totally present in every moment, transforming from one character to another with split-second timing, unbridled passion and virtuosic precision. I experienced firsthand that Jeff was the consummate actor, a living human being with heart and mind nakedly exposed—everything I had aspired to and loved about the theater. A year later Jeff cast me in a play at La MaMa, my first as an actor in New York. Through acting in Jeff's plays *Dark Twist* and *And That's How the Rent Gets Paid, Part III*, I felt like I was at the beginning all over again. A baptism of fire. Sort of like advanced on-the-job downtown-performer-in-training. Performance became a celebration of a kind of family—living, breathing, mysterious, with a whole lot of risk, daring, and tough love. Anything was possible.

Meredith Monk helped me center and distill this sometimes noisy, sometimes wild prescription. Her interdisciplinary theater company, The House, and later her Vocal Ensemble became a home and refuge for me to continue learning my craft as an actor/singer/performer.

I was always a performer first, and continued to be obsessed in the doing of it. In 1987 I had been working on a performance with my partner, Mary Shultz (whom I had met through working on Meredith's *Specimen Days*) at BACA Downtown, called "Odds (or Evens)." The whole idea was for us to work separately and present material to each other at rehearsals. A feature of this piece was "a song our mothers taught us." My mother was eighty-one years old at the time and had left New York to live in the Philippines; as I worked through my sections of the piece, it engendered other stories of her and I began to write. My mother had returned to the Philippines after living in the United States for thirty-five years because she was homesick. Writing about my visits to the Philippines to see her, it was then that my interest in her story became central to my understanding of myself as an adult—a Filipino born in America and an actor/performer living in New York City.

I then began developing this material in performance at spaces like Dixon Place and at Westbeth Theater Center's Monday Night Series. In front of a live audience I saw that the elements of identity, ethnicity, marginality, sexuality, and the search for (a) home became the story that I, as a solo performer, was compelled to tell. As we began to lose lovers, colleagues, friends, and strangers to the specter of AIDS, it was inevitable that the fear of, and acceptance of, human mortality, and the rage and despair at our inability to immediately conquer its onslaught, would color and inform these stories. These early performances, which I called *Filipino Talk,* and sometimes *Filipino Therapy,* were the beginnings of the larger evening-length piece called *Asian Boys.* My experiences and conversations in the early eighties with my friend Jessica Hagedorn gave me a lot of courage to approach these issues. The elegance and passion with which she wrote about her own experience as an immigrant Filipino artist inspired me.

In the summer of 1992 I was asked to perform at the Hot Festival, a festival of queer performance at Dixon Place. In *Asian Boys,* I wanted to explore the full range of my identity—being queer, Asian, Filipino, an artist living in New York City—how all those aspects contributed to a unique understanding of growing up wanting to be "whiter than white." And in an indirect way, confronting issues of prejudice and bias that exist even within sexual- and ethnic-minority communities which perceive themselves as marginal and "outside" the dominant culture. I found, in telling my own story, i.e., growing up ethnic and queer in America, that all these complicated, complex issues became present, were just there in the telling. What is true and authentic in the context of this performance could only come from my own firsthand experiences. I had no intention of constructing a dogmatic, intellectual thesis, but rather, I wanted to allow experience to speak for itself. I hope that the politics of this are implicit and clear; which is not to say that ambivalence and conflict don't arise in the process of confronting these issues—I believe it's part and parcel of questioning and challenging the political and cultural status quo. My own impulses as a performer are to both entertain and enlighten. The audience should be having just as good a time as I'm having performing for them.

In developing *Asian Boys,* I realized that what this particular piece was about for me was my coming to some realization of self-acceptance, actively experiencing what "coming home" really means to me: that through publicly acknowledging that I could be sexually attracted to another Asian man, that I could become comfortable with the "otherness" within myself; and that as a solo performer, I could completely be at home onstage telling this story to others—the audience.

After the initial work-in-progress performances at Dixon Place, it was clear that this collection of monologues, stories, and songs was growing into a full-length evening performance. In June 1993 I was sitting at Pete's Tavern on Irving Place with Chito Jao Garces and Jorge Ortoll and Ching Valdes-Aran of the Ma-Yi Theatre Ensemble, who encouraged me to keep working on *Asian Boys;* Chito and Jorge agreed to produce the full version for Ma-Yi's next season. With the participation of Mark Russell at P.S. 122, *Asian Boys* was presented as part of the Gay Cultural Festival in June 1994 at P.S. 122. My friend Laurie Carlos, herself a wonderful writer and performer, agreed to direct. Laurie created a formal structure for the piece and a choreographic path through which I could get from the beginning to the end; her work with me was inestimable and completely generous. Michael Mazzola did the lighting, Gabriel Berry the costume, James Adlesic was movement coach and inspiration, Don Meissner contributed music, and emerging Filipino artists Paul Pfeiffer (set design) and Angel Velasco Shaw (visual and sound design) collaborated with joy, enthusiasm, and passion. As we went into rehearsal in the spring of 1994, I asked Angel to make a video consisting of interviews of other Asian men of whom we asked questions concerning identity, race, and sexuality. Some of these men were friends, mostly artists and writers, gay and straight. The video of *Asian Boys* created another layer of complexity which I felt the piece needed. We worked very fast. The process always continues.

For me, writing for performance has been a mercurial, elusive craft. It's like writing on the run. Sitting for hours with a notebook—in my room, in cafés in the East Village, on the prowl in gay bars on Second Avenue—everything is grist for inspiration. I've worked best under the pressure of deadline. I remember Tom Murrin the Alien Comic's three dictums for performance—get a date at a performance space, get your flyers and postcards out, and lastly and most important, *show up!* Obviously, these are not always the best of circumstances to write well. The ideal would be to continue to write under less stressful situations and to allow more time to gestate and rewrite. Performance is always of the moment, in the moment, and ethereal that way. I'm hoping to perform *Asian Boys* again, on tour. Maybe this book will help get the good word out to presenters. And I'll keep writing and telling the stories.

The first performances of *Asian Boys* at P.S. 122 were dedicated to three friends who died of AIDS—David Underwood, Ron Vawter, and Paul Walker. They all made a profound impact on my life and work, as they did with many others.

And thanks to some friends and colleagues who are always there, and help me to keep working: Mark Bennett, Yoshiko Chuma, Bill Hart, Angel Shaw, Mary Shultz.

---

from *Asian Boys*
Prologue

My parents were immigrants.

I was born and raised in Flushing, Queens, New York City.

That makes me a first-generation Filipino-American.

I remember how the smell of my mother's cooking permeated the entire house. Strong, pungent smells—of *adobo, pancit, pinakbet*—the pork, the chicken, fish, vegetables, shrimp, *bagoong* (anchovies preserved in jars), hot, steaming rice. Already I felt special.

I was an only child. My parents were already middle-aged when they had me. My mom doted on me. She treated me like her prize possession. The reason she stayed in America for another thirty years. My dad was hard-working. He was a registered nurse. He worked mostly the night shift. Worked all night and slept all day. I could hear him snoring in the bedroom when I came home from school. All day my mother would cook, clean, and pray the rosary. She went to hear Mass every morning of her life.

When I was five I begged my parents to buy a piano so I could have piano lessons. My cousins Mae and Ben Pena took piano from the kindly old lady spinster, Miss Evelyn Olt. They weren't too keen on having lessons. I'd go over to my auntie Serafin and uncle Ben's to hear them practice. Then I went home and played on the radiator cover like it was a keyboard. Miss Olt didn't want to teach me because she thought I was too young at five years old to begin. I proved her wrong.

Music became a special world for me, my universe. My own secret, private galaxy to imagine in, to dream in, to escape to.

The piano is a refuge. An island to come back to. Again and again.

Asian Boy #1

When I see you walking down the street
I tremble

When I see you walking down the street
I avert my eyes

When I see you walking down the street
my heart quakes with fear of uncontrollable passion

When I see you walking down the street
I want to run away

Houseboy

He was my mother's houseboy. He was gaunt and lanky and soft, with more than a trace of that je ne sais quoi. Definitely *bacla*. Efren Martinez was my mother's houseboy. He knew all the secrets of the household. He shared a private world with my mother that no one else knew, that no one neither inside the family nor any stranger from the outside could penetrate or fathom, much less imagine. The intimate knowledge that only he and my mother possessed, with each other, was a source of irritation and jealousy for my aunt Corazon. She hated the closeness and intimacy that Efren achieved by attending to my bedridden mother's needs. He fed her. Gave her her medicine. He clothed her. Undressed her. Emptied her chamber pot. Lifted her up from the bed and took her for walks. Made sure the mosquito net covered her adequately when she slept. Sat beside her while she prayed the rosary. Sometimes he prayed along with her.

He was my mother's confidant. He whispered in her ear and she trusted him. She entrusted the key to her special bureau/closet—the *aparador*—to him. Where her social security checks and American dollars were kept. Her box of jewelry. Her prayerbooks.

I arrive in the middle of rainy season as I always do. Sometimes the streets are flooded up to your knees. Me, the Americano son from New York. The actor, the artiste.

Efren Martinez, my mother's houseboy and confidant, views me with distrust and skepticism. As the days pass, he begins to let his guard down. Because even though he sees how much attention my mother showers on me, he can see clearly that I am not there to intrude on the special, private world that he, and only he, shares with my mother. As much as my mom loves me, and she loves me all too consumingly, I can sense that her bond with Efren Martinez is something else—dark, peculiar, deep, and mysterious.

One still, heavy night in the heat of monsoon August, everyone in the house is asleep. A bloodcurdling scream pierces the silence of the night. It's Efren. He's had a nightmare. The heated babble of Ilocano is heard next. Weeping and wailing and gnashing of teeth. They say that if a houseboy has a nightmare, an evil spirit can steal his soul away.

The next day, my old uncle Ingo accuses Efren, my mother's houseboy, of stealing his gold watch. An argument ensues with shouting on all sides. Efren Martinez packs his clothes into a small luggage case and leaves the house in a fury. We never see him again.

His Filipino Mother Speaks

Nicky. Nicky. This is your mama. Did you pray? You don't pray anymore? Did you go to church last Sunday?

Ay anako! Why don't you call your mama anymore on the telephone?

Did you eat? No matter what happens you must always eat. You must always have enough money to buy food. Eat as much as you can. You must have enough energy to do all your playing and exerting effort.

How is your friend? Is he staying there with you? Maybe he can help you to clean your apartment. You must always be clean. Don't let them see that you're dirty.

Did you get a job yet? Maybe you can stay at that job at the insurance office so you can have something to fall back on. Or you can teach. Teach music.

Don't be always gallivanting in the nighttime. It is very fearful to be out late at night in Manhattan. Be very careful. They might mug you. Don't fight with those boys.

Ala! And what is all this money your father and I spent on your education for? If not so you could be better than the others.

Remember! Your mama is the only one who really loves you. Till my dying days. No one will ever love you like your mother.

Pray to God, dear. Don't ever forget Jesus loves you. And don't give your money to strangers.

Remember your daddy's very forgetful now. Sometimes he forgets to do things around the house. And I am not as young as I used to be. Cleaning and cleaning after your daddy. You should learn how to clean up after yourself already.

Don't fool around with girls. They will cut your thing off. We can find a Filipina for you. Find one like your mama who will look after you. Never leave you.

Don't fool around with anybody! There are those homosexuals in Greenwich Village. We saw them on the television. Screaming and shouting. *Ala!* Do you want to become one of those?

Pray to Jesus, Mary, and Joseph. Ask Jesus to guide you. And keep you away from evil. Pray "Our Father" and "Hail, Mary."

And remember all the time to check the stove and the oven before you go out. You never know what might happen. Or else we will read about you in the *Daily News. Ay!* No more!

Then what is the use of all your education? That is why we sent you to Oberlin College and Conservatory.

And how about that Miss Meredith Monk? Do you like her? Is she married? Maybe you can marry her.

So, *anako!* Trust in God. And pray for your mama and your daddy. So that we can live to see you become famous. Maybe we can see you on the Merv Griffin or Mike Douglas shows. But it's still not too late. You can become a doctor and do your music on the side.

Remember, honey, we love you. Although if your daddy doesn't need me anymore, I will go back to the Philippines. I cannot stand these cold winters anymore.

And my hands are trembling. I cannot move my fingers because of the arthritis. It is too hard to keep the house clean by myself now. And you never come to visit us. Not even once a week. Cannot you visit your mama? We love you so much. You are the one we struggled for. Come and see us once in a while. We know you are very busy with your plays. And your shows.

Remember, your mama is the only one who will always love you.

Asian Boy #3

> For the longest time I couldn't even look at you
> I said to myself he's like my brother
> He's my brother and why would I look at him *that* way
> How could I even think of touching him *that* way
> For the longest time I couldn't even look at you

It would be like sleeping with myself
It would be like making love to myself

With white boys it was so easy
I knew what they wanted from me
They knew what I wanted from them
You could figure that out in a second
The wink of an eye
That's all it would take

But with you
  with my brother
Your skin so smooth
Your skin as brown and tan as mine
Your body slender as a reed
The same angular curves and lines like mine
Your black hair darker than night
  and those eyes
    those eyes like pools of seduction
And the hair just below your lower lip where you haven't shaved
And the nape of your neck where it curves into your shoulder
And those lips that love to kiss and tease

For the longest time I couldn't even look at you
I couldn't return your phone calls
I said to myself you're like my brother
You're my brother and why would I look at you that way
  why should I look at you that way
  why should I touch you that way
How could I even think of touching you *that* way
For the longest time I wouldn't even look at you
It would be like sleeping with myself
It would be like making love to myself

And I heard a voice of reason
  I heard my guardian angel say:
"Sleep with your brother
Make love to him
Learn to love
  your
  self."

Whiter Than White

White middle-class neighborhood. Trees lining the sidewalk. Little red house. You don't have enough saved yet, but you make the down payment for the mortgage. Stability and security. Mama was a schoolteacher and Dad trained as a nurse. Men don't do that. Your daddy's a nurse? I say, "Yeah! And before that he was a Pullman porter on the commuter railroad. He probably served gin and tonics to your dad."

Mama gave up her school-teaching in the islands to travel with my dad to this country.
"Is that your grandmother?"
"No, she's my mom."

Land of the free and home of the brave. When I was growing up they'd speak their language—their dialect—to each other. Ilocano. The young ones would sit around and make fun and imitate their elders and the way they spoke:

"Ebreebody! Time por deener!" The kids, my cousins, would repeat this in unison and crack up rolling on the floor and laughing hysterically.

"Speak English! Speak English! Be an American. You were born here. That's why *we* came here. So you could reap the benefits of our hard work and labor. Go to school. Be the best."

"Be proud. Be proud. *Pero* with the whites, be humble." "I will *not* be put down!" my mother said to me. "Don't ever let them put you down!"

No wonder we kids got schizo and psycho. We had to beat our little white friends at their own game. "Oh! Look at your nose. You have a fine nose. Not flat. Like your father's family!"

Study harder. Play harder. Win them over. Make it big. But don't rock the boat. *Whiter than white!* Clean for Gene! Be James Dean! Dreams of Hollywood. Hollywood and Vine! Everyone knows that Filipino kids know *their* movies and *their* music better than *they* do. Whiter than white.

"What? He's not going to be a doctor like his uncle Tony? He's not going to be a lawyer like his cousin Teddy who went to Yale? How is he going to make money and a decent living?"

Mama, I want to rock, I wanna roll. I want to sing like Smokey oh so sweetly and fine: that aching falsetto sound that makes you know how sweet love is! Ooh baby baby. Ooooh . . .

[*Sings first four bars of "The Way You Do the Things You Do" by William "Smokey" Robinson*]

Bailes de latino! And that keening way you sang those Filipino love songs to me when I was a child. Teach me your language and sing me your music!

What color *am* I, Mama? Black, white, Latino, Asian, yellow, brown, gold?

Prince Charming

My mom was in the kitchen cooking. I was in the dining room watching you dress in front of the mirror above the piano. My cousin Teddy was studying law at Yale. I was seven years old. Old enough to go to confession. Old enough in the eyes of the Church to be capable of sin. My cousin Ted was handsome. You were going to a party. You were going out for the evening. Crisp white dress shirt and blue cravat. I was watching you get dressed. I was a little boy and I was watching you get dressed up going out on a date. Navy blue jacket and your hair slicked back and parted on the side and your cologne smelling sweet and fine. My mom was in the kitchen cooking. "Mama, come look. Come see. Cousin Teddy looks just like Prince Charming. Mama, come see Prince Charming. Come see Prince Charming." My mother came running out of the kitchen and she said, "Yes! Your cousin Teddy is so handsome. Someday he'll be president of the Philippines! He'll represent us as our lawyer! He can have his pick of any beautiful Filipina he wants. Someday you'll be as handsome as he is and get married also. Oh, come, Daddy! Our son said that Teddy looks like Prince Charming! How cute, *naman!*" And I was standing on a chair beaming and applauding. You were handsome. You were my Prince Charming.

Asian Boy #4

When I see you walking down the street
I want kisses from you
I want sexy kisses from you

When I see you walking down the street
I know what I'm feeling

When I see you riding your bike down 7th Street
I could throw myself down at your feet

When I see you walking down my street
I just know what could happen
I know the next thing that could happen

C'mere Asian boy
Be my brother
Be my lover

Come here Asian boy
I want you
I want you so bad

Come here Asian boy
I'm an Asian boy too
I'm an Asian boy too
And I want you
I want you so bad.

Song: Requiem

Ronnie was an actor
He was the best I ever saw
He said, "Let's go down to the disco.
  We'll cruise the boys
  and we'll dance
  We'll dance the night away!"
And he said, "You see those old queens
  sitting at the end of the bar
  Well, I want to grow up and be like them someday"

David was a traveler
He loved to travel to the East
And he loved us Asian boys
And David, he was a master of the eight ball
And he turned to me and he said,
"I can teach you about love
Love complete and full and without bounds
Baby, take a chance with me!"

I do not really understand these times
But I will live the next day through
Oh Lord why do you take the ones I love

Paul was a teacher
He was a pied piper of the imagination
And he loved to laugh through his eyes
With voices of Joyce and Chekhov he dreamed
And let us run wild

Time is a tyrant
And memory, a healer
Oh fisher of souls
Help us unlock the door to this mystery:
I do not really understand these times
But I will see the next day through
Oh Lord why do you take the ones I love
Why do you take my friends so soon?
Oh Lord why do you take the ones we love
Why do you take our friends so soon?

Ronnie was an actor
He was the best I ever saw
And we danced the night away. . . .

PEGGY PETTITT

Name: Peggy Pettitt
Stage Name: Same
Birthdate/Birthplace: February 8, 1950/St. Louis, Missouri
"Raised Up" Where: St. Louis, Missouri
Education: Beaumont High School; B.A. in theater, Antioch College; independent study in England and France
Honors/Grants: NYFA and NEA fellowships; Grants include NYSCA, Vogelstein, Puffin, and Jerome Foundations; honored by New York City's Arts-In-Education Roundtable; Elders Share the Arts; and William Hodson Senior Center
Influences/Mentors/Heroes: The wisdom of ordinary people who deal with life in extraordinary ways; my grandparents and mother. Friends with a vision like J. E. Franklin, Susan Perlstein, Mark Russell, and my husband, Remy Tissier
Places Performed: Hollywood, Broadway, Europe, prisons, community centers, schools, and P.S. 122
Pivotal Performance: Title role in African-American film classic *Black Girl* and "Caught between the Devil and the Deep Blue Sea," my own solo creation
Favorite Performance Experience: Each performance provokes such a strong question in me that when I am able to emerge with a sense of arrival and an openness I feel this is my favorite.
Most Terrifying Performance Experience:
Subject: Civil Rights Movement
Issue: Voter Registration
Place: Oxford, Mississippi
Favorite Prop or Costume: An old woman's cane, an African mask, and a custom-made lavender dress and vest created by my stepdaughter.
Hobbies: Gardening, cooking, and palmistry
Reading List: *Fragments of an Unknown Teaching, The Taste for Things That Are True,* and *No Acting, Please*
Favorite Music: Gospel, classical, and Delta blues
Favorite Quote: "If you don't know how to help somebody just leave 'em alone."

Artist's Notes

I wed the art of solo performance to the experiences and voices of African-American characters of all ages and both genders. I have been working in artistic collaboration with director and visual artist Remy Tissier since 1984 to create more than ten original works, including my most recent pieces, "Wrapped Up, Tied Up, and Tangled," "Tricksters: All over You Like White on Rice," and "Caught between the Devil and the Deep Blue Sea."

I consider my work to be a "creative response" to our social, economical, and cultural environment. Like most people I am unable to control the conditions under which I live. Especially conditions that strike me as being somehow abusive, racist, or unjust. But I am able to "respond" to those conditions creatively. Traditionally in my family, my grandmother did it with storytelling, my grandfather with physical labor, and my mother with song (and I must add they each had a lot of love, humor, and bottom-line com-.passion for all people). I consider storytelling, song, physical labor, and compassion essential elements of my work.

I try to be receptive to the simple expressions of life in all its various forms. The movement of ordinary people actively engaged in their existence is transmitted through a visual and choreographed language that echoes a strong narrative so that the message is able to touch the audience deeply. This wish for a genuine approach and clarity of purpose in my work has given me the capacity to connect with an audience and the ability to effectively inhabit the gesture, speech, and intent of a broad range of characters. Working in the tradition of African-American storytelling I shift from female to male, from old to young, all the while interlacing relationships into densely woven stories addressing important issues of our time, such as child abuse, voter registration, domestic violence, and so on. Tales are worked into full evening performances that both entertain and inform the audience about the commonalities of our struggles here on earth as human beings.

Caught between the Devil and the Deep Blue Sea

"Caught between the Devil and the Deep Blue Sea" is a play written for a solo performer. One actress will play the following characters.
Place: Urban America
Time: Now
HELEN: Single mother, sixty-three years old
HENRY: Laborer, sixty years old
ODETTE: Helen's daughter, twenty-six years old
STEVEN: Helen's son, twenty-nine years old
CARLA: Helen's daughter, nineteen years old

The lights dim as she crosses upstage left into the dark and begins singing.

HELEN: There was a boy
    A very strange, enchanted boy
    They say he wandered very far
    Very far; over land and sea
    One magic day he passed my way . . . etc.

She reenters the light with a cane and in pajamas, crosses to the window, then to the baby's bed. She looks back at the door and then sits on the floor with her back to the audience. She hums Sound #4, Baby's Lullaby, *then creates voice of STEVEN.*

STEVEN: Pssst. Pssst. Helen, let me in. Hey, Helen, let me in.
HELEN: Shut up, boy, and get off that front porch.
STEVEN: Come on, Helen, it's cold! [*No response*] It's cold.
HELEN: You better get off that front porch before I call the police on your ass.
STEVEN: Ah, Helen. Then give me a blanket or somethin'.

[*Helen gets up and takes blanket to door, unlocking, then unhooking screen-door latch. She hands Steven the blanket.*]

STEVEN: Come on, Helen, let me in. I won't do nothin', I promise.
HELEN: [*Locking screen door*] I know you won't do nothin', 'cause you ain't comin' in here to worry my ass to death. I'm sick, boy. I can't be bothered. Now, go 'head . . . you can wrap that blanket around you and sleep out there on the porch.
STEVEN: NO! Then ask Delorse if I can sleep in her car.

[*Yelling through screen past Helen:*]

STEVEN: *Delorse! Hey, Delorse . . .*
HELEN: Shut up, boy, she's asleep. And she don't want you in her car, noway. She has to pick up some of her friends and drive them to work in the morning and when you piss all over yourself like that, it smells. She can't have that. Now just wrap up and go to sleep.
STEVEN: You don't treat the others like this, Helen. You let them sleep inside and be warm and watch TV. Even they ole boyfriends can come in . . . how come I can't come in?
HELEN: You know why. Now let me get some rest. I'm tired.
STEVEN: How come *everybody* else can come inside and I can't?
HELEN: 'Cause I got a restraining order on your ass, nigga, that's why.
STEVEN: Why you got one on me, Helen? I didn't do nothin'. I didn't hurt nobody. Come on, Helen, let me in, I ain't gonna say nothin'. I ain't gonna even say nothin' about that lazy-ass Bernard that you let in the house because of Delorse, or any of Carla's friends. Gaalec! See how you are? And I'm always trying to help you.
HELEN: Help me! You call bustin' that wall out in the back room helping, or flooding the toilet with newspaper, or knocking out the TV, helping? Let me get my rest. I mean it, Steven.
STEVEN: It's cold out here.

HELEN: You been out there long enough. You can manage. You been managing.

STEVEN: Yeah, sleeping in alleys, sleeping in cars and vacant lots . . . it rains.

HELEN: Then wrap yourself in plastic.

STEVEN: Damn, an' you suppose to be my mother.

HELEN: I know that. But *you* don't know that! Every time I let you in here, Steve, you acts a fool. Throwing things around, saying the first thing that comes to your mind. You acts crazy. Using drugs down there in the basement! I can't have that around these grandbabies. There's other people that lives here besides you. You too big to be acting a fool. Can't nobody do nothin' with you. `

STEVEN: I ain't gonna do it no more, Helen. I promise.

HELEN: I know that. The last time I let you in here, you drew your hand back to hit me. I am too old for that. I'm sick. I'm havin' an operation. The doctor said I need my rest and peace and my quiet.

STEVEN: [*Shaking the screen door*] *Then why did you give birth to me, Helen? Then why was I born?*

HELEN: How the hell do I know why you was born? Ask Delorse why she was born. Ask any of my children why they was born. Ask God why was *I* born. You just was. It wasn't up to me.

STEVEN: You don't love me.

HELEN: Who don't love who? How many times have I let you back in here, Steve? Did you appreciate it? Naw! You a grown man, almost thirty years old. I should have put your ass out a long time ago.

STEVEN: You don't tell Delorse that. . . .

HELEN: Shut up! Now get away from that door and to sleep. I'm goin' to sleep. Now, look what you done done. Done woke up the baby.

[*She crosses back to baby's bed, picks up the baby, and sings:*]

> Way down yonder in the itty bitty pool
> Swam three little fishes and the mama fish too.
> "*Stop!*" said the mama fish, "or you'll get lost."
> But the three little fishes didn't want to be bossed.
> So they swam and they swam all over the dam. . . .

[*Lights*]

Tricksters: All over You Like White on Rice

"Tricksters: All over You Like White on Rice" is a play written for a solo performer. One actress will play the following characters, plus various voices. The ages of the characters will change from time to time. The scenes are based on Ann's associations during a trip home from New York to St. Louis, Missouri.

ANN: a dancer, twenty-six years old
ROSE: Ann's mother, fifty-four years old
LAUREEN: Ann's sister, thirty years old
CURTIS: Laureen's husband, thirty years old
AUNT FAITH: Rose's older sister
BARBARA JEAN: Ann's younger sister
ROMAINE: Ann's fiancé
SHELL: Laureen's daughter
COLONEL SANDERS: apparition on the train
WOMAN: Memory from Ann's past
YOUNG ANN: Ann as a child
MR. FATS: an old friend
AUNT CLAUDIA: Rose's younger sister
GRANDMOTHER: Rose's mother
GRANDFATHER: Rose's father
ROY: baggage claim attendant

ANN

He's so high you can't go over
He's so low you can't go under
He's so wide you can't go around
You must come in at the door.

Lights up in compartment. Ann sits on the bed and looks out the window. She blows a toy train whistle. Sound of train moving. Ann puts on an orange shift, becoming ROSE. Lights up full as she stands in front of the bed.

ROSE: As long as your two feets is mates and your asshole points towards the ground, don't you ever let me hear you say anything like that about your sister again!
BARBARA JEAN: All I said was Ann hangs around whitey too much for me. Ain't nothin' no whitey can do for me. They're full of shit. Give 'em two seconds, they'll try and teach you how to be black. They're tricky . . . yeah. I know what I'm talking about . . . right. I work with 'em . . . right. I'm

packin' . . . right. Boom! Boom, Boom, Voom, Voom!! Sheeeit . . . no problem, I know my job, I'm never late . . . right! One day they tried to pull a
trick on me. Call me down to payroll, try to tell me they was gonna have to
cut my check. "Don't take it *personally*, Ms. Wallis. I'm hurting . . ." I said,
"You what? You what? You gonna pay me! Somebody gonna pay me! I'm sick
and tired of being put in a fuckin' trick bag and made to feel like it's my own
damn fault." If Ann wants to hang around whitey, let her. I don't trust 'em,
that's all I got to say. Mama, you know . . .

ROSE: I know you gonna make yourself sick if you keep going on like that,
Barbara Jean. You sound just like you daddy. And you know what happened
to him. You been watchin' too much of that television. Some things are better off left alone. For instance, I just love me a aquarium. You know, with
them little fish that swim around so pretty. Oh, I can sit and look at that all
day. I went to Walgreen's and bought me some fish in a plastic bag. I never
will forget it. Now, them fish was minding their own business, not bothering nobody, but I'm gonna take them home and kill 'em . . . 'cause that's exactly what I did. I thought I knew what I was doin'. I'd take them out of the
bowl to change the water every day . . . and they'd flip-flop on the side of
the sink whilst I rinse out the bowl. I'd watch 'em swim around. Aww, I had
a pretty little black one with great big fins, don'tcha know. Next day, I go to
look at my fish and he floatin' on top of the water on his back, dead as a
doornail. And I kept buying more fish and killing them. It took me a long
time to figure out . . . them fish ain't hurtin' nobody, why don't I just leave
'em alone, since I don't know how to help 'em, just leave 'em alone. "Row,
row, row your boat, merrily down the stream. Merrily, merrily, merrily, merrily. Life is but a dream. . . ."

BARBARA JEAN: Mama, what the hell has that got to do with what I'm
tryin' to say?

ROSE: It's got *everything* to do with what you tryin' to say, Barbara Jean, if
you just listen. If you don't know how to help somebody, just leave 'em
alone. Now, they didn't just get together. There's a history there, and you
was here, remember?

[*Transition into recent past. Characters become slightly younger versions of
themselves.*]

BARBARA JEAN: Ann! There's a Chinese man on the telephone, wants to
talk to you.

ANN: He's not Chinese, he's French. He's got an accent, that's all.

BARBARA JEAN: And then? It all sounds like Chinese to me.

ROSE: When Ann, my oldest girl, came home from college and told us she
was getting married, we couldn't believe it. When she told us he was white,

we didn't know what to think. When she said she was invitin' him home, we didn't know what to *do*! There we were, all seven of us, sittin' around the living room. Every time we heard a car pull up in front of the house, we'd lean, wait, and listen for his shoes to hit those wooden steps. Nothin'. Laureen was seated in the armchair cracking her knuckles, with her two children squeezed in on either side of her. Ann was seated on the floor playing with Little Man, and Shell's smilin' up at me, lookin' sheepish, waitin' to see what I was gonna do. Barbara Jean kept runnin' back and forth to the window, drawing the curtains back just enough to peek onto the porch and give us fair warnin' if she saw him comin'.

BARBARA JEAN: What he look like? How I know it ain't the insurance man?

ROSE: And Curtis, dressed to kill . . .

CURTIS: Girl, you better get away from that window. 'Cause we gonna know when he gets here . . . 'cause Miss Georgia gonna turn a flip out there on her front porch and set every dog in the neighborhood to barkin'.

ROSE: No sooner he said that, a car door slammed. Barbara Jean started runnin' around the room like a chicken with her head cut off, lookin' for a place to sit. Laureen froze stiff and set straight up in her chair with the strangest-looking grin you ever wanted to see in your life painted 'cross her face. I couldn't tell if she was gonna laugh or cry. Ann jumped up and runs toward the door. "Romaine!" You woulda thought it was Christmas and he was Santa Claus. I thought I was gonna lose my teeth if I got caught up in all that scramblin' around, so I held my ground. I knew how to act. This was my home. That was my child he was throwin' his arms around. So I looked him right in the eyes. And he looked back at me and said, "Hello, Ms. Rose." Then he gave me a box that looked like it had been wrapped at Sears and Roebuck's. For a long time nobody knew what to say. It was like we was made out of cardboard. All the questions and answers were thrown into the middle of the room like pebbles into a pond. Plop . . . plop . . . plop . . . from time to time, Curtis stuck his head into the room like a police officer, intent on lockin' somebody up.

CURTIS: How long did you say you was gonna be in St. Louis?

ROSE: Plop! Just then, one of the grandbabies plumb forgot herself and ran right over to him. "What's your name?" he said.

SHELL: Shell.

ROMAINE: Michelle, my belle?

ROSE: Well, when he started talkin' like that, we all broke out laughin'. I laughed like I hadn't laughed in a long time. Even Curtis done thawed and took him on a tour of the neighborhood. When they left, I asked Shell what she thought about her new uncle.

SHELL: Ain't nothin' wrong with Uncle Romaine, he all right.

ROSE: When they got back, they had enough White Castle hamburgers and french fries for everybody.

CURTIS: I told my brother-in-law, I betcha France ain't the only place got castles.

ROSE: He smiled when he looked down at my feet and saw I had taken the house shoes out of the box and had 'em on. Now, let me tell you something, Barbara Jean. That night, that boy ate right . . . pinto beans and cornbread with all us; and when the evening news came on, he sat down on the floor and talked back to the television set better than everybody else could. Every now and then, I saw her slip her hand inside his when she thought nobody else was lookin', and I saw how he responded. Aww, we was havin' a good time, feelin' comfortable in our own home. Lord only knows what this world had in store for the two of them, but for now . . . I said, "I got somethin' for you too, babies, besides the blanket I brought you for your weddin'." I got inspired and I walked over and stood next to the refrigerator. And you all gathered around when I opened my mouth to sing.

> Hush now, don't explain
> Just say you will remain
> I'm glad you're back
> Don't explain
> You know that I love you
> And what love will endure
> I'd do anything for you
> I'm so completely yours
> Hush now, don't explain

Photo copyright © by Dona Ann McAdams

DAVID ROUSSEVE

Name: David Rousseve
Stage Name: Same
Birthdate/Birthplace: November 21, 1959/Houston, Texas
"Raised Up" Where: Houston, Texas
Education: B.A., Princeton University, 1981, magna cum laude
Honors/Grants: NEA Fellowships, 1990–97; NYFA Fellowship, 1991; Rockefeller Foundation, 1994–95; IMZ International Dance Film Festival—First Place, Film Choreography
Influences/Mentors/Heroes: Toni Morrison, Pina Bausch, my grandmother
Places Performed: Brooklyn Academy of Music's Next Wave Festival; P.S. 122; Zellerbach Hall, Berkeley; Carlton Festival, Brazil; Queen Elizabeth Hall/South Bank Center, London; Festival Biennale de la Danse, Lyon, France; American Center, Paris; Hamburg Theater Festival, Germany
Pivotal Performance: Every one
Favorite Performance Experience: Creating a film for *Alive TV* in the swamps of Louisiana
Most Terrifying Performance Experience: In San Francisco: falling off the stage (mid-performance), then rolling out the theater's emergency exit door and finding myself in a pitch-black side alley as the performance went on without me
Favorite Prop or Costume: Any microphone I can stand behind
Reading List: Anything by Toni Morrison, *Crime and Punishment* by Dostoyevsky, *Race Matters* by Cornel West
Favorite Music: The women of jazz: Ella, Sarah, Nina, Dinah . . .

Artist's Notes

The three monologues included here are from the *Creole* series (1988–92), a series of eight dance/theater works written and choreographed by myself for my dance company of eight dancers (REALITY) and a gospel choir. Although listed as excerpts from *Urban Scenes/Creole Dreams* (the last work of the series), the text was written early into the series.

The *Creole* series juxtaposes the life stories of an elderly Creole woman (my grandmother) with our lives in contemporary America. As such, the work jumps back and forth between early 1900s Louisiana and contemporary urban America. Text for the work is likewise in two sets of monologues: my grandmother's stories and my own tales of growing up in Houston, Texas. In performance, the grandmother's "Creole" stories are told more traditionally and formally, and my own autobiographical stories are told informally, almost as stand-up comedy. Both sets of monologues are delivered by myself, the grandmother with a heavy characterization. Thematically, the series grew into a dialogue on loss: The grandmother's loss of her cousin in a brutal rape is likened to our contemporary losses to AIDS.

Urban Scenes/Creole Dreams
Excerpt 1

. . . had a rat . . . had a rat . . . had a rat . . . had a rat . . . had a rat . . . I had this rat when I was young. And it was just your ordinary "white rat": y'all know the kind that kids have as pets sometimes, with the short white hair and the long wiry tail and the big pink ears. Except my rat was " 'flicted"; which is black English for "messed up real bad." 'Cause see, his tail came out about a quarter inch from his body and then it jutted off on a direct right angle. That's 'cause he was born backwards. He came out backwards and his tail got all manked up in the process. He was also missing half of his right ear, from where the mother rat had started to eat him (which they'll do when the li'l rats come out " 'flicted"), but instead, shortly after she'd started the process, she kicked him out the nest, I s'pose thinking he would starve to death.

Which he didn't, y'all, because I found that rat, and I loved that rat, I loved that rat something awful, I loved that rat. But you see the problem was, nobody else loved that rat! And kids used to come over and play with me every day after school, and they would inevitably go running to the den, which was where I kept my ample supply of toys. And when they'd get into that den, they would inevitably go running to the back right-hand corner, 'cause that was where I kept my rat's cage . . . and it was so impressive. It was one of those double-decker Habitrail kind, with two stories and a long spiral staircase so my rat could walk up to the top like he was Bette Davis or Katharine Hepburn.

And those kids would see that cage and their faces would swell with joy (you know how kids' faces will swell with joy when they think they 'bout to see something wonderful), and they would go running to that back right-hand corner of my den and peek inside my rat's cage, and my li'l rat would come crawling out of his Carnation milk carton with the hole in the side and the ripped-up newspaper so he could make himself comfortable and those kids' faces would sink faster than a flat tire on a dirty Mississippi road, and they'd say: "David! My God! How can you keep at it, how can you look at it, how can you touch it, how can you love it?"

And I'd say, "Wait a minute . . . y'all don't understand. I love my rat *because* he's 'flicted. Not in spite of the fact that he's 'flicted, but *because* he's 'flicted." Oh! And the greatest joy of my childhood was, the greatest discovery of my childhood was, I found that if you take this part of your hand [NARRATOR *indicates the bottom of the open palm*] and place it against this part of your thigh [NARRATOR *indicates the top of the right thigh*], and you curve your chest just right, you'll get a hole at the top of your chest just the right size for a fat white rat! [NARRATOR *indicates the hollow of the sternum in a soft, stroking manner*] And I used to put my rat up there in his li'l private "rat spot. . . ." And he would curl his 'flicted tail up towards his big head and stick it inside of his 'flicted ear. And he'd just go to sleep as I'd feel his heart beat into the top of my body through the bottom of his fur. And I would go stand under the moonlight. And I would just stroke my rat, and I would just love my rat. And I would just think: [NARRATOR *switches to the older, raspy voice of the* GRANDMOTHER *character*] "Everybody must got somethin' in life they loves more than theyselfs."

Huh . . . Li'l rat died when I was about eight. Yeah, I lost him very young. He caught rat cancer. At least that's what my parents said. But then again, you know they said the dog caught dog cancer and the cat caught cat cancer, so I don't really know for sure. Except he really did have some sort of tumors all over his body, so I s'pose it was one form of cancer or another.

. . . And I used to miss that rat, y'all. I used to miss that rat something awful, I used to miss that rat. And I would go stand under the moonlight, and stroke that big empty rat spot; but wasn't nothin' there to touch but myself, which I guess should have been enough, but somehow it just wasn't.

Oh! But then, the greatest joy of my adult life, y'all, the greatest discovery of my adult life was: I found, if you're spooned up with somebody in bed at night, and you're curled up in that double fetal position, and they have their arms wrapped tightly around your waist (and you're already in seventh heaven 'cause what more could you ask for?); if their body is positioned just right to where you can feel their abdomen going in, and out, and in against the bottom part of your back; if their body is positioned just right to where you can feel their heart beat against the back of your shoulder blade; if their head is positioned just right, to where you can feel their eyelashes flicker against the soft part of your ear (and you know they must be in that advanced REM state and you hope they're dreamin' about you, 'cause you know you are about them), if their head is positioned just right, y'all, the nostrils will blow hot breath right into your "rat spot"!

[NARRATOR *becomes ecstatic*] Oh! Oh! And that just makes me feel so . . . that just makes me feel so, that just makes me feel like my rat is still there and I can go out under the moonlight and stroke that spot and feel him jumpin' in my heart. . . . [*etc., etc.* . . .]

[*A pause, during which the* NARRATOR *calms down from the excitement*] But then the people started dying; which was kind of like the rat dying, except for it was people dying, which I assumed would be a little more serious, but somehow it just wasn't, because just like with the rat, nobody cared. And I came to realize that nobody cared because instead of 'flicted animals, this time it was 'flicted people: gay people, black people, poor people . . . And they weren't calling it "rat cancer," in fact at first they were calling it "gay cancer," and by the time anybody cared enough to give it a name or simply find out what it was, it was too late 'cause everybody was dead. And the reality is that just like that rat, I'm all alone. And I get so angry, I get so angry, and I don't know if it's because nobody cares or because I'm hurting so bad from being all alone. I get that torrential ball of anger, I get that torrential ball of muck, and it's just rising up from the bottom of my gut, and I don't know if it's because nobody cares or because I'm all alone . . . and it just . . . [NARRATOR *trails off into an incoherent, angry voice, as house music bursts in to interrupt*]

Excerpt 2

[*In the raspy voice of the* GRANDMOTHER]

I remember that bein' alone didn't bother me much when I was very young. Back then, we lived on a white woman's plantation, sharecroppin' as her children of slave children. We was five gal cousins who slept in one bed, in a one-room shack, with no mother, no father, three "sometimey" dogs, and no food. We didn't speak no English, 'cause we was Creole gals, and we had every color gal livin' in that tiny room from pass-for-white Nana to damn-near-nigga-shade Bommie.

Sleepin' was hard 'cause all us childrens had coccaburrow sores speckled over our legs: The kind pickaninny always get; from bein' po' or picking cotton; the kind that ooze out at night and make you holler when you touch 'em.

So every night you'd be woke up by some sleepers' toe scratchin' over your sores. But you couldn't yell out, 'specially not at night, 'cause there was four other people with empty bellies inside tryin' to sleep real quiet in the same sharecropper's room.

So I'd grab Bommie's body sleepin' next to mine; I'd wrap my arms around and hold real tight. I'd spoon up so'st my stomach could cradle her back like a crescent moon at half sunset. I'd caress the curve of her spine with the front of my body. Then I'd cry in her sleep, hopin' I wouldn't wake her with the wet of my tears on the back of her neck. I'd breathe on her rhythm, in and out with her heart, and somehow my leg would stop hurting and my sores would dry up. I'd go back to sleep feelin' her heart beat 'gainst my lips thru the soft part of her neck, knowin' we was joined from someplace way deep inside, where coccaburrow sores ain't nothin' but a nothin' from a nothin' what can't get you in no bed with five cotton-pickin' Creole childs.

. . . and sometimes at night, I'd even want to be alone. Back when I was very young, back in my hometown of Coonville, Louisiana, sometimes at night, I'd even want to be all alone. So I'd wait till we had our fill of cold ash bread and mushy oat stew.

Then I'd run to the middle of the cornfields. And I'd sit in the middle of the cornfields. And I'd mix the spit of my mouth with the fertilizin' soil and rub mud way down deep inside all my sores. First I'd stir it in my palms, then feel the cool help 'gainst my legs.

But then the night air would blow and the stars would shine down and the moon would say, Come on, nigga child, it's your time to fly. And my face would gasp up; point direct towards the sky, and my eyes would slowly rise and lift up the rest of my body; and on my way up, my hands, my arms, my hands would wrap around two cornstalks and hold on tight, 'cause I knew if I didn't I would simply fly away, and when I was on my feet, nearly all the way up, I would just stand . . .

. . . and be . . .

. . . still . . . and listen to the dry cornstalks blowin' in the wind; and see all of us, or at least part of us, five sleepin' pickaninny flyin' thru that sky.

And oh, I know I musta looked a sho' 'nuff mess 'bout that time: yellow, teeth-missin' grin, with caked-up mud fallin' offa my over-sun-blacked-up skin, but I felt mighty fine.

You see, when I was young, bein' alone; sometimes that was somethin' wonderful; 'cuz you knew you never were. We had ourselves, colored children flyin' by; which meant we had each other. And long as I had myself, that part of my soul that could swoop over cornfields or just hold my cousin against my body and love her at night, I was never alone, I was filled with hope, and I was mighty fine, mighty fine.

Part 2

[*Delivered later in the piece*]

When I was fourteen, Bommie got raped by a white man.

He drag her out to the dirt fields, cover her with his white massiveness, and rape her . . . reached his hand down her throat, grabbed her soul and squeezed it till it slowly oozed from her body, as if it had never even existed. I never heard of no human bein' disappearing before, but so much of Bommie was taken on that dirt field, she all but disappeared from us . . . and the torn person we see crawlin' and hobblin' up that back road towards our house would have been enough to yank your heart right out o' your mouth and smash it on the hard gravel floor, were it not for the buffer shock of realizin' our Bommie, my Bommie, was gone and was never comin' back.

We pulled Bommie into the house and tried to wash her body; but she began throwin' a fit the likes of which we'd never seen: Pullin' her own hair, slappin' her own body. We just looked on; tryin' to figure out who it was she despised.

We hunted that white man.

We killed that white man.

We tied his body with rope and drug his mangy carcass out to the cornfields; crushin' the fresh, ready-to-be-nigga-picked stalks with our death procession. When we reached the center, we stuffed dirt in his mouth, then one by one we pissed in his open lids.

That night, the white folks came. When they couldn't find us, they burned our shack, killed all our farm animals, and destroyed all the big-house crops.

As we snuck out of town and into the Lous'ana swamps, I was wearin' the one thing I'd managed to salvage: my Sunday-go-to-meeting yellow velvet hair ribbon. I remember noticin' the difference between the soft crush of yellow velvet between my tremblin' fingers and the poke of wet coccaburrows under my naked feets.

I remember everybody nervously checkin' our direction against the North Star, faces pulled directly up at the moon. As we wiped the tear/sweat rolling drops from our chins, across our faces, and thru our nappy hair, I thought it looked like we slowly decapitated ourselves, pulling back our own heads till they all but disappeared behind our necks; as we chugged on and pulled our heads to the moon.

As I left the group near Lafayette to pull off on my own towards Houston, I looked around me at the tear-covered faces glowing in the moonlight. I was thinkin' I would never again stroke any of these cheeks or kiss my Bommie's lips good night. I heard my own heart break and scream out into the chill of the midnight swamp, as I walked off alone, whispering, "Lord have mercy, what's a nigga go' do, when you all alone, ain't nobody but you?"

Excerpt 3

It was the first day of school. Actually, I should tell you it was the first day of "integrated school," because I was a member of the first class in Houston, Texas, that got bussed across town when they started desegregating the schools.

So it was the first day of integrated school, and I was standing in my living room, waiting for the school bus to come and pick me up and take me across town to the white school. And I was so nervous. I had my face smushed up against our front windowpanes, breathing hard. And the panes began to fog up from my breath and then the fog began to streak, and through the streaks I saw this huge yellow school bus pull up and stop right in front of our house; and I thought to myself: *My God, what a raggedy bus.* And sure enough, we got about three blocks, and then the bus broke down. So not only was it the first day of school, not only were we headed for this strange new world where we had no idea what to expect, but, of course, we were late!

But we were having the time of our lives, anyway; 'cause ya'll know how it is when you get a group of black teenagers together at about that pre-junior high school age and put us on a raggedy rusty yellow bus: We will chant and cheer, and that bus was rockin' as we crossed Houston with our windows open and our heads flyin' out: "Yo' Mama! Yo' Daddy! Yo' greasy

Granny, got holes in her panties!" And all of a sudden we turned one corner, and I was the first one who saw it and I said, "My God, ya'll, that's our school!" Every face on that bus came and pressed against my pane, and the bus started to lean in one direction. And there appeared this massive white building with these huge white columns, and I said, "Uh-oh, y'all, that looks just like where Scarlett O'Hara lived in *Gone with the Wind.*"

And the bus came to an abrupt halt in front of that building. I looked out my window and saw the largest, most imposing white man there. He had a rather abundant belly hangin' down two inches over the top of his pants (that were about three inches too small). He had on a polyester leisure suit and some sort of pseudosuede cowboy hat. His feet were hips'-width apart, his hands were on his hips, and his pelvis was shifting way forward making his lower back virtually nonexistent (I assume so as to accentuate his beer belly). He just nodded his head at each one of us as we got off that bus, "Uh-huh, uh-huh. . . ." And all our chanting and cheering had gotten really serious and switched to "Go . . . go . . . go. . . ." And when my feet reached the bottom step as I got out the bus, I felt someone slap me on my back, and we scattered off by ourselves and completely on our own.

. . . The next thing I can remember is sitting in the back of my first period class: Mrs. Oringderfer's Creative Writing class. They had saved me a seat at the very back of the third row, since I was late. And I can remember looking around that room. I was so nervous. I was so nervous, I was breathing so hard. And I can remember being so nervous, because up to this point, I had never been this close to white people before. Although I guess I knew what they'd be like, since I'd seen every last rerun of *I Love Lucy* and *The Jetsons,* so I knew what they were like; but my God, there were so many of them! And they all had blond hair and blue eyes!

I looked around that room, breathing so hard. I came to notice the back of this little blond boy's head, who was sittin' right in front of me, I noticed that when I would breathe on his hair . . . my God! It would move! Which really tripped me out, because if you remember, the brothers back then were wearing those big afros, and you could blow on those things like a hurricane, they were not moving!

So I'm back there blowing on the back of this little white boy's head, and he kinda started to turn around, and he said, "Well, excuse me, but what are you doing to the back of my head?" And I was so stunned that one of them was actually talking to me, that all I could do was get really sincere and answer him as honestly as possible. I said: "I'm really sorry, but I am so scared, I am so nervous. I feel so alone, and tell you the truth, I've never been this close to a white person before."

And he kinda thought about what I said, looked at me, and said: "Well, come to think of it, I've never been this close to a black person before either. . . . What's your name and where are you from?" And I immediately started to feel better: I felt like I had my first friend in this new environment; my first little bit of human contact. And right when the conversation started to get good, old lady Oringderfer pipes in: ". . . Now, class! . . ." (She was from east Texas, which is always bad news. She had one of those I-moved-from-the-small-town-to-the-big-city-in-search-of-a-better-life-which-I-did-not-find-so-I'm-bitter-as-hell-and-I'm-go'-take-it-out-on-you accents.) ". . . Now, class! Y'all got an assignment. This is a creative writing class, y'all got an assignment: You go' write a essay. And the name of yo' essay is: 'Who I Want to Be.' Now! If you could be somebody (if you could), who would you want to be? Like a hero. Like a hero; who's your hero? You little colored boy back there in the back, you can't keep your trap shut? You stand up right here, right now, you tell me who you want to be!"

Well! I was stunned, as every one of those thirty-some-odd blond heads turned in perfect unison and looked directly at me. But once that initial shock passed, I was completely cool, because I had my answer ready. . . . I knew just what I wanted to be. You see, ever since I have been knee-high to a duck, I have always wanted to be a fat black woman who sings gospel.

Now, I got up out of my chair, grinning like a polecat, so proud of myself at having what I thought was a good answer ready. But I looked up and saw all those blue eyes looking back at me; and all of a sudden I began to feel so alone, and so different and so strange, and by the time my behind stood to rising, I knew there was no way I would ever stand up in a room full of white folks and say I have always wanted to be a fat black woman.

So I said (in that endearing sweet-colored-child voice): "Oh, Mrs. Oringderfer, why, thank you for calling on me, well, I have always wanted to be . . ." and I must have said Martin Luther King or Booker T. Washington, or somebody else I knew good and well she wanted to hear that I wanted to be just like. Old lady Oringderfer nodded her head, smiled, and said, "Oh, well, very good! Why, you are quite a credit to your race."

As I went home that evening, I knew I was going to hate this. I was going to hate living in this new environment. Simply because I'd be entirely too good at it. I mean, I knew I would succeed. And I knew exactly what I was going to have to give up in order to do that.

ABOUT THE AUTHOR

Name: Mark Russell
Stage Name: Same
Birthdate/Birthplace: March 15, 1954/Menominee, Wisconsin
"Raised Up" Where: Owatonna, Minnesota; Java, South Dakota; Redwing, Minnesota; Indianapolis, Indiana; Cleveland, Ohio; Austin, Texas. We moved a lot.
Education: B.F.A. in Theatre Directing, University of Texas at Austin
Honors/Grants: Village Voice Arts Hero Award 1984, NEA panelist, NYSCA panelist, DTW Suitcase Fund Travel Grants
Influences/Mentors/Heroes: Dr. Francis Hodge, Jerzy Grotowski, Peter Brook, David White, Jagienka Zych, John Killacky
Places Performed: P.S. 1; Art on the Beach, 1980; P.S. 122's Avant-Garde-Arama, 1982; the Bessie Ceremony, 1990; Biblio's reading series; St. Mark's Poetry Project; Dixon Place
Pivotal Performance: Playing Prospero in the Texas High School one-act-play contest regionals. Got me hooked. It was also the first time I tried Mexican pot and mixed it with performance, which turned out to not be a very good idea. I soon retired from the stage.
Favorite Performance Experience: Dancing with Frank Conversano at the Bessies
Most Terrifying Performance Experience: Facing the press before Ron Athey's performance
Favorite Prop or Costume: My custom-made black sharkskin suit from Hong Kong and my Psion pocket computer
Hobbies: None. Well, I do write and draw for myself sometimes.
Reading List: Sarah's *New Yorkers*; *PC Magazine;* Michael Ondaatje's *In the Skin of a Lion*
Favorite Music: Van Morrison; R.E.M.; Philip Glass; Nine Inch Nails; Meredith Monk; Patti Smith; the Balenesqu Quartet
Favorite Quote: "Onward into the fog." (Oat Willie)

ACKNOWLEDGMENTS

There are many people to thank for helping me put this book together, foremost the artists who for very little compensation contributed their work for this project and put up with my nagging; the board and staff of Performance Space 122, especially Dominick Balletta and Andrea E. Smith, who allowed me the chance to do this and led the cheering squad; my sweetheart, Sarah Skaggs, who let me act like a possessed artist for a year; Elyce Cheney, who made it happen; Ted Striggles, for all the legal advice I never took; Linda Gross, for taking us on; Jennifer Steinbach, my editor, for making it all fun; Kathy Russo, for all her support; RoseLee Goldberg, for her wise counsel; and Nancy Sakamoto, my associate in this endeavor, who kept things rolling and made it such a pleasant adventure. My compadre, Dona Ann McAdams, who has watched this world from the same street corner as I, for lo, these many years. The angels John, Barry, Bolek, and Ethyl. And last but not least, my folks, Joel and Helen Russell, who taught me all about character.

Terry Galloway's performance text reprinted from *Out All Night and Lost My Shoes* by Terry Galloway (Apalachee Press).

Holly Hughes's *Meat* was previously published in *Between C & D*.

Denis Leary's *More Drugs* reprinted from *No Cure for Cancer* by Denis Leary (An Anchor Book, Published by Doubleday, a division of Bantam Doubleday Dell Publishing Group, Inc.).

Some of Dona Ann McAdams's photographs in this book appear courtesy of the Aperture Foundation, and appear in *Caught in the Act: A Look at Contemporary Multimedia Performance* by Dona Ann McAdams.